Access
My eLab
Literary Horizons

Andy Van Drom

Literary **Horizons**
Analysis and Essay Writing

GSE

TO REGISTER

❶ Go to **mybookshelf.pearsonerpi.com**

❷ Follow the instructions. When asked for your access code, please type the code provided underneath the blue sticker.

❸ To access **My eLab** at any time, go to http://mybookshelf.pearsonerpi.com. **Bookmark this page for quicker access.**

Access to My eLab is valid for 12 months from the date of registration.

STUDENT ACCESS CODE

AEWSTU-SMELL-BENCH-PASTE-COLZA-TUNES

WARNING! This book CANNOT BE RETURNED if the access code has been uncovered.

Note: Once you have registered, you will need to join your online class. Ask your teacher to provide you with the class ID.

TEACHER Access Code

To obtain an access code for My eLab, please contact your Pearson ELT consultant.

 I 800 263-3678, ext. 2
pearsonerpi.com/help

W139522 (A6101504)

1608

Andy Van Drom

Literary **Horizons**

Analysis and Essay Writing

Product Owner
Stephan Leduc

Editor
Lucie Turcotte

Copy Editor
Adam Lawrence

Proofreader
Paula Sarson

Rights and Permissions Coordinator
Aude Maggiori

Text Rights and Permissions
Rachel Irwin

Art Director
Hélène Cousineau

Graphic Design Manager
Estelle Cuillerier

Book Design
Andrée Lauzon

Book Layout
cyclonedesign.ca

Cover Design
Nathalie Giroux

Cover Photo
Juan Álvarez Ajamil on Unsplash

The publisher wishes to thank the following people for their helpful comments and suggestions:

Panagiota Dimakis	Vanier College
Meg Gillespie	Cégep Gérald-Godin
Anthony Granato	Vanier College
Robert Jamieson	Cégep Édouard-Montpetit
Sylvain Jomphe	Cégep de Jonquière
Nathalie Landry	Collège André-Grasset
Karen McCoubrey	Cégep de Sainte-Foy
Tanya-Stephanie Paquette	Cégep de Saint-Hyacinthe
Vanessa Vandergrift	Vanier College
Olga Zavitnevich-Beaulac	Collège de Maisonneuve

1611 Crémazie Boulevard East, 10th Floor
Montréal, Québec H2M 2P2
Canada
Telephone: 1 800 263-3678
Fax: 514 334-4720
information@pearsonerpi.com
pearsonerpi.com

Registration of copyright—Bibliothèque et Archives nationales du Québec, 2019
Registration of copyright—Library and Archives Canada, 2019

Printed in Canada
ISBN 978-2-7613-9522-9   23456789   HLN   23 22 21 20
(82021426)   139522   ABCD   OF10

ACKNOWLEDGEMENTS

A special word of thanks to Anthony Granato from Vanier College for providing me with valuable feedback on text choices and chapter contents. Your contribution has helped me tremendously in making this material relevant for first- and second-language users alike.

Thank you to everyone at Pearson ELT who has contributed to bringing life to *Literary Horizons*, more particularly to Stephan Leduc for entrusting me with this project; Lucie Turcotte for helping me to structure initial ideas and activities into a cohesive manuscript, and Adam Lawrence for so expertly revising it; and the sales representatives for being dedicated ambassadors. Finally, to my colleagues and students at Cégep Limoilou, for inspiring me every day.

Andy Van Drom

Dedication

For Sam, the co-protagonist of my life, whose ability to laugh out loud while reading a story was a great source of inspiration when putting together this book.

"Literature is where I go to explore the highest and lowest places in human society and in the human spirit, where I hope to find not absolute truth but the truth of the tale, of the imagination and of the heart."

—Salman Rushdie

HIGHLIGHTS

Parts I to III are respectively devoted to short stories, drama and poetry. Part IV covers songs, spoken word, graphic novels and speeches.

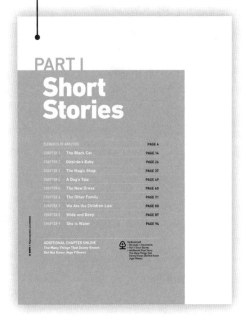

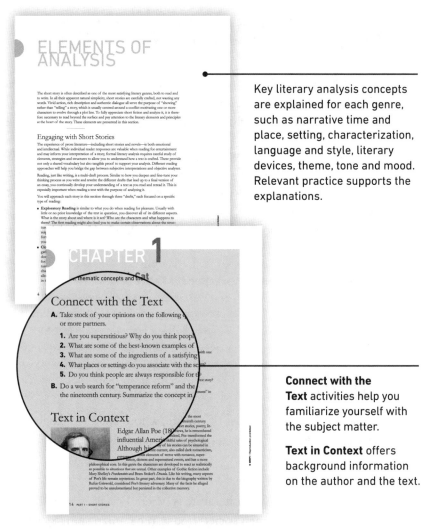

Key literary analysis concepts are explained for each genre, such as narrative time and place, setting, characterization, language and style, literary devices, theme, tone and mood. Relevant practice supports the explanations.

Connect with the Text activities help you familiarize yourself with the subject matter.

Text in Context offers background information on the author and the text.

Through a three-step approach to reading, which consists of an exploratory reading, a close reading and an analytical reading, you will progressively refine your understanding of the text and deepen your analysis.

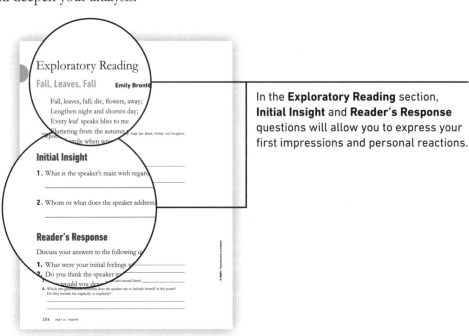

In the **Exploratory Reading** section, **Initial Insight** and **Reader's Response** questions will allow you to express your first impressions and personal reactions.

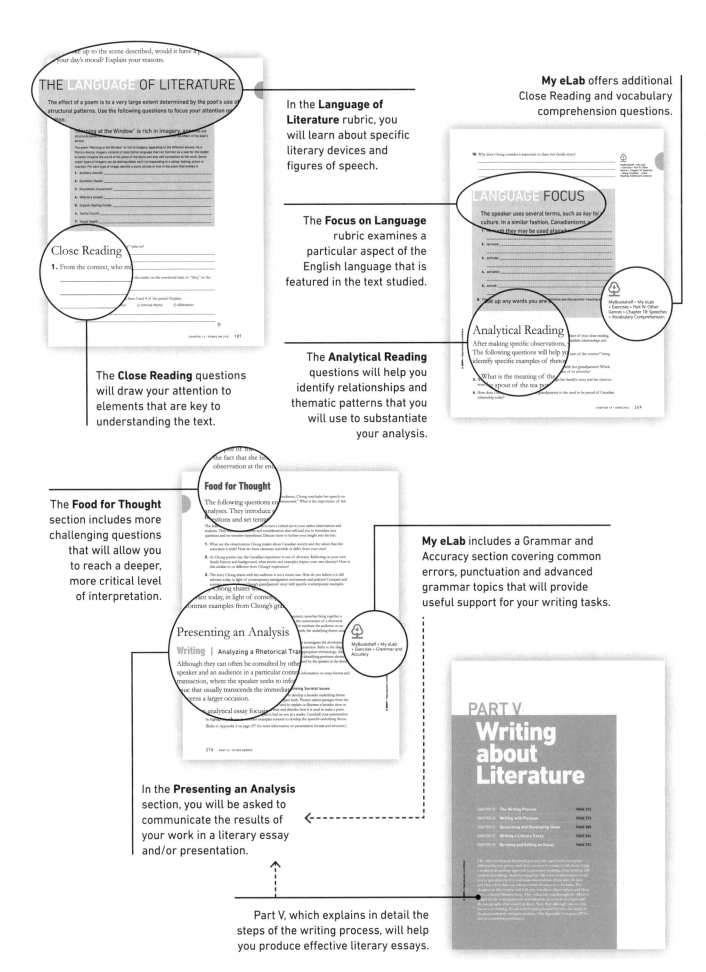

My eLab offers additional Close Reading and vocabulary comprehension questions.

In the **Language of Literature** rubric, you will learn about specific literary devices and figures of speech.

The **Focus on Language** rubric examines a particular aspect of the English language that is featured in the text studied.

The **Close Reading** questions will draw your attention to elements that are key to understanding the text.

The **Analytical Reading** questions will help you identify relationships and thematic patterns that you will use to substantiate your analysis.

The **Food for Thought** section includes more challenging questions that will allow you to reach a deeper, more critical level of interpretation.

My eLab includes a Grammar and Accuracy section covering common errors, punctuation and advanced grammar topics that will provide useful support for your writing tasks.

In the **Presenting an Analysis** section, you will be asked to communicate the results of your work in a literary essay and/or presentation.

Part V, which explains in detail the steps of the writing process, will help you produce effective literary essays.

SCOPE AND SEQUENCE

My eLab includes vocabulary and reading comprehension exercises for all texts studied.

Documents and an online grammar assist students in the production of literary analyses.

Part I: Short Stories
(Chapters 1–9; additional chapter online)

Part II: Drama
(Chapters 10 and 11; additional chapter online)

Reading

Part I: Short Stories
- Considering narrative voice and time
- Analyzing dramatic and narrative structure
- Studying characterization and types of characters
- Exploring setting, mood and atmosphere
- Analyzing tone and style: imagery and symbolism, foreshadowing, irony, figures of speech, level of language
- Examining syntax and diction: vivid and evocative adjectives, sentence types, use of reporting verbs, morphology, word associations generating deeper contextual meaning, prosody
- Identifying thematic concepts and statements

Part II: Drama
- Distinguishing dramatic genres
- Considering narrative point of view and time
- Examining structural and dramatic conventions
- Studying characterization
- Considering place and setting
- Analyzing language and dramatic devices
- Identifying the theme of a play

Writing

Part I: Short Stories
- Analyzing the construction of theme; the expression of theme; theme and mood through character comparison; contrasting perspectives; character psychology; underlying issues and themes in a story; symbols; the implicit meaning of a text

Part II: Drama
- Analyzing the dramatic treatment of a theme

Speaking

Part I: Short Stories
- Presenting a character analysis; an explication focusing on tone; a contemporary reading of a literary theme
- Creating a conference-style presentation on a thematic concept
- Describing setting, mood and atmosphere
- Analyzing supporting themes
- Comparing dystopian societies
- Explaining an unreliable narrative

Part II: Drama
- Presenting contrasting passages
- Explicating thematic duality

Part III: Poetry
(Chapters 12–14)

- Distinguishing poetic genres
- Considering speaker and tone
- Studying rhyming and rhythmic patterns
- Examining structural conventions
- Analyzing language and poetic devices: diction, imagery and symbolism, figures of speech
- Identifying the theme, tone and mood of a poem

- Analyzing the interaction between formal and thematic structure; the development of theme and mood; the contribution of imagery to tone and mood

---

- Comparing internal and external context
- Examining sound devices in free verse poetry
- Revealing themes underlying natural description

Part IV: Other Genres
(Chapters 15–18)

- Considering shared elements in songs, spoken word, graphic novels and speeches: narrative voice and tone, theme and mood, diction and literary devices (figures of speech, imagery and symbolism)
- Studying rhyme, rhythm and sound patterns in songs and spoken word
- Studying specific aspects in graphic novels: plot and narrative, visual elements
- Studying specific aspects in speeches: rhetorical devices and the rhetorical transaction, theme and purpose

---

- Analyzing the development of mood and theme through the combination of words and music in songs; the contribution of performance to the development of mood and theme in spoken word; the development of plot in graphic novels; a rhetorical transaction in a speech

---

- Comparing a listener's response to different songs; spoken word performances
- Examining the visual construction of tone, mood and atmosphere in graphic novels; personal stories underpinning societal issues in speeches

Part V: Writing about Literature

CHAPTER 19
The Writing Process

- Finding ideas
- Producing an outline or mind map
- Developing a thesis statement
- Revising and providing adequate support
- Editing and proofreading

CHAPTER 20
Writing with Purpose

- Determining the proper essay format
- Practising various essay types by writing paragraphs

CHAPTER 21
Generating and Developing Ideas

- Note-taking, freewriting, clustering and listing
- Organizing the steps to create an outline

CHAPTER 22
Writing a Literary Essay

- Writing a thesis statement
- Writing an effective introduction and conclusion
- Writing body paragraphs developing topic sentences and providing supporting details
- Finding a title
- Referencing: direct quotations, paraphrasing and summarizing

CHAPTER 23
Revising and Editing an Essay

- Evaluating development, structure and clarity
- Improving grammar, syntax, spelling and punctuation

TABLE OF CONTENTS

INTRODUCTION

Literary Horizons starts from the premise that literature is not only a form of artistic expression but also a means of communication. Language is central to the human experience, and, regardless of the genre or time period, literary works share the intent to communicate what it means to be human, in all of its rich variety. Literature has the power to move us because we can relate to the experiences it evokes, even if those experiences are very different from our own. When engaging in literary analysis, we gain insight into formal elements, but we also establish with the text a dialogue that allows us to hone our critical thinking skills as we uncover deeper meanings and underlying themes. In this way, broadening our literary horizons transports us and helps us to better know ourselves through reading about others. By engaging with literature, we recognize what is common and appreciate what is different.

I have designed *Literary Horizons* with both native language users and advanced language learners in mind. Through an engaging guided approach applied to a fresh selection of texts across different genres, the book proposes an accessible college-level introduction to literary analysis, and supports students as they learn how to present their observations and insights in speaking and writing formats.

Literature, as a form of language arts, comprises many different forms and genres. *Literary Horizons* not only acknowledges but also celebrates this diversity. It presents the traditional triad of prose, drama and verse in the form of short stories, plays and poems (Parts I–III), as well as a selection of genres that are less commonly studied: pop songs, spoken word, graphic novels and speeches (Part IV). Each part is preceded by an Elements of Analysis section that zooms in on the essential features of the particular genre that follows, and provides contextualized practice exercises that allow students to tackle their subsequent analyses with confidence.

To offer maximum flexibility, these four parts can be taken up in any order; they are also further divided into separate chapters, each of which is based on the same methodological principles and straightforward underlying structure. This approach offers students anchorage as they increase their capacity to draw on pertinent techniques and terminology to inform their analysis. The selection of texts covers a wide variety of themes and vantage points, and spans Canadian and international content ranging from frequently anthologized classics to contemporary contributions, including printed material and recorded performances.

At the outset of each chapter, students are invited to Connect with the Text through discussion and research activities that relate to the work's subject matter, theme and/or format. A Text in Context section further introduces students to the material they are about to engage with by presenting salient sociocultural and historical background information on the author and the text. These considerations lay the foundation for the work students undertake as they further their insight into the text and craft their analysis. Three complementary approaches underpin and structure this process: a first exploratory reading gives students the opportunity to voice and corroborate their initial insight and take stock of their more subjective reader's response. Close reading questions draw attention to specific elements that are significant to understanding the text. The Analytical Reading section, which also includes a subset of more challenging Food for Thought questions, encourages students to reinvest these specific observations into more developed critical interpretations that corroborate their inferences, establish new links and deepen their analysis. At the end of each chapter, two focused presentation tasks invite students to share the result of their work in writing and/or speaking.

In order to analyze and interpret a text, it is of course paramount to understand how the words that make it up are used for specific meaning and effect. In each chapter, a Language of Literature section focuses students' attention on specific literary devices and figures of speech, while a Language Focus section considers a general language feature exemplified in the text, which students will be able to use in their own oral and written production.

Finally, to communicate their responses to a literary work, students need to understand how to express these ideas through language. This involves the study and practice of grammar and syntax, which is conveniently offered in My eLab. In addition to the English language rules that allow students to communicate with accuracy, academic writing also has its own set of conventions. Part V, Writing about Literature, helps students master the different steps of the writing process so they can develop their own ability to craft a text and convey meaning. This transferable skill is also recontextualized in speaking tasks throughout the book.

In My eLab, apart from the Grammar and Accuracy section that offers theoretical content and over one hundred exercises on advanced grammar topics, common errors and punctuation, online extensions are offered for all of the book's chapters. These include practice on literary elements, vocabulary comprehension and additional close reading questions. My eLab Documents contains an additional short story and play, audio and video recordings, worksheets and projects of various scope and nature. A complete answer key and descriptive evaluation grids are also available to teachers.

Literary analysis is not always an easy feat. If it were, we would not need this textbook. That said, I firmly believe that engaging with literature should never be an arduous or daunting task. To this end, *Literary Horizons* presents and explains key tools and strategies in an accessible manner and includes a wide selection of materials to represent the wide variety of the human experience and its artistic expression. Through engaging with these materials and using these tools strategically, you will not only become a better reader, writer and speaker, but you will likely also come to understand more about yourself, culture and society in the process.

Andy Van Drom

PART I
Short Stories

ADDITIONAL CHAPTER ONLINE
The Many Things That Denny Brown
Did Not Know (Age Fifteen)

MyBookshelf
> My eLab > Documents
> Part I: Short Stories
> Additional Short Story:
  The Many Things That
  Denny Brown Did Not Know
  (Age Fifteen)

ELEMENTS OF ANALYSIS

The short story is often described as one of the most satisfying literary genres, both to read and to write. In all their apparent natural simplicity, short stories are carefully crafted, not wasting any words. Vivid action, rich description and authentic dialogue all serve the purpose of "showing" rather than "telling" a story, which is usually centred around a conflict motivating one or more characters to evolve through a plot line. To fully appreciate short fiction and analyze it, it is therefore necessary to read beyond the surface and pay attention to the literary elements and principles at the heart of the story. These elements are presented in this section.

Engaging with Short Stories

The experience of prose literature—including short stories and novels—is both emotional and intellectual. While individual reader responses are valuable when reading for entertainment and may inform your interpretation of a story, formal literary analysis requires careful study of elements, strategies and structures to allow you to understand how a text is crafted. These provide not only a shared vocabulary but also tangible proof to support your analysis. Different reading approaches will help you bridge the gap between subjective interpretations and objective analyses.

Reading, just like writing, is a multi-draft process. Similar to how you deepen and fine-tune your thinking process as you write and rewrite the different drafts that lead up to a final version of an essay, you continually develop your understanding of a text as you read and reread it. This is especially important when reading a text with the purpose of analyzing it.

You will approach each story in this section through three "drafts," each focused on a specific type of reading:

- **Exploratory Reading** is similar to what you do when reading for pleasure. Usually with little or no prior knowledge of the text in question, you discover all of its different aspects. What is the story about and where is it set? Who are the characters and what happens to them? The first reading might also lead you to make certain observations about the structure, style and tone of the text. Finally, you will have an intuitive reaction and an emotional response to the text. This is valuable information. On the one hand, it might inspire your forthcoming analysis. On the other hand, being aware of how you feel about a text will allow you to ensure you analyze it as objectively as possible.

- **Close Reading** allows you to zoom in on specific elements of a text. This is where you gather textual evidence that you can draw on in your forthcoming analysis. It can be broken down into two processes that go hand in hand: noticing and explaining. Close reading can focus on micro-level features (e.g., physical description of a setting, metaphors used, punctuation) as well as macro-level features (e.g., dramatic structure, psychological evolution of a character). Asking critical questions as you examine the elements you consider significant will allow you to explain them based on logical inferences, instead of merely summarizing what is in the text or making assumptions.

- **Analytical Reading** is informed by the insight gleaned from the two previous steps. Once you have identified one or more significant elements of focus for your analysis, critique or explication (i.e., the elements you will want to include in your thesis statement), rereading the entire text or specific passages from this vantage point will allow you to critically reconsider your observations, corroborate your inferences, establish new links and deepen your analysis. This type of reading may also lead you to consult other documents that can help you support your argument.

The Narrative Situation

Literary analysis recognizes that there is no direct and transparent connection between the author's intended meanings and the reader's experience. Explicit information about the author's intentions is rarely available, and even when it is, the text may produce effects that go beyond or differ from these intentions. That said, it is important to consider the historical and social context in which a text was written, as this gives insight into the themes conveyed.

In a similar fashion, it is important to note that the narrator is always a **discursive construct**, observable through traces in the text, and is therefore distinct from the author. For instance, a female author can construct a male narrator. Even in a memoir, the narrative voice represents only the part of the author shown to the reader through the text. The following elements allow you to analyze how a narrative is crafted.

The **narrative situation** of a text relates to how a story is told. More specifically, the narrative situation examines the questions of "who speaks?" and "who sees?" in regard to the narrative. Therefore, this literary element is mostly useful to consider when analyzing prose and poetry, since visual genres such as drama and film tend to directly show interaction between characters, without mediation.

The Narrative Voice

The **narrative voice** can be determined by the narrator's use of pronouns and by the **point of view** used to tell the story:

A **first-person narrator** is inevitably part of the narrative. Although this filters the story from one character's perspective, the first-person narrator can still report on other characters' speech and actions using the third person.

- A first-person narrator can be the **protagonist** of the story:
  > Well, I got a good going-over in the morning from old Miss Watson on account of my clothes; but the widow she didn't scold, but only cleaned off the grease and clay, and looked so sorry that I thought I would behave awhile if I could. (Twain, M., *The Adventures of Huckleberry Finn*)

- The narrator can also be an **onlooker** or secondary character:
  > I had called upon my friend, Mr. Sherlock Holmes, one day in the autumn of last year and found him in deep conversation with a very stout, florid-faced, elderly gentleman with fiery red hair … "You could not possibly have come at a better time, my dear Watson," he said cordially. (Doyle, A. C., "The Red-Headed League")

A **third-person narrator** relates a story without being a part of it. As a result, the entire narrative is in the third person. This type of narrator can focalize the story based on two different points of view.

- An **omniscient narrator** is knowledgeable about the actions and thoughts of the protagonists and relates an overall perspective that goes beyond the sum of the different characters' perspectives:

Elizabeth, having rather expected to affront him, was amazed at his gallantry; but there was a mixture of sweetness and archness in her manner which made it difficult for her to affront anybody; and Darcy had never been so bewitched by any woman as he was by her. He really believed, that were it not for the inferiority of her connections, he should be in some danger. (Austen, J., *Pride and Prejudice*)

- A **limited narrator** acts like a camera lens, following the protagonists' actions from the outside. As such, the narrator can only relay what happens in one given place at one given time. In certain cases, a limited narrator also reports on the thoughts of one focal character.

    He sat back. A sense of complete helplessness had descended upon him. To begin with, he did not know with any certainty that this was 1984. (Orwell, G., *1984*)

PRACTICE

A. For each of the following examples, decide on the type of narrator and point of view used:

1. The bible story of Adam and Eve is not narrated by any of the characters. The narration is factual, and the reader does not know what the protagonists think.

    _____

    _____

2. Greek myths are never narrated by any of the characters. Because the purpose of the myths was instructional, the thoughts of the different characters are often reported and explained.

    _____

    _____

3. The *Curious Incident of the Dog in the Night-Time* (M. Haddon) is narrated by Christopher, who is on the autistic spectrum. The narrative illustrates his incomprehension of other characters' actions.

    _____

    _____

4. The narrator of the Harry Potter novels cannot be identified. Much of the novels' tension is based on the fact that the reader does not know what the antagonists are planning.

    _____

    _____

B. Pay attention to the pronouns and other text features to establish the type of narrator and point of view in these excerpts. If you cannot make a firm choice, explain why.

1. When I was in school, I learned that rivers, creeks, and streams are tributaries.

    _____

2. [The mother] was trying very hard not to cry … The child was now feeling distinctly cornered.

    _____

3. The first human trial was on Patient D, a 56-year-old male, single and childless, who was suffering from colon cancer … The French medical team felt vindicated.

    _____

4. You can see by these things that she was of a rather vain and frivolous character; still, she had virtues, and enough to make up, I think …

    _____

5. She stayed motionless, with gaze riveted upon her child, and her face the picture of fright. Presently her husband entered the room, and without noticing her, went to a table …

_____

C. The following passage from "The Appointment in Samarra" (as retold by W. Somerset Maugham) cleverly uses narration and point of view as literary devices to build tension and surprise. Answer each question before you read further.

Excerpt 1:

There was a merchant in Bagdad who sent his servant to market to buy provisions and in a little while the servant came back, white and trembling, and said, "Master, just now when I was in the marketplace I was jostled by a woman in the crowd and when I turned I saw it was Death that jostled me. She looked at me and made a threatening gesture; now, lend me your horse, and I will ride away from this city and avoid my fate. I will go to Samarra and there, Death will not find me." The merchant lent him his horse, and the servant mounted it, and he dug his spurs in its flanks and as fast as the horse could gallop he went.

1. Considering the use of pronouns and point of view in this excerpt, what type of narrator do you think tells the story? Support your answer with examples.

_____

_____

_____

_____

Excerpt 2:

Then the merchant went down to the marketplace and he saw me standing in the crowd and he came to me and said, "Why did you make a threatening gesture to my servant when you saw him this morning?"

2. Has the use of pronouns changed in this excerpt, and if yes, how? After reading the two preceding excerpts, what type of narrator do you think tells the story? Support your answer with examples.

_____

_____

Excerpt 3:

"That was not a threatening gesture," I said, "it was only a start of surprise. I was astonished to see him in Bagdad, for I had an appointment with him tonight in Samarra."

3. After reading the third excerpt, does your analysis of the type of narrator change? Support your answer with examples.

_____

_____

4. Finally, read through the three excerpts without interruption. Who do you think narrates the story? What does it tell you about the physical aspect of the narrator?

_____

_____

Narrative Time

It is not uncommon for a text to blend different types of narrative voices. In this way, the author can manipulate **narrative time**.

- In **subsequent narration**, the narrator tells what happened in some past time.
- In **prior narration**, the narrator tells what is going to happen at some future time.
- In **simultaneous narration**, the narrator tells the story at the very moment it occurs.

By alternating these forms of narration—for instance, by introducing literary devices such as **flashbacks** and **flashforwards**—the chronological order of the narrative is broken. Another manipulation that affects the reading experience concerns **narrative speed**:

- In a **scene**, the narrative time corresponds to the story's time. Dialogue is a good example of this.
  "I want," I said, "to buy my little boy a few simple tricks."
  "Legerdemain?" he asked. "Mechanical? Domestic?"
  "Anything amusing?" said I. (Wells, H. G., "The Magic Shop")
- In a **pause**, the story is interrupted to make room for narratorial observations, such as descriptions of the setting or the appearance of a character.
  "Lies, lies, lies!" Miss Milan's little workroom was really terribly hot, stuffy, sordid. It smelt of clothes and cabbage cooking ..." (Woolf, V., "The New Dress")
- In a **summary**, the narrator condenses (part of) a story, so the action is accelerated. For instance, a five-day train journey can be related in five sentences.
  "I have watched two whole weeks, and he doesn't come up! This last week a fright has been stealing upon me." (Twain, M., "A Dog's Tale")
- An **ellipsis** skips an entire part of the story—for instance, by indicating that it takes place a certain amount of time beforehand or afterwards.
  "That happened six months ago. And now I am beginning to believe it is all right." (Wells, H. G., "The Magic Shop")

Dramatic Plot Structure

Plot is a term used to describe the structure in which a story's key events, which are part of the narrative, are organized by the author. This structure relates to the order in which the events are presented to the reader, which may be different from their natural or chronological order.

In order to generate tension, the author may use **foreshadowing**, a literary device presaging later plot events through imagery, dialogue or symbols. In the opening scene of the novel *Anna Karenina* by Leon Tolstoi, for instance, the protagonist hears of a man being run over by a train. This event foreshadows her own end when she commits suicide by jumping in front of a train.

The plot is considered to be the foundation of the story around which the settings, characters and actions are constructed in a way to engage the reader. It revolves around one or more **conflicts**, which are typically divided into four groups depending on who or what is involved: **character vs. self, character vs. human, character vs. nature** and **character vs. society**.

Gustav Freytag, a nineteenth-century German author, identified common patterns in literary plots and developed a pyramid-shaped diagram to analyze them. This visual tool will allow you to establish the key moments of a storyline, an important step in literary analysis.

In the **exposition**, the author sets the scene by providing descriptions and background information to introduce the characters and setting.

A single event usually signals the beginning of the main conflict that leads to most of the story's action. This moment is called the **inciting incident** or **complication**.

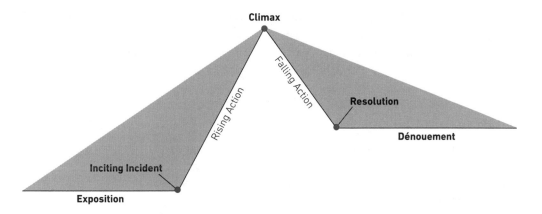

As events unfold, the story builds and gets more exciting. This is the **rising action**.

The **climax** is the moment of greatest tension in a story. It constitutes the tipping point of the action.

As a result of the climax, new events happen and cause **falling action**. The tension gradually dissipates as opportunities and possibilities make their appearance.

This leads to the **resolution** once the main issue is solved. This outcome can be positive or negative for the protagonist.

At the very end of the story arc, called the **dénouement**, the author wraps up any remaining issues and may suggest what happens to the characters after the story finishes or leave the reader to reflect on the story's main theme.

PRACTICE

A. Read the following summary of "Hansel and Gretel" (Grimm Brothers). Identify each sentence with one of the plot moments. Write *E* (exposition), *I* (inciting incident), *RA* (rising action), *C* (climax), *FA* (falling action), *R* (resolution) or *D* (dénouement) in the space provided after each sentence.

There is a great famine in the country and a woodcutter's family is starving. _____ His wife, the children's stepmother, suggests taking Hansel and Gretel into the woods, so they would have two fewer mouths to feed. _____ However, Hansel and Gretel had learned about the plan and use bread crumbs to mark the path. _____ The bread is eaten by the birds, so the children are lost. _____ They find a mysterious cabin made out of gingerbread. _____ It belongs to a cannibalistic witch who captures the children and intends to eat them. _____ Since they are too lean, she decides to lock them up and fatten them first. _____ Finally, the witch prepares the oven and plans to bake both children. _____ Gretel outsmarts her and throws the witch in the oven, where she is burned. _____ The children search the cabin and find gold and jewellery. _____ With the help of birds, they find their way back home. _____ Their stepmother has died in the meantime, and their remorseful father welcomes them. They live happily ever after. _____

B. Work with one or more partners. Choose a fairy tale all of you are familiar with; for instance, "Cinderella," "Little Red Ridinghood," "Jack and the Bean Stalk," or "Beauty and the Beast." First, summarize the story by listing all of the main events in separate sentences, as is done in exercise 1. Then, analyze the story's plot by determining for each event what plot moment it represents, using the abbreviations from exercise 1. Briefly present your summary and plot analysis to your classmates following the format used in the previous activity.

Characterization

Writers shape their characters in different ways, most commonly through the description of physical or psychological traits; the dialogue—either in interactions with other characters or as an inner monologue reporting thoughts and feelings; the actions and behaviours that inform the reader about the character's personality.

In the 1920s, literary critic E. M. Forster developed a typology of literary characters that is still prevalent in literary analysis today.

- **Flat characters** are two-dimensional; they usually have one or a few easily recognizable or stereotypical traits or features that define them.
- **Round characters** are three-dimensional; they are complex, and their nuanced physical and psychological traits are described in rich detail.
- **Static characters** tend to remain unchanged throughout the story.
- **Dynamic characters** evolve, whether positively or negatively, as the story progresses. This can be observed through their verbal and non-verbal behaviour.

For instance, in *Harry Potter and the Philosopher's Stone* (J. K. Rowling), Harry Potter is a round character with a complex personality influenced by his friendships and sense of righteousness, while Draco Malfoy, one of the antagonist characters, is more flat and static, and reduced to his quality of being a mean bully.

The main character of a story is often referred to as the **protagonist**; the **antagonist** is the character in direct conflict with the protagonist. These terms do not make any value judgments in regard to the characters, which can have positive or negative traits. A protagonist with common or negative character traits is referred to as an **antihero**.

PRACTICE

Work with one or more partners. Brainstorm a list of five characters from short stories, novels or films you are familiar with. Taking turns, discuss what you know about each character, then determine if these characteristics make him/her flat or round. Explain your choices. If you have read the story in question, also establish whether the character is static or dynamic.

Setting

Put straightforwardly, the **setting** of a story amounts to its situation in space and time. Other factors may also inform the setting.

Apart from physical environments, places may also be based on mental constructs. For instance, even though *1984* (G. Orwell) and *Mrs. Dalloway* (V. Woolf) are both set in London, the city takes on an entirely different dimension in both novels. In the dystopian *1984*, London is reduced to a grey and grim collection of derelict buildings, literally and figuratively dominated by Big Brother and the Ministry of Truth. In *Mrs. Dalloway*, on the other hand, the city is positively depicted as being lively, dynamic and associated with summer:

> A kilometre away the Ministry of Truth, his place of work, towered vast and white above the grimy landscape. This, he thought with a sort of vague distaste—this was London, chief city of Airstrip One … (*1984*)

In people's eyes, in the swing, tramp, and trudge; in the bellow and the uproar; the carriages, motor cars, omnibuses, vans, sandwich men shuffling and swinging; brass bands; barrel organs; in the triumph and the jingle and the strange high singing of some aeroplane overhead was what she loved; life; London; this moment of June. (*Mrs. Dalloway*)

Similarly, timing can directly affect a story—the same account of events may evoke a different atmosphere when set against the backdrop of a sunny summer's day or a dreary winter evening. Time also has a more indirect impact, notably through the social and cultural context associated with it. A story on black servants has different implications based on whether it is set before or after the Slavery Abolition Act, for instance.

Imagery can be used to complete the setting of a story by appealing to the reader's senses to evoke things like the temperature and weather, as well as the sounds and smells that are part of the environment in which the story is set.

For instance, in *Wuthering Heights*, which is set in two neighbouring houses, Emily Brontë creates a contrasting mood by associating Wuthering Heights with negative, depressing imagery, and Thrushcross Grange with calm and peaceful imagery:

> There was no moon, and everything beneath lay in misty darkness: not a light gleamed from any house, far or near—all had been extinguished long ago; and those at Wuthering Heights were never visible …

> Gimmerton chapel bells were still ringing; and the full, mellow flow of the beck in the valley came soothingly on the ear. It was a sweet substitute for the yet absent murmur of the summer foliage, which drowned that music about the Grange when the trees were in leaf.

Imagery and **symbolism** are often used together, which sometimes makes it difficult to distinguish the two. In the above example, for instance, the descriptive images not only determine the mood of the story but also symbolize the differences between the families who live there. In other words, a symbol is an element in the story that represents another, often more abstract, idea. Common symbols include winter to refer to death or a rose for romance.

All of the above considerations directly affect the **atmosphere** or **mood** that pervades the story. The feelings evoked through the creation of a particular mood transport the reader into the story.

The story's narrator and point of view heavily influence the reader's experience of setting, since it is the construct of the narrator that controls which information is introduced, and how.

PRACTICE

Consider the following passages and determine if the mood is positive or negative. Then, work with a partner to determine what the underlined word or words might symbolize or evoke.

1. The water was <u>deep</u>. No one liked being around that part of The River. (Naponse, D., "She Is Water")

Mood: _____ Symbolic meaning: _____

2. It was such a charming home!—my new one; a fine great house, with pictures, and delicate decorations, and rich furniture, and <u>no gloom</u> anywhere, but all the wilderness of dainty colours lit up with <u>flooding sunshine</u>. (Twain, M., "A Dog's Tale")

Mood: _____ Symbolic meaning: _____

3. She would go to the <u>London Library</u> to-morrow. She would find some wonderful, helpful, astonishing book, quite by chance. (Woolf, V., "The New Dress")

Mood: _____ Symbolic meaning: _____

4. When the little girl came home, it was already <u>getting dark</u>. (Bannerji, H., "The Other Family")

Mood: _____   Symbolic meaning: _____

5. I sit on the <u>bench in the graveyard</u> and I squeeze my hand and make it white and remember about my wife giving birth to my son. (Adams, S., "Wide and Deep")

Mood: _____   Symbolic meaning of "graveyard": _____

Symbolic meaning of "bench": _____

Tone and Style

Apart from the author's choice of characters, events and actions, the author's use of language also has strong influence on the reading experience. The **tone of writing** is an indicator of the author's attitude toward the narrative elements. For instance, through the use of irony, the author can portray an intrinsically trivial event as being of extreme importance. The use of tone brings an additional layer of nuance to a story and may yield genres that sound like a contradiction in terms (e.g., magic realism or horror comedy).

The tone of writing is mostly achieved through the author's stylistic decisions. The **style** of a text is the sum of its linguistic characteristics, including the use of syntax (sentence length and type, word order) and diction (word choice).

An important aspect of literary analysis is to pay attention to diction when performing one or more close readings, because we may presume that the author has carefully made these word choices when conveying ideas to craft a story.

- Words not only have **denotation**—their literal meaning—but also **connotation**—the suggested meaning that can often be inferred from the context.
- Words are part of a register or level of language, ranging from the formal to the informal.
- Words can be associated with written or spoken language.
- Words can be used as **figures of speech** to create a non-literal meaning that differs from their primary usage; for instance, **metaphors** and **similes** both call attention to how two different things are similar. A simile expresses this comparison through the use of the words *as*, *like* or equivalent expressions: "To follow her thought was like following a voice which speaks too quickly" (Virginia Woolf). Metaphors operate in a subtler fashion, without any explicit comparison: "Conscience is a man's compass" (Vincent Van Gogh).
- Words can contribute to **rhythm** and **sound patterns** such as repetition and rhyme, alliteration (repeating the word-initial sound: *Cindy saw six swimmers*), assonance (repeating vowel sounds: *Try to light the fire*) and consonance (repeating consonant sounds: *Max insists he sees ghosts*).

When critics refer to an **author's style**, they highlight the use of these features across texts.

MyBookshelf > My eLab
> Exercises > Part I: Short
Stories > Elements of Analysis

Theme

All of the aforementioned literary elements play a role in the development of the story's theme, which can be said to be the core or motivation of the story. A story can have one or more themes, which are comprehensive statements of a deeper meaning that extends beyond the plot and the characters. Themes usually require being summarized in more abstract terms.

In this regard, a story's theme differs from its **subject matter**, which is what the story is about on a primary, concrete level. In other words, the subject matter can be observed directly, while a theme consists of deeper issues that require analysis to be uncovered.

George Orwell's *Animal Farm* clearly illustrates this distinction. While its subject matter relates to a farm run by animals, the themes of the text have nothing to do with sheep and pigs, but rather concern issues like *the corruption of socialist ideals and the abuse of language as an instrument for indoctrination.*

Both concepts are not entirely separate in the sense that the subject matter is used to express the theme(s) of the story. To determine the theme(s) of a story, you might therefore ask, "What point does the author make through the subject matter of the work?"

When answering this question, it may be helpful to distinguish between broad **thematic concepts** that appear in many different texts—for instance, *love* or *individual vs. society*—and narrow **thematic statements**, which concern the particular argument the author makes about such a concept—e.g., *true love overcomes racial differences*, or *individuals are often powerless against an authoritarian government.*

When conducting literary analysis, it is important to describe the theme(s) as precisely as possible, since the purpose of a literary essay or presentation is to demonstrate how, for instance, a theme develops through the dynamics and mechanics of a text (formulated in a thesis statement). Stating that a short story is about "the difficulty for immigrants to construct an identity that embraces two cultures" is a lot stronger and more compelling than just saying that the story is about "identity." Therefore, "theme" is used in this book to refer to a thematic statement that closely applies to the text under analysis.

PRACTICE

A. Identify the following examples as subject matter (S), thematic concepts (TC) or thematic statements (TS).

1. Two young lovers from feuding families kill themselves because they do not want to live without the other person. _____

2. Love _____

3. The forcefulness of love can lead people to prefer death over being separated from the person they love. _____

4. The danger of totalitarian regimes _____

5. A man goes to great lengths to oppose the regime of Big Brother, but finally succumbs. _____

6. Through the abuse of power and control, totalitarian regimes annihilate personal freedom of their citizens. _____

B. Determine the subject matter, thematic concept and thematic statement (or theme) of the excerpt of *The Appointment in Samarra*, found on page 7.

Subject matter: _____

Thematic concept: _____

Thematic statement/theme: _____

CHAPTER 1

The Black Cat

– Edgar Allan Poe

This chapter focuses on the following:

- Setting and atmosphere
- Characterization and types of characters
- Symbolism
- Language Focus: vivid and evocative adjectives
- The Language of Literature: foreshadowing and style
- Theme: thematic concepts and thematic statements

Connect with the Text

A. Take stock of your opinions on the following questions. Discuss them with one or more partners.

1. Are you superstitious? Why do you think people believe in superstitions?
2. What are some of the best-known examples of superstitions?
3. What are some of the ingredients of a satisfying horror story or film?
4. What places or settings do you associate with the scariest scenes in a horror story?
5. Do you think people are always responsible for their actions? Why?

B. Do a web search for "temperance reform" and the "temperance movement" in the nineteenth century. Summarize the concept in a few sentences.

Text in Context

Edgar Allan Poe (1809–1849) was one of the most influential American writers of the nineteenth century. Although his works include many short stories, poetry, literary criticism essays and book reviews, he is remembered mostly for his tales of terror. Indeed, Poe transformed the horror story genre with his skilful tales of psychological depth and insight. Many of his stories can be situated in the Gothic literature current, also called dark romanticism, which blends elements of terror with romance, superstition, distress and supernatural events, and has a more philosophical core. In this genre the characters are developed to react as realistically as possible to situations that are unreal. Other examples of Gothic fiction include Mary Shelley's *Frankenstein* and Bram Stoker's *Dracula*. Like his writing, many aspects of Poe's life remain mysterious. In great part, this is due to the biography written by Rufus Griswold, considered Poe's literary adversary. Many of the facts he alleged proved to be unsubstantiated but persisted in the collective memory.

Exploratory Reading

Read the text a first time without interruption. Keep an open mind and take a mental note of your reactions and observations. Soak up the mood and atmosphere without looking for any specific elements. When you are finished, answer the questions below the text.

The Black Cat   **Edgar Allan Poe**

1 For the most wild, yet most **homely** narrative which I am about to pen, I neither expect nor solicit belief. Mad indeed would I be to expect it, in a case where my very senses reject their own evidence. Yet, mad am I not—and very surely do I not dream. But to-morrow I die, and to-day I would unburden my soul. My immediate purpose is to place before the world, plainly, succinctly, and without comment, a series of mere household events. In their consequences, these events have terrified—have tortured—have destroyed me. Yet I will not attempt to expound them. To me, they have presented little but horror—to many they will seem less terrible than baroques. Hereafter, perhaps, some intellect may be found which will reduce my phantasm to the commonplace—some intellect more calm, more logical, and far less excitable than my own, which will perceive, in the circumstances I detail with awe, nothing more than an ordinary succession of very natural causes and effects.

2 From my infancy I was noted for the docility and humanity of my disposition. My tenderness of heart was even so conspicuous as to make me the jest of my companions. I was especially fond of animals, and was indulged by my parents with a great variety of pets. With these I spent most of my time, and never was so happy as when feeding and caressing them. This peculiarity of character grew with my growth, and, in my manhood, I derived from it one of my principal sources of pleasure. To those who have cherished an affection for a faithful and **sagacious** dog, I need hardly be at the trouble of explaining the nature or the intensity of the gratification thus derivable. There is something in the unselfish and self-sacrificing love of a brute, which goes directly to the heart of him who has had frequent occasion to test the **paltry** friendship and gossamer fidelity of mere Man.

3 I married early, and was happy to find in my wife a disposition not **uncongenial** with my own. Observing my partiality for domestic pets, she lost no opportunity of procuring those of the most **agreeable** kind. We had birds, gold-fish, a fine dog, rabbits, a small monkey and a cat.

4 This latter was a remarkably large and beautiful animal, entirely black, and sagacious to an astonishing degree. In speaking of his intelligence, my wife, who at heart was not a little tinctured with superstition, made frequent allusion to the ancient popular notion, which regarded all black cats as witches in disguise. Not that she was ever serious upon this point—and I mention the matter at all for no better reason than that it happens, just now, to be remembered.

5 Pluto—this was the cat's name—was my favourite pet and playmate. I alone fed him, and he attended me wherever I went about the house. It was even with difficulty that I could prevent him from following me through the streets.

6 Our friendship lasted, in this manner, for several years, during which my general temperament and character—through the instrumentality of the fiend Intemperance—had (I blush to confess it) experienced a radical alteration for the worse. I grew, day by day, more moody, more irritable, more regardless of the feelings of others. I suffered myself to use intemperate language to my wife. At length, I even offered her personal violence. My pets, of course, were made to feel the change in my disposition. I not only neglected, but ill-used them. For Pluto, however, I still retained sufficient regard to restrain me from maltreating him, as I made no scruple of maltreating the rabbits, the monkey, or even the dog, when by accident, or through affection, they came in my way. But my disease grew upon me—for what disease is like Alcohol?—and at length even Pluto, who was now becoming old, and consequently somewhat **peevish**—even Pluto began to experience the effects of my ill temper.

7 One night, returning home, much intoxicated, from one of my haunts about town, I fancied that the cat avoided my presence. I seized him; when, in his fright at my violence, he inflicted a slight wound upon my hand with his teeth. The fury of a demon instantly possessed me. I knew myself no longer. My original soul seemed, at once, to take its flight from my body; and a more than **fiendish** malevolence, gin-nurtured,

thrilled every fibre of my frame. I took from my waistcoat pocket a pen-knife, opened it, grasped the poor beast by the throat, and deliberately cut one of its eyes from the socket! I blush, I burn, I shudder, while I pen the damnable atrocity.

8 When reason returned with the morning—when I had slept off the fumes of the night's debauch—I experienced a sentiment half of horror, half of remorse, for the crime of which I had been guilty; but it was, at best, a feeble and equivocal feeling, and the soul remained untouched. I again plunged into excess, and soon drowned in wine all memory of the deed.

9 In the meantime the cat slowly recovered. The socket of the lost eye presented, it is true, a frightful appearance, but he no longer appeared to suffer any pain. He went about the house as usual, but, as might be expected, fled in extreme terror at my approach. I had so much of my old heart left, as to be at first grieved by this evident dislike on the part of a creature which had once so loved me. But this feeling soon gave place to irritation. And then came, as if to my final and irrevocable overthrow, the spirit of Perverseness. Of this spirit philosophy takes no account. Yet I am not more sure that my soul lives, than I am that perverseness is one of the primitive impulses of the human heart—one of the indivisible primary faculties, or sentiments, which give direction to the character of man. Who has not, a hundred times, found himself committing a **vile** or a silly action, for no other reason than because he knows he should not? Have we not a perpetual inclination, in the teeth of our best judgment, to violate that which is Law, merely because we understand it to be such? This spirit of perverseness, I say, came to my final overthrow. It was this unfathomable longing of the soul to vex itself—to offer violence to its own nature—to do wrong for the wrong's sake only—that urged me to continue and finally to consummate the injury I had inflicted upon the unoffending brute. One morning, in cool blood, I slipped a noose about its neck and hung it to the limb of a tree—hung it with the tears streaming from my eyes, and with the bitterest remorse at my heart—hung it because I knew that it had loved me, and because I felt it had given me no reason of offence—hung it because I knew that in so doing I was committing a sin—a deadly sin that would so jeopardize my immortal soul as to place it—if such a thing were possible—even beyond the reach of the infinite mercy of the Most Merciful and Most Terrible God.

10 On the night of the day on which this cruel deed was done, I was aroused from sleep by the cry of "Fire!"

The curtains of my bed were in flames. The whole house was blazing. It was with great difficulty that my wife, a servant, and myself, made our escape from the conflagration. The destruction was complete. My entire worldly wealth was swallowed up, and I resigned myself thenceforward to despair.

11 I am above the weakness of seeking to establish a sequence of cause and effect between the disaster and the atrocity. But I am detailing a chain of facts, and wish not to leave even a possible link imperfect. On the day succeeding the fire, I visited the ruins. The walls, with one exception, had fallen in. This exception was found in a compartment wall, not very thick, which stood about the middle of the house, and against which had rested the head of my bed. The plastering had here, in great measure, resisted the action of the fire—a fact which I attributed to its having been recently spread. About this wall a dense crowd were collected, and many persons seemed to be examining a particular portion of it with every minute and eager attention. The words "strange!" "singular!" and other similar expressions, excited my curiosity. I approached and saw, as if graven in bas-relief upon the white surface, the figure of a gigantic cat. The impression was given with an accuracy truly marvellous. There was a rope about the animal's neck.

12 When I first beheld this apparition—for I could scarcely regard it as less—my wonder and my terror were extreme. But at length reflection came to my aid. The cat, I remembered, had been hung in a garden adjacent to the house. Upon the alarm of fire, this garden had been immediately filled by the crowd—by some one of whom the animal must have been cut from the tree and thrown, through an open window, into my chamber. This had probably been done with the view of arousing me from sleep. The falling of other walls had compressed the victim of my cruelty into the substance of the freshly-spread plaster; the lime of which, with the flames and the ammonia from the carcass, had then accomplished the portraiture as I saw it.

13 Although I thus readily accounted to my reason, if not altogether to my conscience, for the startling fact just detailed, it did not the less fail to make a deep impression upon my fancy. For months I could not rid myself of the phantasm of the cat; and, during this period, there came back into my spirit a half-sentiment that seemed, but was not, remorse. I went so far as to regret the loss of the animal, and to look about me, among the vile haunts which I now habitually frequented, for another pet of the same species, and of somewhat similar appearance, with which to supply its place.

14 One night as I sat, half stupefied, in a den of more than infamy, my attention was suddenly drawn to some black object, reposing upon the head of one of the immense hogsheads of gin, or of rum, which constituted the chief furniture of the apartment. I had been looking steadily at the top of this hogshead for some minutes, and what now caused me surprise was the fact that I had not sooner perceived the object thereupon. I approached it, and touched it with my hand. It was a black cat—a very large one—fully as large as Pluto, and closely resembling him in every respect but one. Pluto had not a white hair upon any portion of his body; but this cat had a large, although indefinite, splotch of white, covering nearly the whole region of the breast.

15 Upon my touching him, he immediately arose, purred loudly, rubbed against my hand, and appeared delighted with my notice. This, then, was the very creature of which I was in search. I at once offered to purchase it of the landlord; but this person made no claim to it—knew nothing of it—had never seen it before.

16 I continued my caresses, and when I prepared to go home, the animal evinced a disposition to accompany me. I permitted it to do so; occasionally stooping and patting it as I proceeded. When it reached the house it domesticated itself at once, and became immediately a great favourite with my wife.

17 For my own part, I soon found a dislike to it arising within me. This was just the reverse of what I had anticipated; but—I know not how or why it was—its evident fondness for myself rather disgusted and annoyed me. By slow degrees, these feelings of disgust and annoyance rose into the bitterness of hatred. I avoided the creature; a certain sense of shame, and the remembrance of my former deed of cruelty, preventing me from physically abusing it. I did not, for some weeks, strike, or otherwise violently ill-use it; but gradually—very gradually—I came to look upon it with unutterable loathing, and to flee silently from its **odious** presence, as from the breath of a pestilence.

18 What added, no doubt, to my hatred of the beast, was the discovery, on the morning after I brought it home, that, like Pluto, it also had been deprived of one of its eyes. This circumstance, however, only endeared it to my wife, who, as I have already said, possessed, in a high degree, that humanity of feeling which had once been my distinguishing trait, and the source of many of my simplest and purest pleasures.

19 With my aversion to this cat, however, its partiality for myself seemed to increase. It followed my footsteps with a pertinacity which it would be difficult to make the reader comprehend. Whenever I sat, it would crouch beneath my chair, or spring upon my knees, covering me with its loathsome caresses. If I arose to walk, it would get between my feet, and thus nearly throw me down, or, fastening its long and sharp claws in my dress, clamber, in this manner, to my breast. At such times, although I longed to destroy it with a blow, I was yet withheld from so doing, partly by a memory of my former crime, but chiefly—let me confess it at once—by absolute dread of the beast.

20 This dread was not exactly a dread of physical evil—and yet I should be at a loss how otherwise to define it. I am almost ashamed to own—yes, even in this felon's cell, I am almost ashamed to own—that the terror and horror with which the animal inspired me, had been heightened by one of the merest chimeras it would be possible to conceive. My wife had called my attention, more than once, to the character of the mark of white hair, of which I have spoken, and which constituted the sole visible difference between the strange beast and the one I had destroyed. The reader will remember that this mark, although large, had been originally very indefinite; but, by slow degrees—degrees nearly imperceptible, and which for a long time my reason struggled to reject as fanciful—it had, at length, assumed a rigorous distinctness of outline. It was now the representation of an object that I shudder to name—and for this, above all, I loathed, and dreaded, and would have rid myself of the monster had I dared—it was now, I say, the image of a hideous—of a **ghastly** thing—of the Gallows!—oh, mournful and terrible engine of horror and of crime—of agony and of death!

21 And now was I indeed wretched beyond the wretchedness of mere humanity. And a brute beast—whose fellow I had contemptuously destroyed—a brute beast to work out for me—for me, a man, fashioned in the image of the High God—so much of insufferable woe! Alas! neither by day nor by night knew I the blessing of rest any more! During the former the creature left me no moment alone; and, in the latter, I started, hourly, from dreams of unutterable fear, to find the hot breath of the thing upon my face, and its vast weight—an incarnate nightmare that I had no power to shake off—incumbent eternally upon my heart!

22 Beneath the pressure of torments such as these, the feeble remnant of the good within me succumbed. Evil thoughts became my sole intimates—the darkest and most evil of thoughts. The moodiness of my usual temper increased to hatred of all things and of all mankind; while, from the sudden, frequent and

ungovernable outbursts of a fury to which I now blindly abandoned myself, my uncomplaining wife, alas! was the most usual and the most patient of sufferers.

23 One day she accompanied me, upon some household errand, into the cellar of the old building which our poverty compelled us to inhabit. The cat followed me down the steep stairs, and, nearly throwing me headlong, exasperated me to madness. Uplifting an axe, and forgetting, in my wrath, the childish dread which had hitherto stayed my hand, I aimed a blow at the animal which, of course, would have proved instantly fatal had it descended as I wished. But this blow was arrested by the hand of my wife. Goaded, by the interference, into a rage more than demoniacal, I withdrew my arm from her grasp, and buried the axe in her brain. She fell dead upon the spot, without a groan.

24 This hideous murder accomplished, I set myself forthwith, and with entire deliberation, to the task of concealing the body. I knew that I could not remove it from the house, either by day or by night, without the risk of being observed by the neighbours. Many projects entered my mind. At one period I thought of cutting the corpse into minute fragments, and destroying them by fire. At another, I resolved to dig a grave for it in the floor of the cellar. Again, I deliberated about casting it in the well in the yard—about packing it in a box, as if merchandise, with the usual arrangements, and so getting a porter to take it from the house. Finally I hit upon what I considered a far better expedient than either of these. I determined to wall it up in the cellar—as the monks of the Middle Ages recorded to have walled up their victims.

25 For a purpose such as this the cellar was well adapted. Its walls were loosely constructed, and had lately been plastered throughout with a rough plaster, which the dampness of the atmosphere had prevented from hardening. Moreover, in one of the walls was a projection, caused by a false chimney, or fireplace, that had been filled up, and made to resemble the rest of the cellar. I made no doubt that I could readily displace the bricks at this point, insert the corpse, and wall the whole up as before, so that no eye could detect anything suspicious.

26 And in this calculation I was not deceived. By means of a crowbar I easily dislodged the bricks, and, having carefully deposited the body against the inner wall, I propped it in that position, while, with little trouble, I relaid the whole structure as it originally stood. Having procured mortar, sand, and hair, with every possible precaution, I prepared a plaster which could not be distinguished from the old, and with this I very carefully went over the new brickwork. When I had finished, I felt satisfied that all was right. The wall did not present the slightest appearance of having been disturbed. The rubbish on the floor was picked up with the minutest care. I looked around triumphantly, and said to myself, "Here at least, then, my labour has not been in vain."

27 My next step was to look for the beast which had been the cause of so much wretchedness; for I had, at length, firmly resolved to put it to death. Had I been able to meet with it, at the moment, there could have been no doubt of its fate; but it appeared that the crafty animal had been alarmed at the violence of my previous anger, and forebore to present itself in my present mood. It is impossible to describe, or to imagine, the deep, the blissful sense of relief which the absence of the detested creature occasioned in my bosom. It did not make its appearance during the night—and thus for one night at least, since its introduction into the house, I soundly and tranquilly slept; aye, slept even with the burden of murder upon my soul!

28 The second and the third day passed, and still my tormentor came not. Once again I breathed as a free man. The monster, in terror, had fled the premises forever! I should behold it no more! My happiness was supreme! The guilt of my dark deed disturbed me but little. Some few inquiries had been made, but these had been readily answered. Even a search had been instituted—but of course nothing was to be discovered. I looked upon my future felicity as secured.

29 Upon the fourth day of the assassination, a party of the police came, very unexpectedly, into the house, and proceeded again to make rigorous investigation of the premises. Secure, however, in the inscrutability of my place of concealment, I felt no embarrassment whatever. The officers bade me accompany them in their search. They left no nook or corner unexplored. At length, for the third or fourth time, they descended into the cellar. I quivered not in a muscle. My heart beat calmly as that of one who slumbers in innocence. I walked the cellar from end to end. I folded my arms upon my bosom, and roamed easily to and fro. The police were thoroughly satisfied, and prepared to depart. The glee at my heart was too strong to be restrained. I burned to say if but one word, by way of triumph, and to render doubly sure their assurance of my guiltlessness.

30 "Gentlemen," I said at last, as the party ascended the steps, "I delight to have allayed your suspicions. I wish you all health, and a little more courtesy. By-the-bye, gentlemen, this—this is a very well-constructed

house." (In the rabid desire to say something easily, I scarcely knew what I uttered at all.) "I may say an excellently well-constructed house. These walls—are you going, gentlemen?—these walls are solidly put together;" and here, through the mere frenzy of bravado, I rapped heavily, with a cane which I held in my hand, upon that very portion of the brickwork behind which stood the corpse of the wife of my bosom.

31 But may God shield and deliver me from the fangs of the Arch-Fiend! No sooner had the reverberation of my blows sunk into silence, than I was answered by a voice from within the tomb!—by a cry, at first muffled and broken, like the sobbing of a child, and then quickly swelling into one long, loud, and continuous scream, utterly anomalous and inhuman—a howl—a wailing shriek, half of horror and half of triumph, such as might have arisen only out of hell, conjointly from the throats of the damned in their agony and of the demons that exult in the damnation.

32 Of my own thoughts it is folly to speak. Swooning, I staggered to the opposite wall. For one instant the party upon the stairs remained motionless, through extremity of terror and of awe. In the next, a dozen stout arms were toiling at the wall. It fell bodily. The corpse, already greatly decayed and clotted with gore, stood erect before the eyes of the spectators. Upon its head, with red extended mouth and solitary eye of fire, sat the hideous beast whose craft had seduced me into murder, and whose informing voice had consigned me to the hangman. I had walled the monster up within the tomb!

(3913 words)

Source: Poe, E. A. "The Black Cat." *United States Saturday Post*, 19 Aug. 1843, poestories.com/read/blackcat.

Initial Insight

1. What is the story about? Write down anything that intuitively comes to you.

_____

_____

2. How would you describe the narrator of the story?

_____

_____

_____

Reader's Response

Consider the following questions. Discuss your answers with one or more partners.

1. What are some of the controversial elements and events in the story? Are they necessary to further the storyline?

2. What emotional response(s) or reaction(s) did these events evoke in you?

3. What sort of impression did the narrator make on you?

4. Beyond "unburden[ing his] soul," why do you think the narrator might write down and share his story?

5. Do you think some of the story's inexplicable elements, such as the imprint of Pluto on the narrator's bedroom wall after the fire, are supernatural, or is there some logical explanation, as the narrator suggests?

6. Does the story end the way you expected? How? Why?

The author uses vivid adjectives that go beyond mere description to evoke the intensity of his moral evaluation of the thing or person being described. Refer to the context, and use a reputable unilingual dictionary to define the following words (identified in bold) as they are used in the text. Pay attention to the value judgment they imply; is it positive or negative, and to what degree?

1. homely (par. 1): _____

2. sagacious (par. 2): _____

3. paltry (par. 2): _____

4. uncongenial (par. 3): _____

5. agreeable (par. 3): _____

6. peevish (par. 6): _____

7. fiendish (par. 7): _____

8. vile (par. 9): _____

9. odious (par. 17): _____

10. ghastly (par. 20): _____

Look up any other words you are unsure of.

MyBookshelf > My eLab > Exercises > Part I: Short Stories > Chapter 1: The Black Cat > Vocabulary Comprehension

Close Reading

As you read the text again, pay attention to elements that seem significant to understanding and interpreting the story. The following guided reading questions will help you.

1. What type of narrator does this story have?

   a) First-person narrator (the protagonist)

   b) First-person narrator (an onlooker or secondary character)

   c) Third-person narrator (omniscient point of view)

   d) Third-person narrator (limited point of view)

2. From where does the narrator share his story?

_____

3. From which peculiarity of character does the narrator say he draws one of his principal sources of pleasure?

_____

4. How does the narrator define the spirit of perverseness?

_____

_____

5. How does the narrator "consummate" Pluto's injury? What is a synonym of "consummate" in this context?

_____

6. What does the narrator find many people examining in the ruins of his house?

_____

7. What is the only difference between the second cat and Pluto? How is this an important detail?

_____

_____

8. How does the narrator feel about the second cat, and why does he feel this way?

_____

_____

9. How does the narrator feel in the aftermath of the murder in the basement?

a) He feels the heavy burden of guilt weighing down his soul.

b) He feels furious with the world and descends into a dark rage.

c) He feels nothing ever again.

d) He sleeps tranquilly and feels free and happy.

10. What causes the police to start tearing down the wall? Who or what do they find behind it?

_____

_____

MyBookshelf > My eLab > Exercises > Part I: Short Stories > Chapter 1: The Black Cat > Close Reading: Additional Questions

THE LANGUAGE OF LITERATURE

The effect of any text is to a very large extent determined by the author's diction and use of figures of speech and other literary devices. Use the following questions to focus your attention on how the author uses language in the story.

A. **Foreshadowing** is a literary device used to generate tension by presaging later plot events. It gives the reader a clue of what is to come—for instance, through the use of imagery, dialogue or symbols. In "The Black Cat," the image of a hanging at the gallows is evoked three times. First, identify these three recurrences in the text. Then, discuss how they serve as a foreshadowing technique.

B. Poe uses **style** to contribute to the construction of the narrator's character. The story features a heavy use of dashes to create long, cumbersome sentences as the narrator voices his thoughts. What does this use of **syntax** reveal about the narrator?

C. Another element of style concerns the narrator's **capitalization** of certain nouns, such as Fiend Intemperance, Alcohol, Horror and Perverseness. What is the immediate impact of capitalizing a noun? What does it suggest about the narrator's view of these words?

D. In the following excerpt from the penultimate paragraph, underline two similes. Discuss how they illustrate the narrator's state of mind.

I was answered by a voice from within the tomb!—by a cry, at first muffled and broken, like the sobbing of a child, and then quickly swelling into ... a wailing shriek, half of horror and half of triumph, such as might have arisen only out of hell, conjointly from the throats of the damned in their agony and of the demons that exult in the damnation.

Analytical Reading

After making specific observations, you are ready to analyze the subject of your close reading. The following questions will help you look for thematic patterns, establish relationships and identify specific examples of literary devices or principles.

1. In this story, Poe provides few details about **setting**. In contrast with many of his stories featuring intricate imagery, this story focuses more on the action of the main character. That said, the atmosphere changes as the setting of the story shifts. First, draw on the narrator's account to describe each of the following settings in one or two sentences.

Setting	Description / Atmosphere
The narrator's first home	
The second house	
The bar (den) where the second cat is found	
The cellar	
The prison cell	

Explain the change in atmosphere you observe and what it may signify.

2. The story's **plot** is articulated around four types of **conflict**. For each conflict, explain in one or two sentences how it is illustrated in the story. Underline a passage in the text that supports your explanation and write the number of the paragraph(s) where the passage can be found. Then, determine which conflict holds the most importance.

a. Character vs. human

Explanation: _____

_____

Paragraph(s) containing a support passage: _____

b. Character vs. nature

Explanation: _____

_____

Paragraph(s) containing a support passage: _____

c. Character vs. self

Explanation: _____

_____

Paragraph(s) containing a support passage: _____

d. Character vs. society

Explanation: _____

_____

Paragraph(s) containing a support passage: _____

The conflict that is most important in the story is:

_____

3. Explain how the causal relationship that exists between the story's most important conflict and the other three types of conflict help the reader understand the story on a deeper level.

4. As the story develops, does the narrator change, and if so, how? Does that make him a **static** or **dynamic character**? Is he **flat** or **round**? Provide evidence from the story to support your claims.

5. **Active characters** move the story along by consciously making changes to their surroundings. **Passive characters** mostly undergo the changes going on around them—which does not mean they do not complete any actions at all. Characters may be active in some ways and passive in others, or they may change from one to the other as the story progresses.

Determine if each of the four main characters in "The Black Cat" is active, passive or both. Support each box you check with evidence from the story. Once you have completed the table, discuss your choices and evidence with one or more partners.

Character	Character Type	Evidence
Narrator	☐ Active ☐ Passive	
Wife	☐ Active ☐ Passive	
Pluto	☐ Active ☐ Passive	

Character	Character Type	Evidence
Second cat	☐ Active ☐ Passive	

6. An **unreliable narrator** tells the reader a story that cannot be taken at face value because he or she displays characteristics that undermine their credibility. Is the narrator reliable or unreliable? Why?

7. The **thematic concepts** below are central to "The Black Cat." Explain how they manifest themselves in the story. Pay attention to the specific way(s) in which each one is taken up. Is there a progression? Support your explanations with evidence from the text.

Violence   Freedom vs. confinement   Love and hatred
Alcohol   Psychological transformation

Food for Thought

The following questions encourage you to turn a critical eye to your earlier observations and analyses. They introduce elements and considerations that will lead you to formulate new questions and set tentative hypotheses. Discuss these to further your insight into the text.

1. After analyzing the story, look back at its title. The title only references one black cat. Does this mean that there is only one cat in the story? What hypotheses can you put forward? Support each hypothesis with evidence from the text.

2. The narrator pretends that he never had any troubles until he began drinking alcohol, yet there is evidence in the story that alcohol is not the only thing to blame for his sociopathic actions. Describe other details the reader knows about the narrator that likely contribute to his slide into violence and insanity.

3. How does the narrative fit in with the temperance movement?

4. There are two types of blindness on display in this story. The two cats are partially blind, but the narrator also suffers from a sort of blindness. How so? Explain.

5. Poe rarely named characters in his stories, so when he did give them names, this should be considered of importance to the story. Do a web search for "Pluto + Greek mythology" and explain the possible symbolism of this name.

6. The character of Pluto also shows striking similarities with Odin in Norse mythology. Do a web search to find which three characteristics Pluto shares with Odin. What might this suggest in regard to the second cat? Paraphrase information in your own words. Remember to record your sources, so you can use them as references, should you decide to include this information in an essay or presentation. (Refer to the Referencing and Plagiarism section on pages 289–291 for more details.)

7. Refer to the Text in Context section on page 14 or do a web search to pinpoint the most common features of Gothic fiction. Then, try to find an example from the text to illustrate each of these features. Work in a small group; put together and compare what you have found in order to present one complete list of features, with the most eloquent examples.

Presenting an Analysis

Writing | Analyzing the Construction of Theme

Write a literary analysis essay around a thesis statement focusing on the construction of theme(s) in "The Black Cat." For instance, you may wish to analyze how a particular symbol or image recurs throughout the story to evoke one or more of the themes identified in the Analytical Reading section. You can also analyze how the different types of conflicts contribute to this theme/these themes. Make sure you investigate the themes specific to the story (thematic statements) rather than the thematic concepts that underpin them.

Example:

In "The Black Cat," Edgar Allan Poe underscores the narrator's descent into madness by setting the story in physical spaces that gradually deteriorate as the story progresses.

In the body paragraphs, use an analysis structure to provide evidence and examples from the text to point out the use of one of your selected elements and its role in the construction of your chosen theme(s). Refer to the work you did in the Analytical Reading section. Make sure to provide clear examples from the text to illustrate and support your analysis.

(Refer to Part V, Writing about Literature, on page 271 for more information on essay format and structure.)

Speaking | Presenting a Character Analysis

In order to explain their role, purpose and meaning within the storyline, present a character analysis of the narrator, the black cat(s) or the wife. The following questions may guide you; however, you should give a cohesive presentation that is not a mere addition to the answers to each question. As with an essay, focus on a central thesis that you break up into smaller topics.

- What are the character's most important physical and psychological traits?
- Is the character (mostly) flat or round, dynamic or static?
- Is the character (mostly) active or passive?
- What type(s) of conflict is the character involved in?
- Does the character or any of its actions represent a symbol?
- How does the character fit into the theme(s) of the story?

(Refer to Appendix 2 on page 297 for more information on presentation format and structure.)

MyBookshelf > My eLab
> Exercises > Grammar
and Accuracy

CHAPTER 2

Désirée's Baby

– Kate Chopin

This chapter focuses on the following:

- Setting
- Dramatic and narrative structure
- Symbolism
- Language Focus: understanding regional realities
- The Language of Literature: irony and tone
- Theme

Connect with the Text

Before you read the story, do a web search to find the answers to the questions below. This will help you visualize the setting of the story and contextualize its themes. Summarize or paraphrase information in your own words. Remember to record your sources so you can use them as references, should you decide to include this information in an essay or presentation. (Refer to the Referencing and Plagiarism section on pages 289–291 for more details.)

1. When was slavery abolished in Louisiana? What was the role of the Civil War in this?

2. In the Louisiana context, what are Creoles?

3. What does a Creole plantation typically look like? What types of buildings does it usually feature? Research historical information and images to support your description.

4. What were the slaves' roles on a plantation?

5. What was the social status of American women like in the first half of the nineteenth century?

6. When did the women's rights movement come about in the United States?

Text in Context

Kate Chopin (1850–1904) was born Katherine O'Flaherty in St. Louis, Missouri. She was of French and Irish descent. After the death of her father when she was five years old, Chopin grew up in an all-female household, and she is often considered one of the first modern feminist authors. That said, Chopin followed a conventional path as a housewife until her husband, Oscar Chopin, died at age 32. Chopin moved back to St. Louis and started writing as therapy, to fight her state of depression. She quickly became a prolific writer, publishing almost 100 short stories, three novels and a play. Being set in Louisiana, her short stories are fine examples of Southern regionalist fiction inspired by her own life in New Orleans living on a plantation. Chopin's writing style was influenced by French author Guy de Maupassant. In 1899, her novel *The Awakening* received much negative criticism because of its strong female protagonist. Afterwards, Chopin remained on a quest for artistic acceptance until her sudden passing. Her writing was overlooked until the 1960s, when it was rediscovered under the influence of the modern feminist movement.

Exploratory Reading

Read the text a first time without interruption. Keep an open mind and take a mental note of your reactions and observations. Soak up the mood and atmosphere without looking for any specific elements. When you are finished, answer the questions below the text.

Désirée's Baby

Kate Chopin

1 As the day was pleasant Madame Valmondé drove over to L'Abri to see Désirée and the baby.

2 It made her laugh to think of Désirée with a baby. Why, it seemed but yesterday that Désirée was little more than a baby herself; when Monsieur in riding through the gateway of Valmondé had found her lying asleep in the shadow of the big stone pillar.

3 The little one awoke in his arms and began to cry for "Dada." That was as much as she could do or say. Some people thought she might have strayed there of her own accord, for she was of the toddling age. The prevailing belief was that she had been purposely left by a party of Texans, whose canvas-covered wagon, late in the day, had crossed the ferry that Coton-Maïs kept, just below the plantation. In time Madame Valmondé abandoned every speculation but the one that Désirée had been sent to her by a beneficent **Providence** to be the child of her affection, seeing that she was without child of the flesh. For the girl grew to be beautiful and gentle, affectionate and sincere; the idol of Valmondé.

4 It was no wonder, when she stood one day against the stone pillar in whose shadow she had lain asleep, eighteen years before, that Armand Aubigny riding by and seeing her there, had fallen in love with her. That was the way all the Aubignys fell in love, as if struck by a pistol shot. The wonder was, that he had not loved her before; for he had known her since his father brought him home from Paris, a boy of eight, after his mother died there. The passion that awoke in him that day, when he saw her at the gate, swept along like an avalanche, or like a prairie fire, or like anything that drives headlong over all obstacles.

5 Monsieur Valmondé grew practical and wanted things well considered: that is, the girl's obscure origin. Armand looked into her eyes and did not care. He was reminded that she was nameless. What did it matter about a name when he could give her one of the oldest and proudest in Louisiana? He ordered the **corbeille** from Paris, and contained himself with what patience he could until it arrived; then they were married.

6 Madame Valmondé had not seen Désirée and the baby for four weeks. When she reached L'Abri she shuddered at the first sight of it, as she always did. It was a sad looking place, which for many years had not known the gentle presence of a mistress. Old Monsieur Aubigny having married and buried his wife in France, and she having loved her own land too well ever to leave it. The roof came down steep and black like a cowl reaching out beyond the wide galleries that encircled the yellow stuccoed house. Big, solemn oaks grew close to it, and their thick-leaved, far-reaching branches shadowed it like a pall. Young Aubigny's rule was a strict one, too, and under it his **negroes** had forgotten how to be gay, as they had been during the old master's easy-going and indulgent lifetime.

7 The young mother was recovering slowly, and lay full length, in her soft white muslins and laces, upon a couch. The baby was beside her, upon her arm, where he had fallen asleep at her breast. The **yellow** nurse woman sat beside a window fanning herself.

8 Madame Valmondé bent her portly figure over Désirée and kissed her, holding her an instant tenderly in her arms. Then she turned to the child.

9 "This is not the baby!" she exclaimed, in startled tones. French was the language spoken at Valmondé in those days.

10 "I knew you would be astonished," laughed Désirée, "at the way he has grown. The little **cochon de lait**! Look at his legs, mamma, and his hands and finger-nails,—real finger-nails. Zandrine had to cut them this morning. Isn't it so, Zandrine?"

11 The woman bowed her turbaned head majestically, "Mais si, madame."

12 "And the way he cries," went on Désirée, "is deafening. Armand heard him the other day as far away as La Blanche's cabin."

13 Madame Valmondé had never removed her eyes from the child. She picked it up and walked with it over to the window that was lightest. She scanned it narrowly, then looked as searchingly at Zandrine, whose face was turned to look across the fields.

14 "Yes, the child has grown, has changed," said Madame Valmondé, slowly, as she replaced it beside its mother. "What does Armand say?"

15 Désirée's face became suffused with a glow that was happiness itself.

16 "Oh, Armand is the proudest father in the parish, I believe, chiefly because it is a boy, to bear his name; though he says, not—that he would have loved a girl as well. But I know it isn't true. I know he says that to please me. And, mamma," she added, drawing Madame Valmondé's head down to her, and speaking in a whisper, "he hasn't punished one of them—not one of them—since baby is born. Even Négrillon, who pretended to have burnt his leg that he might rest from work—he only laughed, and said Négrillon was a great scamp. Oh, mamma, I'm so happy; it frightens me."

17 What Désirée said was true. Marriage, and later the birth of his son, had softened Armand Aubigny's imperious and exacting nature greatly. This was what made the gentle Désirée so happy, for she loved him desperately. When he frowned she trembled, but loved him. When he smiled, she asked no greater blessing of God. But Armand's dark, handsome face had not often been disfigured by frowns since the day he fell in love with her.

18 When the baby was about three months old Désirée awoke one day to the conviction that there was something in the air menacing her peace. It was at first too subtle to grasp. It had only been a disquieting suggestion; an air of mystery among the blacks; unexpected visits from far-off neighbours who could hardly account for their coming. Then a strange, an awful change in her husband's manner, which she dared not ask him to explain. When he spoke to her, it was with averted eyes, from which the old love-light seemed to have gone out. He absented himself from home; and when there, avoided her presence and that of her child, without excuse. And the very spirit of Satan seemed suddenly to take hold of him in his dealing with the slaves. Désirée was miserable enough to die.

19 She sat in her room, one hot afternoon, in her peignoir, listlessly drawing through her fingers the strands of her long, silky brown hair that hung about her shoulders. The baby, half naked, lay asleep upon her own great mahogany bed, that was like a sumptuous throne, with its satin-lined half-canopy. One of La Blanche's little **quadroon** boys—half naked too— stood fanning the child slowly with a fan of peacock feathers. Désirée's eyes had been fixed absently and sadly upon the baby, while she was striving to penetrate the threatening mist that she felt closing about her. She looked from her child to the boy who stood beside him, and back again; over and over. "Ah!" It was a cry that she could not help; which she was not conscious of having uttered. The blood turned like ice in her veins, and a clammy moisture gathered upon her face.

20 She tried to speak to the little quadroon boy; but no sound would come, at first. When he heard his name uttered, he looked up, and his mistress was pointing to the door. He laid aside the great, soft fan, and obediently stole away, over the polished floor, on his bare tiptoes.

21 She stayed motionless, with gaze riveted upon her child, and her face the picture of fright.

22 Presently her husband entered the room, and without noticing her, went to a table and began to search among some papers which covered it.

23 "Armand," she called to him, in a voice which must have stabbed him, if he was human. But he did not notice. "Armand," she said again. Then she rose and tottered toward him. "Armand," she panted once more, clutching his arm, "look at our child. What does it mean? tell me."

24 He coldly but gently loosened her fingers from about his arm and thrust the hand away from him. "Tell me what it means!" she cried despairingly.

25 "It means," he answered lightly, "that the child is not white; it means that you are not white."

26 A quick conception of all that this accusation meant for her, nerved her with unwonted courage to deny it. "It is a lie—it is not true, I am white! Look at my hair, it is brown; and my eyes are grey, Armand, you know

they are grey. And my skin is fair," seizing his wrist. "Look at my hand—whiter than yours, Armand," she laughed hysterically.

27 "As white as La Blanche's," he said cruelly; and went away leaving her alone with their child.

28 When she could hold a pen in her hand, she sent a despairing letter to Madame Valmondé.

29 "My mother, they tell me I am not white. Armand has told me I am not white. For God's sake tell them it is not true. You must know it is not true. I shall die. I must die. I cannot be so unhappy, and live."

30 The answer that came was as brief:

31 "My own Désirée: Come home to Valmondé—back to your mother who loves you. Come with your child."

32 When the letter reached Désirée she went with it to her husband's study, and laid it open upon the desk before which he sat. She was like a stone image: silent, white, motionless after she placed it there.

33 In silence he ran his cold eyes over the written words. He said nothing. "Shall I go, Armand?" she asked in tones sharp with agonized suspense.

34 "Yes, go."

35 "Do you want me to go?"

36 "Yes, I want you to go."

37 He thought Almighty God had dealt cruelly and unjustly with him; and felt, somehow, that he was paying Him back in kind when he stabbed thus into his wife's soul. Moreover, he no longer loved her, because of the unconscious injury she had brought upon his home and his name.

38 She turned away like one stunned by a blow, and walked slowly toward the door, hoping he would call her back.

39 "Good-bye, Armand," she moaned.

40 He did not answer her. That was his last blow at fate. After it was dealt he felt like a remorseless murderer.

41 Désirée went in search of her child. Zandrine was pacing the sombre **gallery** with it. She took the little one from the nurse's arms with no word of explanation, and descending the steps, walked away, under the live oak branches.

42 It was an October afternoon. Out in the still fields the negroes were picking cotton; and the sun was just sinking.

43 Désirée had not changed the thin white garment nor the slippers which she wore. Her head was uncovered and the sun's rays brought a golden gleam from its brown meshes. She did not take the broad, beaten road which led to the far-off plantation of Valmondé. She walked across a deserted field, where the stubble bruised her tender feet, so delicately shod, and tore her thin gown to shreds.

44 She disappeared among the reeds and willows that grew thick along the banks of the deep, sluggish **bayou**; and she did not come back again.

* * *

45 Some weeks later there was a curious scene enacted at L'Abri. In the centre of the smoothly swept back-yard was a great bonfire. Armand Aubigny sat in the wide hallway that commanded a view of the spectacle; and it was he who dealt out to a half-dozen negroes the material which kept this fire ablaze.

46 A graceful cradle of willow, with all its dainty furbishings, was laid upon the pyre, which had already been fed with the richness of a priceless **layette**. Then there were silk gowns, and velvet and satin ones added to these; laces, too, and embroideries; bonnets and gloves—for the corbeille had been of rare quality.

47 The last thing to go was a tiny bundle of letters; innocent little scribblings that Désirée had sent to him during the days of their **espousal**. There was the remnant of one back in the drawer from which he took them. But it was not Désirée's. It was part of an old letter from his mother to his father. He read it. She was thanking God for the blessing of her husband's love;

48 "But, above all," she wrote, "night and day, I thank the good God for having so arranged our lives that our dear Armand will never know that his mother, who adores him, belongs to the race that is cursed with the brand of slavery."

(2161 words)

Source: Chopin, K. "Désirée's Baby." *Vogue*, 1893, www.gutenberg. org//files/160/160-h/160-h.html.

Initial Insight

1. What is the story about? Write down anything that intuitively comes to you.

_____

_____

2. Does the story take place before or after the American Civil War? How do you know?

_____

_____

_____

3. Who narrates the story? Does the narrator take sides, or is the presented point of view objective?

_____

_____

_____

Reader's Response

Consider the following questions. Discuss your answers with one or more partners.

1. What emotional response(s) or reaction(s) did the story evoke in you?

2. Do you empathize with Désirée and/or with Armand? Why or why not?

3. How is Désirée's behaviour different from that of women today?

4. What do you think happens when Désirée disappears in the bayou?

5. Do you believe Désirée's decision to leave is warranted? Why do you think she acts the way she does?

LANGUAGE FOCUS

In line with the characteristics of regionalist—sometimes also called local colour—fiction, Chopin uses southern dialect and descriptions of the south to portray regional aspects, such as cultural and social values as well as imagery and settings. Because they are essential to a deep understanding of the events and issues at the heart of the story, it is paramount to know precisely what these words mean in the context of nineteenth-century Louisiana. First, refer to the context to infer the most likely meaning of each word (identified in bold). Take a note of it in the margin or on a separate sheet of paper. Then use credible online sources and a reputable unilingual dictionary to precisely define the words as they are used in the text. If there is a discrepancy between the inferred and researched meaning, ask yourself how the new information affects your comprehension and interpretation of the story.

1. Providence (par. 3) _____

2. corbeille (de mariage) (par. 5) _____

3. negroes (par. 6) _____

4. yellow (nurse woman) (par. 7) _____

5. cochon de lait (par. 10) _____

6. quadroon (par. 19) _____

7. gallery (par. 41) _____

8. bayou (par. 44) _____

9. layette (par. 46) _____

10. espousal (par. 47) _____

Look up any other words you are unsure of.

MyBookshelf > My eLab
> Exercises > Part I: Short
Stories > Chapter 2:
Désirée's Baby > Vocabulary
Comprehension

Close Reading

As you read the text again, pay attention to elements that seem significant to understanding and interpreting the story. The following guided reading questions will help you.

1. How did Désirée come to live with the Valmondés?

_____

_____

_____

_____

2. The Valmondés considered that …

a) God had given them Désirée as a blessing.

b) God had given them Désirée as a curse.

c) God had no part in Désirée being abandoned nearby.

3. What concerns does Monsieur Valmondé bring up before consenting to the marriage of Armand and Désirée? What are the cultural cues we can pick up from this concern?

_____

_____

_____

4. How does Armand treat the slaves on his plantation as opposed to how his father treated them?

a) He is generally very strict and mean to them while his father had been kind to them.

b) He is very kind and treats them like equals while his father was cruel to them.

c) He is very kind and treats them like equals just like his father did.

d) He is very strict and mean to them just like his father was.

5. Once the baby is about three months old, what three changes in Armand does Désirée observe?

_____

_____

_____

6. What other unusual behaviours does Désirée notice, making her suspect that things are changing in her happy home?

_____

_____

7. At what precise moment does Désirée finally realize that something is different about her child?

_____

_____

8. When Désirée confronts Armand, what is his response? Why?

_____

_____

9. When Désirée decides to leave L'Abri, where exactly does she go?

_____

_____

MyBookshelf > My eLab > Exercises > Part I: Short Stories > Chapter 2: > Désirée's Baby > Close Reading: Additional Questions

10. The letter from Armand's mother to Armand's father reveals

a) his mother is black.   b) his father is black.   c) his mother is white.   d) he is white.

THE LANGUAGE OF LITERATURE

The effect of any text is to a very large extent determined by the author's diction and use of figures of speech and other literary devices. Use the following questions to focus your attention on how the author uses language in the story.

A. Irony is a contrast or incongruity between expectations for a situation and its reality. Irony can manifest itself in three different ways. **Verbal irony** involves the speaker saying something in sharp contrast to the actual meaning of an utterance. **Situational irony** consists of a situation in which the outcome is very different from what was expected. **Dramatic irony** occurs when the audience has more information than the characters in a work of literature. For each of the following passages from the text, determine what type of irony it illustrates and explain your choice.

1. "This is not the baby!" [Madame Valmondé] exclaimed, in startled tones.

2. One of La Blanche's little quadroon boys—half naked too—stood fanning the child slowly with a fan of peacock feathers.

3. "But, above all," [Madame Aubigny] wrote, "night and day, I thank the good God for having so arranged our lives that our dear Armand will never know that his mother, who adores him, belongs to the race that is cursed with the brand of slavery."

B. Tone is the writer's attitude toward the subject matter of a literary work. It is generally conveyed through diction and other literary and stylistic devices. In "Désirée's Baby," although the narrator objectively reports the events that make up the story, Chopin's attitude toward them can be inferred from her word choice, which creates imagery along the light/warm-dark/cold continuum, as well as her use of metaphor and simile.

"The passion that awoke in him that day ... swept along like an avalanche, or like a prairie fire."

→ This simile suggests Armand's love is destructive.

"... she was striving to penetrate the threatening mist that she felt closing about her."

→ This metaphor likens Désirée's problematic situation to mist that blocks out the light in her life.

> "Désirée had not changed the thin <u>white</u> garment ... her head was uncovered and the <u>sun's rays</u> brought a <u>golden gleam</u> from its brown meshes."
>
> → In this passage, several elements evoke light to underline Désirée's purity and innocence.
>
> In the text, underline at least five more examples of diction, metaphor or simile that contribute to the story's tone by associating light or warm qualities with Désirée and cold or dark qualities with Armand.

Analytical Reading

After making specific observations, you are ready to analyze the subject of your close reading. The following questions will help you look for thematic patterns, establish relationships and identify specific examples of literary devices or principles.

1. The following fourteen points make up the **dramatic plot structure (plot line)** of "Désirée's Baby." After referring to the Dramatic Plot Structure section in Elements of Analysis (pages 8–10), write the corresponding plot moments in the right-hand column. First, determine the **climax** of the story by considering at what point the tension is highest. What information serves as the **exposition** of the story, and what **inciting incident(s)** enable(s) the central conflict? At the end of the story, what **resolution** ends the central conflict? Is there more than one resolution? How does the story conclude in a **dénouement**? Finally, determine which of the remaining points make up the **rising action** and the **falling action**.

Events	Plot moments
(1) Madame Valmondé sets out to visit Désirée and her baby.	
(2) Désirée is found next to a stone pillar by Monsieur Valmondé.	
(3) Armand Aubigny falls in love with Désirée when he sees her standing against a stone pillar.	
(4) Monsieur Valmondé proposes that before they marry, Désirée's origin should be examined. Armand declines.	
(5) Madame Valmondé is visibly shocked when she sees the baby's appearance.	
(6) Armand's attitude toward the slaves softens considerably.	
(7) Désirée senses there is something wrong; the mood in the house changes.	
(8) Désirée notices a similarity between her baby and the slave boy fanning it.	
(9) Désirée confronts Armand about the baby's skin colour. He accuses her.	
(10) Désirée writes to her mother, Madame Valmondé, asking for help.	
(11) Madame Valmondé sends Désirée a letter in response, telling her to come back home.	
(12) Désirée takes her baby and leaves the house, disappearing into a bayou.	
(13) Armand sets up a bonfire to burn Désirée's belongings.	
(14) Armand finds and reads a letter from his mother to his father.	

2. Complete the narrative timeline by putting the plot moment numbers from question 1 in chronological order (i.e., the order in which they would have occurred rather than the order in which they are presented to the reader).

___ ___ ___ ___ ___ ___ ___ ___ ___ ___ ___ ___ ___ ___

Where does the dramatic structure (plot) differ from the narrative timeline? Circle the numbers on the timeline on page 33. Are these instances of flashbacks or flashforwards? Explain why the author may have arranged the plot in this manner.

3. In the text, find the time indicators that allow the reader to understand the events that make up the dramatic plot structure in spite of them not being introduced in a linear fashion in chronological order.

(1) As the day was pleasant …	(6)	(11)
(2)	(7)	(12)
(3)	(8)	(13)
(4) No specific time indicator is associated with event 4.	(9)	(14)
(5)	(10)	

Consider the time indicators for points 1, 8 and 12. In which way do they reflect the plot line of the story?

4. Analyze the characters of Désirée and Armand by considering the following elements:

- Meaning of first name
- Character's physical appearance
- Character's principal actions
- Character traits at outset
- Character traits as conflict unfolds

Explain how Désirée's and Armand's traits can be seen to represent human duality. A graphic organizer is available in My eLab Documents.

5. If, on a primary level, the **conflict** at the centre of the plot opposes Désirée and Armand (character vs. human), then what other type of conflict do these two characters represent? Think of why both characters act the way they do.

6. The regionalist **setting** of "Désirée's Baby" is centred around two plantations—Valmondé and L'Abri. Answer the following questions about the setting.

a. What is Madame Valmondé's impression of L'Abri as she arrives?

b. How does this description contrast with what you know about Valmondé?

c. What is the importance of the third-person narrator describing this setting from Madame Valmondé's perspective? What does it suggest?

d. The name of the Aubigny plantation, "L'Abri," literally translates into English as "the shelter." What or who might "L'Abri" offer shelter to?

7. Kate Chopin uses several settings and characters as **symbols** for one or more of the story's themes. Closely read the passages in which the symbols listed below are described. Work with a partner to discuss your interpretations. Then complete the chart provided in My eLab Documents. Make sure to support your explanations with evidence from the text.

The stone pillar	The corbeille	La Blanche's cabin
The quadroon boys	The bayou	The bonfire

MyBookshelf > My eLab > Documents > Part I: Short Stories > Chapter 2: Désirée's Baby

MyBookshelf > My eLab > Documents > Part I: Short Stories > Chapter 2: Désirée's Baby

8. In the text, identify three instances of **foreshadowing** that provide clues about Armand's lineage. Explain what type of clue each passage presents.

9. A higher power is evoked twice in regard to Désirée—once by Madame Valmondé and once by Armand Aubigny. In what context does this happen? Is their attitude toward God and Providence the same? What might this higher power symbolize?

Food for Thought

The following questions encourage you to turn a critical eye to your earlier observations and analyses. They introduce elements and considerations that will lead you to formulate new questions and set tentative hypotheses. Discuss these to further your insight into the text.

1. After analyzing the story, look back at its title. Why does the title only refer to the baby as being Désirée's? What do you think the author tries to achieve with this?

2. Why do you think Chopin, toward the end of the story, explains Désirée's journey in great detail, and yet does not specifically state her ultimate fate? Could this walk symbolize something else?

> "She walked across a deserted field, where the stubble bruised her tender feet, so delicately shod, and tore her thin gown to shreds. She disappeared among the reeds and willows that grew thick along the banks of the deep, sluggish bayou; and she did not come back again."

3. Madame Valmondé knew, upon seeing the child early on, that he was not white. She was also aware this could cause her daughter trouble. In her letter, she does not offer any advice or consolation, but only incites her daughter to return home. Does she bear any responsibility in the outcome of Désirée and her baby? Why do you think Madame Valmondé acts the way she does?

4. Do you think Armand knew about his origins? Provide evidence from the text to support your opinion.

5. Chopin does not clearly state whether or not Armand had some knowledge of his lineage prior to disclosing the contents of the letter in the end of the story. If you theorize that he was unaware of this information, and consider his position, the time period, and the culture he was raised in, does this cause you to sympathize with the antagonist? Do you think it likely he would have acted differently if he had had this information before? Why?

Presenting an Analysis

Writing | Analyzing the Expression of Theme

Write a literary analysis essay around a thesis statement focusing on the depiction and inherent criticism of racism and/or gender inequality in "Désirée's Baby." Kate Chopin draws on many literary elements and techniques to express these themes, and you can narrow down your topic by zooming in on one of them. For instance, you can decide to look at the roles played by one or more characters, the symbols associated with key plot moments or the use of irony.

Example:

> By drawing on situational irony to uncover parallels between La Blanche and Désirée, including their dependence on and relationships with Armand, Kate Chopin criticizes the racial and gender inequality characteristic of the nineteenth-century American South.

In each of the body paragraphs, use an analysis structure to provide evidence and examples from the text to point out the use of one of your selected elements, and explain how this element contributes to Chopin's criticism of racism and gender inequality. Refer to the work you did in the Analytical Reading section. Make sure to provide clear examples from the text to illustrate and support your analysis.

(Refer to Part V, Writing about Literature, on page 271 for more information on essay format and structure.)

Speaking | Presenting an Explication Focusing on Tone

"Désirée's Baby" is very rich in its use of symbols, literary and stylistic devices that contribute to the tone Kate Chopin wished to convey. Choose a passage that you find especially evocative in this regard, and present an explication of it.

- Point out meaningful descriptions of settings and characters, explaining how and why these contribute and fit into the overall story line.
- Point out and explain any particular word choices, uses of imagery, symbols, metaphors or similes.
- Establish links between the observations you make and the central themes of gender inequality and racism.

(Refer to Appendix 2 on page 297 for more information on presentation format and structure.)

MyBookshelf > My eLab
> Exercises > Grammar and
Accuracy

CHAPTER 3

The Magic Shop

– H. G. Wells

This chapter focuses on the following:

- Setting, mood and atmosphere
- Dramatic structure and narrative structure
- Types of narrators and characters
- Language Focus: interpreting meaning from a social and historical perspective
- The Language of Literature: imagery and symbols
- Theme

Connect with the Text

Take stock of your opinions on the following questions. Discuss them with one or more partners.

1. Do you believe in magic? Why or why not?

2. Have you ever attended a magic show or seen magic tricks being performed? What were your impressions?

3. Do you consider magic dangerous or benign entertainment?

4. Do you think stories featuring magic are for children, adults, or both? Give examples of stories you have read or watched.

Text in Context

Herbert George Wells (1866–1946) was a prolific British author best known for science fiction, even though he wrote novels and short stories in many different genres. Wells's writing was heavily influenced by the *zeitgeist*, or spirit, of the Victorian and Edwardian eras, which were characterized by political and economic change brought on by British imperialism, liberal political ideologies, and the industrial revolution. Realizing that people had lost their capacity to wonder at the possibilities of magic, he infused his writing with scientific ideas and theories to justify the impossible. His training as a scientist and his left-wing political views may explain his use of futuristic tropes and utopian or dystopian environments. Virginia Woolf infamously criticized Wells for writing fiction in order to promote his social and political ideals—something he actually took pride in. In many of his stories, Wells turned the fears haunting his contemporaries into strong symbols of liberal optimism whilst giving ordinary people a voice, often illustrated by the presence of lower-middle-class vernacular speech in his dialogue.

Exploratory Reading

Read the text a first time without interruption. Keep an open mind and take a mental note of your reactions and observations. Soak up the mood and atmosphere without looking for any specific elements. When you are finished, answer the questions below the text.

The Magic Shop

H. G. Wells

1 I had seen the Magic Shop from afar several times; I had passed it once or twice, a shop window of alluring little objects, magic balls, magic hens, wonderful cones, ventriloquist dolls, the material of the basket trick, packs of cards that *looked all right,* and all that sort of thing, but never had I thought of going in until one day, almost without warning, Gip hauled me by my finger right up to the window, and so conducted himself that there was nothing for it but to take him in. I had not thought the place was there, to tell the truth—a modest-sized frontage in Regent Street, between the picture shop and the place where the chicks run about just out of patent incubators, but there it was sure enough. I had **fancied** it was down nearer the Circus, or round the corner in Oxford Street, or even in Holborn; always over the way and a little inaccessible it had been, with something of the mirage in its position; but here it was now quite indisputably, and the fat end of Gip's pointing finger made a noise upon the glass.

2 "If I was rich," said Gip, dabbing a finger at the Disappearing Egg, "I'd buy myself that. And that"—which was The Crying Baby, Very Human—"and that," which was a mystery, and called, so a neat card asserted, "Buy One and Astonish Your Friends."

3 "Anything," said Gip, "will disappear under one of those cones. I have read about it in a book.

4 "And there, dadda, is the Vanishing Halfpenny—only they've put it this way up so's we can't see how it's done."

5 Gip, dear boy, inherits his mother's **breeding**, and he did not propose to enter the shop or worry in any way; only, you know, quite unconsciously, he lugged my finger doorward, and he made his interest clear.

6 "That," he said, and pointed to the Magic Bottle.

7 "If you had that?" I said; at which promising inquiry he looked up with a sudden radiance.

8 "I could show it to Jessie," he said, thoughtful as ever of others.

9 "It's less than a hundred days to your birthday, Gibbles," I said, and laid my hand on the door-handle.

10 Gip made no answer, but his grip tightened on my finger, and so we came into the shop.

11 It was no common shop this; it was a magic shop, and all the prancing precedence Gip would have taken in the matter of mere toys was wanting. He left the **burthen** of the conversation to me.

12 It was a little, narrow shop, not very well lit, and the door-bell pinged again with a plaintive note as we closed it behind us. For a moment or so we were alone and could glance about us. There was a tiger in *papier-mâché* on the glass case that covered the low counter —a grave, kind-eyed tiger that waggled his head in a methodical manner; there were several crystal spheres, a china hand holding magic cards, a stock of magic fish-bowls in various sizes, and an immodest magic hat that shamelessly displayed its springs. On the floor were magic mirrors; one to draw you out long and thin, one to swell your head and vanish your legs, and one to make you short and fat like a draught; and while we were laughing at these the shopman, as I suppose, came in.

13 At any rate, there he was behind the counter—a curious, sallow, dark man, with one ear larger than the other and a chin like the toe-cap of a boot.

14 "What can we have the pleasure?" he said, spreading his long magic fingers on the glass case; and so with a start we were aware of him.

15 "I want," I said, "to buy my little boy a few simple tricks."

16 "**Legerdemain?**" he asked. "Mechanical? Domestic?"

17 "Anything amusing?" said I.

18 "Um!" said the shopman, and scratched his head for a moment as if thinking. Then, quite distinctly, he drew from his head a glass ball. "Something in this way?" he said, and held it out.

19 The action was unexpected. I had seen the trick done at entertainments endless times before—it's part of the common stock of conjurers—but I had not expected it here. "That's good," I said, with a laugh.

20 "Isn't it?" said the shopman.

21 Gip stretched out his disengaged hand to take this object and found merely a blank palm.

22 "It's in your pocket," said the shopman, and there it was!

23 "How much will that be?" I asked.

24 "We make no charge for glass balls," said the shopman politely. "We get them"—he picked one out of his elbow as he spoke—"free." He produced another from the back of his neck, and laid it beside its predecessor on the counter. Gip regarded his glass ball sagely, then directed a look of inquiry at the two on the counter, and finally brought his round-eyed scrutiny to the shopman, who smiled. "You may have those two," said the shopman, "and, if you *don't* mind one from my mouth. *So!*"

25 Gip counselled me mutely for a moment, and then in a profound silence put away the four balls, resumed my reassuring finger, and nerved himself for the next event.

26 "We get all our smaller tricks in that way," the shopman remarked.

27 I laughed in the manner of one who subscribes to a jest. "Instead of going to the wholesale shop," I said. "Of course, it's cheaper."

28 "In a way," the shopman said. "Though we pay in the end. But not so heavily—as people suppose ... Our larger tricks, and our daily provisions and all the other things we want, we get out of that hat ... And you know, sir, if you'll excuse my saying it, there *isn't* a wholesale shop, not for Genuine Magic goods, sir. I don't know if you noticed our inscription—the Genuine Magic Shop." He drew a business-card from his cheek and handed it to me. "Genuine," he said, with his finger on the word, and added, "There is absolutely no deception, sir."

29 He seemed to be carrying out the joke pretty thoroughly, I thought.

30 He turned to Gip with a smile of remarkable affability. "You, you know, are the Right Sort of Boy."

31 I was surprised at his knowing that, because, in the interests of discipline, we keep it rather a secret even at home; but Gip received it in unflinching silence, keeping a steadfast eye on him.

32 "It's only the Right Sort of Boy gets through that doorway."

33 And, as if by way of illustration, there came a rattling at the door, and a squeaking little voice could be faintly heard. "Nyar! I *warn* 'a go in there, dadda, I WARN 'a go in there. Ny-a-a-ah!" and then the accents of a downtrodden parent, urging consolations and propitiations. "It's locked, Edward," he said.

34 "But it isn't," said I.

35 "It is, sir," said the shopman, "always—for that sort of child," and as he spoke we had a glimpse of the other youngster, a little, white face, pallid from sweet-eating and over-sapid food, and distorted by evil passions, a ruthless little egotist, pawing at the enchanted pane. "It's no good, sir," said the shopman, as I moved, with my natural helpfulness, doorward, and presently the spoilt child was carried off howling.

36 "How do you manage that?" I said, breathing a little more freely.

37 "Magic!" said the shopman, with a careless wave of the hand, and behold! sparks of coloured fire flew out of his fingers and vanished into the shadows of the shop.

38 "You were saying," he said, addressing himself to Gip, "before you came in, that you would like one of our 'Buy One and Astonish your Friends' boxes?"

39 Gip, after a gallant effort, said "Yes."

40 "It's in your pocket."

41 And leaning over the counter—he really had an extraordinarily long body—this amazing person produced the article in the customary conjurer's manner. "Paper," he said, and took a sheet out of the empty hat with the springs; "string," and behold his mouth was a string box, from which he drew an unending thread, which when he had tied his parcel he bit off— and, it seemed to me, swallowed the ball of string. And then he lit a candle at the nose of one of the ventriloquist's dummies, stuck one of his fingers (which had become sealing-wax red) into the flame, and so sealed the parcel. "Then there was the Disappearing Egg," he remarked, and produced one from within my coat-breast and packed it, and also The Crying Baby, Very Human. I handed each parcel to Gip as it was ready, and he clasped them to his chest.

42 He said very little, but his eyes were eloquent; the clutch of his arms was eloquent. He was the playground of unspeakable emotions. These, you know, were *real* Magics.

43 Then, with a start, I discovered something moving about in my hat—something soft and jumpy. I whipped it off, and a ruffled pigeon—no doubt a confederate— dropped out and ran on the counter, and went, I fancy, into a cardboard box behind the *papier-mâché* tiger.

44 "Tut, tut!" said the shopman, dexterously relieving, me of my headdress; "careless bird, and—as I live— nesting!"

45 He shook my hat, and shook out into his extended hand, two or three eggs, a large marble, a watch, about half a dozen of the inevitable glass balls, and then crumpled, crinkled paper, more and more and more, talking all the time of the way in which people neglect to brush their hats inside as well as out—politely, of course, but with a certain personal application. "All sorts of things accumulate, sir ... Not *you*, of course, in particular ... Nearly every customer ... Astonishing what they carry about with them ..." The crumpled paper rose and billowed on the counter more and more and more, until he was nearly hidden from us, until he was altogether hidden, and still his voice went on and on. "We none of us know what the fair semblance of a human being may conceal, sir. Are we all then no better than brushed exteriors, whited **sepulchres**—"

46 His voice stopped—exactly like when you hit a neighbour's gramophone with a well-aimed brick, the same instant silence—and the rustle of the paper stopped, and everything was still ...

47 "Have you done with my hat?" I said, after an interval.

48 There was no answer.

49 I stared at Gip, and Gip stared at me, and there were our distortions in the magic mirrors, looking very **rum**, and grave, and quiet ...

50 "I think we'll go now," I said. "Will you tell me how much all this comes to? ...

51 "I say," I said, on a rather louder note, "I want the bill; and my hat, please."

52 It might have been a sniff from behind the paper pile ...

53 "Let's look behind the counter, Gip," I said. "He's making fun of us."

54 I led Gip round the head-wagging tiger, and what do you think there was behind the counter? No one at all! Only my hat on the floor, and a common conjurer's lop-eared white rabbit lost in meditation, and looking as stupid and crumpled as only a conjurer's rabbit can do. I resumed my hat, and the rabbit lolloped a lollop or so out of my way.

55 "Dadda!" said Gip, in a guilty whisper.

56 "What is it, Gip?" said I.

57 "I *do* like this shop, dadda."

58 "So should I," I said to myself, "if the counter wouldn't suddenly extend itself to shut one off from the door." But I didn't call Gip's attention to that. "Pussy!" he said, with a hand out to the rabbit as it came lolloping past us; "Pussy, do Gip a magic!" and his eyes followed it as it squeezed through a door I had certainly not

remarked a moment before. Then this door opened wider, and the man with one ear larger than the other appeared again. He was smiling still, but his eye met mine with something between amusement and defiance. "You'd like to see our showroom, sir," he said, with an innocent suavity. Gip tugged my finger forward. I glanced at the counter and met the shopman's eye again. I was beginning to think the magic just a little too genuine. "We haven't *very* much time," I said. But somehow we were inside the showroom before I could finish that.

59 "All goods of the same quality," said the shopman, rubbing his flexible hands together, "and that is the Best. Nothing in the place that isn't genuine Magic, and warranted thoroughly rum. Excuse me, sir!"

60 I felt him pull at something that clung to my coat-sleeve, and then I saw he held a little, wriggling red demon by the tail—the little creature bit and fought and tried to get at his hand—and in a moment he tossed it carelessly behind a counter. No doubt the thing was only an image of twisted indiarubber, but for the moment—! And his gesture was exactly that of a man who handles some petty biting bit of vermin. I glanced at Gip, but Gip was looking at a magic rocking-horse. I was glad he hadn't seen the thing. "I say," I said, in an undertone, and indicating Gip and the red demon with my eyes, "you haven't many things like *that* about, have you?"

61 "None of ours! Probably brought it with you," said the shopman—also in an undertone, and with a more dazzling smile than ever. "Astonishing what people *will* carry about with them unawares!" And then to Gip, "Do you see anything you fancy here?"

62 There were many things that Gip fancied there.

63 He turned to this astonishing tradesman with mingled confidence and respect. "Is that a Magic Sword?" he said.

64 "A Magic Toy Sword. It neither bends, breaks, nor cuts the fingers. It renders the bearer invincible in battle against any one under eighteen. Half a crown to seven and **sixpence**, according to size. These panoplies on cards are for juvenile knights-errant and very useful—shield of safety, sandals of swiftness, helmet of invisibility."

65 "Oh, dadda!" gasped Gip.

66 I tried to find out what they cost, but the shopman did not heed me. He had got Gip now; he had got him away from my finger; he had embarked upon the exposition of all his confounded stock, and nothing was going to stop him. Presently I saw with a qualm of

distrust and something very like jealousy that Gip had hold of this person's finger as usually he has hold of mine. No doubt the fellow was interesting, I thought, and had an interestingly faked lot of stuff, really *good* faked stuff, still—

67 I wandered after them, saying very little, but keeping an eye on this prestidigital fellow. After all, Gip was enjoying it. And no doubt when the time came to go we should be able to go quite easily.

68 It was a long, rambling place, that showroom, a gallery broken up by stands and stalls and pillars, with archways leading off to other departments, in which the queerest-looking assistants loafed and stared at one, and with perplexing mirrors and curtains. So perplexing, indeed, were these that I was presently unable to make out the door by which we had come.

69 The shopman showed Gip magic trains that ran without steam or clockwork, just as you set the signals, and then some very, very valuable boxes of soldiers that all came alive directly you took off the lid and said—I myself haven't a very quick ear, and it was a tongue-twisting sound, but Gip—he has his mother's ear—got it in no time. "Bravo!" said the shopman, putting the men back into the box unceremoniously and handing it to Gip. "Now," said the shopman, and in a moment Gip had made them all alive again.

70 "You'll take that box?" asked the shopman.

71 "We'll take that box," said I, "unless you charge its full value. In which case it would need a Trust Magnate—"

72 "Dear heart! *No!*" and the shopman swept the little men back again, shut the lid, waved the box in the air, and there it was, in brown paper, tied up and—*with Gip's full name and address on the paper!*

73 The shopman laughed at my amazement.

74 "This is the genuine magic," he said. "The real thing."

75 "It's a little too genuine for my taste," I said again.

76 After that he fell to showing Gip tricks, odd tricks, and still odder the way they were done. He explained them, he turned them inside out, and there was the dear little chap nodding his busy bit of a head in the sagest manner.

77 I did not attend as well as I might. "Hey, presto!" said the Magic Shopman, and then would come the clear, small "Hey, presto!" of the boy. But I was distracted by other things. It was being borne in upon me just how tremendously rum this place was; it was, so to speak, inundated by a sense of rumness. There was something a little rum about the fixtures even, about the ceiling, about the floor, about the casually distributed chairs. I had a **queer** feeling that whenever

I wasn't looking at them straight they went askew, and moved about, and played a noiseless puss-in-the-corner behind my back. And the cornice had a serpentine design with masks—masks altogether too expressive for proper plaster.

78 Then abruptly my attention was caught by one of the odd-looking assistants. He was some way off and evidently unaware of my presence—I saw a sort of three-quarter length of him over a pile of toys and through an arch—and, you know, he was leaning against a pillar in an idle sort of way doing the most horrid things with his features! The particular horrid thing he did was with his nose. He did it just as though he was idle and wanted to amuse himself. First of all it was a short, blobby nose, and then suddenly he shot it out like a telescope, and then out it flew and became thinner and thinner until it was like a long, red flexible whip. Like a thing in a nightmare it was! He flourished it about and flung it forth as a fly-fisher flings his line.

79 My instant thought was that Gip mustn't see him. I turned about, and there was Gip quite preoccupied with the shopman, and thinking no evil. They were whispering together and looking at me. Gip was standing on a little stool, and the shopman was holding a sort of big drum in his hand.

80 "Hide and seek, dadda!" cried Gip. "You're He!"

81 And before I could do anything to prevent it, the shopman had clapped the big drum over him.

82 I saw what was up directly. "Take that off," I cried, "this instant! You'll frighten the boy. Take it off!"

83 The shopman with the unequal ears did so without a word, and held the big cylinder toward me to show its emptiness. And the little stool was vacant! In that instant my boy had utterly disappeared! ...

84 You know, perhaps, that sinister something that comes like a hand out of the unseen and grips your heart about. You know it takes your common self away and leaves you tense and deliberate, neither slow nor hasty, neither angry nor afraid. So it was with me.

85 I came up to this grinning shopman and kicked his stool aside.

86 "Stop this folly!" I said. "Where is my boy?"

87 "You see," he said, still displaying the drum's interior, "there is no deception—"

88 I put out my hand to grip him, and he eluded me by a dexterous movement. I snatched again, and he turned from me and pushed open a door to escape. "Stop!" I said, and he laughed, receding. I leapt after him—into utter darkness.

89 *Thud!*

90 "Lor' bless my 'eart! I didn't see you coming, sir!"

91 I was in Regent Street, and I had collided with a decent-looking working man; and a yard away, perhaps, and looking a little perplexed with himself, was Gip. There was some sort of apology, and then Gip had turned and come to me with a bright little smile, as though for a moment he had missed me.

92 And he was carrying four parcels in his arm!

93 He secured immediate possession of my finger.

94 For the second I was rather at a loss. I stared round to see the door of the Magic Shop, and, behold, it was not there! There was no door, no shop, nothing, only the common pilaster between the shop where they sell pictures and the window with the chicks! ...

95 I did the only thing possible in that mental tumult; I walked straight to the kerbstone and held up my umbrella for a cab.

96 "'Ansoms," said Gip, in a note of culminating exultation.

97 I helped him in, recalled my address with an effort, and got in also. Something unusual proclaimed itself in my tail-coat pocket, and I felt and discovered a glass ball. With a petulant expression I flung it into the street.

98 Gip said nothing.

99 For a space neither of us spoke.

100 "Dadda!" said Gip, at last, "that *was* a proper shop!"

101 I came round with that to the problem of just how the whole thing had seemed to him. He looked completely undamaged—so far, good; he was neither scared nor unhinged, he was simply tremendously satisfied with the afternoon's entertainment, and there in his arms were the four parcels.

102 Confound it! what could be in them?

103 "Um!" I said. "Little boys can't go to shops like that every day."

104 He received this with his usual stoicism, and for a moment I was sorry I was his father and not his mother, and so couldn't suddenly there, *coram publico*, in our **hansom**, kiss him. After all, I thought, the thing wasn't so very bad.

105 But it was only when we opened the parcels that I really began to be reassured. Three of them contained boxes of soldiers, quite ordinary lead soldiers, but of so good a quality as to make Gip altogether forget that originally these parcels had been Magic Tricks of the only genuine sort, and the fourth contained a kitten, a little living white kitten, in excellent health and appetite and temper.

106 I saw this unpacking with a sort of provisional relief. I hung about in the **nursery** for quite an unconscionable time ...

107 That happened six months ago. And now I am beginning to believe it is all right. The kitten had only the magic natural to all kittens, and the soldiers seemed as steady a company as any colonel could desire. And Gip—?

108 The intelligent parent will understand that I have to go cautiously with Gip.

109 But I went so far as this one day. I said, "How would you like your soldiers to come alive, Gip, and march about by themselves?"

110 "Mine do," said Gip. "I just have to say a word I know before I open the lid."

111 "Then they march about alone?"

112 "Oh, *quite*, dadda. I shouldn't like them if they didn't do that."

113 I displayed no unbecoming surprise, and since then I have taken occasion to drop in upon him once or twice, unannounced, when the soldiers were about, but so far I have never discovered them performing in anything like a magical manner ...

114 It's so difficult to tell.

115 There's also a question of finance. I have an incurable habit of paying bills. I have been up and down Regent Street several times looking for that shop. I am inclined to think, indeed, that in that matter honour is satisfied, and that, since Gip's name and address are known to them, I may very well leave it to these people, whoever they may be, to send in their bill in their own time.

(3994 words)

Source: Wells, H. G. "The Magic Shop." *The Strand Magazine*, June 1903, www.gutenberg.org/files/1743/1743-h/1743-h.htm.

Initial Insight

1. What is the story about? Write down anything that intuitively comes to you.

_____

_____

2. How would you describe the mood and atmosphere of the story?

_____

_____

Reader's Response

Consider the following questions. Discuss your answers with one or more partners.

1. Do you think the magic tricks in the story are real? What impact might your attitude have on your interpretation of the story? What impact might the opposite attitude have?

2. What is unusual about the magic shop? Do you think the shopman has any bad intentions?

3. How does the story end for each of the three main characters? How do you feel about that ending? Does it bring closure or leave you with any doubts as to what might happen afterwards?

LANGUAGE FOCUS

The author's use of language is inevitably informed by the historical and social context in which the story was written. The story is set in London, England, at the beginning of the twentieth century. As a result, some of the words and expressions used may have a different meaning than the one you might be familiar with in their contemporary usage. Refer to the context, and use a reputable unilingual dictionary to define the following words (identified in bold) as they are used in the text.

1. fancied (par. 1): _____

2. breeding (par. 5): _____

3. burthen (par. 11): _____

4. legerdemain (par. 16): _____

5. sepulchre (par. 45): _____

6. rum (par. 49): _____

7. sixpence (par. 64): _____

8. queer (par. 77): _____

9. hansom* (par. 104): _____

10. nursery (par. 106): _____

*This word is also written as 'ansom (par. 96) to reflect the common pronunciation in the London vernacular of the time.

Look up any other words you are unsure of.

MyBookshelf > My eLab > Exercises > Part I: Short Stories > Chapter 3: The Magic Shop > Vocabulary Comprehension

Close Reading

As you read the text again, pay attention to elements that seem significant to understanding and interpreting the story. The following guided reading questions will help you.

1. Who is Gip and approximately how old is he? What is his relationship to the narrator? Use information from the text to support your answer.

_____

_____

2. How does Gip feel about magic? And the narrator? Support your answer with quotes from paragraph 1.

_____

_____

_____

_____

3. What does the shopman suggest when he says, "We make no charge for glass balls. We get them, … free … though we pay in the end." (par. 24 and 28)

_____

_____

_____

4. What does the narrator imply when he describes that he "laughed in the manner of one who subscribes to a jest"? (par. 27)

_____

_____

5. How is Gip different from the boy who is not allowed into the shop?

_____

_____

6. What does the shopman make appear from the narrator's hat?

_____

_____

7. In response to these items appearing from the hat, what does the shopman refer to when he tells the narrator that "all sorts of things accumulate … Nearly every customer … Astonishing what they carry about with them"? (par. 45)

_____

_____

_____

8. In reference to the little red demon, what accusation does the shopman make when he tells the narrator "None of ours!"

_____

9. What is the implication of the shopman's knowing Gip's address?

_____

_____

10. What are the two main preoccupations of the narrator throughout the story?

_____

_____

MyBookshelf > My eLab > Exercises > Part I: Short Stories > Chapter 3: The Magic Shop > Close Reading: Additional Questions

THE LANGUAGE OF LITERATURE

The effect of any text is to a very large extent determined by the author's diction and use of figures of speech and other literary devices. Use the following questions to focus your attention on how the author uses language in the story.

A. Wells uses rich **imagery** to describe the magic shop, mostly referring to one of the five senses—vision (e.g., "a little, narrow shop," "on the floor were magic mirrors"). These images have the particularity of also evoking a sixth sense, or a feeling of eeriness and unease. Establish a list of words and phrases used by the narrator that you consider particularly charged in this way. Work with a partner to compare your choices and explain how they contribute to the story's mood.

B. The "magic sword" can be interpreted as a **symbol** for magic in general. Closely examine the description in the following conversation between Gip and the shopman:

"Is that a Magic Sword?" [Gip] said.

"A Magic Toy Sword. It neither bends, breaks, nor cuts the fingers. It renders the bearer invincible in battle against any one under eighteen. Half a crown to seven and sixpence, according to size ..."

Pinpoint the difference between Gip's and the shopman's reference to the sword. In its description, which aspects of the sword make it magic?

C. Two small mammals appear in the story: a rabbit and a kitten. Working individually, use a separate sheet of paper to compare their descriptions and characteristics. What might these animals symbolize? Then, discuss your hypothesis with one or more partners.

Analytical Reading

After making specific observations, you are ready to analyze the subject of your close reading. The following questions will help you look for thematic patterns, establish relationships and identify specific examples of literary devices or principles.

1. "The Magic Shop" features three main characters. Use the following questions to guide you in analyzing the story's **narrative situation**.

   a. Are the characters flat or round, static or dynamic? For each, elaborate a list of their most important physical, mental, moral and behavioural traits.

b. Who narrates the story? What type of narrator is this?

c. How would the story be affected if it had a different narrator? Discuss how alternative points of view would alter the information and impressions the reader has.

d. What can you observe about the narrative time of the story's main events? Does the author use prior, simultaneous or subsequent narration? At what point in the story does the reader become aware of this? How does this affect the mood of the story?

2. Consider these questions on **plot line**, and use your answers to complete the mind map of Freytag's Pyramid.

a. What is the story's central conflict, and what is at stake for the protagonist and other characters?

b. At what moment in the story is the tension highest?

c. What are the most important events that build up to the climax? Pay attention to changes in the story's mood.

d. What are the outcomes that make up the falling action?

e. What is the situation at the very beginning and at the very end of the story? These situations represent the exposition and resolution, respectively.

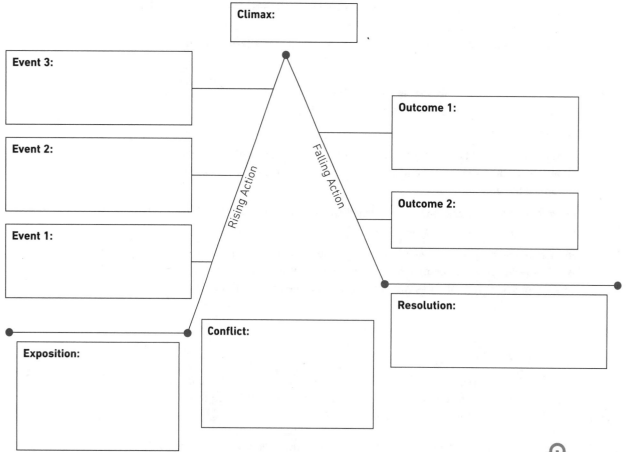

3. For each of the key plot events you established, identify the actions and attitudes of the three main **characters**. Use the chart provided in My eLab Documents. Compare their similarities and differences.

MyBookshelf > My eLab > Documents > Part I: Short Stories > Chapter 3: The Magic Shop

4. Discuss how this specific conflict, as well as the characters' different actions and attitudes toward it, can be distilled into a broader theme for the story.

Food for Thought

The following questions encourage you to turn a critical eye to your earlier observations and analyses. They introduce elements and considerations that will lead you to formulate new questions and set tentative hypotheses. Discuss these to further your insight into the text.

1. After analyzing the story, look back at its title. From what you have read, what does it indicate?

2. When describing the magic shop, the author introduces several dynamic special effects reminiscent of those used in films. For instance, the shopman turns himself into a rabbit, and the shop opens up to reveal other departments. Which other examples can you find? Discuss the action sequences they evoke.

3. H. G. Wells's son was called George Phillip. It is therefore sometimes hypothesized that the two of them are the story's protagonists. Discuss how knowing this hypothesis may impact a literary analysis of the story.

4. Other stories such as *Willy Wonka and the Chocolate Factory* (R. Dahl), *Mary Poppins* (P. L. Travers) and, more recently, *Harry Potter* (J. K. Rowling) take up similar themes of children evolving in magical environments. Choose one such story that you have already read. Compare it with "The Magic Shop," focusing on the mood, the children's relationships with magic and the adults' attitudes toward it.

5. "The Magic Shop" is also available as an illustrated book and a short film (I. Emes, 1982). Consult one of these versions, and discuss any similarities and differences with the atmosphere you experienced when reading the story.

Presenting an Analysis

Writing | Analyzing Theme and Mood through Character Comparison

Write a literary analysis essay around a thesis statement focusing on how the mood and characters in "The Magic Shop" contribute to one of the story's major themes, such as reality vs. fantasy or childish worrying vs. adult worrying.

Examples:

By narrating "The Magic Shop" through the lens of a worried father, H. G. Wells makes the reader wonder where the line lies between fantasy and reality.

In "The Magic Shop," H. G. Wells uses the protagonists' reactions to magic to contrast the capacity for children to wonder at simple things with the tendency for adults to worry.

In the body paragraphs, use a comparison and contrast structure to describe how the different characters interact with one another and react to the events that unfold at the magic shop. Refer to the work you did in exercises 2 and 3 of the Analytical Reading section. Explain the tension these interactions generate and how this tension fits into the theme. Make sure to provide clear examples from the text to illustrate and support your analysis.

(Refer to Part V, Writing about Literature, on page 271 for information on essay format and structure.)

Speaking | Describing Setting, Mood and Atmosphere

Based on your insight into the mood and atmosphere of the story and how the setting and characters contribute to it, prepare a word cloud or mood board, focusing on the story as a whole or on a specific scene, setting or character (e.g., the hidden showroom, the shopman).

A mood board is a collage or composition of images and other visual elements, often created by designers or artists to give an idea of the mood, style or theme they wish to give to a project, such as a play, a film or an interior design. A word cloud can be used for the same purpose; it regroups words that represent the concept instead of images.

Example of a mood board for London
at the beginning of the twentieth century:

Example of a word cloud based
on the concept of London:

Use your creation as visual support to prepare and deliver a cohesive presentation in which you analyze and explain the construction of the story's mood and atmosphere.

(Refer to Appendix 2 on page 297 for more information on presentation and structure.)

MyBookshelf > My eLab
> Exercises > Grammar and
Accuracy

CHAPTER 4

A Dog's Tale

– Mark Twain

This chapter focuses on the following:

- Narrator and point of view
- Dramatic structure
- Language Focus: synonyms
- The Language of Literature: personification and allegory
- Theme

Connect with the Text

A. Before you read the story, take stock of your opinions on the following questions. Discuss them with one or more partners.

1. Do you have any pets? How would you describe your relationship with them?
2. What does the phrase "man's best friend" mean to you? Be specific.
3. In certain countries, the law defines animals as objects, while in others, the law defines them as sentient beings. Discuss what characteristics warrant one or the other of these legal definitions. What are the consequences of each definition?
4. How do you feel about a vegan lifestyle? Is it something everyone should aspire to? Are vegans morally superior to meat eaters? Why or why not?
5. Do you consider that animal rights organizations play a useful role in society? Why or why not?

B. Consider the following two quotes attributed to Mark Twain. What opinions on humans, animals and their relationships can you infer?

> "It is just like man's vanity and impertinence to call an animal dumb because it is dumb to his dull perceptions."

> "I believe I am not interested to know whether Vivisection produces results that are profitable to the human race or doesn't."

Text in Context

Born in 1835 as Samuel Langhorne Clemens, Mark Twain himself was his own first literary character, so to speak. He was as contradictory a person as the difference between his real name and pen name suggests. He grew up in Missouri in a family of Irish and English heritage. After working as a typesetter at various newspapers, he became a steamboat captain on the Mississippi River. "Mark Twain" was the boatmen's cry to indicate two fathoms (12 feet) of safe water. Later in life, he moved East, first to New York and then to Connecticut. This is reflected in his work, which looks nostalgically to the South for its literary landscape and to the more progressive East for its values. Twain published fiction, poetry and nonfiction and was known for his black humour, wit and mastery of vernacular English. He also delivered many speeches, including one in Montreal in 1881.

In 1884, *The Adventures of Huckleberry Finn* quickly became a best-seller and, in spite of its initial censorship, has become one of the most widely read and taught novels in American literature. In the years that followed, Twain was plagued by financial trouble and lost his wife and a daughter. He continued to write, but most of his later material was not published until after his death in 1910 because of its pessimistic tone, scathing social criticism and nihilistic philosophy.

Exploratory Reading

Read the text a first time without interruption. Keep an open mind and take a mental note of your reactions and observations. Soak up the mood and atmosphere without looking for any specific elements. When you are finished, answer the questions below the text.

A Dog's Tale   **Mark Twain**

CHAPTER 1

1 My father was a St. Bernard, my mother was a collie, but I am a Presbyterian. This is what my mother told me; I do not know these nice distinctions myself. To me they are only fine large words meaning nothing. My mother had a fondness for such; she liked to say them, and see other dogs look surprised and envious, as wondering how she got so much education. But, indeed, it was not real education; it was only show: she got the words by listening in the dining-room and drawing-room when there was company, and by going with the children to Sunday-school and listening there; and whenever she heard a large word she said it over to herself many times, and so was able to keep it until there was a **dogmatic** gathering in the neighbourhood, then she would get it off, and surprise and distress them all, from pocket-pup to mastiff, which rewarded her for all her trouble. If there was a stranger he was nearly sure to be suspicious, and when he got his breath again he would ask her what it meant. And she always told him. He was never expecting this, but thought he would catch her; so when she told him, he was the one that looked ashamed, whereas he had thought it was going to be she. The others were always waiting for this, and glad of it and proud of her, for they knew what was going to happen, because they had had experience. When she told the meaning of a big word they were all

so taken up with admiration that it never occurred to any dog to doubt if it was the right one; and that was natural, because, for one thing, she answered up so promptly that it seemed like a dictionary speaking, and for another thing, where could they find out whether it was right or not? for she was the only cultivated dog there was. By and by, when I was older, she brought home the word Unintellectual, one time, and worked it pretty hard all the week at different gatherings, making much unhappiness and **despondency**; and it was at this time that I noticed that during that week she was asked for the meaning at eight different **assemblages**, and flashed out a fresh definition every time, which showed me that she had more presence of mind than culture, though I said nothing, of course. She had one word which she always kept on hand, and ready, like a life-preserver, a kind of emergency word to strap on when she was likely to get washed overboard in a sudden way—that was the word Synonymous. When she happened to fetch out a long word which had had its day weeks before and its prepared meanings gone to her dump-pile, if there was a stranger there of course it knocked him groggy for a couple of minutes, then he would come to, and by that time she would be away down the wind on another tack, and not expecting anything; so when he'd **hail** and ask her to cash in, I (the only dog on the inside of her game) could see her canvas flicker a moment—but only just a moment, —then it would belly out taut and full, and she would say, as calm as a summer's day, "It's synonymous with supererogation," or some godless long reptile of a word like that, and go **placidly** about and skim away on the next tack, perfectly comfortable, you know, and leave that stranger looking **profane** and embarrassed, and the initiated slatting the floor with their tails in unison and their faces **transfigured** with a holy joy.

2 And it was the same with phrases. She would drag home a whole phrase, if it had a grand sound, and play it six nights and two matinees, and explain it a new way every time,—which she had to, for all she cared for was the phrase; she wasn't interested in what it meant, and knew those dogs hadn't wit enough to catch her, anyway. Yes, she was a daisy! She got so she wasn't afraid of anything, she had such confidence in the ignorance of those creatures. She even brought anecdotes that she had heard the family and the dinner guests laugh and shout over; and as a rule she got the nub of one chestnut hitched onto another chestnut, where, of course, it didn't fit and hadn't any point; and when she delivered the nub she fell over and rolled on the floor and laughed and barked in the most insane way, while I could see that she was wondering to herself why it didn't seem as funny as it did when she first heard it. But no harm was done; the others rolled and barked too, privately ashamed of themselves for not seeing the point, and never suspecting that the fault was not with them and there wasn't any to see.

3 You can see by these things that she was of a rather vain and frivolous character; still, she had virtues, and enough to make up, I think. She had a kind heart and gentle ways, and never harboured resentments for injuries done her, but put them easily out of her mind and forgot them; and she taught her children her kindly way, and from her we learned also to be brave and prompt in time of danger, and not to run away, but face the **peril** that threatened friend or stranger, and help him the best we could without stopping to think what the cost might be to us. And she taught us, not by words only, but by example, and that is the best way and the surest and the most lasting. Why, the brave things she did, the splendid things! she was just a soldier; and so modest about it—well, you couldn't help admiring her, and you couldn't help imitating her; not even a King Charles spaniel could remain entirely despicable in her society. So, as you see, there was more to her than her education.

CHAPTER 2

4 When I was well grown, at last, I was sold and taken away, and I never saw her again. She was broken-hearted, and so was I, and we cried; but she comforted me as well as she could, and said we were sent into this world for a wise and good purpose, and must do our duties without repining, take our life as we might find it, live it for the best good of others, and never mind about the results; they were not our affair. She said men who did like this would have a noble and beautiful reward by and by in another world, and although we animals would not go there, to do well and right without reward would give to our brief lives a worthiness and dignity which in itself would be a reward. She had gathered these things from time to time when she had gone to the Sunday-school with the children, and had laid them up in her memory more carefully than she had done with those other words and phrases; and she had studied them deeply, for her good and ours. One may see by this that she had a wise and thoughtful head, for all there was so much lightness and vanity in it.

5 So we said our farewells, and looked our last upon each other through our tears; and the last thing she said—keeping it for the last to make me remember it the better, I think—was, "In memory of me, when there is a time of danger to another do not think of yourself, think of your mother, and do as she would do."

6 Do you think I could forget that? No.

CHAPTER 3

7 It was such a charming home!—my new one; a fine great house, with pictures, and delicate decorations, and rich furniture, and no gloom anywhere, but all the wilderness of dainty colours lit up with flooding sunshine; and the spacious grounds around it, and the great garden—oh, greensward, and noble trees, and flowers, no end! And I was the same as a member of the family; and they loved me, and petted me, and did not give me a new name, but called me by my old one that was dear to me because my mother had given it me—Aileen Mavourneen. She got it out of a song; and the Grays knew that song, and said it was a beautiful name.

8 Mrs. Gray was thirty, and so sweet and so lovely, you cannot imagine it; and Sadie was ten, and just like her mother, just a darling slender little copy of her, with auburn tails down her back, and short frocks; and the baby was a year old, and plump and dimpled, and fond of me, and never could get enough of hauling on my tail, and hugging me, and laughing out its innocent

happiness; and Mr. Gray was thirty-eight, and tall and slender and handsome, a little bald in front, alert, quick in his movements, businesslike, prompt, decided, unsentimental, and with that kind of trim-chiselled face that just seems to glint and sparkle with frosty intellectuality! He was a renowned scientist. I do not know what the word means, but my mother would know how to use it and get effects. She would know how to depress a rat-terrier with it and make a lap-dog look sorry he came. But that is not the best one; the best one was Laboratory. My mother could organize a Trust on that one that would skin the tax-collars off the whole herd. The laboratory was not a book, or a picture, or a place to wash your hands in, as the college president's dog said—no, that is the lavatory; the laboratory is quite different, and is filled with jars, and bottles, and electrics, and wires, and strange machines; and every week other scientists came there and sat in the place, and used the machines, and discussed, and made what they called experiments and discoveries; and often I came, too, and stood around and listened, and tried to learn, for the sake of my mother, and in loving memory of her, although it was a pain to me, as realizing what she was losing out of her life and I gaining nothing at all; for try as I might, I was never able to make anything out of it at all.

9   Other times I lay on the floor in the mistress's workroom and slept, she gently using me for a footstool, knowing it pleased me, for it was a caress; other times I spent an hour in the nursery, and got well tousled and made happy; other times I watched by the crib there, when the baby was asleep and the nurse out for a few minutes on the baby's affairs; other times I romped and raced through the grounds and the garden with Sadie till we were tired out, then slumbered on the grass in the shade of a tree while she read her book; other times I went visiting among the neighbour dogs,—for there were some most pleasant ones not far away, and one very handsome and courteous and graceful one, a curly haired Irish setter by the name of Robin Adair, who was a Presbyterian like me, and belonged to the Scotch minister.

10   The servants in our house were all kind to me and were fond of me, and so, as you see, mine was a pleasant life. There could not be a happier dog than I was, nor a gratefuller one. I will say this for myself, for it is only the truth: I tried in all ways to do well and right, and honour my mother's memory and her teachings, and earn the happiness that had come to me, as best I could.

11   By and by came my little puppy, and then my cup was full, my happiness was perfect. It was the dearest little waddling thing, and so smooth and soft and velvety, and had such cunning little awkward paws, and such **affectionate** eyes, and such a sweet and innocent face; and it made me so proud to see how the children and their mother adored it, and fondled it, and exclaimed over every little wonderful thing it did. It did seem to me that life was just too lovely to—

12   Then came the winter. One day I was standing a watch in the nursery. That is to say, I was asleep on the bed. The baby was asleep in the crib, which was alongside the bed, on the side next the fireplace. It was the kind of crib that has a lofty tent over it made of a gauzy stuff that you can see through. The nurse was out, and we two sleepers were alone. A spark from the wood-fire was shot out, and it lit on the slope of the tent. I suppose a quiet interval followed, then a scream from the baby woke me, and there was that tent flaming up toward the ceiling! Before I could think, I sprang to the floor in my fright, and in a second was half-way to the door; but in the next half-second my mother's farewell was sounding in my ears, and I was back on the bed again. I reached my head through the flames and dragged the baby out by the waistband, and tugged it along, and we fell to the floor together in a cloud of smoke; I snatched a new hold, and dragged the screaming little creature along and out at the door and around the bend of the hall, and was still tugging away, all excited and happy and proud, when the master's voice shouted:

13   "Begone, you cursed beast!" and I jumped to save myself; but he was wonderfully quick, and chased me up, striking furiously at me with his cane, I dodging this way and that, in terror, and at last a strong blow fell upon my left fore-leg, which made me shriek and fall, for the moment, helpless; the cane went up for another blow, but never descended, for the nurse's voice rang wildly out, "The nursery's on fire!" and the master rushed away in that direction, and my other bones were saved.

14   The pain was cruel, but, no matter, I must not lose any time; he might come back at any moment; so I limped on three legs to the other end of the hall, where there was a dark little stairway leading up into a garret where old boxes and such things were kept, as I had heard say, and where people seldom went. I managed to climb up there, then I searched my way through the dark among the piles of things, and hid in the secretest place I could find. It was foolish to be afraid there, yet still I was; so afraid that I held in and hardly even whimpered, though it would have been such a comfort to whimper, because that eases the

pain, you know. But I could lick my leg, and that did me some good.

15 For half an hour there was a commotion down-stairs, and shoutings, and rushing footsteps, and then there was quiet again. Quiet for some minutes, and that was grateful to my spirit, for then my fears began to go down; and fears are worse than pains,—oh, much worse. Then came a sound that froze me! They were calling me—calling me by name—hunting for me!

16 It was muffled by distance, but that could not take the terror out of it, and it was the most dreadful sound to me that I had ever heard. It went all about, everywhere, down there: along the halls, through all the rooms, in both stories, and in the basement and the cellar; then outside, and further and further away—then back, and all about the house again, and I thought it would never, never stop. But at last it did, hours and hours after the vague twilight of the garret had long ago been blotted out by black darkness.

17 Then in that blessed stillness my terror fell little by little away, and I was at peace and slept. It was a good rest I had, but I woke before the twilight had come again. I was feeling fairly comfortable, and I could think out a plan now. I made a very good one; which was, to creep down, all the way down the back stairs, and hide behind the cellar door, and slip out and escape when the iceman came at dawn, while he was inside filling the refrigerator; then I would hide all day, and start on my journey when night came; my journey to—well, anywhere where they would not know me and betray me to the master. I was feeling almost cheerful now; then suddenly I thought, Why, what would life be without my puppy!

18 That was despair. There was no plan for me; I saw that; I must stay where I was; stay, and wait, and take what might come—it was not my affair; that was what life is—my mother had said it. Then—well, then the calling began again! All my sorrows came back. I said to myself, the master will never forgive. I did not know what I had done to make him so bitter and so unforgiving, yet I judged it was something a dog could not understand, but which was clear to a man and dreadful.

19 They called and called—days and nights, it seemed to me. So long that the hunger and thirst near drove me mad, and I recognized that I was getting very weak. When you are this way you sleep a great deal, and I did. Once I woke in an awful fright—it seemed to me that the calling was right there in the garret! And so it was: it was Sadie's voice, and she was crying; my name was falling from her lips all broken, poor thing, and

I could not believe my ears for the joy of it when I heard her say,

20 "Come back to us—oh, come back to us, and forgive—it is all so sad without our—"

21 I broke in with *such* a grateful little yelp, and the next moment Sadie was plunging and stumbling through the darkness and the lumber and shouting for the family to hear, "She's found! she's found!"

22 The days that followed—well, they were wonderful. The mother and Sadie and the servants—why, they just seemed to worship me. They couldn't seem to make me a bed that was fine enough; and as for food, they couldn't be satisfied with anything but game and delicacies that were out of season; and every day the friends and neighbours flocked in to hear about my heroism—that was the name they called it by, and it means agriculture. I remember my mother pulling it on a kennel once, and explaining it that way, but didn't say what agriculture was, except that it was synonymous with intramural incandescence; and a dozen times a day Mrs. Gray and Sadie would tell the tale to new-comers, and say I risked my life to save the baby's, and both of us had burns to prove it, and then the company would pass me around and pet me and exclaim about me, and you could see the pride in the eyes of Sadie and her mother; and when the people wanted to know what made me limp, they looked ashamed and changed the subject, and sometimes when people hunted them this way and that way with questions about it, it looked to me as if they were going to cry.

23 And this was not all the glory; no, the master's friends came, a whole twenty of the most distinguished people, and had me in the laboratory, and discussed me as if I was a kind of discovery; and some of them said it was wonderful in a dumb beast, the finest exhibition of instinct they could call to mind; but the master said, with **vehemence**, "It's far above instinct; it's *reason*, and many a man, privileged to be saved and go with you and me to a better world by right of its possession, has less of it than this poor silly quadruped that's **foreordained** to **perish**"; and then he laughed, and said, "Why, look at me—I'm a sarcasm! Bless you, with all my grand intelligence, the only thing I inferred was that the dog had gone mad and was destroying the child, whereas but for the beast's intelligence—it's *reason*, I tell you!—the child would have perished!"

24 They disputed and disputed, and *I* was the very centre and subject of it all, and I wished my mother could know that this grand honour had come to me; it would have made her proud.

25 Then they discussed optics, as they called it, and whether a certain injury to the brain would produce blindness or not, but they could not agree about it, and said they must test it by experiment by and by; and next they discussed plants, and that interested me, because in the summer Sadie and I had planted seeds—I helped her dig the holes, you know,—and after days and days a little shrub or a flower came up there, and it was a wonder how that could happen; but it did, and I wished I could talk,—I would have told those people about it and shown them how much I knew, and been all alive with the subject; but I didn't care for the optics; it was dull, and when they came back to it again it bored me, and I went to sleep.

26 Pretty soon it was spring, and sunny and pleasant and lovely, and the sweet mother and the children patted me and the puppy good-bye, and went away on a journey and a visit to their kin, and the master wasn't any company for us, but we played together and had good times, and the servants were kind and friendly, so we got along quite happily and counted the days and waited for the family.

27 And one day those men came again, and said now for the test, and they took the puppy to the laboratory, and I limped three-leggedly along, too, feeling proud, for any attention shown the puppy was a pleasure to me, of course. They discussed and experimented, and then suddenly the puppy shrieked, and they set him on the floor, and he went staggering around, with his head all bloody, and the master clapped his hands, and shouted:

28 "There, I've won—confess it! He's as blind as a bat!"

29 And they all said,

30 "It's so—you've proved your theory, and suffering humanity owes you a great debt from henceforth," and they crowded around him, and wrung his hand cordially and thankfully, and praised him.

31 But I hardly saw or heard these things, for I ran at once to my little darling, and snuggled close to it where it lay, and licked the blood, and it put its head against mine, whimpering softly, and I knew in my heart it was a comfort to it in its pain and trouble to feel its mother's touch, though it could not see me. Then it drooped down, presently, and its little velvet nose rested upon the floor, and it was still, and did not move any more.

32 Soon the master stopped discussing a moment, and rang in the footman, and said, "Bury it in the far corner of the garden," and then went on with the discussion, and I trotted after the footman, very happy and grateful, for I knew the puppy was out of its pain now, because it was asleep. We went far down the garden to the furthest end, where the children and the nurse and the puppy and I used to play in the summer in the shade of a great elm, and there the footman dug a hole, and I saw he was going to plant the puppy, and I was glad, because it would grow and come up a fine handsome dog, like Robin Adair, and be a beautiful surprise for the family when they came home; so I tried to help him dig, but my lame leg was no good, being stiff, you know, and you have to have two, or it is no use. When the footman had finished and covered little Robin up, he patted my head, and there were tears in his eyes, and he said, "Poor little doggie, you SAVED *his* child."

33 I have watched two whole weeks, and he doesn't come up! This last week a fright has been stealing upon me. I think there is something terrible about this. I do not know what it is, but the fear makes me sick, and I cannot eat, though the servants bring me the best of food; and they pet me so, and even come in the night, and cry, and say, "Poor doggie—do give it up and come home; *don't* break our hearts!" and all this terrifies me the more, and makes me sure something has happened. And I am so weak; since yesterday I cannot stand on my feet any more. And within this hour the servants, looking toward the sun where it was sinking out of sight and the night chill coming on, said things I could not understand, but they carried something cold to my heart.

34 "Those poor creatures! They do not suspect. They will come home in the morning, and eagerly ask for the little doggie that did the brave deed, and who of us will be strong enough to say the truth to them: 'The humble little friend is gone where go the beasts that perish.'"

(4339 words)

Source: Twain, M. "A Dog's Tale." *Harper's Magazine*, 1903, www.loa.org/images/pdf/Twain_Dogs-Tale.pdf.

Initial Insight

1. What is the story about? Write down anything that intuitively comes to you.

_____

_____

2. Why is the short story divided into three chapters? How are they related? Which character features in all three chapters?

_____

_____

_____

3. Who narrates the story? Do you consider the narrator to be reliable or unreliable? Explain.

_____

_____

_____

_____

Reader's Response

Consider the following questions. Discuss your answers with one or more partners.

1. What emotional response(s) or reaction(s) did the story evoke in you?

2. Did you find the idea of a dog telling a story to be convincing as a literary device? Why or why not?

3. Why do you think the author dedicates the entire first chapter to the narrator's mother and her behaviour?

4. What do you think happens after the story ends?

5. This story was written in 1903. Is it still relevant today? Why or why not?

LANGUAGE FOCUS

In the first chapter of the story, Twain draws attention to the mother's use of the expression "it's synonymous with ..." to explain complex words she does not genuinely understand. Match the words from the text in the left-hand column with their plain English synonyms in the right-hand column. Refer to the paragraph numbers in parentheses to see the words in context.

1. dogmatic (par. 1) _____	a) ask
2. despondency (par. 1) _____	b) calmly
3. assemblage (par. 1) _____	c) changed
4. hail (par. 1) _____	d) danger
5. placidly (par. 1) _____	e) destined
6. profane (par. 1) _____	f) die
7. transfigured (par. 1) _____	g) hopelessness
8. peril (par. 3) _____	h) intensity
9. affectionate (par. 11) _____	i) kind
10. vehemence (par. 23) _____	j) meeting
11. foreordained (par. 23) _____	k) opinionated
12. perish (par. 23) _____	l) ignorant of esoteric or expert knowledge

Look up any other words you are sure of.

MyBookshelf > My eLab
> Exercises > Part I: Short
Stories > Chapter 4:
A Dog's Tale > Vocabulary
Comprehension

Close Reading

As you read the text again, pay attention to elements that seem significant to understanding and interpreting the story. The following guided reading questions will help you.

1. In which three places does the narrator's mother pick up complex words, and from whom?

_____

_____

2. Does this make her a more intelligent dog?   □ Yes   □ No   Explain.

_____

3. Why do all of the other dogs admire her for using these words?

_____

_____

4. What life lesson does the narrator learn from her mother? Why does the mother consider this the most important advice?

_____

_____

5. Why does the narrator feel happy and loved in her new environment? Check all that apply.

a) The house and garden are bright and big.
b) She gets a new nickname, Aileen.
c) She gets a lot of affection.
d) She gets to do all the same things as the members of the family.

6. What is Mr. Gray's job? What is the narrator's understanding of it?

_____

_____

7. Why does Aileen hide after pulling the baby out of its crib?

a) She is scared because she thinks she will get punished.
b) She is scared because she did something wrong.
c) She is scared because there is a big commotion and a lot of noise.

8. What happens to the puppy in the laboratory? Be as specific as possible.

_____

9. What does Aileen think will happen with the puppy once it is buried?

_____

10. At the very end of the story, what does Aileen do?

a) She digs a deep hole.
b) She impatiently waits for the children to come back.
c) She gets sick from all the food the servants bring her.
d) She stops eating and dies of hunger.

MyBookshelf > My eLab
> Exercises > Part I: Short
Stories > Chapter 4:
A Dog's Tale > Close Reading:
Additional Questions

THE LANGUAGE OF LITERATURE

The effect of any text is to a very large extent determined by the author's diction and use of figures of speech and other literary devices. Use the following questions to focus your attention on how the author uses language in the story.

A. **Personification** is a figure of speech in which an abstract concept or an animal is associated with human attributes; e.g., "the flowers beside them, chill and shiver" (R. Frost); "blushing birds go down to drink" (E. Dickinson). Repeated personification can be used to support a related concept, **anthropomorphism**, in which a non-human character is depicted as being human. For instance, famous literary characters like Pinocchio and Winnie-the-Pooh are anthropomorphic because they behave like humans. In "A Dog's Tale," the sentence "We [the dogs] looked our last upon each other through our tears" includes a form of personification because associating tears with sadness is a human trait. Making the dogs "speak" rather than "bark" is a form of anthropomorphism, because it makes the reader think of them as humans rather than animals.

1. Choose the excerpts that are examples of personification. Explain your choices.

   a) It was foolish to be afraid there, yet still I was.

   b) So we said our farewells.

   c) I romped and raced through the grounds and the garden with Sadie.

   d) And I was the same as a member of the family.

   e) When he got his breath again he would ask her what it meant.

2. Answer the following questions about elements that contribute to anthropomorphism of the dogs. Do a web search if needed.

   a. Which of the three words referring to the narrator's pedigree (St. Bernard, collie, Presbyterian) is not actually a dog breed? What does it mean?

   b. The narrator is called Aileen Mavourneen and one of her friends is called Robin Adair. What is the origin of these names?

3. In the text, find five more examples of personification and/or anthropomorphism. Work with one or more partners, explaining why you consider your examples to be personification or anthropomorphism.

B. Personification and anthropomorphism allow the author to create an **allegory**, a literary construct in which the literal actions and events that are reported refer to a second level of meaning. It is often used to represent abstract ideas or to criticize sociopolitical situations or events. Who and what does the author criticize through the dogs' behaviour?

Analytical Reading

After making specific observations, you are ready to analyze the subject of your close reading. The following questions will help you look for thematic patterns, establish relationships and identify specific examples of literary devices or principles.

1. In Chapter 1 of the story, the author uses a **play on words** with the phrase "a dogmatic gathering." Explain in what sense the narrator uses the word *dogmatic*. What is its actual meaning, and how does this indicate the tone and author's attitude toward the events narrated?

2. Complete the table with the narrator's mother's positive and negative **character traits**.

Positive traits	Negative traits

Consider the character traits you identified. Which ones would you typically associate with a dog? Which character traits only apply to humans?

3. What is the central event related in Chapter 2? What does the mother pass on to Aileen, and why is this important for the remainder of the story?

4. Where does Aileen's mother's advice originally come from? Considering the events that unfold in Chapter 3, explain how the origin of the advice is **ironic**.

5. In Chapter 3, the second paragraph **foreshadows** some of the tragic events that are to happen. Which two pieces of information are important in this regard?

6. In Chapter 3, how is the **narrative speed** increased and decreased to serve the plot line? Refer to the four techniques described on page 8.

7. The narrator alternates between descriptions of what happens and her understanding of these events. Explain how alternating between these two types of accounts generates **situational irony**.

8. Explain how the behaviour of the footman and servants is used by the author to criticize societal class roles.

Food for Thought

The following questions encourage you to turn a critical eye to your earlier observations and analyses. They introduce elements and considerations that will lead you to formulate new questions and set tentative hypotheses. Discuss these to further your insight into the text.

1. Though the title is very brief, it evokes several aspects and themes of the story. It also contains a play on words. Look up the word "tale" if need be, and discuss the different interpretations the title offers.

2. Why do you think the author chose to tell the story from the dog's perspective? What other points of view would have been possible? How would these have affected the narrative and its tone?

3. The very last paragraph of the story is in quotation marks. Why do you think that is? Who or what do the words *creatures* and *us* refer to?

4. Why do you think Twain decided to make Mrs. Gray and the children absent themselves for the last part of the story?

5. Apart from being invested in the anti-vivisection movement, Mark Twain was also a fervent critic of religious institutions, slavery and the lack of women's rights. Can you find traces of these themes in "A Dog's Tale," either literally in the story or suggested on a secondary level through the events and what they represent? How are they treated? Find examples and discuss your observations.

Example:

Twain criticizes the concept of Sunday school, for instance, by highlighting that a moral often repeated and considered an important life lesson by the protagonist is actually not followed by most people.

Presenting an Analysis

Writing | Analyzing Contrasting Perspectives

Write a literary analysis essay around a thesis statement focusing on the contrast between animal selflessness and human selfishness. Mark Twain constructs this theme throughout the story through the use of irony and the description of situations and events that contribute to an allegorical or secondary-level reading.

Example:

In "A Dog's Tale," Mark Twain emphasizes human hypocrisy by contrasting the dog's proud application of morals learned at Sunday school with humans' utter disrespect for these guidelines.

In each of the body paragraphs, use an analysis structure to provide evidence and examples from the text to point out how Twain creates this contrast. You can present your analysis of the human and animal perspectives in separate paragraphs or compare and contrast different aspects within each paragraph. Refer to the work you did in the Analytical Reading section. Make sure to provide clear examples from the text to illustrate and support your analysis.

(Refer to Part V, Writing about Literature, on page 271 for more information on essay format and structure.)

Speaking | Analyzing Supporting Themes

Your work in the Analytical Reading and Food for Thought sections showed that Twain does not only focus on the relationship between animals and humans. He also criticizes religion and social structures by evoking thematic concepts like loyalty, freedom, hypocrisy and morality. Choose one of these thematic concepts—or another that you observed—and explain how precisely it is taken up in the story by adding one or more controlling ideas to your thesis.

- Point out meaningful descriptions of symbols and characters, explaining how and why these contribute to the theme you explore.
- Point out and explain any particular word choices or examples of metaphors or similes.
- Establish links between the observations you make and the theme you present on.

(Refer to Appendix 2 on page 297 for more information on presentation format and structure.)

MyBookshelf > My eLab
> Exercises > Grammar and
Accuracy

CHAPTER 5

The New Dress

– Virginia Woolf

This chapter focuses on the following:

- Narrative situation and types of narrators
- Symbolism
- Language Focus: analyzing complex sentences
- The Language of Literature: symbol, repetition, metaphor and simile
- Theme

Connect with the Text

A. Discuss your opinions on the following questions with one or more partners.

1. Are clothing or fashion in general important to you? Why or why not?
2. How important do you think looks are in determining someone's identity?
3. What does the term "fashion victim" evoke for you?
4. When interacting with others in social settings, what (if anything) makes you feel uncomfortable or shy?

B. Before you read the story, do a web search to find the answers to the following questions. This will help you visualize the setting and themes of the story. Remember to record your sources so you can use them as references.

1. What did women's fashion look like in the 1920s in the United Kingdom?
2. Why was this period also called "the roaring twenties"?
3. What does Virginia Woolf's concept of "frock consciousness" refer to?
4. What exactly is "stream of consciousness," and what are some of its defining features? Find an example of this narrative mode online. Work with a partner to discuss how the features you researched are represented in both of your examples.

Text in Context

Growing up at the turn of the twentieth century, Virginia Woolf (1882–1941) had witnessed important societal changes. After World War I, increased communication, social mobility and affordable commodities dramatically transformed people's lives. Literacy rates improved, and the 1918 Representation of the People Act gave all men over twenty-one and all women over thirty the right to vote. Intellectual and scientific advances also contributed to a change in how people viewed themselves. Darwin's evolutionary theory and Freud's concept of the unconscious, for instance, led to a heightened interest in the human psyche. In 1923, Woolf's novel *Mrs. Dalloway* reflected the fading of Victorian values, and its typical stream-of-consciousness narrative focused the reader's attention on the protagonist's psyche rather than an intricate plot line. Woolf also had a considerable impact on cultural life through her publishing house; she regularly hosted gatherings for intellectuals of the time. Woolf's personal life also had a dark side as she struggled with mental health issues and attempted suicide. Although Woolf is often hailed as one of the most important modern feminist writers, she started exploring the question of women's nature and social role long before making it a political issue. "The New Dress" is representative of Woolf's writing, both in its narrative style and its desire to explore the female psyche. There is no logical progression of ideas in the story; rather, they occur randomly, as the narrator's thoughts drift to and from the party.

Exploratory Reading

Read the text a first time without interruption. Keep an open mind and take a mental note of your reactions and observations. Soak up the mood and atmosphere without looking for any specific elements. When you are finished, answer the questions below the text.

The New Dress **Virginia Woolf**

1 Mabel had her first serious suspicion that something was wrong as she took her cloak off and Mrs. Barnet, while handing her the mirror and touching the brushes and thus drawing her attention, perhaps rather markedly, to all the appliances for tidying and improving hair, complexion, clothes, which existed on the dressing table, confirmed the suspicion—that it was not right, not quite right, which growing stronger as she went upstairs and springing at her, with conviction as she greeted Clarissa Dalloway, she went straight to the far end of the room, to a shaded corner where a looking-glass hung and looked. No! It was not *right*. And at once the misery which she always tried to hide, the profound dissatisfaction—the sense she had had, ever since she was a child, of being inferior to other people—set upon her, relentlessly, remorselessly, with an intensity which she could not beat off, as she would when she woke at night at home, by reading Borrow or Scott; for oh these men, oh these women, all were thinking—"What's Mabel wearing? What a fright she looks! What a hideous new dress!"—their eyelids flickering as they came up and then their lids shutting rather tight. It was her own appalling inadequacy; her cowardice; her mean, water-sprinkled blood that depressed her. And at once the whole of the room where, for ever so many hours, she had planned with the little dressmaker how it was to go,

seemed sordid, repulsive; and her own drawing-room so shabby, and herself, going out, puffed up with vanity as she touched the letters on the hall table and said: "How dull!" to show off—all this now seemed unutterably silly, paltry, and provincial. All this had been absolutely destroyed, shown up, exploded, the moment she came into Mrs. Dalloway's drawing-room.

2 What she had thought that evening when, sitting over the teacups, Mrs. Dalloway's invitation came, was that, of course, she could not be fashionable. It was absurd to pretend it even—fashion meant cut, meant style, meant thirty guineas at least—but why not be original? Why not be herself, anyhow? And, getting up, she had taken that old fashion book of her mother's, a Paris fashion book of the time of the Empire, and had thought how much prettier, more dignified, and more womanly they were then, and so set herself—oh, it was foolish—trying to be like them, pluming herself in fact, upon being modest and old-fashioned, and very charming, giving herself up, no doubt about it, to an orgy of self-love, which deserved to be chastised, and so rigged herself out like this.

3 But she dared not look in the glass. She could not face the whole horror—the pale yellow, idiotically old-fashioned silk dress with its long skirt and its high sleeves and its waist and all the things that looked so

charming in the fashion book, but not on her, not among all these ordinary people. She felt like a dressmaker's dummy standing there, for young people to stick pins into.

4 "But, my dear, it's perfectly charming!" Rose Shaw said, looking her up and down with that little satirical pucker of the lips which she expected—Rose herself being dressed in the height of fashion, precisely like everybody else, always.

5 We are all like flies trying to crawl over the edge of the saucer, Mabel thought, and repeated the phrase as if she were crossing herself, as if she were trying to find some spell to annul this pain, to make this agony endurable. Tags of Shakespeare, lines from books she had read ages ago, suddenly came to her when she was in agony, and she repeated them over and over again. "Flies trying to crawl," she repeated. If she could say that over often enough and make herself see the flies, she would become numb, chill, frozen, dumb. Now she could see flies crawling slowly out of a saucer of milk with their wings stuck together; and she strained and strained (standing in front of the looking-glass, listening to Rose Shaw) to make herself see Rose Shaw and all the other people there as flies, trying to hoist themselves out of something, or into something, meagre, insignificant, toiling flies. But she could not see them like that, not other people. She saw herself like that—she was a fly, but the others were dragonflies, butterflies, beautiful insects, dancing, fluttering, skimming, while she alone dragged herself up out of the saucer. (Envy and spite, the most detestable of the vices, were her chief faults.)

6 "I feel like some dowdy, decrepit, horribly dingy old fly," she said, making Robert Haydon stop just to hear her say that, just to reassure herself by furbishing up a poor weak-kneed phrase and so showing how detached she was, how witty, that she did not feel in the least out of anything. And, of course, Robert Haydon answered something, quite polite, quite insincere, which she saw through instantly, and said to herself, directly he went (again from some book), "Lies, lies, lies!" For a party makes things either much more real, or much less real, she thought; she saw in a flash to the bottom of Robert Haydon's heart; she saw through everything. She saw the truth. *This* was true, this drawing-room, this self, and the other false. Miss Milan's little workroom was really terribly hot, stuffy, sordid. It smelt of clothes and cabbage cooking; and yet, when Miss Milan put the glass in her hand, and she looked at herself with the dress on, finished, an extraordinary bliss shot through her heart. Suffused with light, she sprang into existence.

Rid of cares and wrinkles, what she had dreamed of herself was there—a beautiful woman. Just for a second (she had not dared look longer, Miss Milan wanted to know about the length of the skirt), there looked at her, framed in the scrolloping mahogany, a grey-white, mysteriously smiling, charming girl, the core of herself, the soul of herself; and it was not vanity only, not only self-love that made her think it good, tender, and true. Miss Milan said that the skirt could not well be longer; if anything the skirt, said Miss Milan, puckering her forehead, considering with all her wits about her, must be shorter; and she felt, suddenly, honestly, full of love for Miss Milan, much, much fonder of Miss Milan than of any one in the whole world, and could have cried for pity that she should be crawling on the floor with her mouth full of pins, and her face red and her eyes bulging—that one human being should be doing this for another, and she saw them all as human beings merely, and herself going off to her party, and Miss Milan pulling the cover over the canary's cage, or letting him pick a hemp-seed from between her lips, and the thought of it, of this side of human nature and its patience and its endurance and its being content with such miserable, scanty, sordid, little pleasures filled her eyes with tears.

7 And now the whole thing had vanished. The dress, the room, the love, the pity, the scrolloping looking-glass, and the canary's cage—all had vanished, and here she was in a corner of Mrs. Dalloway's drawing-room, suffering tortures, woken wide awake to reality.

8 But it was all so paltry, weak-blooded, and petty-minded to care so much at her age with two children, to be still so utterly dependent on people's opinions and not have principles or convictions, not to be able to say as other people did, "There's Shakespeare! There's death! We're all weevils in a captain's biscuit"—or whatever it was that people did say.

9 She faced herself straight in the glass; she pecked at her left shoulder; she issued out into the room, as if spears were thrown at her yellow dress from all sides. But instead of looking fierce or tragic, as Rose Shaw would have done—Rose would have looked like Boadicea—she looked foolish and self-conscious, and simpered like a schoolgirl and slouched across the room, positively slinking, as if she were a beaten mongrel, and looked at a picture, an engraving. As if one went to a party to look at a picture! Everybody knew why she did it—it was from shame, from humiliation.

10 "Now the fly's in the saucer," she said to herself, "right in the middle, and can't get out, and the milk," she thought, rigidly staring at the picture, "is sticking its wings together."

11 "It's so old-fashioned," she said to Charles Burt, making him stop (which by itself he hated) on his way to talk to some one else.

12 She meant, or she tried to make herself think that she meant, that it was the picture and not her dress, that was old-fashioned. And one word of praise, one word of affection from Charles would have made all the difference to her at the moment. If he had only said, "Mabel, you're looking charming to-night!" it would have changed her life. But then she ought to have been truthful and direct. Charles said nothing of the kind, of course. He was malice itself. He always saw through one, especially if one were feeling particularly mean, paltry, or feeble-minded.

13 "Mabel's got a new dress!" he said, and the poor fly was absolutely shoved into the middle of the saucer. Really, he would like her to drown, she believed. He had no heart, no fundamental kindness, only a veneer of friendliness. Miss Milan was much more real, much kinder. If only one could feel that and stick to it, always. "Why," she asked herself—replying to Charles much too pertly, letting him see that she was out of temper, or "ruffled" as he called it ("Rather ruffled?" he said and went on to laugh at her with some woman over there)—"Why," she asked herself, "can't I feel one thing always, feel quite sure that Miss Milan is right, and Charles wrong and stick to it, feel sure about the canary and pity and love and not be whipped all round in a second by coming into a room full of people?" It was her odious, weak, vacillating character again, always giving at the critical moment and not being seriously interested in conchology, etymology, botany, archeology, cutting up potatoes and watching them fructify like Mary Dennis, like Violet Searle.

14 Then Mrs. Holman, seeing her standing there, bore down upon her. Of course a thing like a dress was beneath Mrs. Holman's notice, with her family always tumbling downstairs or having the scarlet fever. Could Mabel tell her if Elmthorpe was ever let for August and September? Oh, it was a conversation that bored her unutterably!—it made her furious to be treated like a house agent or a messenger boy, to be made use of. Not to have value, that was it, she thought, trying to grasp something hard, something real, while she tried to answer sensibly about the bathroom and the south aspect and the hot water to the top of the house; and all the time she could see little bits of her yellow dress in the round looking-glass which made them all the size of boot-buttons or tadpoles; and it was amazing to think how much humiliation and agony and self-loathing and effort and passionate ups and downs of feeling

were contained in a thing the size of a threepenny bit. And what was still odder, this thing, this Mabel Waring, was separate, quite disconnected; and though Mrs. Holman (the black button) was leaning forward and telling her how her eldest boy had strained his heart running, she could see her, too, quite detached in the looking-glass, and it was impossible that the black dot, leaning forward, gesticulating, should make the yellow dot, sitting solitary, self-centred, feel what the black dot was feeling, yet they pretended.

15 "So impossible to keep boys quiet"—that was the kind of thing one said.

16 And Mrs. Holman, who could never get enough sympathy and snatched what little there was greedily, as if it were her right (but she deserved much more for there was her little girl who had come down this morning with a swollen knee-joint), took this miserable offering and looked at it suspiciously, grudgingly, as if it were a halfpenny when it ought to have been a pound and put it away in her purse, must put up with it, mean and miserly though it was, times being hard, so very hard; and on she went, creaking, injured Mrs. Holman, about the girl with the swollen joints. Ah, it was tragic, this greed, this clamour of human beings, like a row of cormorants, barking and flapping their wings for sympathy—it was tragic, could one have felt it and not merely pretended to feel it!

17 But in her yellow dress to-night she could not wring out one drop more; she wanted it all, all for herself. She knew (she kept on looking into the glass, dipping into that dreadfully showing-up blue pool) that she was condemned, despised, left like this in a backwater, because of her being like this a feeble, vacillating creature; and it seemed to her that the yellow dress was a penance which she had deserved, and if she had been dressed like Rose Shaw, in lovely, clinging green with a ruffle of swansdown, she would have deserved that; and she thought that there was no escape for her— none whatever. But it was not her fault altogether, after all. It was being one of a family of ten; never having money enough, always skimping and paring; and her mother carrying great cans, and the linoleum worn on the stair edges, and one sordid little domestic tragedy after another—nothing catastrophic, the sheep farm failing, but not utterly; her eldest brother marrying beneath him but not very much—there was no romance, nothing extreme about them all. They petered out respectably in seaside resorts; every watering-place had one of her aunts even now asleep in some lodging with the front windows not quite facing the sea. That was so like them—they had to

squint at things always. And she had done the same—she was just like her aunts. For all her dreams of living in India, married to some hero like Sir Henry Lawrence, some empire builder (still the sight of a native in a turban filled her with romance), she had failed utterly. She had married Hubert, with his safe, permanent underling's job in the Law Courts, and they managed tolerably in a smallish house, without proper maids, and hash when she was alone or just bread and butter, but now and then—Mrs. Holman was off, thinking her the most dried-up, unsympathetic twig she had ever met, absurdly dressed, too, and would tell every one about Mabel's fantastic appearance—now and then, thought Mabel Waring, left alone on the blue sofa, punching the cushion in order to look occupied, for she would not join Charles Burt and Rose Shaw, chattering like magpies and perhaps laughing at her by the fireplace—now and then, there did come to her delicious moments, reading the other night in bed, for instance, or down by the sea on the sand in the sun, at Easter—let her recall it—a great tuft of pale sand-grass standing all twisted like a shock of spears against the sky, which was blue like a smooth china egg, so firm, so hard, and then the melody of the waves—"Hush, hush," they said, and the children's shouts paddling—yes, it was a divine moment, and there she lay, she felt, in the hand of the Goddess who was the world; rather a hard-hearted, but very beautiful Goddess, a little lamb laid on the altar (one did think these silly things, and it didn't matter so long as one never said them). And also with Hubert sometimes she had quite unexpectedly—carving the mutton for Sunday lunch, for no reason, opening a letter, coming into a room—divine moments, when she said to herself (for she would never say this to anybody else), "This is it. This has happened. This is it!" And the other way about it was equally surprising—that is, when everything was arranged—music, weather, holidays, every reason for happiness was there—then nothing happened at all. One wasn't happy. It was flat, just flat, that was all.

18 Her wretched self again, no doubt! She had always been a fretful, weak, unsatisfactory mother, a wobbly wife, lolling about in a kind of twilight existence with nothing very clear or very bold, or more one thing than another, like all her brothers and sisters, except perhaps Herbert—they were all the same poor water-veined creatures who did nothing. Then in the midst of this creeping, crawling life, suddenly she was on the crest of a wave. That wretched fly—where had she read the story that kept coming into her mind about the fly and the saucer?—struggled out. Yes, she

had those moments. But now that she was forty, they might come more and more seldom. By degrees she would cease to struggle any more. But that was deplorable! That was not to be endured! That made her feel ashamed of herself!

19 She would go to the London Library to-morrow. She would find some wonderful, helpful, astonishing book, quite by chance, a book by a clergyman, by an American no one had ever heard of; or she would walk down the Strand and drop, accidentally, into a hall where a miner was telling about the life in the pit, and suddenly she would become a new person. She would be absolutely transformed. She would wear a uniform; she would be called Sister Somebody; she would never give a thought to clothes again. And for ever after she would be perfectly clear about Charles Burt and Miss Milan and this room and that room; and it would be always, day after day, as if she were lying in the sun or carving the mutton. It would be it!

20 So she got up from the blue sofa, and the yellow button in the looking-glass got up too, and she waved her hand to Charles and Rose to show them she did not depend on them one scrap, and the yellow button moved out of the looking-glass, and all the spears were gathered into her breast as she walked toward Mrs. Dalloway and said "Good night."

21 "But it's too early to go," said Mrs. Dalloway, who was always so charming.

22 "I'm afraid I must," said Mabel Waring. "But," she added in her weak, wobbly voice which only sounded ridiculous when she tried to strengthen it, "I have enjoyed myself enormously."

23 "I have enjoyed myself," she said to Mr. Dalloway, whom she met on the stairs.

24 "Lies, lies, lies!" she said to herself, going downstairs, and "Right in the saucer!" she said to herself as she thanked Mrs. Barnet for helping her and wrapped herself, round and round and round, in the Chinese cloak she had worn these twenty years.

(3205 words)

Source: Woolf, V. "The New Dress." *The Forum*, May 1927, ebooks. adelaide.edu.au/w/woolf/virginia/w91h/chapter7.html.

Initial Insight

1. What is the story about? Summarize the plot in one sentence.

_____

_____

2. As it has a limited plot line, what explains the length of the story?

_____

_____

_____

Reader's Response

Consider the following questions. Discuss your answers with one or more partners.

1. Do you find Mabel to be a likeable character? Why or why not?
2. Did you find the story to be an easy or a challenging read? Why?
3. Do you consider the story and/or the main character to be superficial or profound? Why?
4. Would you have liked the story to include any other elements or perspectives? Which ones?
5. How does the story end? Do you interpret this ending to be positive, negative or neutral? Explain.

LANGUAGE FOCUS

Virginia Woolf is known for her use of **stream of consciousness**, a narrative mode in which the language mimics a character's internal thoughts and feelings. This writing style gained traction at the beginning of the twentieth century and incorporates the natural chaos of thoughts and feelings that occur in our minds at any given time. This is rendered, for instance, through the use of long and **complex sentence structures**. Improve your comprehension by being attentive to the following elements of syntax.

A. Highlight the grammatical subjects of each of the underlined verbs. In the margin, write the number of the verb next to the corresponding subject.

> Mabel had her first serious suspicion that something was wrong as she took her cloak off and Mrs. Barnet, while handing her the mirror and touching the brushes and thus drawing her attention, perhaps rather markedly, to all the appliances for tidying and improving hair, complexion, clothes, which <u>existed</u> [1] on the dressing table, <u>confirmed</u> [2] the suspicion—that it was not right, not quite right, which <u>growing</u> [3] stronger as she went upstairs and springing at her, with conviction as she greeted Clarissa Dalloway, she went straight to the far end of the room, to a shaded corner where a looking-glass hung and <u>looked</u> [4].

B. Underline the word(s) that can replace "it" in the following sentence.

> But it was all so paltry, weak-blooded, and petty-minded to care so much at her age with two children, to be still so utterly dependent on people's opinions and not have principles or convictions ...

MyBookshelf > My eLab
> Exercises > Part I: Short
Stories > Chapter 5: The
New Dress > Vocabulary
Comprehension

MyBookshelf > My eLab
> Exercises > Grammar
and Accuracy > Syntax
> Sentence Structure

Close Reading

As you read the text again, pay attention to elements that seem significant to understanding and interpreting the story. The following guided reading questions will help you.

1. In the opening paragraph, what exactly is "not right"?

a) Mabel's hair got undone on her way to the party.
b) Mabel's dress got damaged while she walked up the stairs.
c) Mabel feels uncomfortable in her dress.

2. What is the first thing Mabel does after greeting the hostess?

_____

3. When receiving the invitation, why did Mabel believe she could not be fashionable?

_____

4. What is the main difference between Mabel's dress and Rose Shaw's?

_____

5. Who is Miss Milan? How does Mabel feel toward her?

_____

6. Why does Mabel dislike Mrs. Holman?

_____

7. Which moments make Mabel the happiest?

a) Simple moments that come unexpectedly
b) Social events where she is the centre of attention
c) Moments that she has been able to plan meticulously to her liking

8. Why exactly does Mabel leave the party?

_____

_____

9. What does Mabel tell Mrs. Dalloway before she goes downstairs?

    a) "I'm afraid I'm not feeling very well."

    b) "I have enjoyed myself enormously."

    c) "Lies, lies, lies!"

10. What does Mabel put on when she leaves?

MyBookshelf > My eLab > Exercises > Part I: Short Stories > Chapter 5: The New Dress > Close Reading: Additional Questions

THE LANGUAGE OF LITERATURE

The effect of any text is to a very large extent determined by the author's diction and use of figures of speech and other literary devices. Use the following questions to focus your attention on how the author uses language in the story.

A. The "new dress" is clearly a **symbol** that has a central place in the story. Which adjectives are used to describe it? Write them in the table below—in the left-hand column if the adjective is used by the protagonist, and in the right-hand column if another character uses it.

Mabel Waring	Other characters

What do you observe? _____

_____

B. As part of the stream-of-consciousness narrative mode, words or phrases are sometimes repeated within the same sentence or passage. This **repetition** draws attention to words and thoughts Mabel feels particularly strongly about, or which are important in the story:

> And, of course, Robert Haydon answered something, <u>quite</u> polite, <u>quite</u> insincere, …
>
> <u>"Why," she asked herself</u>—replying to Charles much too pertly, letting him see that she was out of temper, or "ruffled" as he called it … —<u>"Why," she asked herself</u>, "can't I feel one thing always …?"

With a partner, find five more examples of repetition and discuss their impact. Which thoughts or ideas does the repetition draw attention to?

C. On several occasions, Mabel likens the people at the party to insects in a saucer. Identify whether the following sentences are **metaphors** (M) or **similes** (S).

1. _____ We are all like flies trying to crawl over the edge of the saucer, Mabel thought, …

2. _____ … she was a fly, but the others were dragonflies, butterflies, beautiful insects, dancing, fluttering, skimming, …

3. _____ … to make herself see Rose Shaw and all the other people there as flies, trying to hoist themselves out of something, or into something, meagre, insignificant, toiling flies.

4. _____ … she was condemned, despised, left like this in a backwater, …

Analytical Reading

After making specific observations, you are ready to analyze the subject of your close reading. The following questions will help you look for thematic patterns, establish relationships and identify specific examples of literary devices or principles.

1. The **narrative situation** of the story is quite particular. Analyze it more closely by answering the following questions:

    a. Is the narrator the protagonist? What type of pronouns are used?

    b. Does the reader have access to the protagonist's thoughts and feelings? How?

    c. Does the reader have access to the other characters' thoughts and feelings? How?

    d. Whose comments do passages in between dashes represent?
       E.g., "… and so set herself—oh, it was foolish—trying to be like them …"

    e. Whose comments do passages in parentheses represent?
       E.g., "But she could not see them like that, not other people. … (Envy and spite, the most detestable of the vices, were her chief faults.)"

2. Most of the information available to the reader is filtered through the thoughts of the protagonist, Mabel Waring. In order to get a subtler understanding of what objectively **characterizes** her and how she feels about each of these characteristics, complete the table below.

Mabel's …	Information	Thoughts or feelings
Age		
Clothing worn to the party		
Financial situation		
Family situation		
Social class		

Based on the information above, distill Mabel's thoughts or feelings into at least three themes that inform her behaviour.

3. Where in the house does the party take place? Consider the passages where Mabel arrives at the party and leaves again, and explain what this might represent.

4. In the story, Mabel looks into a mirror on two different occasions. What are these two moments, and how does Mabel feel about her reflection? Explain any similarities or differences.

5. Which moments does Mabel revisit in the story's flashbacks? (See paragraphs 2, 6 and 17.) How does she feel about these moments, and how do they compare to the present situation?

6. Explain the significance of Mabel's extended "flies in a saucer" metaphor. What does the saucer represent? What does the milk represent? Who or what does the fly refer to? Who or what do the other insects refer to?

7. Consider the last few paragraphs, starting at paragraph 19. Why does Mabel decide to leave the party, and what is her intention? Although the outcome is not mentioned explicitly, the last few lines of the story provide two important clues. Closely examine the answer Mabel gives Mrs. Dalloway and the garment she puts on. What do these suggest? Explain.

8. Considering Mabel's thoughts and feelings, as analyzed in the previous questions, what does the yellow dress symbolize in the story?

Food for Thought

The following questions encourage you to turn a critical eye to your earlier observations and analyses. They introduce elements and considerations that will lead you to formulate new questions and set tentative hypotheses. Discuss these to further your insight into the text.

1. Mabel's last name is Waring. Which word(s) does this name evoke? What information does this give in regard to the protagonist?

2. Do you think the other characters in attendance at the party are as mean and unsympathetic toward Mabel as she believes? Explain why or why not, using precise examples from the text.

3. Imagine a very similar storyline focusing not on a female but on a male protagonist. Keeping in mind this story was published in 1927, how do you think this change would affect the protagonist's situation and thoughts?

4. As illustrated by the quotation below, Virginia Woolf herself had a fascination for clothing. This relationship was not always a positive one. Do a web search to find out more about Woolf's complicated relationship with fashion. Remember to record your sources so you can use them as references, should you decide to include this information in an essay or presentation. Then, discuss any similarities and differences you observe between Woolf and Mabel, the protagonist of "The New Dress."

> "But I must remember to write about my clothes next time I have an impulse to write. My love of clothes interests me profoundly: only it is not love; & what it is I must discover." – May 1925.
>
> Woolf, V. *The Diary of Virginia Woolf*, edited by Anne Olivier Bell, Penguin, 1978.

5. "The New Dress" is also a fine example of intertextuality; its storyline intersects with Woolf's novel *Mrs. Dalloway*, as well as six other short stories grouped in the collection *Mrs. Dalloway's Party*.[1] The characters recur within the different stories, and all but one feature a female protagonist. Read one of these stories and compare the protagonist's thoughts to those of Mabel Waring. How are they similar or different?

---

1. Woolf, V. *Mrs Dalloway's Party: A Short Story Sequence*, edited by Stella McNichol, Hogarth Press, 1973.

Presenting an Analysis

Writing | Analyzing Character Psychology

In "The New Dress," Virginia Woolf uses a stream-of-consciousness narrative mode to address the tormented interiority of Mabel Waring. In line with this technique, thoughts are presented randomly rather than logically, in the order the protagonist lingers on them. As Mabel's anxiety and paranoia increase, thoughts may seem more chaotic and fragmented. In order to truly understand the protagonist and her behaviour, the reader needs to actively establish connections between the hints in the text and insight presented throughout the story.

Prepare an analytical essay in which you explain one or more of the mental states or character traits that inform Mabel's behaviour, clearly illustrating your point with examples from different passages in the text.

(Refer to Part V, Writing about Literature, on page 271 for information on essay format and structure.)

Speaking | Presenting a Contemporary Reading of a Literary Theme

Even though "The New Dress" was published in 1927, most of its themes still clearly resonate in today's society. Using salient passages from the text, establish a parallel between the party described in the story and today's use of social media. You can explore this from different angles. For instance, you might want to compare the character's behaviour at the party with the way in which people conduct themselves on social media. Another possible angle consists in comparing people's desire to conform to fashion ideals promoted by so-called "influencers" with Mabel's aspiration to fully belong at the party.

After establishing one specific topic and angle for your comparison, prepare a cohesive presentation in which you demonstrate insight not only in the short story you have analyzed but also in its relevance to a current sociocultural phenomenon.

(Refer to Appendix 2 on page 297 for more information on presentation format and structure.)

MyBookshelf > My eLab
> Exercises > Grammar and
Accuracy

CHAPTER 6

The Other Family

– Himani Bannerji

This chapter focuses on the following:

- Narrative situation
- Symbolism
- Types of conflicts
- Language Focus: reporting verbs
- The Language of Literature: imagery, deictic expressions, characterization
- Theme

Connect with the Text

A. Make a quick sketch or drawing of your family. Then, work in a small group to compare your work. Who did you include? In what manner did you draw them? Observe and discuss any similarities and differences.

B. Working with one or more partners, discuss the meaning of the concepts below. Do a web search to document yourself if need be.

- Immigrant
- Multiculturalism
- Systemic racism

C. Take stock of your opinions on the following questions. Discuss them with one or more partners.

1. What does it mean to be Canadian? Find as many defining elements as possible.
2. Think of your family tree. Were your parents born here? How about your grandparents, your great-grandparents?
3. In what terms would you define your identity? Consider elements that are important to you; e.g., beliefs, gender, origin, religion, sexual orientation, etc.
4. Have you ever been discriminated against or witnessed discrimination in any way? Expand.

Text in Context

Himani Bannerji (1942) was born in what is now Bangladesh and received her bachelor's and master's degrees from the University of Calcutta, where she also taught. She earned her PhD from the University of Toronto and is currently a professor in the Department of Sociology at York University. Her research focuses on the expression of identity in Canadian literature, and she has also written theoretical essays and books on gender, race and multiculturalism, including *The Dark Side of the Nation: Essays on Multiculturalism, Nationalism, and Gender* (2000) and

Demography and Democracy: Essays on Nationalism, Gender, and Ideology (2011). She was awarded the Rabindra Memorial Prize for her work on Bengal culture. As a creative author, she has published several short stories, children's literature and two collections of poetry.

Exploratory Reading

Read the text a first time without interruption. Keep an open mind and take a mental note of your reactions and observations. Soak up the mood and atmosphere without looking for any specific elements. When you are finished, answer the questions below the text.

The Other Family

Himani Bannerji

1 When the little girl came home it was already getting dark. The winter twilight had transformed the sheer blue sky of the day into the colour of steel, on which were etched a few stars, the bare winter trees and the dark wedges of the house tops. A few lit windows cast a faint glow on the snow outside. The mother stood at her window and watched the little hooded figure walking toward the house. The child looked like a shadow, her blue coat blended into the shadows of the evening. This child, her own, how small and insubstantial she seemed, and how alone, walking home through a pavement covered with ice and snow! It felt unreal. So different was this childhood from her own, so far away from the sun, the trees and the peopled streets of her own country! What did I do, she thought, I took her away from her own people and her own language, and now here she comes walking alone, through an alien street in a country named Canada.

2 As she contemplated the solitary, moving figure, her own solitude rushed over her like a tide. She had drifted away from a world that she had lived in and understood, and now she stood here at the same distance from her home as from the homes which she glimpsed while walking past the sparkling clean windows of the sandblasted houses. And now the door bell rang, and here was her daughter scraping the snow off her boots on the doormat.

3 Dinner time was a good time. A time of warmth, of putting hot, steaming food onto the table. A time to chat about the important things of the day, a time to show each other what they had acquired. Sometimes, however, her mother would be absent-minded, worried perhaps about work, unsettled perhaps by letters that had arrived from home, scraping her feelings into a state of rawness. This was such an evening. She had

served herself and her child, started a conversation about their two cats and fallen into a silence after a few minutes.

4 "You aren't listening to me, Mother."

5 The complaining voice got through to her, and she looked at the indignant face demanding attention from the other side of the table. She gathered herself together.

6 "So what did he do, when you gave him dried food?"

7 "Oh, I don't quite remember, I think he scratched the ground near his bowl and left."

8 The child laughed.

9 "That was smart of him! So why don't we buy tinned food for them?"

10 "Maybe we should," she said, and tried to change the topic.

11 "So what did you do in your school today?"

12 "Oh, we drew pictures like we do every day. We never study anything—not like you said you did in your school. We drew a family—our family. Want to see it?"

13 "Sure, and let's go to the living room, OK? This is messy." Scraping of chairs and the lighting of the lamps in the other room. They both made a rush for the most comfortable chair, both reached it at the same time and made a compromise.

14 "How about you sit in my lap? No? OK, sit next to me then and we will squeeze in somehow."

15 There was a remarkable resemblance between the two faces, except that the face of the child had a greater intensity, given by the wide open eyes. She was fine boned, and had black hair framing her face. Right now she was struggling with the contents of her satchel, apparently trying to feel her way to the paintings.

Presenting an Analysis

Writing | Analyzing Underlying Issues and Themes

In "The Other Family," Himani Bannerji uses an at-first-sight banal event as a symbol and vehicle to depict more profound questions of identity. Prepare an analytical essay in which you discuss the surface-level events and conflicts that concern the drawing, and explain how these are representative of the mother's deeper thoughts and feelings. For instance, you can focus on the imagery and symbols that mirror physical and psychological observations, or you can expand on the conflict between the mother and the daughter and how it relates to the mother's conflict with society. Refer to the work you did in the Analytical Reading section.

(Refer to Part V, Writing about Literature, on page 271 for information on essay format and structure.)

Speaking | Creating a Conference-Style Presentation on a Thematic Concept

"The Other Family" is a story about identity and acceptance—accepting yourself for who you are, accepting your culture, your family, your uniqueness. Prepare a TED-style talk that draws on the power of narrative by using examples from the short story to illustrate and support a positive and motivational message that relates to the thematic concept of acceptance. You may apply this to culture and ethnicity as in the story, but you can also transfer this message onto the acceptance of another type of identity—for instance, gender identity. Refer to your work in the Food for Thought section. Adapt your presentation to your intended audience. For instance, recent immigrants will relate differently to the story than people who were born and raised in the country they currently live in.

MyBookshelf > My eLab
> Exercises > Grammar and
Accuracy

(Refer to Appendix 2 on page 297 for more information on presentation format and structure.)

CHAPTER 7

We Ate the Children Last

– Yann Martel

This chapter focuses on the following:

- Dramatic structure
- Symbolism
- Setting
- Language Focus: morphology
- The Language of Literature: metaphor and diction
- Theme

Connect with the Text

Before you read the story, consider the following questions. Do a web search if necessary. Then, discuss your answers with one or more partners.

1. What is a utopia? What is a dystopia? How are the two concepts similar? How are they different?

2. Find three examples of dystopian literature. What are they about? Summarize the story and main theme(s) in a few sentences.

3. Which films or TV series have you seen recently that could be considered dystopian? What characteristics make them fit into this genre? How is the society they depict similar to ours? How is it different?

4. What sort of social function is often attributed to dystopian texts?

5. Examine the title of the short story and make a prediction. What do you think it is about?

Text in Context

Yann Martel (1963–) is of Québécois descent, but was born in Salamanca, Spain. As a result of his parents being part of the Canadian foreign service, he grew up in Spain, France, Costa Rica and Mexico. He attended university in Ontario, and, after obtaining a degree in philosophy, he continued to travel, spending time in South America, Iran, Turkey and India. Although his first language is French, Martel writes exclusively in English. His first book was published in 1993, but it is his 2001 novel *Life of Pi* that brought Martel literary fame. This allegorical survival story of an Indian teenager trying to emigrate to Canada by crossing the Pacific in a lifeboat, accompanied by several animals including a royal Bengal tiger, was awarded the prestigious Man Booker prize. It has been published in over forty countries and more than thirty languages, and was adapted for cinema by Ang Lee in 2012. Most of Martel's stories share with *Life of Pi* their imaginative writing, formal experimentation and unusual themes. Between 2007 and 2011, Martel sent Canadian prime minister Stephen Harper a book every two weeks, accompanied by an explanatory letter meant to draw attention to the importance of literature to inform our world view. "We Ate the Children Last" illustrates Martel's power of imagination as well as his social engagement.

Exploratory Reading

Read the text a first time without interruption. Keep an open mind and take a mental note of your reactions and observations. Take in the setting and soak up the atmosphere without looking for any specific elements. When you are finished, answer the questions below the text.

We Ate the Children Last   Yann Martel

1 The first human trial was on Patient D, a 56-year-old male, single and childless, who was suffering from colon cancer. He was a skeletal man with white, bloodless skin who could no longer ingest even clear fluids. He was aware that his case was terminal and he waived all rights to legal redress should the procedure go wrong. His recovery was astounding. Two days after the operation, he ate six lunch meals in one sitting. He gained 24 kilos in two weeks. Clearly, his liver, pancreas and gall bladder, the source of greatest worry, had adapted to the transplant. The only side-effect noted at the time concerned his diet. Patient D rapidly came to dislike sweet dishes, then spicy ones, then cooked food altogether. He began to eat bananas and oranges without peeling them. A nurse reported that one morning she found him eating the flowers in his room.

2 The French medical team felt vindicated. Until then, the success rate of full-organ xenografts was zero; all transplants of animal organs to humans—the hearts, livers and bone marrow of baboons, the kidneys of chimpanzees—had failed. The only real achievement in the field was the grafting of pigs' heart valves to repair human hearts and, to a lesser extent, of pigs' skin on to burn victims. The team decided to examine the species more closely. But the process of rendering pigs' organs immunologically inert proved difficult, and few organs were compatible. The potential of the pig's digestive system, despite its biological flexibility, stirred little interest in the scientific community, especially among the Americans; it was assumed that the porcine organ would be too voluminous and that its high caloric output would induce obesity in a human.

The French were certain that their simple solution to the double problem—using the digestive system of a smaller, pot-bellied species of pig—would become the stuff of scientific legend, like Newton's apple. "We have put into this man a source of energy both compact and powerful—a Ferrari engine!" boasted the leader of the medical team.

3 Patient D was monitored closely. When asked about what he ate, he was evasive. A visit to his apartment three months after the operation revealed that his kitchen was barren; he had sold everything in it, including fridge and stove, and his cupboards were empty. He finally confessed that he went out at night and picked at garbage. Nothing pleased him more, he said, than to gorge himself on putrid sausages, rotten fruit, mouldy brie, baguettes gone green, skins and carcasses, and other soured leftovers and kitchen waste. He spent a good part of the night doing this, he admitted, since he no longer felt the need for much sleep and was embarrassed about his diet. The medical team would have been concerned except that his haemoglobin count was excellent, his blood pressure was ideal, and further tests revealed what was plain to the eye: the man was bursting with good health. He was stronger and fitter than he had been in all his life.

4 Regulatory approval came swiftly. The procedure replaced chemotherapy as the standard treatment for all cancers of the digestive tract that did not respond to radiotherapy.

5 Les Bons Samaritains, a lobby group for the poor, thought to apply this wondrous medical solution to a social problem. They suggested that the operation

be made available to those receiving social assistance. The poor often had unwholesome diets, at a cost both to their health and to the state, which had to spend so much on medical care. What better, more visionary remedy than a procedure that in reducing food budgets to nothing created paragons of fitness? A cleverly orchestrated campaign of petitions and protests— "Malnutrition: zéro! Déficit: zéro!" read the banners— easily overcame the hesitations of the government.

6 The procedure caught on among the young and the bohemian, the chic and the radical, among all those who wanted a change in their lives. The opprobrium attached to eating garbage vanished completely. In short order, the restaurant became a retrograde institution, and the eating of prepared food a sign of attachment to deplorable worldly values. A revolution of the gut was sweeping through society. "Liberté! Liberté!" was the cry of the operated. The meaning of wealth was changing. It was all so heady. The telltale mark of the procedure was a scar at the base of the throat; it was a badge we wore with honour.

7 Little was made at the time of a report by the Société protectrice des animaux on the surprising drop in the number of stray cats and dogs. Garbage became a sought-after commodity. Unscrupulous racketeers began selling it. Dumps became dangerous places. Garbage collectors were assaulted. The less fortunate resorted to eating grass.

8 Then old people began vanishing without a trace. Mothers who had turned away momentarily were finding their baby carriages empty. The government reacted swiftly. In a matter of three days, the army descended upon every one of the operated, without discrimination between the law-abiding and the criminal. The newspaper *Le Cochon Libre* tried to put out a protest, but the police raided their offices and only a handful of copies escaped destruction. There were terrible scenes during the round-up: neighbours denouncing neighbours, children being separated from their families, men, women and children being stripped in public to look for telling scars, summary executions of people who tried to escape. Internment camps were set up, nearly always in small, remote towns: Les Milles, Gurs, Le Vernet d'Ariège, Beaune-la-Rolande, Pithiviers, Recebedou.

9 No provisions were made for food in any of the camps. The story was the same in all of them: first the detainees ate their clothes and went naked. Then the weaker men and women disappeared. Then the rest of the women. Then more of the men. Then we ate those we loved most. The last known prisoner was an exceptional brute by the name of Jean Proti. After 41 days without a morsel of food except his own toes and ears, and after 30 hours of incessant screaming, he died.

10 I escaped. I still have a good appetite, but there is a moral rot in this country that even I can't digest. Everyone knew what happened, and how and where. To this day everyone knows. But no one talks about it and no one is guilty. I must live with that

---

(1073 words)

Source: Martel, Y. "We Ate the Children Last." *The Guardian*, 17 July 2004, theguardian.com/books/2004/jul/17/originalwriting.fiction4.

Initial Insight

1. What is the story about? Write down anything that intuitively comes to you.

_____

_____

2. When and where is the story set?

_____

_____

_____

3. Would you say the tone of the story is positive, neutral or negative? Why?

_____

_____

Reader's Response

Consider the following questions. Discuss your answers with one or more partners.

1. Did you consider the story to be believable or possible? Why or why not?

2. Which aspects of the setting felt familiar to you, and which didn't?

3. Did the story make you reflect on its topics? How?

4. How do you imagine the narrator, physically and personality-wise?

5. What is the narrator's attitude toward the story that is told? What is yours?

LANGUAGE FOCUS

Morphology, the linguistic study interested in word structures, allows us to observe how base parts, called word roots, can often be combined with affixes—usually short elements with an abstract meaning—to form a new word with a related meaning. Affixes placed before the root are called prefixes; those that follow the root are suffixes.

Examples:

Regulate – **de**regulate – regulat**ory**   approve – **dis**approve – approv**al**

Being attentive to word roots, prefixes and suffixes may allow you to understand words you have not encountered before.

A. Consider the related word pairs below. Relate the meaning of the second word to the definition of the word above. Then, infer the abstract meaning of the prefix or suffix indicated in bold and write it down. Work with a partner to find two other words that contain the same affix.

Example:

Skeleton [structure consisting of all the bones in a human or animal body]

Skelet**al**: _having the form or character of_

1. Graft [part of a body or plant attached elsewhere]

   Xenograft: _____

2. Pork [the meat from pigs]

   Porc**ine**: _____

3. Evade [avoid talking about something]

   Evas**ive**: _____

4. therapy [treatment of an illness or injury]

   radiotherapy: _____

5. Vision [idea of what something could or should be like]

   Vision**ary**: _____

B. In the text, find five more words that contain a prefix or suffix. Follow the approach above to identify the affix and determine its meaning. Discuss your examples with a partner.

Look up any words you are unsure of.

MyBookshelf > My eLab > Exercises > Part I: Short Stories > Chapter 7: We Ate the Children Last > Vocabulary Comprehension

Close Reading

As you read the text again, pay attention to elements that seem significant to understanding and interpreting the story. The following guided reading questions will help you.

1. Initially, what is the procedure described in the story a treatment for?

_____

2. What exactly explains the change in patient D's dietary preferences?

_____

_____

3. After visiting patient D's apartment, why is the medical team not concerned?

_____

4. What social problem was the procedure supposed to resolve?

_____

5. What becomes highly prized after the procedure's invention?

_____

6. What specific event made the government decide to intervene?

_____

7. What was done with those who had undergone the medical procedure?

_____

8. At the end of the story, what is revealed about the narrator?

   a) The narrator underwent the procedure.
   b) The narrator is patient D.
   c) The narrator is a woman.
   d) The narrator escaped being attacked by the operated.

MyBookshelf > My eLab > Exercises > Part I: Short Stories > Chapter 7: We Ate the Children Last > Close Reading: Additional Questions

THE LANGUAGE OF LITERATURE

The effect of any text is to a very large extent determined by the author's diction and use of figures of speech and other literary devices. Use the following questions to focus your attention on how the author uses language in the story.

A. Consider what you know about characters such as the narrator, patient D and Jean Proti. What does this allow you to conclude about the story's level of **characterization**?

B. In paragraph 2, find an example of a **metaphor**. What does this metaphor suggest about the scientists' attitude?

C. What is the importance of **diction** or, more specifically, the use of French words and expressions in the story?

D. Which two strategies does the author use to allow a reader who does not speak French to still understand the story? Consider the following two examples.

   1. "'Malnutrition: zéro! Déficit: zéro!' read the banners."

   2. "Les Bons Samaritains, a lobby group for the poor ..."

Analytical Reading

After making specific observations, you are ready to analyze the subject of your close reading. The following questions will help you look for thematic patterns, establish relationships and identify specific examples of literary devices or principles.

1. How do the last three sentences of the first paragraph **foreshadow** the events to come?

2. What type of **narrator** and **perspective** is used to tell the story? What does the reader know about the narrator? How is he or she involved in the story?

3. Because of its concision and chronological dramatic **structure**, the story has a clear plot.

First, on a separate sheet of paper, summarize the main event(s) of each paragraph into one brief sentence. Then, complete the plot diagram below with the paragraph numbers that correspond to each of the plot moments indicated.

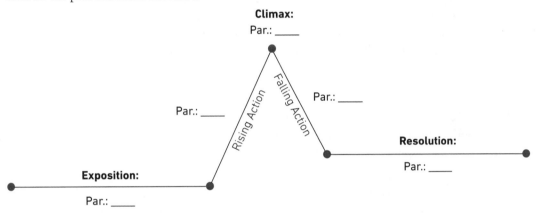

4. What exactly is the "revolution of the gut" described by the narrator, and what does it **symbolize**?

5. What is the importance of **setting** the story in France?

6. The story portrays different social actors: the scientific community, the government, lobby groups (for the poor and for animal rights) and the people. For each social actor, describe what they do (or don't do) and their attitude. How does this affect the sequence of events in the story? Whom does the author criticize?

Food for Thought

The following questions encourage you to turn a critical eye to your earlier observations and analyses. They introduce elements and considerations that will lead you to formulate new questions and set tentative hypotheses. Discuss these to further your insight into the text.

1. Why is the short story titled "We Ate the Children Last"? How does it relate to the events described in the story? What is the title's connotation? Consider every word of the title separately and discuss its implications.

2. In the last paragraph, who does the narrator accuse of "moral rot"? Explain how this "moral rot" manifests itself in the story.

3. What is the significance of the "internment camps" mentioned in the story? Think of the episodes in history as well as current events that have involved such camps. What might the author be trying to say about them?

4. In light of the actions perpetrated by the narrator, do you feel he or she is in a position to judge others on moral grounds? Why or why not?

5. Director Andrew Cividino turned "We Ate the Children Last" into a short film that won awards at the Toronto International Film Festival (TIFF) and Vancouver International Film Festival. After watching it, discuss the differences between the story and its film adaptation. Did the film version alter your interpretation of the story? If yes, how? Did you feel the dystopian atmosphere to be stronger in the story or in the film? Why?

Presenting an Analysis

Writing | Reading between the Lines

In "We Ate the Children Last," the narrator reports on events in a detached, objective manner. However, the last paragraph clearly signals the author's desire to criticize certain societal aspects, regrouped under what the narrator calls "moral rot." Identify one or more of the thematic concepts that constitute an element of criticism. Then, turn them into thematic statements by illustrating how they are taken up in the story. Finally, establish a parallel with contemporary society to highlight exactly how the author criticizes it.

Example:

"We Ate the Children Last" can be read as a warning against unnecessary medical interventions, such as gastric banding and other cosmetic surgeries, which may have far-reaching consequences that are impossible or difficult to predict.

In each of the body paragraphs, provide evidence and examples from the text to point out the treatment of your chosen thematic statements. You may wish to use an analytical paragraph structure or an argumentative paragraph structure, depending on your desire to focus more on the story or on the real-life social issues. Refer to the work you did in the Analytical Reading and Food for Thought sections. Illustrate and support your analysis with clear examples from the text.

(Refer to Part V, Writing about Literature, on page 271 for more information on essay format and structure.)

Speaking | Comparing Dystopian Societies

Prepare a presentation that compares the treatment of a social situation represented as being problematic in "We Ate the Children Last" and another dystopian short story, novel, television series or film. Use examples from each text to illustrate your observations. The following questions may guide you.

- Which actions or events are depicted as being problematic, and how are they treated as a theme in the work?
- What is the narrator's role and involvement in this situation, and how does this affect the story?
- Where is the story set, and how is that important?
- How does the story end? Does this ending provide closure?

Structure your presentation in such a way as to point out any similarities and differences between the two examples you discuss. As in a comparative essay, you can identify different topics, then illustrate each point with examples from your two texts, or you can focus about half of your presentation on each example and conclude by pointing out similarities and differences. As you prepare an outline, take the time to analyze which of these two structures will flow best.

(Refer to Appendix 2 on page 297 for more information on presentation format and structure.)

MyBookshelf > My eLab > Exercises > Grammar and Accuracy

CHAPTER 8

Wide and Deep

– Socrates Adams

This chapter focuses on the following:

- Absurdity
- Symbolism
- Narrative voice
- Language Focus: word associations generating deeper contextual meaning
- The Language of Literature: prosody, narration and setting
- Theme

Connect with the Text

A. Take stock of your opinions on the following questions. Discuss them with one or more partners.

1. Examine the title of the short story and make a prediction. What do you think it is about? What could be qualified as being "wide" and "deep"?

2. What are some of your happiest childhood memories? What can you observe about the level of detail in which you remember them?

3. If you had to select three moments that you consider the most important or meaningful in your life so far, what would they be, and why are they meaningful?

B. Before you read the story, do a web search to find the answers to the questions below. Remember to record your sources so you can use them as references, should you decide to include this information in an essay or presentation.

1. What is absurdity in literature? What is its purpose? How can it be used?

2. How are memories formed? Where in the brain are they stored? Are there different types of memory and memories? Research a visual representation of the brain, and work with one or more partners to discuss the answers you found and complete one another's understanding of them.

Text in Context

Socrates Adams (1984–) was born in Bath, England. He spent time in Greece as a child, with his maternal grandparents. He attended university at King's College in London, but never graduated. After travelling the north of England in a canal barge for half a year, he decided to make Manchester his home, writing his first two novels while working at an academic bookstore. His first novel, *Everything's Fine*, was published in 2011. It was nominated for the Guardian's First Book Award. Adams has also worked in film. He co-wrote and starred in *Wizard's Way*, a feature film that won the London Comedy Festival Discovery Award. He now lives in Bristol with his wife and young son and writes full time. In regard to his writing, Adams says, "I love to be alive and able to express myself in all that I do […] I love to think of all the things I love and love to write them down." Adams's stories carry a lot of pathos, often blending humour and elements of the absurd in order to explore deep human emotions and troubling situations.

Exploratory Reading

Read the text a first time without interruption. Keep an open mind and take a mental note of your reactions and observations. Take in the descriptions and soak up the mood and atmosphere without looking for any specific elements. When you are finished, answer the questions below the text.

Wide and Deep

Socrates Adams

1 I am five and a half years old. I am holding my wife's hand as she gives birth to our son. My wife is six years old. I am her toy boy. The nurse, who is eight years old, is saying things to my wife like, "Keep pushing. You are nearly there." I keep hold of my wife's hand even though she is gripping me as hard as she can. My fingers are white as my son is born. The nurse places the tiny boy into my wife's arms and she starts to breastfeed him, automatically. I am swelling with pride.

2 I feel a triangle of love. The triangle is connecting my wife, the baby, me. The triangle seems like a beam of green light, made of love.

3 My wife is crying as she breastfeeds the baby. The family I have is the greatest family in the history of families. I imagine my son's life, stretching out in front of me, and I am immeasurably happy.

* * *

4 My son is two weeks old and it is time for him to go to school. My son's first words were "Feed me." He said the words and then my wife/his mother started to immediately feed him. Whenever she feeds him she is so overcome with emotion that she cries. She doesn't stop crying maybe for one or two hours after she feeds him. Then she feeds him again.

5 I drive to the school and I talk to my son as we drive along. I tell him about school being an important place. My son quietly sits and thinks about the big issues of life. When we get to the school the head teacher is waiting for my son and she takes him and moves him into the school. I worry about my son suffering from separation anxiety.

6 When I get home my wife is standing in the corner of the kitchen. She is facing the corner and crying. I go upstairs and work because I have taken my work home with me.

* * *

7 My wife and I are at my son's first birthday party. His friends are here. He is about to cut his cake and pop open the champagne and drink it with them and then go out on the town. I look at my wife who is looking at the cake. We are both proud of my son and each other. I think about the way I have changed since he was born. I think about the way my wife has changed. My wife is a tiny and thin creature.

8 My wife collapses onto the floor, silently. My son and his friends have a great time drinking the champagne and cutting the cake. I lie down on the floor next to my wife and whisper to her quietly as the boys trample on top of us. I look at her face and it is drawn and pale. I touch her face with my hand and keep whispering to her.

* * *

9 It is three months since the party. We are at the graveyard and we are burying my wife. I have found it difficult since she died. I rely on my son now. When I look at him I can often imagine her older face. I am six and three-quarters years old. My son is one and one-quarter years old. My wife would be seven and one-quarter years old. My son's girlfriend comes up to me after the funeral and says to me that my wife had a good innings. My son's girlfriend is one and two-thirds years old.

10 I can rely on my son. He and his girlfriend leave me at the church. I sit on the bench in the graveyard and I squeeze my hand and make it white and remember about my wife giving birth to my son.

* * *

11 I live in an old people's home. I am totally mad because of my dementia. I don't understand human emotions/responsibilities/family structures any more. I sit in a rocking chair on the lawn. I watch a ten-year-old shuffle along the lawn and fall down dead. I start singing the song that I sing every day:

> *dig me my grave both wide and deep*
> *put marble slabs at my head and feet*
> *upon my breast put a turtle white dove*
> *to show the whole world that I died of love*

(725 words)

Source: Adams, S. "Wide and Deep." *The Best British Short Stories 2012*, edited by N. Royle, Salt Publishing, 2012.

Initial Insight

1. What is the story about? Write down anything that intuitively comes to you.

_____

_____

2. Which elements of the story struck you as odd?

_____

_____

_____

3. How would you describe the mood of the story? Is it comical, dramatic, sad, …? Why?

_____

_____

_____

_____

Reader's Response

Consider the following questions. Discuss your answers with one or more partners.

1. Did you find any of the story's events difficult to understand or make sense of? Why?
2. Which aspects of the story stood out to you? Why?
3. How do you imagine the narrator, physically and mentally?
4. Beyond the events reported, what do you think the story is truly about?
5. What do you imagine the song at the end of the story to sound like?

LANGUAGE FOCUS

The experience and interpretation of a phrase, sentence or passage in a text is not merely the sum of the individual meanings of the words that make it up. These words also interact with one another to generate associations and connotations that allow the reader to infer deeper meanings. Consider the following sentences. Explain the relationship between the underlined words, and discuss the images and deeper meaning they evoke.

1. ... she starts to <u>breastfeed</u> him, automatically. I am <u>swelling</u> with pride.

2. I imagine my son's life, <u>stretching out</u> in front of me, and I am <u>immeasurably</u> happy.

3. My wife collapses onto the floor, <u>silently</u>. I [...] <u>whisper</u> to her <u>quietly</u> as the boys trample on top of us.

4. I watch a ten-year-old <u>shuffle</u> along the lawn and <u>fall down</u> dead.

Look up any words you are unsure of.

MyBookshelf > My eLab > Exercises > Part I: Short Stories > Chapter 8: Wide and Deep > Vocabulary Comprehension

Close Reading

As you read the text again, pay attention to elements that seem significant to understanding and interpreting the story. The following guided reading questions will help you.

1. Who does the love triangle described by the narrator involve?

_____

2. What is the first thing the narrator remembers his wife doing after giving birth?

_____

3. What is the narrator worried about when he takes his son to school for the first time?

_____

4. What does the narrator do when he finds his wife crying at their son's first day of school?

a) He does nothing.

b) He comforts her the best he can.

c) He goes upstairs to work.

d) He starts crying, too.

5. What does the narrator reflect on at his son's birthday party?

_____

_____

6. What unexpected event happens at the birthday party?

_____

_____

7. How does the narrator's son remind him of his wife?

a) They both had good innings.

b) The narrator sees his wife's face in his son's.

c) The son has his mother's kindness.

d) The narrator's son accompanies him to church, as his wife did.

8. What does the narrator say explains his erratic behaviour?

_____

_____

MyBookshelf > My eLab > Exercises > Part I: Short Stories > Chapter 8: Wide and Deep > Close Reading: Additional Questions

THE LANGUAGE OF LITERATURE

The effect of any text is to a very large extent determined by the author's diction and use of figures of speech and other literary devices. Use the following questions to focus your attention on how the author uses language in the story.

A. An **unreliable narrator** displays characteristics that undermine their credibility and tells a story that cannot be taken at face value. What are the textual characteristics that make this story's narrator unreliable? Give an example of how they manifest themselves.

B. Is the story an example of **subsequent**, **prior** or **simultaneous narration**? In what tense is the narrative written? What is unusual about this, and what does it suggest about the events described?

C. Each part of the story, indicated by asterisks, has a different **setting**. What elements are repeatedly used to describe the setting, and where can they be found?

D. **Prosody** is an aspect of diction that concerns the sound patterns resulting from the author's choice of words, and the ways in which they are combined. While it is an essential feature of poetry, prosody can also be observed in prose. The repetition of consonant sounds in successive words, as in "end up in the deep darkness" is called **consonance**; the repetition of vowel sounds is called **assonance**, as in "Mai likes white lilacs."

Decide whether the following phrases from the text contain examples of assonance or consonance. Underline the vowels or consonants that are repeated to create this prosodic effect.

1. I am her toy boy. _____

2. ... she breastfeeds the baby. _____

3. The triangle seems like a beam of green light. _____

4. I worry about my son suffering from separation anxiety. _____

5. ... cut his cake and pop open the champagne _____

Analytical Reading

After making specific observations, you are ready to analyze the subject of your close reading. The following questions will help you look for thematic patterns, establish relationships and identify specific examples of literary devices or principles.

1. The story includes five distinct **scenes**. Identify each scene, then discuss which elements that make up its action seem plausible, and which ones seem affected by the narrator's unreliable state of mind.

2. Referring to the scenes identified in question 1, which common thread(s) do you observe in scenes 1–4? Consider what happens and who is involved. What does this information suggest about the narrator and what he considers important in life?

3. Explain how breastfeeding acts as a **symbol** for the relationship between the mother and her son. Consider the mother's actions as well as her feelings.

4. Which of the son's actions makes the narrator say he can rely on him? To the reader, what might this observation actually suggest?

5. Explain how *fingers squeezed until they are white* is used as a **symbol** that bridges life and death.

6. The adjectives "wide" and "deep" can be found in the song lyrics at the end of the story describing the measurements of a grave. Considering the story's narrator, what can these adjectives refer to in a **figurative sense**?

Food for Thought

The following questions encourage you to turn a critical eye to your earlier observations and analyses. They introduce elements and considerations that will lead you to formulate new questions and set tentative hypotheses. Discuss these to further your insight into the text.

1. The son and wife are clearly central figures in the narrator's life. Between the two of them, which person seems more important to the narrator? Explain your choice.

2. Time references, more specifically references to age, are omnipresent in the story. Is there a logic to them? What do you think they represent, and why does the narrator mention them so often?

3. The lyrics that appear at the end of the story are based on a folk song known as "The Railroad Boy" or "The Butcher Boy." Do a web search for the lyrics or a rendition of this song. Discuss the story and mood of the song, and how it fits in with the short story.

4. How would you describe the mood of the story and the narrator's dealing with his dementia?

    a. Which elements in the text support this reading?

    b. How much of the mood you described is based on your own emotional response to the story? Explain.

    c. Do a web search on the behavioural and psychological symptoms of dementia. How does this information inform your interpretation of the narrator's attitude and the story's mood?

Presenting an Analysis

Writing | Reading into the Narrator's Mind

"Wide and Deep" can be read as a meditation on life as the narrator starts by recounting his son's birth and ends with his wife's passing and looking toward his own death. Examining relevant passages from the story, analyze the narrator's vision of what makes life important and why he sings a song about dying every day. You may wish to focus on the narrator himself, or on the relationship he has with the other characters.

Example:

By looking back on the key moments of his life, the narrator in "Wide and Deep" draws attention to the fact that life is made of memories shared with others, and that losing those memories is also losing a part of life.

In each of the body paragraphs, use an analytical structure to provide evidence and examples from the text to point out the narrator's implicit musings. Refer to the work you did in the Analytical Reading and Food for Thought sections. Since you are presenting an analysis, make sure not to include any personal opinions that you cannot back up or explain with evidence from the text itself.

(Refer to Part V, Writing about Literature, on page 271 for more information on essay format and structure.)

MyBookshelf > My eLab
> Exercises > Grammar and
Accuracy

Speaking | Explaining an Unreliable Narrative and Its Effect on the Reader

Because of his dementia, the narrator in "Wide and Deep" is unreliable. Based on the research you did in Connect with the Text and any additional sources you deem necessary, prepare a presentation that provides explanations as to why the narrator describes the story's events in the way he does. Comment on the authenticity of this behaviour, and present an explication of a passage to explain how these narrative features affected you as a reader.

Structure your presentation from general to more specific.

- Start by describing the narrator, and point out passages that illustrate your description.
- Then, use information from your research to explain why the narrator may experience and recount his memories in this way.
- End your presentation with a more detailed explication of one passage to point out the impact it had on you as a reader and what themes it made you reflect on.

Use visual support to help the audience follow along as you present passages and research. Include references for all of the content that is not your own. This includes quotations from the story, information from your research as well as any images or other visuals you include in your slides. Apply MLA guidelines to present these references on your slides.

A sample MLA-style slideshow presentation is available in My eLab Documents.

Refer to Appendix 2 on page 297 for more information on presentation format and structure.

MyBookshelf > My eLab
> Documents > Chapter 22:
Writing a Literary Essay
> MLA Referencing Guidelines

MyBookshelf > My eLab
> Documents > Appendix 2:
Presentation Checklist >
Presenting an Analysis –
MLA-Style Slideshow
Presentation

CHAPTER 9

She Is Water

– Darlene Naponse

This chapter focuses on the following:

- Setting
- Imagery and symbolism
- Narrative voice
- Language Focus: informal and colloquial speech
- The Language of Literature: narrative situation, figures of speech
- Theme

Connect with the Text

A. Take stock of your opinions on the following questions. Discuss them with one or more partners.

1. What associations does the concept of "water" evoke in you? Brainstorm as many answers as possible, considering water in all of its different forms.
2. What are some of the stereotypes and challenges facing First Nations people, and why should they matter to Canadians?
3. Discuss the meaning, usage and connotations of the terms "Indian," "Native," "Aboriginal," "Indigenous" and "First Nations."

B. Before you read the story, do a web search to find the answers to the questions below. Remember to record your sources so you can use them as references.

1. Who are the Anishinaabe and the Ojibwe peoples? Where do they live? Summarize the most important facts you find about their history and culture.
2. Darlene Naponse lives on the Atikameksheng Anishnawbek reserve. Where is it located? Visit the website to get an idea of the story's setting.

3. In Indigenous cultures, what do the following totem animals symbolize?

- Fish   - Ants   - Eagle   - Crow   - Salamander

Text in Context

Darlene Naponse (1973–) is an Anishinaabe kwe from Atikameksheng Anishnawbek, Ontario. She was born and raised in her community, where she still lives and works today. Naponse is a firm believer in education for all women, especially Indigenous women. She holds a certificate, a bachelor's degree and a master's degree in creative writing and film from three different Canadian and American universities. She has also lectured on Indigenous literature at Laurentian University, focusing on issues concerning Indigenous women in Canada. Naponse describes herself as an independent artist. She keeps complete creative control over all of her work in order to protect the stories, imagery, history and traditions of First Nations people. She is not only a writer but also a film director and video artist. In addition to her artistic work, Naponse has acted as a band councillor in her community, and as a governmental consultant in the field of First Nations governance and social structures. All of Naponse's undertakings are deeply rooted in her community, First Nations realities of the twenty-first century and her spiritual relationship with Mother Earth. "She Is Water" perfectly illustrates the power of Naponse's poetic storytelling as it evokes life, love and hate on a reserve.

Exploratory Reading

Read the text a first time without interruption. Keep an open mind and take a mental note of your reactions and observations. Take in the events and soak up the mood and atmosphere without looking for any specific elements. When you are finished, answer the questions below the text.

She Is Water   **Darlene Naponse**

She lived by The River. She loved
by The River, felt pain
by The River,
bathed in The River, dreamed
in The River,
fished
in The River,
told stories
to The River, found her first moment of true joy
by The River, discovered how to listen by The River.
In The River, she sleeps.

1 The River ran along the border of the reserve and the township. It was once a popular area to paddle down. Freshwater trout swam the river. In 1957, the plywood plant on the north shore of Lake Dark started production, dumping liquid garbage, from employee's shit and piss to formaldehyde, into the lake. Chemicals humans can't even pronounce were pushed, pumped, and forgotten. Thirty-five years later, an implausible number of puked-out litres of toxic waste in Lake Dark, the company closed its doors, yet it never cleaned up a drop of their hate. Lake Dark's natural outflow is The River.

*   *   *

2 Edna Redfoot once found a two-headed trout, or so she says at every band meeting, when she was fishing in the Lake. Robert Hurf once found a pickerel infested with vile, open sores. I believe that story 'cause I saw

it in his garage. The pickerel had few scales left. As I stared at the sores, I felt them mutating, like alien heads rising from the circular, oozing tombs.

3 Every now and then, people sank cars, skidoos, bikes, washing machines, old love letters, boats, ashes, cans of Spam, cups, canoes, pants, panties, dresses, shoes, cowboy boots, fishing rods, beer bottles, cigarette butts, pop cans, and bodies in Lake Dark, the deepest lake in the region.

4 Kids swam at the beach in a roped-off area. The water was so turbulent and deep; I imagine it never has time to warm up. The last August swim is the most important. It is the one day you float on your back and watch the horizon disappear. You spend the day soaking in the sun and the water. You and your friends stay late at the beach. Once the sun falls behind the cedars, you know it is fall. The cool breeze makes the water unbearable to swim after that day.

*   *   *

5 In the winter of 1989, two boys from town were crossing frozen Lake Dark. It was a warm winter, and many of the lakes in the area hadn't frozen over. The boys were heading home from a party and instead of driving around the lake, they decided to drive across. Their bodies and truck were never found. All that remained was their tracks and one eyewitness who saw them crossing about six in the morning. I imagined they found a better place to live, away from this small town.

6 My grandmother told me eight canoers died on Lake Dark in 1954. They went in the water too early. Spring is a bitch sometimes. The winds shifted them into the water.

7 Bodies began to be discovered, south of Lake Dark, in The River. Suzy Highground was found face up, naked, stuck in Tom Hunt's dock. She was twelve and from the reserve. The police never investigated; they said it was a swimming accident. Suzy won every swim contest on the reserve. She was walking home from school, twenty-one kilometres away from The River when she disappeared.

8 Annie TwoToes never had time to tell her story. She was found upriver by the Mayor's farm. No one ever heard what happened to her. Her parents closed their eyes and were never seen again.

* * *

9 When I was in school, I learned that rivers, creeks, and streams are tributaries. The word sounds like it should be known as greatness. These tributaries, the branches of Lake Dark, all had greatness.

10 The creek that ran north had the best trout run around. Me and my dad once pulled a fifteen-pound trout from that creek; my family ate for four days.

11 West of Lake Dark, was a small stream that had this distant way of being. It was hard to walk along and full of rocks and deadfall. My brother James once found a bear cub stuck in the rocks. He watched him for fifteen minutes and waited for the cub's mother to come back. As he was going to move the rocks, the mother bear returned. She walked around the cub, then started to dig. My brother hid behind a boulder. The mother bear growled, which my dad later told us was a moan of fear as it ripped apart the rocks. The mother bear and her cub ran away. James ran home to tell us his tale.

12 The western stream was the one area most townies never went. In the spring me and my cousins pick fiddleheads along the shoreline. My aunt June Feather would buy them for five cents a fiddlehead. She'd make a stew from them or fry them up. I never tried them. Aunt June said fiddleheads are the most wonderful thing in the world. I always thought Saturdays with my mom and brothers were the most wonderful thing in the world.

13 In the south is a small river and rapids. We liked to camp there. The water runs constantly, and my mom says "It's the best place to catch Whitefish." She told me the water is the cleanest in the area, because the water is always moving. I was confused till one hot day I watched the water in Lake Dark, and it never moved. I'm sure it did, but as the sweat dropped off my forehead into the water, the ripple was the only movement I saw.

14 We always gathered, fished, hunted, and lived near water when I was young. In the summer, we were never at our house. We often set camp out on The River for weeks. We ate fish and swam the whole summer. All my cousins would either stay with us, or their parents would set up camp. At night we played kick the can and hid in the hardwood bush. When the person who was IT finished counting to twenty by the can, they would go around looking for everyone and when they saw you they would run back to the can and say "I see Julia." Then Julia would be out. If you were not good at finding people or not a fast runner, your cousin would come running out of the bush and kick the can then you are IT again. The older cousins always cheated and teamed up against us young ones. Then we teamed up and 'cause we were faster, we managed to be the ones hiding, not looking for everyone.

15 I asked my grandfather about The River. He said his mother was born across The River downstream. We lived where the water changed direction. In school, it is referred to the area that separates the Atlantic and Arctic watersheds. They say the water starts to run north from this point.

16 He told me about the natural borders, the divides, and the height of land. He told me stories about the settlers divvying up land using the natural divides. I wondered how they could do that if the land wasn't theirs to give away?

* * *

17 In the east, I was left to sleep. The water was deep. No one liked being around that part of The River. It always seems to take more away than you imagined.

* * *

18 My grandfather lived on The River. He had a small farm along The River that ran two kilometres along the bend. The bend is where all the fun starts. After the bend, the rapids begin. It's not like the Colorado River, but it was our rapids. When you paddled down it, you often lost a paddle or put a good dent or hole in your canoe.

19 When I was eleven, I tried taking an inflatable tube down The River. My cousins, my brother Davis, and I were pumped. Cousin Jack hit the jagged rocks in the front part of the rapids and never made it down; my other cousin Gent watched on the shoreline;

Davis rode the tube like a knee board. He was fearless. Then right after the last calm, he dove into the water and knocked himself out on a boulder. I was following him, so I swam to get him. He was a big boy, always was. When he was born, he looked like a four-month baby boy. By age two, he stood taller than any of his cousins.

20 I jumped in and swam to him. He floated to the surface face down. Jack ran to get my grandfather. I tried flipping him over. Gent jumped in and helped me drag him to the shore. We turned him over. Davis didn't breathe. Gent ran home. I kept screaming at Davis, hitting his chest, moving him sideways. I breathed into his mouth. I looked inside his mouth and asked the fish, the ants, the eagle, the crow to help him breathe but they all disappeared.

21 My grandfather sold his farm after Davis died. He moved us closer to the village, on the flattest, driest land, away from The River. My mother didn't say a word to me for seven days.

22 Weeks and months after Davis died I wondered why the fish, the ants, the eagle, the crow all went away? They were always with me, aside from that evil salamander, who always seemed to escape my sight, the fish, the ants, the eagle, the crow watched over me.

*   *   *

23 The truck came from behind me. I was trying to remember the words to "We got the beat" when he grabbed me. I was walking into town to meet up with my study group. I never saw him, nor did I know him. His large rough hands smelled of old ashtrays and gasoline.

24 When he put his hands over my mouth, I gagged and started to get sick. He pulled my arms and tied them behind my back. I was screaming. No one was around to hear. He tied a cloth over my eyes and pushed me into his truck. I threw up all over the truck and he punched me in the face.

25 By the time I started to breathe we were driving away. My stomach convulsed as he was shouting at me. Death metal rang and phased out his voice.

26 "Jumpin' get down we got the beat. Round and round and round, We got the beat." I repeated over and over.

*   *   *

27 The River ran through the reserve, with its many creeks and streams running into it. We always seemed to be running south, following the creek. The reserve was a small area, a few houses, a band office, and a clinic. The clinic was in a rundown portable. We were all shipped out every morning on the yellow bus into town to go to school. School was fun for me. I liked all the classes. I never really liked the teachers; they were mean, but I liked the books. Science class was always interesting.

28 I imagined myself being an astronaut. I wanted to search the sky for intelligent life. I wanted to explore, like Captain Janeway, Captain of the Starfleet starship USS *Voyager*. I wanted to float in space, and walk on another planet. My mother bought me books on space.

29 We lived with my grandpa for a few years and my mother was making decent money at the truck stop. All the truckers liked it when she talked back. My mother had the worst potty mouth. She swore just like them. The truck stop was the perfect place to make tips. The men loved her comic rudeness and rewarded her for her antics.

30 When she came home she was exhausted. She would come in and kiss me goodnight. My mother wasn't that great with money so she gave me her tips and told me to hide them till Christmas or for school clothes for me and my brother.

31 I was thirteen, hiding money in a space book. The one space book I never really liked because its pictures were childish. I cut out an area and stashed the loonies, toonies, and five dollar bills in the book. It filled quickly, so I cut up the encyclopedias we had. I was the only one who read in the house. My brother or my grandpa would never look in the books.

32 My grandpa had satellite. There were so many channels it was ridiculous. You could watch old films, new films, channels just for sports, channels just for music, channels in Spanish and lots of commercials.

33 Each week we watched *Star Trek: Voyager*. My grandfather sat in his La-Z-Boy and I lay on the floor. I could smell the maple wood burning and the heat was constant. I didn't need a blanket or a pillow. During the commercial, I heard the cast-iron lever creak open; Grandpa was putting more wood in the fireplace. I loved watching the red-hot embers roll around. It was hypnotizing. Grandpa was slow putting the wood in and I always got extra seconds to see the embers turn to flame.

34 We watched as Captain Janeway and her crew travelled through space, moving past every obstacle challenging them. Would they make it home? They were diplomatic, saved lives, and kept to the Starfleet's ethical code of conduct. I wanted to work on a spaceship like the Captain. She kicked ass. She also sounded like she smoked a hundred Export A's a day. Captain Janeway

had a thing with Chakotay, the hunky Native American who was her First Officer. It was the first time I saw a native character that didn't have a loincloth and speak like a stoic illiterate on TV. I loved satellite TV.

35 Everything was aligning for me. I felt like I was a planet in the solar system.

* * *

36 My first kiss was under a full moon. I stood still waiting for something to happen in my body, a sign he was the one. He drove a dirt bike and sang with the Eagle Claw drum group. His hair was longer than mine. His lips were small and so soft, I wanted to plump them like a goose. We dated for a bit and had more fun running around in the bush than making out. We broke up and I decided to search only for boys with luscious lips and strong hands. It was a tall order, but I knew there was someone out there.

37 Davis always teased me about boys and said I would marry an ugly man with no teeth and have ten babies. I knew I was going to marry the hottest Indian at the Pow Wow and may not have any babies.

* * *

38 Our Mother worked three jobs. She worked at the truck stop, was a part-time librarian, and sometimes she sold Tupperware. After Davis died, I went to work with her and didn't go to school for six months. She told the teachers she was homeschooling me. The school fought with my mother and said she didn't have the skills to homeschool me. She said to test me when I returned and then if I was not up to their standards, I would lose my year.

39 The months after Davis died were strange. I liked being with my mom but when we had moments of fun, we stopped quickly, and started to do a chore. We both kinda looked at each other, then turned around, and went our separate ways. I often found her outside in the yard looking west.

40 My older brother James was in his last year of high school and worked in a garage. We only saw him at breakfast or, when he was broke, he was home for dinner. He never spoke of Davis nor of our father, who disappeared one night on the reserve when I was seven. It was better our father had left; he wasn't that nice to our mother. He was an asshole from the drink.

41 I helped my mother at the truck stop in the mornings then I read all afternoon, while she worked at the library. She ordered so many books about space and aliens that year, the librarian had created a special section titled, The Universe, The Cosmos, and Extraterrestrials.

The magazines were the most popular thing for people to read at the library, and the librarian put the space collection, with a huge globe and planets hanging from the ceiling, right beside the magazines. It was the best place in the world.

42 Lake Dark recognized my obsession with space and aliens. I was walking to my friend's house, it was a cold December night and I was not dressed properly. I cut through old man Bob's farm and walked along the shoreline. I kept hearing this noise. It felt like it was under me. At first, I thought I was on the frozen lake. I stopped and looked for some ailing cow. Nothing was around me but the cold. The cows were in the barn. I was still along the farmland.

43 I listened in the darkness. I understood that under the water, aliens were speaking to me. No, I was not high; I never did that stuff. I was only thirteen. Drones and murmurs echoed through my brain. The curved rhythms whirled and rose. It was a code. No, it was an unwritten message to me. Yes, it was the air escaping and the ice forming, but maybe it was from Davis or an alien calling out to me to play them a Pow Wow song. After an hour, I understood it. The water was speaking to me. I had to dream.

* * *

44 I returned to school in the winter and left at lunch and spent afternoons at the library.

45 They tried to expel me, but my mom dared them to test me. I passed every test, with high marks. The principal was so upset he walked out of the room.

46 My mom laughed and we ran out of the school straight to the car. On the way home, she bought a bucket of fried chicken for dinner. It was a celebration. We never had takeout; the only time we had fried chicken was at feasts and birthdays.

47 James came home that evening and after the greasy bucket of chicken, we told funny stories from the past. James finally told a story about Davis and hunting. In the middle he cried. It was the first time I saw him cry. Mom and I watched him cry. Then he looked up, said he missed Davis. It was the first time we all cried together.

48 Davis was the emptiness we all carried; he was the love we all understood. James finished his story. We laughed so much my mom fell off her chair.

* * *

49 A month later, four owls sat outside my mother's door. She never saw more than two beside each other. The owls only came to her door when people she loved died.

50 She ran out the door and followed the owls down to The River.

      *   *   *

51 When the large man dumped me in the water, he held me under. The weeds rubbed against my bare legs. The River was cold; he broke the ice when he dropped me in The River. The pickerel came and sang an ancient song.

52 The tiny molecules of bacteria perfectly arranged themselves on my body, holding together all my skin.

53 My eyes were open and I saw everything. His face was filled with hate. His hands were still dirty. His hair was light brown and greasy.

54 It was Saturday, the spring of '97.

55 After he left, ice covered The River. A muskrat swam to me and closed my eyes with his tiny feet.

      *   *   *

56 I asked the fish, the ants, the eagle, the crow, and Davis to help me breathe. They floated with me. We were on the starship USS *Voyager* travelling a million light years away.

———————

(3314 words)

Source: Naponse, D. "She Is Water." *The Malahat Review*, 2016, web.uvic.ca/malahat/issues/197.html.

Initial Insight

1. What is the story about? Write down anything that intuitively comes to you.

_____

2. What do you know about the narrator? State as many facts as you can remember.

_____

_____

_____

_____

_____

_____

Reader's Response

Consider the following questions. Discuss your answers with one or more partners.

1. Did you find it easy or difficult to picture the story's setting? Why?

2. What are the issues portrayed in the story that stood out to you?

3. How do you imagine the narrator? Did you find it easy or difficult to relate to her? Why?

4. Do you think the narrator has a happy life or not? Explain your answer.

5. How would you describe the overall mood of the story? Why is that?

6. Would you say the story is about death or about life? Why?

LANGUAGE FOCUS

The narrator's language use reflects her voice as a teenager. The text contains several instances of more informal grammatical and syntactical constructions as well as colloquial words and expressions. In each of the sentences below, underline one informal grammatical form, word or phrase. Discuss why it is considered colloquial, and replace it with a more formal synonym.

1. I believe that story 'cause I saw it in his garage. _____

2. Me and my dad once pulled a fifteen-pound trout from that creek [...]. _____

3. The western stream was the one area most townies never went. _____

4. She'd make a stew from them or fry them up. _____

5. He told me stories about the settlers divvying up land [...]. _____

6. My cousins, my brother Davis, and I were pumped. _____

7. We lived with my grandpa for a few years [...]. _____

8. My mother had the worst potty mouth. _____

9. She gave me her tips and told me to hide them till Christmas [...]. _____

10. No, I was not high; I never did that stuff. _____

Look up any words you are unsure of.

MyBookshelf > My eLab
> Exercises > Part I: Short
Stories > Chapter 9: She
Is Water > Vocabulary
Comprehension

Close Reading

As you read the text again, pay attention to elements that seem significant to understanding and interpreting the story. The following guided reading questions will help you.

1. What resulted from the proximity of the plywood plant?

    a) More employment opportunities for the Indigenous population

    b) Pollution of the water bodies surrounding the reserve

    c) Increasing popularity of the area for paddling and fishing trout

    d) More suspicious deaths found in the lake

2. What two anomalies does the narrator report about the pickerel she sees in Robert Hurf's garage?

_____

3. In which two distinct categories can the incidents reported in paragraphs 5–8 be placed?

_____

_____

4. What do the narrator and her aunt, respectively, consider to be the most wonderful thing in the world?

_____

_____

5. Why does the narrator's grandfather sell his farm to live closer to the village?

_____

_____

_____

_____

6. Who does the narrator feel has abandoned her after her brother's accident?

_____

_____

_____

7. What happens to the narrator as she is on her way to meet with her study group, singing a song?

_____

8. Why does the narrator like science class?

_____

9. How do the narrator, her mother and brother finally manage to deal with the loss of Davis?

a) By trying to forget about him as much as possible

b) By making offerings near the river in his honour

c) By talking about him, crying and laughing together

d) By eating his favourite meal, fried chicken

10. Who does the narrator feel accompany her on her final journey?

_____

_____

MyBookshelf > My eLab > Exercises > Part I: Short Stories > Chapter 9: She Is Water > Close Reading: Additional Questions

THE LANGUAGE OF LITERATURE

The effect of any text is to a very large extent determined by the author's diction and use of figures of speech and other literary devices. Use the following questions to focus your attention on how the author uses language in the story.

A. What **type of narrator** and **narrative time** does the author use to tell the story? What is particular about this in the story?

B. In paragraph 1, what **metaphor** does the narrator use as a synonym for "toxic waste"? How does this **foreshadow** events to come?

C. In paragraph 3, the author plays with the **literary devices of climax** (a figure of speech in which words, phrases or clauses are arranged in order of increasing importance) and **anti-climax** (a figure of speech in which statements gradually descend in order of importance) when the narrator lists all of the items abandoned in the lake. Explain this affirmation and how it highlights how suspected deaths are trivialized.

D. A **euphemism** is a figure of speech that substitutes an inoffensive term for one considered offensive or too explicit. Which word or phrase constitutes a euphemism in paragraph 17?

E. The river plays a central role in the story. In the following passage, identify two elements that contribute to its **personification**: "The River ran through the reserve, with its many creeks and streams running into it. We always seemed to be running south, following the creek."

Analytical Reading

After making specific observations, you are ready to analyze the subject of your close reading. The following questions will help you look for thematic patterns, establish relationships and identify specific examples of literary devices or principles.

1. The story starts with a poem. Explain its function and meaning in regard to the short story that follows.

2. Dark Lake and its tributaries play a central role in the story, in a literal and figurative sense. The narrator repeatedly situates events in regard to the lake, by mentioning one of the cardinal directions. Use the mind map below to take note of this information.

North: _____

_____

West: _____

_____

_____

Dark Lake

East: _____

_____

_____

South: _____

_____

_____

3. The story spans two distinct time frames. The first is a chronological account of the narrator's childhood memories and musings on life at the reserve. The second concerns the final moments of her life. Which paragraphs are part of the second time frame? Explain the impact this has on the plot line.

4. In paragraph 15, explain how the watershed also symbolizes the division between two cultures.

5. What implicit criticism can be found in the narrator's accounts of four accidents on the lake and in the river?

6. Why is the narrator fascinated by space and the television show *Star Trek: Voyager*?

7. What parallel can you establish between the relationship of the narrator's mother and father and the events that unfold between her and her attacker?

8. Examine the context to explain the meaning of the sentence "I had to dream" at the end of paragraph 43.

9. The pickerel appears at the very beginning (par. 2) and very end of the story (par. 51). What does it symbolize, and what is the importance of its presence in the final scene?

10. The narrator calls upon her totem animals—the fish, the ants, the eagle and the crow— on two occasions in the story. What do they symbolize? How is their behaviour different between the first mention and the second?

Food for Thought

The following questions encourage you to turn a critical eye to your earlier observations and analyses. They introduce elements and considerations that will lead you to formulate new questions and set tentative hypotheses. Discuss these to further your insight into the text.

1. After reading and analyzing the story, how do you interpret its metaphorical title, "She Is Water"? Think of the associations you brainstormed in Connect with the Text, as well as the different occurrences of water as a symbol in the text.

2. What do you imagine happens after the story concludes? Explain your reasoning based on your insight into the events that occur in the story.

3. In the story, the narrator's mother is often found looking west when thinking of her dead son. The narrator "was left to sleep […] in the east." What might the opposing cardinal directions symbolize in both of these cases?

Presenting an Analysis

Writing | Analyzing the Symbolism of Water

Water is omnipresent in this short story, set at a reserve bordered by a lake and a river. Water also acts as a strong and profound symbol. It is no coincidence that "The River" is consistently capitalized; its presence in the story can be likened to a character in its own right. Pinpoint what you consider to be the most important characteristics of the lake and the river, and examine relevant passages from the story to support your analysis. Then, write a thesis statement focusing on the importance of their symbolism in light of the story's final scene.

Example:

In "She Is Water," Naponse draws a parallel between the toxic waste dumped in the lake and the narrator's body dumped in the river by referring to both of them as products of "hate" toward the First Nations community.

In each of the body paragraphs, use an analytical structure. In the first paragraph, provide evidence and examples from the text to support the characteristics and symbolic meanings of water you decide to focus on. Refer to the work you did in the Analytical Reading and Food for Thought sections. In the second paragraph, explain the link between these meanings and the events that make up the story's dénouement. Make sure to clearly explain and support your interpretation. Since you are presenting an analysis, do not include any personal opinions that you cannot back up or explain with evidence from the text itself.

(Refer to Part V, Writing about Literature, on page 271 for more information on essay format and structure.)

Speaking | Discussing Opposing Forces

Several of the themes evoked in "She Is Water" are developed in terms of opposing forces:

- Life and death
- Men and women
- Nature and human activity
- Indigenous and white cultures

Prepare a presentation on one such pair of opposing forces.

- Discuss how the theme is represented in the story and what its importance is in regard to the overall narrative.
- Then, point out how exactly this theme is taken up in the story. Which characters, plot moments or other literary devices relate to it, and how? Present relevant passages of the story to support your analysis.
- End your presentation by opening up the topic to a discussion of a real-life issue related to this theme facing First Nations people, now or in the past.

Present a cohesive presentation that transitions smoothly between your explanation of the theme's representation in the story, your detailed analysis of one or more pertinent passages and the real-life issue. Make sure it is easy for your audience to distinguish between analysis and interpretation, between fiction and reality.

(Refer to Appendix 2 on page 297 for more information on presentation format and structure.)

PART II
Drama

ADDITIONAL CHAPTER ONLINE
The Revenger's Tragedy

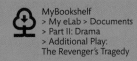

MyBookshelf
> My eLab > Documents
> Part II: Drama
> Additional Play:
The Revenger's Tragedy

ELEMENTS OF ANALYSIS

Drama differs considerably from prose or poetry since it is written to be performed on a stage. Stage performances present the audience with a version of the play that has already been interpreted (and possibly adapted) by the director and actors of a particular production. Reading a play, however, gives first-hand access to the author's stage directions and other written information on the play's setting, characters, etc. By imagining and interpreting these features, readers can then "see" and "hear" a representation of the play that has not been coloured by anyone else. This is also the form in which dramatic texts first appear to the director and the cast of any production. Finally, reading a play also allows for closer literary analysis, as it is not as ephemeral as watching a particular performance. The elements presented in the following section inform such an analysis.

Engaging with Drama

A dramatic text contains many elements also found in fiction: plot, setting, characters, themes, symbols and other literary devices. However, when watching a theatre performance, the audience sees and hears the actors deliver the lines written by the author, also called the playwright; these compose the play's **primary text**. Rather than simply reading these lines out loud, the actors, guided by a director, rely on **secondary texts** to give life to the characters and the story in which they evolve. These include the author's scene descriptions, stage directions and the *dramatis personae*. In a performance, these texts are not spoken but rather enacted, or visible through costume and set design. To fully understand a dramatic text, the reader therefore needs to consider all of the information contained in the script.

Formal literary analysis requires careful study of elements, strategies and structures to allow you to understand how a text is crafted. Similar to how you deepen and fine-tune your thinking process as you write and rewrite the different drafts that lead up to a final version of an essay, you continually develop your understanding of a text as you read and reread it. This will help you bridge the gap between subjective interpretations and objective analyses.

You will approach each dramatic text in this section through three "drafts," each focused on a specific type of reading:

- **Exploratory Reading** allows you to discover the different aspects of a dramatic text to get a general understanding of it. What is the play about and where is it set? Who are the characters and what happens to them? In order to answer these questions, first read the secondary texts usually found at the beginning of the script and at the beginning of the different acts and scenes. These will give you valuable insight into the play's structure, setting and characters. Then, read through the entire play for pleasure, but remain attentive to stage directions that complement the characters' lines. Finally, take stock of your emotional response to the text.

- **Close Reading** allows you to zoom in on specific elements or passages of a dramatic text. This is where you gather textual evidence that you can draw on in your forthcoming analysis. Close reading can focus on micro-level features (e.g., a character's use of language or that character's actions and non-verbal language as described in the secondary text) as well as macro-level features (e.g., dramatic structure, the psychological evolution of a character). When analyzing dramatic texts that are voluminous, feature many characters or are written in challenging language, carefully select which passages of the text are pertinent in light of your focus.

- **Analytical Reading** is informed by the two previous steps. Once you have identified one or more significant elements of focus for your analysis (i.e., the elements you will want to include in your thesis statement), rereading the entire text or specific passages from this vantage point will allow you to critically reconsider your observations, corroborate your inferences, establish new links and deepen your analysis.

Dramatic Genres

The oldest definition of dramatic genres can be retraced to Aristotle's *Poetics*, written around 335 BCE. Aristotle's distinction between tragedy and comedy still exists today, although several subgenres have been introduced over the centuries.

Tragedy introduces the audience to a heroic protagonist who undergoes a reversal of fortune. Tragedies typically involve intense action and conflicts, arouse emotions such as pity and fear and end in a catastrophe (such as the death of the protagonist). The objective of this, according to Aristotle, is catharsis, a purgation and purification of the audience's strong emotions through art.

- **Senecan tragedies** were recited rather than staged in the Roman era, but their five-act structure became a model for English playwrights.
- **Revenge tragedies** were popular in the Elizabethan era and employed many elements of the Senecan tragedy such as murder, revenge, ghosts and madness. They often contained a play-within-the-play.
- **Domestic tragedies**, focusing on lower- or middle-class protagonists, gained popularity from the eighteenth century onward, in line with social shifts. They sought to arouse empathy rather than fear in the audience.
- **Modern tragedies** often follow the new conventions of domestic tragedy (ordinary conflict, characters and language) and may feature an anti-hero, who does not display the dignity and courage of a traditional hero.

Comedy aims at amusing and entertaining the audience; the genre implicitly reassures the audience that no disaster will occur and that the play's outcome will be positive. High comedy appeals to the intellect and has a serious purpose (e.g., to criticize), while low comedy focuses on situational humour.

- **Romantic comedies** focus on lovers and their struggle to come together.
- **Satiric comedies** criticize social, political or philosophical notions or practices.
- **Comedies of manners** ridicule the artificial and sophisticated behaviour of the higher social classes.
- **Farces** present highly exaggerated and caricatured characters, an unlikely plot and verbal humour.
- **Melodrama**, which became popular in the nineteenth century, often reinforces a romantic or sensational plot with musical elements.

The boundaries of dramatic genres are often blurred. **Tragicomedy** draws on dramatic conventions from both tragedy and comedy. Tragicomedies present characters of all social ranks and may zoom in on conflicts of epic proportions as well as day-to-day problems. The conflict they present can end in catastrophe or be diffused into a happy ending. Many contemporary plays, as well as television and cinema productions, can be considered forms of tragicomedy.

MyBookshelf > My eLab
> Documents > Part II: Drama
> The Revenger's Tragedy

The Narrative Situation

Narrative Point of View

In drama, there is **usually no narrator** who tells the reader or spectator what is going on in the story-world. The audience gains information directly from what can be seen and heard on stage or, when reading a play, from the primary and secondary texts.

In some plays, one of the characters may occasionally act as a narrator to move the plot forward, by describing certain actions and events that are not shown, or by commenting on the action in the form of an aside in which the character addresses the audience directly, unheard by the other characters that may be on the stage.

Being witness to all of the scenes making up a play, the reader or spectator usually benefits from an **omniscient point of view**, an overall perspective that goes beyond the sum of the different characters' perspectives. Some plays offer a **limited point of view**, by only relaying what happens in one given place at one given time, or by only giving access to the scenes that involve a focal character.

Narrative Time

Dramatic texts are primarily composed of **scenes**, in which the story unfolds in real time in the form of the characters' actions and dialogues. Although scenes are inevitably performed in a successive fashion on stage, the reader or audience should consider that they may take place simultaneously on the narrative timeline.

That said, the play's **narrative speed** can also be slowed down or sped up. This creates a discrepancy between the narrative time, or **played time**, and the real **playing time**, or duration of the play.

Dramatic devices such as the aside or the soliloquy can be used to interrupt the action and generate a **pause**, allowing characters to voice their inner thoughts or intentions.

A character can present a **summary** of events that are not directly included in the play, for instance, by reporting them to another character. This accelerates the action.

An **ellipsis** skips an entire part of the story—for instance, by indicating that a scene takes place a certain amount of time before or after the previous one. This indicator can be given directly to the reader or the audience, symbolized by a stage prop such as a clock, or it can be part of the dialogue.

Finally, the chronological order of the story can be broken through the introduction of **flashbacks** and **flashforwards**. This strategic arrangement of narrative elements and events makes up the **dramatic plot**.

PRACTICE

A. The following words are spoken by the chorus at the very beginning of Shakespeare's *Romeo and Juliet*. What dramatic device does this represent and how does it affect the plot?

> Two households, both alike in dignity,
>   In fair Verona, where we lay our scene,
> From ancient grudge break to new mutiny,
>   Where civil blood makes civil hands unclean.
> From forth the fatal loins of these two foes
>   A pair of star-cross'd lovers take their life;
> Whose misadventur'd piteous overthrows

Do with their death bury their parents' strife.
The fearful passage of their death-mark'd love,
 And the continuance of their parents' rage,
Which, but their children's end, nought could remove,
 Is now the two hours' traffic of our stage;
The which if you with patient ears attend,
 What here shall miss, our toil shall strive to mend.

_____

_____

_____

B. Consider the following excerpt from Henrik Ibsen's *A Doll's House*. In which way is the ellipsis between the opening dialogue and the second scene represented in the setting?

Nora. Hide the Christmas Tree carefully, Helen. Be sure the children do not see it until this evening, when it is dressed. [To the PORTER, taking out her purse.] How much?

Porter. Sixpence.

Nora. There is a shilling. No, keep the change.

[…]

[**THE SAME SCENE**.—The Christmas Tree is in the corner by the piano, stripped of its ornaments and with burnt-down candle-ends on its dishevelled branches. NORA'S cloak and hat are lying on the sofa. She is alone in the room, walking about uneasily. She stops by the sofa and takes up her cloak.]

_____

_____

_____

_____

C. In this excerpt from *Romeo and Juliet*, Romeo is hidden in the darkness of the gardens as Juliet appears at a balcony and voices her thoughts. What purpose does the aside serve?

Juliet
O Romeo, Romeo! wherefore art thou Romeo?
Deny thy father and refuse thy name;
Or, if thou wilt not, be but sworn my love,
And I'll no longer be a Capulet.

Romeo
[aside] Shall I hear more, or shall I speak at this?

Juliet
'Tis but thy name that is my enemy:
Thou art thyself, though not a Montague.

_____

_____

_____

Dramatic Plot Structure

Plot is a term used to describe the structure in which a play's events and scenes, which are part of the narrative, are organized by the author and may be different from their natural or chronological order. The plot structure is designed to engage the reader or audience and revolves around one or more **conflicts**. These can be **internal**, representing a character's mental or emotional struggle (character vs. self), or **external**, involving several characters (character vs. human) or a broader concept, such as religion, the environment or society at large (character vs. society). In some plays, the plot can be divided into distinct **subplots** (also called **plot lines**), which piece together to form the story.

Classical and traditional plays typically employ a set of plot-related conventions, while modern plays only follow them partly or not at all.

Structural Conventions

Traditional plays usually follow a **five-act structure**. Based on ancient Greek and Shakespearean drama, nineteenth-century author Gustav Freytag developed a pyramid-shaped diagram to analyze and understand the function of each act. Although modern plays have moved away from this rigid format, this visual tool will still allow you to establish the key moments of a plot, regardless of its division into acts and scenes.

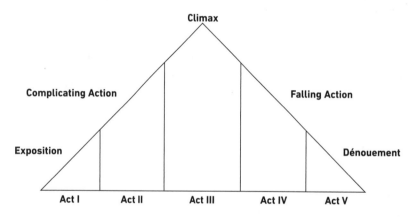

Act I, the **exposition**, introduces the play by providing descriptions and background information on the setting and characters, and by presenting a conflict. In other words, the reader or audience is usually informed about the "who," "what," "where," "when" and "why" of the story at the beginning of the play. Some plays do not follow this convention in order to spark curiosity or generate tension.

Act II develops on further circumstances related to the main conflict. These **complicating actions** present the characters in more detail and may introduce new characters. They can also lead to subplots that unfold alongside the play's central conflict. Complicating actions evoke a specific **dramatic question** (which may remain implicit) for the reader or audience to seek an answer to.

The **climax** constitutes the tipping point of the action; act III presents the crisis that ultimately leads to the dénouement of the play.

In act IV, new events happen and may delay the final dénouement of the play. These events maintain tension and are called the **falling action**.

Act V, the final act in traditional plays, presents the end of the story arc, called the **dénouement**. This offers a solution to the play's central conflict, in the form of a catastrophe in tragedies, or a happy ending in comedies.

PRACTICE

Consider the following synopsis of William Shakespeare's *Hamlet*, which follows the traditional five-act structure outlined above:

> Prince Hamlet has been summoned home to Denmark to attend his father's funeral. One night, a Ghost reveals itself to Hamlet, claiming to be the ghost of Hamlet's father, and alleges that he was murdered by Hamlet's uncle, Claudius, who has since married Hamlet's mother and assumed the throne. Hamlet decides to uncover the truth for himself. He makes himself appear mad, mistreating his girlfriend Ophelia to deflect Claudius' suspicion. Queen Gertrude, however, is convinced that only the late king's death and her recent remarriage could upset Hamlet. Hamlet leads a troupe of players to perform a play that re-enacts King Hamlet's death by poisoning, causing King Claudius to react in a way that convinces Hamlet his uncle did indeed poison his father. Claudius sends Hamlet to England on a diplomatic mission, and secretly arranges for him to be executed on arrival. Hamlet escapes and returns to the court. Claudius organizes a duel involving Hamlet. During the duel, Gertrude drinks from a poisoned goblet intended for Hamlet. Hamlet is nonetheless wounded with a poisoned weapon. Right before he dies, Hamlet manages to avenge his father and kills Claudius.

Make an assumption as to how these events may unfold across the five acts of the play. In the synopsis above, place four slash marks to indicate the division between acts.

Dramatic Conventions

Classical plays also convey a sense of authenticity and cohesion, expressed through the law of the three unities—**unity of plot**, **unity of place** and **unity of time**. This convention states that a play should only have one single plot line, taking place in a single place over the span of one day. The purpose of this is to imitate life as authentically as possible. Again, modern plays often do not follow (all of) these conventions, and even traditional playwrights, including Shakespeare, used them in a flexible manner.

PRACTICE

Read the following short summary of Susan Glaspell's one-act play *Trifles*.

> The play starts when the local sheriff, accompanied by attorney George Henderson and neighbour Lewis Hale, enter the Wrights' farmhouse to investigate the murder of its owner, John. John's wife, Minnie, is suspected of the murder and Mrs. Hale and Mrs. Peters come along to collect some of Minnie's personal belongings to bring to her in jail. While the men search the house for evidence, the two women start their own investigation in the kitchen, which the men overlooked. First, they find a piece of sewing, and postulate that a particularly erratic design offers evidence of Minnie's solitude and frustration in her married life. Then, the women find a dead canary, which might be the motif for the murder. The women sympathize with Minnie, realizing that her husband was abusive, and hide the evidence from the men.

On a separate sheet of paper, explain how this play respects the three unities.

Characters

Dramatis Personae

Drama can be considered a character-driven genre, since it presents the audience directly with scenes that are only based on characters' actions and interactions, which convey all plot-related information. The characters in plays can generally be divided into **major characters** and **minor characters**, depending on how important they are for the plot. This importance can be measured through the amount of stage presence and the number of lines the character has.

The lead character of a story is referred to as the **protagonist**. Some plays have **dual protagonists**—two characters, having similar amounts of stage presence, each with their own story arc (e.g., *Romeo and Juliet*). The **antagonist** is the character in direct conflict with the protagonist(s). In some plays, the **antagonistic force** may be a more abstract concept, such as societal values or the environment. These terms do not make any value judgments in regard to the characters, which can have positive or negative traits. In other words, the protagonist may be unlikeable and the antagonist may be a charismatic character.

PRACTICE

A. Consider the following list of characters from *Hamlet* (Shakespeare). Based on the information on the *dramatis personae* provided at the beginning of the script, complete the mind map.

> **CLAUDIUS**, King of Denmark.
> **GERTRUDE**, Queen of Denmark and Mother to Hamlet.
> **GHOST** of Hamlet's Father.
> **HAMLET**, Son to the late, and Nephew to the present King.
> **HORATIO**, Friend to Hamlet.
> **OPHELIA**, Daughter to Polonius.
> **POLONIUS**, Lord Chamberlain.
> **LAERTES**, his Son.
> **ROSENCRANTZ & GUILDENSTERN**: Courtiers to Claudius.
> *(Lords, Ladies, Officers, Soldiers, Sailors, Messengers and Attendants.)*

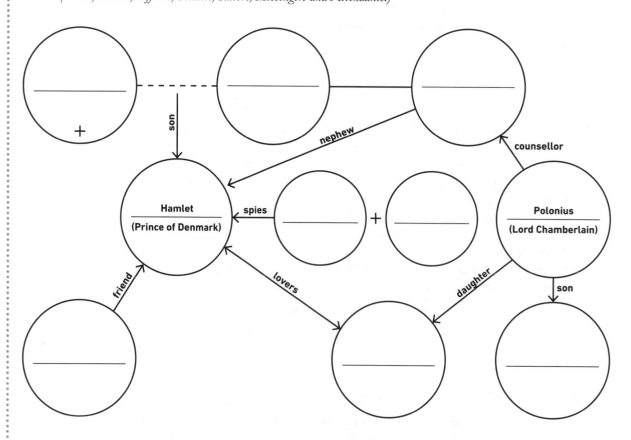

B. Referring to the brief summary of the play on page 111, identify the major and minor characters in *Hamlet*. Identify the protagonist(s) and antagonist(s).

_____

_____

Characterization

Character development in a play is conveyed in the primary and secondary texts, and can mainly be achieved in three ways:

- Through language—either in dialogue and interactions with other characters, as an inner monologue reporting thoughts and feelings (a soliloquy) or through description by another character;
- Through actions and behaviours that inform the audience about the character's personality;
- Through appearance—including a character's looks and dress—and body language.

In the 1920s, literary critic E. M. Forster developed a typology of literary characters that is still prevalent in literary analysis today.

- **Flat characters** are two-dimensional; they usually have one or a few easily recognizable or stereotypical traits or features that define them.
- **Round characters** are three-dimensional; they are complex, and their nuanced physical and psychological traits are described in rich detail.
- **Static characters** tend to remain unchanged throughout the play.
- **Dynamic characters** evolve, whether positively or negatively, as the play progresses.

For instance, in *Macbeth*, the protagonist is a round and dynamic character affected by a range of emotions including ambition, guilt and paranoia. The three witches that appear to Macbeth and make prophecies encouraging him to commit murder are flat and static; their only role in the play is to represent fate and evil.

PRACTICE

In the following passage from *Pygmalion* (G. Bernard Shaw, Act II), underline examples of characterization of the flower girl through language (L), through actions (AC) and through appearance (AP). Write the appropriate abbreviations in the margin.

MRS. PEARCE [hesitating, evidently perplexed]. A young woman wants to _____
see you, sir.

HIGGINS. A young woman! What does she want?

MRS. PEARCE. Well, sir, she says you'll be glad to see her when you know _____
what she's come about. She's quite a common girl, sir. Very common indeed. I should have sent her away, only I thought perhaps you wanted her to talk into your machines. I hope I've not done wrong; but really you see such queer people sometimes—you'll excuse me, I'm sure, sir—

HIGGINS. Oh, that's all right, Mrs. Pearce. Has she an interesting accent?

MRS. PEARCE. Oh, something dreadful, sir, really. I don't know how you can take an interest in it.

The flower girl enters in state. She has a hat with three ostrich feathers, orange, sky-blue and _____
red. She has a nearly clean apron, and the shoddy coat has been tidied a little. The pathos of this deplorable figure, with its innocent vanity and consequential air, touches Pickering, who _____
has already straightened himself in the presence of Mrs. Pearce. But as to Higgins, the only

distinction he makes between men and women is that when he is neither bullying nor exclaim-
ing to the heavens against some featherweight cross, he coaxes women as a child coaxes its
nurse when it wants to get anything out of her.

HIGGINS [brusquely, recognizing her with unconcealed disappointment, and at once, babylike, making an intolerable grievance of it]. Why, this is the girl I jotted down last night. She's no use: I've got all the records I want of the Lisson Grove lingo; and I'm not going to waste another cylinder on it. [To the girl] Be off with you: I don't want you.

THE FLOWER GIRL. Don't you be so saucy. You ain't heard what I come for yet. [To Mrs. Pearce, who is waiting at the door for further instruction] Did you tell him I come in a taxi?

Place

Space

Space is an important element in drama since the stage itself also represents a place where the action is presented. Stage types and technical possibilities have changed over time, which has influenced the way plays are written and performed. While historically, plays were performed in daylight on stages that were at least partially surrounded by the audience, in the nineteenth century there was a shift to a picture-frame stage, also called **proscenium stage**. This provides the same perspective as contemplating an image, painting or film. The front of the stage is often referred to as the **fourth wall**, virtually separating the audience from the action. The late twentieth century saw the birth of **immersive theatre**, which aims to eliminate all barriers between the play and the audience members, as they become a part of the playing space and setting.

Plays differ significantly with regard to how space is presented and how much information about it is provided. The appearance of the set is usually described in **stage directions** or **descriptions** at the beginning of acts or scenes. They also list all the essential **stage props** such as furniture and accessories.

The level of descriptive detail informs analysis as it serves as a meaningful indicator of the functions and importance of the play's setting. A more detailed stage set creates an illusion of **realism**, while a bare stage set gives more imaginative freedom to the audience and may suggest that the action depicted could take place anywhere and affect anyone.

Of course, stage productions can reinterpret or reinvent the staging instructions—for instance, based on **cultural and economic considerations**. Victorian theatres sometimes even brought horses on stage to make the play more spectacular and engaging but also to show off the theatre's wealth. Contemporary performances of Shakespearean plays have been known to set the action in different eras, such as the 1960s, or different places, such as India. These have an important impact on the **set design**.

PRACTICE

A. Consider and compare the following stage directions and descriptions from *Macbeth* and *Pygmalion*. What do you observe about their level of description? Closely examine the different elements mentioned, and make assumptions and inferences on their purpose and meaning. Discuss them with a partner.

1. *Macbeth* (W. Shakespeare, Act 1)

SCENE 1. A desert place.
Thunder and lightning. Enter three Witches

SCENE 2. A camp near Forres.

Alarum within. Enter DUNCAN, MALCOLM, DONALBAIN, LENNOX, with Attendants, meeting a bleeding Sergeant

2. *Pygmalion* (G. Bernard Shaw, Act 2)

Next day at 11 a.m. Higgins's laboratory in Wimpole Street. It is a room on the first floor, looking on the street, and was meant for the drawing-room. The double doors are in the middle of the back hall; and persons entering find in the corner to their right two tall file cabinets at right angles to one another against the walls. In this corner stands a flat writing-table, on which are a phonograph, a laryngoscope, a row of tiny organ pipes with a bellows, a set of lamp chimneys for singing flames with burners attached to a gas plug in the wall by an indiarubber tube, several tuning-forks of different sizes, a life-size image of half a human head, showing in section the vocal organs, and a box containing a supply of wax cylinders for the phonograph.

Further down the room, on the same side, is a fireplace, with a comfortable leather-covered easy-chair at the side of the hearth nearest the door, and a coal-scuttle. There is a clock on the mantelpiece. Between the fireplace and the phonograph table is a stand for newspapers. […]

B. How would the level of detail of the directions affect a director staging these plays? Imagine and discuss the different possibilities they leave for stage productions.

Setting

The **setting** of a play amounts to its situation in place and time. Other factors, such as the social and political background portrayed in the play, may also inform the setting. The plot is presented against the background of a specific setting, which often reinforces the story that is told through action and dialogue. In this way, the setting often acts as a **symbol** that points to other levels of meaning in the play. For instance, the storm at the beginning of Shakespeare's *The Tempest* not only functions as a dramatic background to the action but also reflects the characters' state of disorder. **Stage business** is a non-verbal action that draws the attention of the audience to a character through gestures and/or to an element of the setting through a character's interactions with a stage prop—for instance, to get them to notice or think about a symbol.

Imagery can also be used to complete the setting of a play by appealing to the reader's senses to evoke things like the temperature and weather, as well as the sounds and smells that are part of the environment in which the play is set. While in contemporary plays such elements might be showed directly through the use of lighting, sound and special effects, in classical plays it is common to hear characters describe these parts of the setting that could not otherwise be rendered at the time.

All of the above considerations directly affect the **atmosphere** or **mood** that pervades the play.

Language and Dramatic Devices

Apart from the development of plot, setting and characters, the playwright's use of language has a strong influence on the audience's or reader's experience of a play. Although dramatic language is modelled on real-life interactions, it is inevitably artificially constructed and also serves a specific purpose. Dramatic language is often rhetorical and includes many figures of speech and stylistic forms to draw attention to the play's symbols and themes. While playwrights such as Shakespeare also used **verse**, most contemporary plays only contain dialogue in the form of regular **prose**.

Language

The tone of a play is affected by the language use of its characters. The **style** of a character's speech is the sum of its linguistic characteristics, including the use of syntax (sentence length and type, word order) and diction (word choice). An important aspect of literary analysis of a play therefore consists in paying close attention to diction when performing one or more close readings, because we may presume that the author has carefully made these word choices when crafting the characters' utterances.

- Words not only have **denotation**—their literal meaning—but also connotation—the suggested meaning that can often be inferred from the context.
- Words are typically part of a **register** or level of language, ranging from the formal to the informal.
- Words can be used as **figures of speech** to create a non-literal meaning that differs from their primary usage; for instance, **metaphors** and **similes** both call attention to how two different things are similar. A simile expresses this comparison through the use of the words *as*, *like* or equivalent expressions: "It seems she hangs upon the cheek of night as a rich jewel in an Ethiop's ear" (Shakespeare, *Romeo and Juliet*, act 1, scene 4). Metaphors operate without any explicit comparison: "All the world's a stage, / and all the men and women merely players" (Shakespeare, *As You Like It*, act 2, scene 7).

Words can contribute to **rhythm** and **sound patterns** such as repetition and rhyme, alliteration (repeating the word-initial sound: *Cindy saw six swimmers*), assonance (repeating vowel sounds: *Try to light the fire*) and consonance (repeating consonant sounds: *Max insists he sees ghosts*).

PRACTICE

A. In the excerpt from *Pygmalion* on page 114, explain how the flower girl's use of "saucy" and "ain't" are indicators of her social status. What level of language do they belong to?

_____

_____

B. In the same excerpt, explain the denotation and connotation of the sentence "… I come in a taxi."

_____

_____

C. In the prologue to *Romeo and Juliet* on pages 108–109, identify one line that contains alliteration and one line that contains an example of assonance.

Alliteration: _____

Assonance: _____

D. In the same excerpt, what do you observe about the last word of each line?

_____

MyBookshelf > My eLab
> Exercises > Part II: Drama
> Elements of Analysis

Dramatic Devices

Although language is (almost) exclusively presented to the audience through the characters' utterances, these can take different forms:

- **Dialogue**, the verbal exchange between two or more characters, also implies **turn-taking**. Characters may have shorter or longer turns, may interrupt one another or engage in more structured forms of conversation, such as the **repartee**—a brief, usually witty response.
- A **soliloquy**, a type of monologue, is often used to allow the audience to know a character's inner thoughts.

- An **aside** allows a character to address the audience directly, unheard by the other characters.
- In classical plays, the **chorus**, a group of unnamed individuals standing to the side of the stage, comment on the action and give advice to characters.
- If there is a discrepancy between the audience's and characters' knowledge of certain information, this can lead to **dramatic irony**. For instance, while a character may lack sufficient insight to understand a pun, the audience may possess the background knowledge to do so.

Theme

All of the aforementioned elements play a role in the development of the play's **theme(s)**, or the core motivation of the play. A play can have one or more themes, which are comprehensive statements of a deeper meaning that extends beyond the plot and the characters. In this regard, a play's theme differs from its subject matter, which is what the play is about on a primary, concrete level. In other words, the subject matter can be observed directly, while a theme consists of deeper issues that require analysis to be uncovered.

For instance, a story of a family coming together to mourn the loss of a parent can focus on parenting and emotional violence, as in *August: Osage County* (T. Letts), while *Death of a Salesman* (A. Miller) addresses themes like choice, ambition and disillusionment and *Scorched* [*Incendies*] (W. Mouawad) brings up questions of identity and acceptance.

Both concepts are not entirely separate in the sense that the subject matter is used to express the theme(s) of the play. To determine the theme(s) of a play, you might therefore ask, "What point does the author make through the subject matter of the work?" When answering this question, it may be helpful to distinguish between broad thematic concepts that appear in many different texts—for instance, love or revenge—and narrow thematic statements, which concern the particular argument the playwright makes about such a concept—e.g., true love overcomes social conventions, or revenge leads people to question their sense of ethics—what is right or wrong.

PRACTICE

Consider some of the plays that are discussed in this chapter. For each, identify the theme (T) and subject matter (S). Then, write one or more thematic concepts that underpin the more precise thematic statement given.

1. *Pygmalion*

A phonetics expert makes a bet that he can pass a flower girl as a duchess by altering her accent. _____

Social identity and class are informed through appearance and speech patterns. _____

Thematic concepts: _____

_____

2. *Macbeth*

The thirst for power can corrupt even the most noble of men. _____

After being told by three witches that he will become king, a soldier seeks the crown regardless of the consequences. _____

Thematic concepts: _____

_____

CHAPTER 10

A Midsummer Night's Dream

– William Shakespeare

This chapter focuses on the following:

- Plot structure
- Characters and characterization
- Symbolism
- Language Focus: personal pronouns
- The Language of Literature: dramatic devices and conventions
- Theme

Connect with the Text

A. Take stock of your opinions on the following questions. Discuss them with one or more partners.

1. What do you enjoy about a theatre performance? What aspects do you not like?

2. Have you read or seen a Shakespeare play or film adaptation before? How do you feel about its language, level of difficulty and relevance today?

3. How do you feel about dreams? Are they significant to real life in any way?

4. How do you feel about the representation of love in stories, plays and films? Is it usually credible? Why or why not? Think of a few "good" and a few "poor" examples of love stories, and discuss your choices.

B. Before you read *A Midsummer Night's Dream*, do a web search to find the answers to the following questions. This will help you understand the social and historical background of the play. Remember to record your sources so you can use them as references, should you decide to include this information in an essay or presentation.

1. What are the main characteristics of Elizabethan theatre? In Shakespeare's time, where and when were plays performed? What did theatres look like? Who attended performances?

2. Several of the characters in *A Midsummer Night's Dream* were not invented by Shakespeare himself. Theseus and Hippolyta are figures from Greek mythology. Oberon is a character present in medieval literature. Puck, also known as Robin Goodfellow, is rooted in English folklore. Summarize the origins and main traits of these four characters in a few sentences each.

3. Magic plays an important role in *A Midsummer Night's Dream*. What beliefs and superstitions prevailed in Elizabethan England? Discuss how these attitudes might have influenced Shakespeare's writing.

Text in Context

William Shakespeare (1564–1616), nicknamed "the Bard," is considered by many the quintessential playwright. He grew up in Stratford-upon-Avon, a relatively small town in England. His father was a shop owner, which meant Shakespeare was able to attend grammar school until the age of 15. At age 18, he married Anne Hathaway and the couple had three children. Little is known about the next decade of his life, until he established himself as an actor and playwright in London. He was a prolific writer during the Elizabethan and Jacobean ages; he wrote 38 plays between 1590 and 1611, as well as 154 sonnets and several other types of poems. In his works, he introduced hundreds of new words to the English language, many of which are still frequently used today; e.g., addiction, downstairs, educate and puppy. In 1599, his theatre group built the famous Globe Theatre on London's south bank, of which a replica can be visited today. Many of Shakespeare's best-known plays, such as *Hamlet* and *Macbeth*, were purposely written to be performed there. While Shakespeare's earlier plays, including *A Midsummer Night's Dream*, were comedies, his work evolved toward darker themes and tragedies in the second half of his writing career. No original manuscripts of Shakespeare's plays have been conserved; the actors from Shakespeare's company brought together 36 plays in what is known as the *First Folio* in 1623.

Exploratory Reading

Read the play a first time without interruption. Keep an open mind and take a mental note of your reactions and observations. Soak up the events, atmosphere and language without looking for any specific elements. When you are finished, answer the questions below the text.

Note: You will find the complete play in My eLab Documents.

MyBookshelf > My eLab > Documents > Part II: Drama > Chapter 10: A Midsummer Night's Dream

A Midsummer Night's Dream

William Shakespeare

(act 1, scenes 1 and 2, and act 2, scene 1)

Dramatis Personæ

THESEUS, Duke of Athens.
EGEUS, Father to Hermia.
LYSANDER, DEMETRIUS, in love with Hermia.
PHILOSTRATE, Master of the Revels to Theseus.
QUINCE, a Carpenter.
SNUG, a Joiner.
BOTTOM, a Weaver.
FLUTE, a Bellows-mender.
SNOUT, a Tinker.
STARVELING, a Tailor.

HIPPOLYTA, Queen of the Amazons, betrothed to Theseus.

HERMIA, Daughter to Egeus, in love with Lysander.
HELENA, in love with Demetrius.

OBERON, King of the Fairies.
TITANIA, Queen of the Fairies.
PUCK, or Robin Goodfellow.
PEASE-BLOSSOM, COBWEB, MOTH, MUSTARD-SEED, Fairies.
Other Fairies attending their King and Queen.
Attendants on Theseus and Hippolyta.

SCENE.—Athens, and a Wood near it.

ACT I. SCENE I.

Athens. The Palace of THESEUS.

Enter THESEUS, HIPPOLYTA, PHILOSTRATE,
and Attendants

THESEUS

Now, fair Hippolyta, our nuptial hour
Draws on apace; four happy days bring in
Another moon: but, O, methinks, how slow
This old moon wanes! she lingers my desires,
5 Like to a step-dame or a dowager
Long withering out a young man's revenue.

HIPPOLYTA

Four days will quickly steep themselves in night;
Four nights will quickly dream away the time;
And then the moon, like to a silver bow
10 New-bent in heaven, shall behold the night
Of our solemnities.

THESEUS

      Go, Philostrate,
Stir up the Athenian youth to merriments;
Awake the pert and nimble spirit of mirth;
Turn melancholy forth to funerals;
15 The pale companion is not for our pomp.

Exit PHILOSTRATE

Hippolyta, I woo'd thee with my sword,
And won thy love, doing thee injuries;
But I will wed thee in another key,
With pomp, with triumph and with revelling.

Enter EGEUS, HERMIA, LYSANDER,
and DEMETRIUS

EGEUS

20 Happy be Theseus, our renowned duke!

THESEUS

Thanks, good Egeus: what's the news with thee?

EGEUS

Full of vexation come I, with complaint
Against my child, my daughter Hermia.
Stand forth, Demetrius. My noble lord,
25 This man hath my consent to marry her.
Stand forth, Lysander: and my gracious duke,
This man hath bewitch'd the bosom of my child;
Thou, thou, Lysander, thou hast given her rhymes,
And interchanged love-tokens with my child:
30 Thou hast by moonlight at her window sung,

With feigning voice verses of feigning love,
And stolen the impression of her fantasy
With bracelets of thy hair, rings, gawds, conceits,
Knacks, trifles, nosegays, sweetmeats, messengers
35 Of strong prevailment in unharden'd youth:
With cunning hast thou filch'd my daughter's heart,
Turn'd her obedience, which is due to me,
To stubborn harshness: and, my gracious duke,
Be it so she; will not here before your grace
40 Consent to marry with Demetrius,
I beg the ancient privilege of Athens,
As she is mine, I may dispose of her:
Which shall be either to this gentleman
Or to her death, according to our law
45 Immediately provided in that case.

THESEUS

What say you, Hermia? be advised fair maid:
To you your father should be as a god;
One that composed your beauties, yea, and one
To whom you are but as a form in wax
50 By him imprinted and within his power
To leave the figure or disfigure it.
Demetrius is a worthy gentleman.

HERMIA

So is Lysander.

THESEUS

      In himself he is;
But in this kind, wanting your father's voice,
55 The other must be held the worthier.

HERMIA

I would my father look'd but with my eyes.

THESEUS

Rather your eyes must with his judgment look.

HERMIA

I do entreat your grace to pardon me.
I know not by what power I am made bold,
60 Nor how it may concern my modesty,
In such a presence here to plead my thoughts;
But I beseech your grace that I may know
The worst that may befall me in this case,
If I refuse to wed Demetrius.

THESEUS

65 Either to die the death or to abjure
For ever the society of men.
Therefore, fair Hermia, question your desires;
Know of your youth, examine well your blood,
Whether, if you yield not to your father's choice,

70 You can endure the livery of a nun,
   For aye to be in shady cloister mew'd,
   To live a barren sister all your life,
   Chanting faint hymns to the cold fruitless moon.
   Thrice-blessed they that master so their blood,
75 To undergo such maiden pilgrimage;
   But earthlier happy is the rose distill'd,
   Than that which withering on the virgin thorn
   Grows, lives and dies in single blessedness.

HERMIA

   So will I grow, so live, so die, my lord,
80 Ere I will my virgin patent up
   Unto his lordship, whose unwished yoke
   My soul consents not to give sovereignty.

THESEUS

   Take time to pause; and, by the next new moon—
   The sealing-day betwixt my love and me,
85 For everlasting bond of fellowship—
   Upon that day either prepare to die
   For disobedience to your father's will,
   Or else to wed Demetrius, as he would;
   Or on Diana's altar to protest
90 For aye austerity and single life.

DEMETRIUS

   Relent, sweet Hermia: and, Lysander, yield
   Thy crazed title to my certain right.

LYSANDER

   You have her father's love, Demetrius;
   Let me have Hermia's: do you marry him.

EGEUS

95 Scornful Lysander! true, he hath my love,
   And what is mine my love shall render him.
   And she is mine, and all my right of her
   I do estate unto Demetrius.

LYSANDER

   (*to* THESEUS) I am, my lord, as well derived as he,
100 As well possess'd; my love is more than his;
   My fortunes every way as fairly rank'd,
   If not with vantage, as Demetrius';
   And, which is more than all these boasts can be,
   I am beloved of beauteous Hermia:
105 Why should not I then prosecute my right?
   Demetrius, I'll avouch it to his head,
   Made love to Nedar's daughter, Helena,
   And won her soul; and she, sweet lady, dotes,
   Devoutly dotes, dotes in idolatry,
110 Upon this spotted and inconstant man.

THESEUS

   I must confess that I have heard so much,
   And with Demetrius thought to have spoke thereof;
   But, being over-full of self-affairs,
   My mind did lose it. But, Demetrius, come;
115 And come, Egeus; you shall go with me,
   I have some private schooling for you both.
   For you, fair Hermia, look you arm yourself
   To fit your fancies to your father's will;
   Or else the law of Athens yields you up—
120 Which by no means we may extenuate—
   To death, or to a vow of single life.
   Come, my Hippolyta: what cheer, my love?
   Demetrius and Egeus, go along:
   I must employ you in some business
125 Against our nuptial and confer with you
   Of something nearly that concerns yourselves.

EGEUS

   With duty and desire we follow you.

Exeunt all but LYSANDER and HERMIA

LYSANDER

   How now, my love! why is your cheek so pale?
   How chance the roses there do fade so fast?

HERMIA

130 Belike for want of rain, which I could well
   Beteem them from the tempest of my eyes.

LYSANDER

   Ay me! for aught that I could ever read,
   Could ever hear by tale or history,
   The course of true love never did run smooth;
135 But, either it was different in blood,—

HERMIA

   O cross! too high to be enthrall'd to low.

LYSANDER

   Or else misgraffed in respect of years,—

HERMIA

   O spite! too old to be engaged to young.

LYSANDER

   Or else it stood upon the choice of friends,—

HERMIA

140 O hell! to choose love by another's eyes.

LYSANDER

   Or, if there were a sympathy in choice,
   War, death, or sickness did lay siege to it,

Making it momentany as a sound,
Swift as a shadow, short as any dream;
145 Brief as the lightning in the collied night,
That, in a spleen, unfolds both heaven and earth,
And ere a man hath power to say 'Behold!'
The jaws of darkness do devour it up:
So quick bright things come to confusion.

HERMIA

150 If then true lovers have been ever cross'd,
It stands as an edict in destiny:
Then let us teach our trial patience,
Because it is a customary cross,
As due to love as thoughts and dreams and sighs,
155 Wishes and tears, poor fancy's followers.

LYSANDER

A good persuasion: therefore, hear me, Hermia.
I have a widow aunt, a dowager
Of great revenue, and she hath no child:
From Athens is her house remote seven leagues;
160 And she respects me as her only son.
There, gentle Hermia, may I marry thee;
And to that place the sharp Athenian law
Cannot pursue us. If thou lovest me then,
Steal forth thy father's house to-morrow night;
165 And in the wood, a league without the town,
Where I did meet thee once with Helena,
To do observance to a morn of May,
There will I stay for thee.

HERMIA

My good Lysander!
I swear to thee, by Cupid's strongest bow,
170 By his best arrow with the golden head,
By the simplicity of Venus' doves,
By that which knitteth souls and prospers loves,
And by that fire which burn'd the Carthage queen,
When the false Troyan under sail was seen,
175 By all the vows that ever men have broke,
In number more than ever women spoke,
In that same place thou hast appointed me,
To-morrow truly will I meet with thee.

LYSANDER

Keep promise, love. Look, here comes Helena.

Enter HELENA

HERMIA

180 God speed fair Helena! whither away?

HELENA

Call you me fair? that fair again unsay.

Demetrius loves your fair: O happy fair!
Your eyes are lode-stars; and your tongue's sweet air
More tuneable than lark to shepherd's ear,
185 When wheat is green, when hawthorn buds appear.
Sickness is catching: O, were favour so,
Yours would I catch, fair Hermia, ere I go;
My ear should catch your voice, my eye your eye,
My tongue should catch your tongue's sweet melody.
190 Were the world mine, Demetrius being bated,
The rest I'd give to be to you translated.
O, teach me how you look, and with what art
You sway the motion of Demetrius' heart.

HERMIA

I frown upon him, yet he loves me still.

HELENA

195 O that your frowns would teach my smiles such skill!

HERMIA

I give him curses, yet he gives me love.

HELENA

O that my prayers could such affection move!

HERMIA

The more I hate, the more he follows me.

HELENA

The more I love, the more he hateth me.

HERMIA

200 His folly, Helena, is no fault of mine.

HELENA

None, but your beauty: would that fault were mine!

HERMIA

Take comfort: he no more shall see my face;
Lysander and myself will fly this place.
Before the time I did Lysander see,
205 Seem'd Athens as a paradise to me:
O, then, what graces in my love do dwell,
That he hath turn'd a heaven unto a hell!

LYSANDER

Helen, to you our minds we will unfold:
To-morrow night, when Phoebe doth behold
210 Her silver visage in the watery glass,
Decking with liquid pearl the bladed grass,
A time that lovers' flights doth still conceal,
Through Athens' gates have we devised to steal.

HERMIA

(*to* HELENA) And in the wood, where often you and I

215 Upon faint primrose-beds were wont to lie,
Emptying our bosoms of their counsel sweet,
There my Lysander and myself shall meet;
And thence from Athens turn away our eyes,
To seek new friends and stranger companies.
220 Farewell, sweet playfellow: pray thou for us;
And good luck grant thee thy Demetrius!
Keep word, Lysander: we must starve our sight
From lovers' food till morrow deep midnight.

LYSANDER
I will, my Hermia.

Exit HERMIA

Helena, adieu:
225 As you on him, Demetrius dote on you!

Exit

HELENA
How happy some o'er other some can be!
Through Athens I am thought as fair as she.
But what of that? Demetrius thinks not so;
He will not know what all but he do know:
230 And as he errs, doting on Hermia's eyes,
So I, admiring of his qualities:
Things base and vile, folding no quantity,
Love can transpose to form and dignity:
Love looks not with the eyes, but with the mind;
235 And therefore is wing'd Cupid painted blind:
Nor hath Love's mind of any judgment taste;
Wings and no eyes figure unheedy haste:
And therefore is Love said to be a child,
Because in choice he is so oft beguiled.
240 As waggish boys in game themselves forswear,
So the boy Love is perjured every where:
For ere Demetrius look'd on Hermia's eyne,
He hail'd down oaths that he was only mine;
And when this hail some heat from Hermia felt,
245 So he dissolved, and showers of oaths did melt.
I will go tell him of fair Hermia's flight:
Then to the wood will he to-morrow night
Pursue her; and for this intelligence
If I have thanks, it is a dear expense:
250 But herein mean I to enrich my pain,
To have his sight thither and back again.

Exit

ACT I. SCENE II. Athens. QUINCE'S house.

*Enter QUINCE, SNUG, BOTTOM, FLUTE,
SNOUT, and STARVELING*

QUINCE
Is all our company here?

BOTTOM
You were best to call them generally, man by man,
according to the scrip.

QUINCE
Here is the scroll of every man's name, which is
thought fit, through all Athens, to play in our
interlude before the duke and the duchess, on his
wedding-day at night.

BOTTOM
First, good Peter Quince, say what the play treats
on, then read the names of the actors, and so grow
to a point.

QUINCE
5 Marry, our play is, The most lamentable comedy, and
most cruel death of Pyramus and Thisby.

BOTTOM
A very good piece of work, I assure you, and a
merry. Now, good Peter Quince, call forth your
actors by the scroll. Masters, spread yourselves.

QUINCE
Answer as I call you. Nick Bottom, the weaver.

BOTTOM
Ready. Name what part I am for, and proceed.

QUINCE
You, Nick Bottom, are set down for Pyramus.

BOTTOM
10 What is Pyramus? a lover, or a tyrant?

QUINCE
A lover, that kills himself most gallant for love.

BOTTOM
That will ask some tears in the true performing of
it: if I do it, let the audience look to their
eyes; I will move storms, I will condole in some
measure. To the rest: yet my chief humour is for a
tyrant: I could play Ercles rarely, or a part to
tear a cat in, to make all split.
*The raging rocks
And shivering shocks
Shall break the locks
Of prison gates;
And Phibbus' car
Shall shine from far*

And make and mar
The foolish Fates.

This was lofty! Now name the rest of the players. This is Ercles' vein, a tyrant's vein; a lover is more condoling.

QUINCE
Francis Flute, the bellows-mender.

FLUTE
15 Here, Peter Quince.

QUINCE
Flute, you must take Thisby on you.

FLUTE
What is Thisby? a wandering knight?

QUINCE
It is the lady that Pyramus must love.

FLUTE
Nay, faith, let me not play a woman; I have a beard coming.

QUINCE
20 That's all one: you shall play it in a mask, and you may speak as small as you will.

BOTTOM
An I may hide my face, let me play Thisby too, I'll speak in a monstrous little voice. 'Thisne, Thisne;' 'Ah, Pyramus, lover dear! thy Thisby dear, and lady dear!'

QUINCE
No, no; you must play Pyramus: and, Flute, you Thisby.

BOTTOM
Well, proceed.

QUINCE
Robin Starveling, the tailor.

STARVELING
25 Here, Peter Quince.

QUINCE
Robin Starveling, you must play Thisby's mother. Tom Snout, the tinker.

SNOUT
Here, Peter Quince.

QUINCE
You, Pyramus' father: myself, Thisby's father:

Snug, the joiner; you, the lion's part: and, I hope, here is a play fitted.

SNUG
Have you the lion's part written? pray you, if it be, give it me, for I am slow of study.

QUINCE
30 You may do it extempore, for it is nothing but roaring.

BOTTOM
Let me play the lion too: I will roar, that I will do any man's heart good to hear me; I will roar, that I will make the duke say 'Let him roar again, let him roar again.'

QUINCE
An you should do it too terribly, you would fright the duchess and the ladies, that they would shriek; and that were enough to hang us all.

ALL
That would hang us, every mother's son.

BOTTOM
I grant you, friends, if that you should fright the ladies out of their wits, they would have no more discretion but to hang us: but I will aggravate my voice so that I will roar you as gently as any sucking dove; I will roar you an 'twere any nightingale.

QUINCE
35 You can play no part but Pyramus; for Pyramus is a sweet-faced man; a proper man, as one shall see in a summer's day; a most lovely gentleman-like man: therefore you must needs play Pyramus.

BOTTOM
Well, I will undertake it. What beard were I best to play it in?

QUINCE
Why, what you will.

BOTTOM
I will discharge it in either your straw-colour beard, your orange-tawny beard, your purple-in-grain beard, or your French-crown-colour beard, your perfect yellow.

QUINCE
Some of your French crowns have no hair at all, and then you will play bare-faced. But, masters, here are your parts: and I am to entreat you, request

you and desire you, to con them by to-morrow night; and meet me in the palace wood, a mile without the town, by moonlight; there will we rehearse, for if we meet in the city, we shall be dogged with company, and our devices known. In the meantime I will draw a bill of properties, such as our play wants. I pray you, fail me not.

BOTTOM

40 We will meet; and there we may rehearse most obscenely and courageously. Take pains; be perfect: adieu.

QUINCE

At the duke's oak we meet.

BOTTOM

Enough; hold or cut bow-strings.

Exeunt

ACT II. SCENE I. A wood near Athens.

Enter, from opposite sides, a Fairy, and PUCK

PUCK

How now, spirit! whither wander you?

FAIRY

    Over hill, over dale,
    Thorough bush, thorough brier,
    Over park, over pale,
    Thorough flood, thorough fire,
    I do wander everywhere,
    Swifter than the moon's sphere;
    And I serve the fairy queen,
    To dew her orbs upon the green.
    The cowslips tall her pensioners be:
    In their gold coats spots you see;
    Those be rubies, fairy favours,
    In those freckles live their savours:
    I must go seek some dewdrops here
    And hang a pearl in every cowslip's ear.
Farewell, thou lob of spirits; I'll be gone:
Our queen and all our elves come here anon.

PUCK

The king doth keep his revels here to-night:
5 Take heed the queen come not within his sight;
For Oberon is passing fell and wrath,
Because that she as her attendant hath
A lovely boy, stolen from an Indian king;
She never had so sweet a changeling;
10 And jealous Oberon would have the child

Knight of his train, to trace the forests wild;
But she perforce withholds the loved boy,
Crowns him with flowers and makes him all her joy:
And now they never meet in grove or green,
15 By fountain clear, or spangled starlight sheen,
But, they do square, that all their elves for fear
Creep into acorn-cups and hide them there.

FAIRY

Either I mistake your shape and making quite,
Or else you are that shrewd and knavish sprite
20 Call'd Robin Goodfellow: are not you he
That frights the maidens of the villagery;
Skim milk, and sometimes labour in the quern
And bootless make the breathless housewife churn;
And sometime make the drink to bear no barm;
25 Mislead night-wanderers, laughing at their harm?
Those that Hobgoblin call you and sweet Puck,
You do their work, and they shall have good luck:
Are not you he?

PUCK

    Thou speak'st aright;
I am that merry wanderer of the night.
30 I jest to Oberon and make him smile
When I a fat and bean-fed horse beguile,
Neighing in likeness of a filly foal:
And sometime lurk I in a gossip's bowl,
In very likeness of a roasted crab,
35 And when she drinks, against her lips I bob
And on her wither'd dewlap pour the ale.
The wisest aunt, telling the saddest tale,
Sometime for three-foot stool mistaketh me;
Then slip I from her bum, down topples she,
40 And "Tailor!" cries, and falls into a cough;
And then the whole quire hold their hips and laugh,
And waxen in their mirth and neeze and swear
A merrier hour was never wasted there.
But, room, fairy! here comes Oberon.

FAIRY

45 And here my mistress. Would that he were gone!

*Enter, from one side, OBERON, with his train;
    from the other, TITANIA, with hers*

OBERON

Ill met by moonlight, proud Titania.

TITANIA

What, jealous Oberon! Fairies, skip hence:
I have forsworn his bed and company.

OBERON

Tarry, rash wanton: am not I thy lord?

TITANIA

50 Then I must be thy lady: but I know
When thou hast stolen away from fairy land,
And in the shape of Corin sat all day,
Playing on pipes of corn and versing love
To amorous Phillida. Why art thou here,
55 Come from the farthest Steppe of India?
But that, forsooth, the bouncing Amazon,
Your buskin'd mistress and your warrior love,
To Theseus must be wedded, and you come
To give their bed joy and prosperity.

OBERON

60 How canst thou thus for shame, Titania,
Glance at my credit with Hippolyta,
Knowing I know thy love to Theseus?
Didst thou not lead him through the
glimmering night
From Perigenia, whom he ravished?
And make him with fair Ægle break his faith,
65 With Ariadne and Antiopa?

TITANIA

These are the forgeries of jealousy:
And never, since the middle summer's spring,
Met we on hill, in dale, forest or mead,
By paved fountain or by rushy brook,
70 Or in the beached margent of the sea,
To dance our ringlets to the whistling wind,
But with thy brawls thou hast disturb'd our sport.
Therefore the winds, piping to us in vain,
As in revenge, have suck'd up from the sea
75 Contagious fogs; which falling in the land
Have every pelting river made so proud
That they have overborne their continents:
The ox hath therefore stretch'd his yoke in vain,
The ploughman lost his sweat, and the green corn
80 Hath rotted ere his youth attain'd a beard;
The fold stands empty in the drowned field,
And crows are fatted with the murrion flock;
The nine men's morris is fill'd up with mud,
And the quaint mazes in the wanton green
85 For lack of tread are undistinguishable:
The human mortals want their winter here;
No night is now with hymn or carol blest:
Therefore the moon, the governess of floods,
Pale in her anger, washes all the air,
90 That rheumatic diseases do abound:
And thorough this distemperature we see
The seasons alter: hoary-headed frosts
Far in the fresh lap of the crimson rose,
And on old Hiems' thin and icy crown
95 An odorous chaplet of sweet summer buds

Is, as in mockery, set: the spring, the summer,
The childing autumn, angry winter, change
Their wonted liveries, and the mazed world,
By their increase, now knows not which is which:
100 And this same progeny of evils comes
From our debate, from our dissension;
We are their parents and original.

OBERON

Do you amend it then; it lies in you:
Why should Titania cross her Oberon?
105 I do but beg a little changeling boy,
To be my henchman.

TITANIA

Set your heart at rest:
The fairy land buys not the child of me.
His mother was a votaress of my order:
And, in the spiced Indian air, by night,
110 Full often hath she gossip'd by my side,
And sat with me on Neptune's yellow sands,
Marking the embarked traders on the flood,
When we have laugh'd to see the sails conceive
And grow big-bellied with the wanton wind;
115 Which she, with pretty and with swimming gait
Following,—her womb then rich with my
young squire,—
Would imitate, and sail upon the land,
To fetch me trifles, and return again,
As from a voyage, rich with merchandise.
120 But she, being mortal, of that boy did die;
And for her sake do I rear up her boy,
And for her sake I will not part with him.

OBERON

How long within this wood intend you stay?

TITANIA

Perchance till after Theseus' wedding-day.
125 If you will patiently dance in our round
And see our moonlight revels, go with us;
If not, shun me, and I will spare your haunts.

OBERON

Give me that boy, and I will go with thee.

TITANIA

Not for thy fairy kingdom. Fairies, away!
130 We shall chide downright, if I longer stay.

Exit TITANIA with her train

OBERON

Well, go thy way: thou shalt not from this grove

Till I torment thee for this injury. (*to* PUCK)
My gentle Puck, come hither. Thou rememberest
Since once I sat upon a promontory,
135 And heard a mermaid on a dolphin's back
Uttering such dulcet and harmonious breath
That the rude sea grew civil at her song
And certain stars shot madly from their spheres,
To hear the sea-maid's music.

PUCK

I remember.

OBERON

140 That very time I saw, but thou couldst not,
Flying between the cold moon and the earth,
Cupid all arm'd: a certain aim he took
At a fair vestal throned by the west,
And loosed his love-shaft smartly from his bow,
145 As it should pierce a hundred thousand hearts;
But I might see young Cupid's fiery shaft
Quench'd in the chaste beams of the watery moon,
And the imperial votaress passed on,
In maiden meditation, fancy-free.
150 Yet mark'd I where the bolt of Cupid fell:
It fell upon a little western flower,
Before milk-white, now purple with love's wound,
And maidens call it love-in-idleness.
Fetch me that flower; the herb I shew'd thee once:
155 The juice of it on sleeping eye-lids laid
Will make or man or woman madly dote
Upon the next live creature that it sees.
Fetch me this herb; and be thou here again
Ere the leviathan can swim a league.

PUCK

160 I'll put a girdle round about the earth
In forty minutes.

Exit

OBERON

Having once this juice,
I'll watch Titania when she is asleep,
And drop the liquor of it in her eyes.
The next thing then she waking looks upon,
165 Be it on lion, bear, or wolf, or bull,
On meddling monkey, or on busy ape,
She shall pursue it with the soul of love:
And ere I take this charm from off her sight,
As I can take it with another herb,
170 I'll make her render up her page to me.
But who comes here? I am invisible;
And I will overhear their conference.

Enter DEMETRIUS, HELENA, *following him*

DEMETRIUS

I love thee not, therefore pursue me not.
Where is Lysander and fair Hermia?
175 The one I'll slay, the other slayeth me.
Thou told'st me they were stolen unto this wood;
And here am I, and wode within this wood,
Because I cannot meet my Hermia.
Hence, get thee gone, and follow me no more.

HELENA

180 You draw me, you hard-hearted adamant;
But yet you draw not iron, for my heart
Is true as steel: leave you your power to draw,
And I shall have no power to follow you.

DEMETRIUS

Do I entice you? do I speak you fair?
185 Or, rather, do I not in plainest truth
Tell you, I do not, nor I cannot love you?

HELENA

And even for that do I love you the more.
I am your spaniel; and, Demetrius,
The more you beat me, I will fawn on you:
190 Use me but as your spaniel, spurn me, strike me,
Neglect me, lose me; only give me leave,
Unworthy as I am, to follow you.
What worser place can I beg in your love,—
And yet a place of high respect with me,—
195 Than to be used as you use your dog?

DEMETRIUS

Tempt not too much the hatred of my spirit;
For I am sick when I do look on thee.

HELENA

And I am sick when I look not on you.

DEMETRIUS

You do impeach your modesty too much,
200 To leave the city and commit yourself
Into the hands of one that loves you not;
To trust the opportunity of night
And the ill counsel of a desert place
With the rich worth of your virginity.

HELENA

205 Your virtue is my privilege: for that
It is not night when I do see your face,
Therefore I think I am not in the night;
Nor doth this wood lack worlds of company,
For you in my respect are all the world:

210 Then how can it be said I am alone,
When all the world is here to look on me?

DEMETRIUS
I'll run from thee and hide me in the brakes,
And leave thee to the mercy of wild beasts.

HELENA
The wildest hath not such a heart as you.
215 Run when you will, the story shall be changed:
Apollo flies, and Daphne holds the chase;
The dove pursues the griffin; the mild hind
Makes speed to catch the tiger; bootless speed,
When cowardice pursues and valour flies.

DEMETRIUS
220 I will not stay thy questions; let me go:
Or, if thou follow me, do not believe
But I shall do thee mischief in the wood.

HELENA
Ay, in the temple, in the town, the field,
You do me mischief. Fie, Demetrius!
225 Your wrongs do set a scandal on my sex:
We cannot fight for love, as men may do;
We should be wood and were not made to woo.

Exit DEMETRIUS

I'll follow thee and make a heaven of hell,
To die upon the hand I love so well.

Exit

OBERON
230 Fare thee well, nymph: ere he do leave this grove,
Thou shalt fly him and he shall seek thy love.

Re-enter PUCK

Hast thou the flower there? Welcome, wanderer.

PUCK
Ay, there it is.

OBERON
        I pray thee, give it me.
I know a bank where the wild thyme blows,
235 Where oxlips and the nodding violet grows,
Quite over-canopied with luscious woodbine,
With sweet musk-roses and with eglantine:
There sleeps Titania sometime of the night,
Lull'd in these flowers with dances and delight;
240 And there the snake throws her enamell'd skin,
Weed wide enough to wrap a fairy in:
And with the juice of this I'll streak her eyes,
And make her full of hateful fantasies.
Take thou some of it, and seek through this grove:
245 A sweet Athenian lady is in love
With a disdainful youth: anoint his eyes;
But do it when the next thing he espies
May be the lady: thou shalt know the man
By the Athenian garments he hath on.
250 Effect it with some care, that he may prove
More fond on her than she upon her love:
And look thou meet me ere the first cock crow.

PUCK
Fear not, my lord, your servant shall do so.

Exeunt

(5114 words)
Source: Shakespeare, W. *A Midsummer Night's Dream. (1595–96) The Complete Works of William Shakespeare*, http://shakespeare.mit.edu/midsummer/full.html.

Initial Insight

1. What is the story about? Write down anything that intuitively comes to you.

_____

_____

_____

_____

_____

2. In which settings does the play take place?

_____

3. Who are the main characters?

_____

_____

4. What is the mood and atmosphere of the play? Write down any adjectives you associate with it.

_____

_____

_____

Reader's Response

Consider the following questions. Discuss your answers with one or more partners.

1. Was your reading experience of the play more positive or more negative? Which elements contributed to that impression?

2. After reading the play, how would you explain its title?

3. Who do you consider to be the most important character of the play?

4. Did you find it difficult to distinguish between certain characters? Which ones, and why?

5. What are your thoughts on the representation of men and women in the play?

6. Does the play's ending qualify as an example of "and they lived happily ever after"? Why or why not?

LANGUAGE FOCUS

While modern English has only one second person pronoun—"you"—Middle English had two: "thou" in singular and "you" in plural. Parallel to what can be observed in contemporary French and Spanish, over time, people also started employing "you" in singular to convey politeness or formality. In the early-modern English of Shakespeare's time, "thou" and "you" could indicate fine distinctions of social status and interpersonal relationships:

You	Thou (subject) / Thee (object)
• addresses social superiors	• addresses social inferiors
• addresses social equals of the upper class	• addresses social equals of the lower class
• used in public	• used in private
• expresses formality and politeness	• expresses familiarity or intimacy
• shows respect and admiration	• shows scorn or contempt

1. Which pronoun would you expect the group of craftsmen preparing a play to use? Which pronoun do they actually use, and how does this fit into the play?

2. In act 1, scene 1, what could explain Theseus's use of _thee_ and _you_ to address Egeus and his daughter? (See 1.1.21 and 1.1.46.)

3. In act 2, scene 1, explain the pronoun shift that occurs as Titania and Oberon quarrel over the changeling boy. (See 2.1.123-129.)

4. In the exchange between Demetrius and Helena, what do you observe regarding the use of pronouns, and how does this support what you know about the situation between them? (See 2.1.205–213.)

MyBookshelf > My eLab
> Exercises > Part II: Drama
> Chapter 10: A Midsummer
Night's Dream > Vocabulary
Comprehension

Close Reading

As you read the text again, pay attention to elements that seem significant to understanding and interpreting the story. The following guided reading questions will help you.

ACT 1, SCENE 1

1. What is the event Theseus and Hippolyta are preparing at the outset of the play?

2. Who is Hermia in love with? Who does Egeus want Hermia to marry?

3. What three choices does Theseus give to Hermia? What is Hermia's response?

4. What is Lysander's plan to circumvent Egeus's wish?

5. How does Helena feel toward Hermia? What does she decide to do at the end of the scene, and why?

ACT 1, SCENE 2

6. Why is the group of craftsmen meeting?

7. Who seems to be in charge of the meeting, and why?

8. Why does Flute not want to play Thisbe?

9. Why does the role of the lion worry Quince and Bottom?

10. Where do the men agree to rehearse, and why?

_____

_____

ACT 2, SCENE 1

11. What kind of reputation does Puck have, and why?

_____

_____

_____

12. What are Oberon and Titania fighting about?

_____

_____

13. What does Oberon send Puck to find?

_____

_____

14. What does Oberon overhear in the woods?

_____

_____

15. What does Oberon decide when Puck returns?

_____

_____

MyBookshelf > My eLab
> Exercises > Part II: Drama
> Chapter 10: A Midsummer
Night's Dream > Close Reading:
Additional Questions

THE LANGUAGE OF LITERATURE

The effect of any text is to a very large extent determined by the author's diction and use of figures of speech and other literary devices. Use the following questions to focus your attention on how the author uses language in the story.

A. What **genre** and subgenre best describes this play?

a) domestic tragedy   b) farce   c) romantic comedy   d) tragicomedy

B. In act 1, scene 1, Theseus uses the rose as a **metaphor** to describe the options Hermia has if she refuses to marry Demetrius. Explain the metaphor by linking it to two of the three possible choices, which you identified in Close Reading question 3 (page 130).

But earthlier happy is the rose distill'd,
Than that which withering on the virgin thorn
Grows, lives and dies in single blessedness. (1.1.78–80)

C. _Pyramus and Thisby_, which a group of actors is preparing to stage in act 1, scene 2, is an example of

a) a secondary text   b) a chorus   c) a play-within-the-play   d) a satire

Analytical Reading

After making specific observations, you are ready to analyze the subject of your close reading. The following questions will help you look for thematic patterns, establish relationships and identify specific examples of literary devices or principles.

Questions 11 to 14 pertain to passages of the play that are not included in this chapter. To answer those questions, you may wish to read the entire play, which is included in My eLab Documents.

MyBookshelf > My eLab
> Documents > Part II: Drama
> Chapter 10: A Midsummer
Night's Dream

1. In order to help you analyze the play more effectively, complete the List of Characters chart available in My eLab. Use the information gleaned from act 1.

2. In order to help you analyze the play more effectively, summarize the action, the characters and the setting in each scene after reading it more closely. Use the scene summary charts provided in My eLab Documents. Use them as reference charts to keep track of the action and how it is structured in the plot.

3. *A Midsummer Night's Dream* follows the five-act structure explained on page 110. For each act, explain in a few sentences which action(s) or event(s) represent the key moments in the plot.

   a. Act 1: Exposition   **d.** Act 4: Falling action
   b. Act 2: Complicating action   **e.** Act 5: Dénouement
   c. Act 3: Climax

4. What is the **central plot** of the play, and what are the **subplots**? How do the minor characters in the subplots influence the central plot?

5. In *A Midsummer Night's Dream*, several characters are not clearly distinguishable as **protagonists** or **antagonists**. Explain this by considering the relationships between the different characters.

6. The four lovers, Hermia, Helena, Lysander and Demetrius, closely resemble one another in different ways. Examine their situation, personality traits and ambitions. What do they have in common, and how are they different?

7. **Conflict** is the driving force behind the plot. It also plays a key role in the theme, as the conflicts faced by the characters concern their troublesome experience of love. Explain how each type of conflict listed below is taken up in the play.

Character vs. human: _____

_____

_____

Character vs. society: _____

_____

Character vs. self: _____

_____

8. **Setting** refers not only to the physical location of a story, but also to the atmosphere and time. What do the woods represent? What is the mood of the scenes set in the woods? What time of the year and what time of the day do they take place?

9. In act 1, scene 1, Lysander tells Hermia that "The course of true love never did run smooth." What does this imply, and how does it **foreshadow** the action in the play?

10. In act 2, scene 1, what point does Titania make about her relationship with Oberon in her soliloquy? Pay special attention to the following lines:

> The childing autumn, angry winter, change
> Their wonted liveries, and the mazed world,
> By their increase, now knows not which is which:
> And this same progeny of evils comes
> From our debate, from our dissension; (2.1.97-101)

11. In act 2, scene 2, what does Hermia dream about? How does this dream act as a **metaphor** for her real circumstances?

12. In act 3, scene 1, why does Bottom's idea of a Prologue appear ridiculous?

13. Summarize the orders Oberon gives to Puck toward the end of act 3 to ensure that "all things shall be peace" and that the play's conflicts are resolved.

14. Explain how each quotation represents an important event in act 4, scene 1.

"I know you two are rival enemies."	(Speaker: _____)
"I beg the law, the law, upon his head."	(Speaker: _____)
"It seems to me / That yet we sleep, we dream."	(Speaker: _____)
"I have had a most rare vision."	(Speaker: _____)

In which way do these events dissipate the conflict?

_____

_____

15. How does Shakespeare use the fairy world to create **dramatic irony** in the play?

Food for Thought

The following questions encourage you to turn a critical eye to your earlier observations and analyses. They introduce elements and considerations that will lead you to formulate new questions and set tentative hypotheses. Discuss these to further your insight into the text.

1. A short video excerpt of a contemporary performance of *A Midsummer Night's Dream*, directed by Julie Taymor (2014), is available in My eLab Documents. Watch the recording and discuss your answers to the following questions with one or more partners.

    a. Which characters appear in the excerpt?

    b. Do any of the characters look or behave differently from what you expected based on your reading of the play?

    c. Did you prefer reading the lines or hearing them being spoken? Why?

    d. In what way does the stage setting render the magical and whimsical aspect of the woods?

    e. Why do you think the audience laughs at the line, "But who comes here? I am invisible; / And I will overhear their conference"?

    f. Which elements of the stage design and props would have been impossible in Shakespeare's time? What do you feel they contribute to the play, if anything?

    g. Which aspect of the performance do you feel enhances the play the most?

MyBookshelf > My eLab
> Documents > Part II: Drama
> A Midsummer Night's Dream

2. Dreams play a large part in this play. Not only are they mentioned several times throughout the play, but Puck's speech at the end of the play also refers explicitly to the act of dreaming. What are the different implications of dreaming portrayed in the play?

3. How does the **play-within-the-play** *Pyramus and Thisby* allow Shakespeare to reflect upon the nature of the theatre?

4. How do the different couples depicted in the play represent the various stages in a relationship, and what different aspects of love do these couples implicitly represent?

5. Hermia and Helena seem just as foolish in love as Demetrius and Lysander, although they are not under an enchantment. Discuss how this may act as a reflection on societal values and on gender.

6. Is the "love-juice"—the potion extracted from the love-in-idleness flower—as magical and unlikely as it sounds? What can it be considered a metaphor of?

7. The worlds of the court, the Athenian lovers, the craftsmen actors and the fairies intersect, but remain mostly separate. Referring to the list of *dramatis personae* and the work you have done in this chapter, complete the chart with the characters. Identify the characters that pass from their world to another.

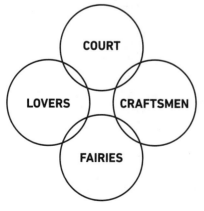

    a. Court: _____

    b. Athenian lovers: _____

       Which character passes to the world of the court? _____

    c. Craftsmen actors: _____

       Which character passes to the world of the fairies? _____

    d. Fairies: _____

       Which characters pass to the world of the lovers? _____

8. Based on your understanding of the play, would you argue that Shakespeare had a positive or negative view of the themes presented in the play and on life in general? Why?

Presenting an Analysis

Writing | Analyzing the Treatment of a Central Theme

In *A Midsummer Night's Dream*, the central theme of love can be broken down into different conflicts that may arise in the quest for love. Prepare an analytical essay with a thesis statement that investigates how the theme is taken up in the main plot and the subplots, and how the conflicts between the characters help to develop different aspects of the theme.

Example:

By introducing fairies who intervene in human relationships that seem hopeless at the outset of the play, Shakespeare not only suggests that love is often inexplicable but he also emphasizes that any love is worth pursuing, however foolish it may seem.

In each of the body paragraphs, provide evidence and examples from the text to point out the importance of your chosen subplot(s) and character(s). Refer to the work you did in the Analytical Reading and Food for Thought sections. Make sure to provide clear examples from the text to illustrate and support your analysis.

(Refer to Part V, Writing about Literature, on page 271 for more information on essay format and structure.)

Speaking | Presenting Contrasting Passages

A Midsummer Night's Dream is heavily based on contrasts. Many characters, situations or settings have a double or an opposite. Pinpoint three to five examples of such contrasts, supported with textual evidence. Briefly summarize each, pointing out similarities and differences between the two elements that make up the contrast. Then, explain how these contrasts further the plot or the themes of the play.

Prepare a cohesive presentation in which you demonstrate insight into the play through your selection and discussion of contrasting elements and relevant passages. Practise reading these passages out loud so you can effectively include them in your presentation.

(Refer to Appendix 2 on page 297 for more information on presentation format and structure.)

MyBookshelf > My eLab
> Exercises > Grammar and
Accuracy

Lungs

– Duncan Macmillan

This chapter focuses on the following:

- Narrative situation
- Characters and characterization
- Symbolism
- Language Focus: speech features
- The Language of Literature: dramatic devices and figures of speech
- Theme

Connect with the Text

Take stock of your opinions on the following questions. Discuss them with one or more partners.

1. Based on the play's title, what do you expect it to be about?

2. What is your outlook on the future? What are your hopes, your fears?

3. What do you believe people can do to limit or reduce their environmental footprint? What do you believe you can personally do?

4. What are some of the things you do to deal with stress or stressful situations?

5. Consider the stage set design for *Lungs* in the photo. What questions or expectations does it spark in you?

Text in Context

Duncan Macmillan (1980–) began writing plays while completing a bachelor's degree in film and theatre at Reading University (United Kingdom). Rather than writing for the big screen, he was drawn to playwriting, which he describes as "live decision-making" because the characters' decisions and actions are what moves the plot forward. Macmillan's characters tend to question themselves on issues of personal responsibility—are they to blame? Is there anything they can do about their situation? Macmillan has focused such reflections on contemporary anxieties in his acclaimed plays on parenthood and climate change (*Lungs*), addiction (*People, Places, and Things*) and anxiety and suicide (*The Most Humane Way to Kill a Lobster, Every Brilliant Thing*). Due to his choice of themes, he has been called the playwright for the millennial generation, and has received several prestigious awards for his work, including Best Play for *Lungs*

at London's 2013 Off West End Awards as well as UK Theatre Best Director Award for his adaptation of George Orwell's *1984*. Seeking inspiration in his own fears and anxieties as he approached age 30, Macmillan wrote the script of *Lungs* in a two-day span, before further polishing it while actors rehearsed it live on stage.

Exploratory Reading

Read the play a first time without interruption. Keep an open mind and take a mental note of your reactions and observations. Soak up the events, atmosphere and language without looking for any specific elements. When you are finished, answer the questions below the text.

Note: The following is an abridged version of the play. You will find the complete play in My eLab Documents.

MyBookshelf > My eLab
> Documents > Part II: Drama
> Chapter 11: Lungs

Lungs   **Duncan Macmillan**

This play is written to be performed on a bare stage. There is no scenery, no furniture, no props and no mime. There are no costume changes. Light and sound should not be used to indicate a change in time or place.

A forward slash mark (/) marks the point of interruption in overlapping dialogue.

A comma on a separate line (,) indicates a pause, a rest or a silence, the length of which should be determined by the context.

The absence of a full stop at the end of a line indicates a point of interruption, a trailing off or an interruption of thought.

There is no interval.

Lights up.

W	A baby?
M	Breathe.
W	A baby?
M	I was just thinking.
5 W	About the future.
M	We'd have to change how we live.
W	The planet, use less
M	no, that's, well yes but that's not
W	okay.
10 M	I'm freaking you out.
W	Not / freaking me out.
M	Completely. You thought you'd be the one.
W	No.
M	The one to say it, yes. To say yes, yes okay, I'm
15	ready, yes, let's do it, yes.
W	That's
M	to put the pressure on, yes, / to try to convince me to

W	pressure? Put the pressure on, I'm not a a a a
20 M	we're having a conversation. That's all that's happening. All that's happening is we're having a conversation.
W	You're having a conversation.
M	We're having a conversation.
25 W	A conversation you're starting.
M	A conversation I'm, yes, that I'm trying to start.
W	A conversation that you're deciding to start now.
M	Yes.
W	In Ikea.
30 M	I hadn't planned to.
W	No. Okay. Yes. Okay.
M	Do you want some water / or
W	that kid with the panda is staring.
M	You're hyperventilating.
35 W	Don't exaggerate.
M	If it's too much
W	it's not / too much.
M	If it's too much we can put it back in the box,

just put a lid on it and lock it away and then later when
40 you're feeling less freaked out / we can

W   I'm not freaked out.

M   Alright fine okay.

W   I'm not freaked out I'm just surprised. I'm surprised I'm fucking shocked actually. I'm

45 M   freaked out.

W   I'm not.

M   You are.

W   I'm completely freaked out yes because why don't you ever, how can you, why didn't you, why would you

50 not talk to me about this / I wish you'd let me IN I wish you'd let me IN to your head. Into your fucking impenetrable fucking

M   I'm talking to you now. I'm telling you now. We're talking, we're talking now, we're having a conversation.

55 When should I have

W   we're not. We're not. This isn't a conversation.

M   Okay.

W   It just isn't.

M   Okay.

60 W   I don't know what it is but I know for fucking certain it's not a

M   right okay okay.

W   Can we at least get out of the queue? Everybody's

M   of course, I'm sorry, I didn't mean to just

65   ,

W   yes. I need a minute. Can we put it back in the box?

M   There's no rush.

W   Just to

M   there's no hurry.

70 W   Catch my breath.

M   It's a conversation.

W   Bit of a walk or something. Ten minutes. Meet you back at the car.

M   Okay. **[ellipsis 1]**

75 W   What's wrong?

M   You said ten minutes.

W   I needed to think.

M   It's pitch dark. You stink of fags.

W   It's snowing. Is it snowing?

80 M   You've not got a coat.

W   This weather is insane.

M   Coldest winter ever they've just said. Hottest summer, coldest winter.

W   And you left the engine running.

85 M   I was listening to the radio.

W   I'm okay.

M   I know I just worried.

W   No need.

M   Good.

90   ,

W   Did we get any of the stuff we came here for?

M   I went back but they'd

W   shit.

M   Yeah.

95   ,

W   A baby?

       ,

M   I was just thinking.

       ,

100 W   Can we just we will talk about it but

M   I know.

W   not right now. I'm too

M   yeah, me too.

105 W   Can I drive?

M   Course.

W   You can play your tape. Let me hear your new songs.

M   They're not finished.

110 W   Okay, well, let's just sit and not say anything then okay? Just be silent, just not have to deal with this right away because

M   good.

W   I don't have the

115 M   it's okay. Whenever you want to talk about it we / can

W   no okay of course good but not now I don't have anything to say about it right now because it's such a shock, it's such an enormous, you can't just say

120 something like that to someone you can't just say that to me and expect me to just be fine and rational and clear-headed / and not

M   when would be the right time to / mention

W   I don't know I don't have the answers I just know

125 that that wasn't it.

       ,

    I'm sorry.

M   I'm sorry too.

130 W　You're right. It is. It is

M　yes.

W　Something we should

M　we should.

W　We should be, yes, be talking about. We should.

135 Yes.

M　Good.

W　Because, fuck, we're not getting

M　I know.

W　Any younger.

140 M　No.

'

So are we talking about it or

W　no.

'

145 Yes.

'

Go on.

M　With what?

W　With, you were saying, with, you know, what?

150 What were you saying?

M　I've said it all.

W　Then say it again because I couldn't hear you before because people were staring and I was pushing a trolley and holding a lamp and I couldn't breathe.

155 M　You got the gist.

W　I think so.

M　Or you wouldn't have got as freaked out as you did.

W　Touché.

'

160 Touché.

'

So.

Where do we go from here?

M　Well, we should try to leave the car park.

165 W　Sarcasm? Right now? You think that's going to

M　I'd like to hear your opinion.

W　Yes.

M　Of course.

W　Of course yes.

170 M　It's a two-way

W　I know.

M　It's a two-way thing and so

W　but

M　go on.

175 W　Alright, it's this it's

I have no idea. I don't opinion? I don't have it's like you've punched me in the face then asked me a maths question / while I'm still on the

M　like I punched you in the face?

180 W　You know what I mean.

M　No.

W　Okay. Yes. Let's do it. Let's do it. Yes. Let's do it. Yes.

M　I'm not

185 W　I'm saying yes.

M　I'm not asking a question.

W　Aren't you?

M　No.

W　You're starting a conversation.

190 M　I'm trying to.

W　Well it's started and now it's happening and I'm saying yes.

M　Right.

W　Look, alright, listen, you have to understand

195 alright, I'm thinking out loud here so please just let me talk just let me think it through out loud please alright don't just jump in if I say something wrong or stupid just let me think okay because I've always wanted alright and I'm talking in the abstract I've always wanted

200 I've always had a sense or an idea of myself always defined myself okay as a person who would,

that my purpose in life that my function on this planet would be to and not that I ever thought about it like that it's only now because you're asking or not

205 asking but mentioning, starting the conversation only because of that that I'm now even thinking about it but it's always sort of been a given for me an assumption ever since I was a little girl playing with dolls I mean long long long before I met you, it's never been

210 what I guess it should be which is a a a a a a an extension of an expression of you know, fucking love or whatever, a coming together of two people it's always been this alright and this sounds stupid and naïve but it's always been an image,

215 I guess, of myself with a bump and glowing in that motherly or pushing a pram or a cot with a mobile above it or singing to it reading Beatrix Potter or Dr Seuss, I don't care, never cared about it being a boy

or girl just small and soft and adorable and with that
milky head smell and the tiny socks and giggles and
yes vomit even it's all part of it, looking after

      it, caring for it that's I think that's the impulse
and there's always been a father in the picture but sort
of a blurry background generic man, I'm sorry, it's just
this picture of my life I've always had since I was able
to think and I've never ever questioned it. Never.

      And I've pushed it all down and focused on my
career, on my studies, on myself and now it's becoming,
potentially becoming a bit real I'm going to have to
think about it for a second please just a a a a a or
much longer in fact because well because I'm not an
idiot, I'm a thoughtful, very thoughtful person and I
want to do everything for the right reason or at least
a good reason and I believe in questioning and never
just blindly accepting or and it's going to take a lot of
effort to unravel or to to to to to to excavate not
excavate but excavate all of those

      previously held beliefs and assumptions because
it's important probably the most important thing you
could do to bring another person a yes a person an
actually living breathing thinking because they won't
stay small forever and I think don't they I think a lot
of people think about them being small, just tiny and
sweet and unconditional with their eyes and giggles
and tiny little fingers gripping your thumb and I do I
did I think I thought like that because it's too hard like
we're not quite designed to be able to fully comprehend
the the the the

M   enormity

W   or whatever which is a maybe it's a survival mech-
anism perhaps an inbuilt thing because, fuck, if you
thought about it if you really properly thought about it
before actually doing it then you'd never

      ever actually fucking do it because it's too fucking
too fucking

M   enormous

W   it is it is it is it's fucking enormous, fucking
enormous fucking the purpose of life itself, the
purpose, the meaning, the meaninglessness, the love
and the horror and the hope and the fear and everything the volume of all of it turned right up, the rest
of your life the rest of someone else's life committing
someone to something forever, ancestry, the seven

and a half thousand

      generations of human history and I don't even
know much about my own grandparents, let alone my
great grandparents or or or or and it's their genes, their
genetic stuff, really, them, these dead people moving
around making choices for this little, this tiny, but
that's not the whole thing,

M   breathe.

W   This is what I'm saying this is what I'm saying
because they don't stay small, they grow up and
become people, they become grown-ups like everyone
else, they become their own grown-up people and
they think their own thoughts and they buy their own
clothes and they leave home and they hate you.

      Alright, because I'm thinking out loud.
      I'm thinking and talking.

M   I didn't say anything.

W   We're having a conversation.

M   Yes.

W   That's all that's happening.

M   Look, let's get home and drink some gin and see
if we want to talk about it. **[ellipsis 2]**

W   And the planet.

M   I don't want ice. Take my ice.

W   The planet. Because you worry about the same
things I do, you care about the same

M   right, yes.

W   And they say don't they that if you really care
about the planet, if you really care about the future of
mankind then don't have children.

M   Do they?

W   I mean, they actually say if you really care about
the planet then kill yourself but I'm
      I mean, I'm not going to do that.
      So,
      because there's, what, there's seven billion people
or so, there's too many people and there's not enough
of everything so really the right thing to do, the ethical
thing to do is to not contribute to that, particularly
people like us.

M   People like

W   car driving, plastic bag using, aerosol spraying,
avocado importing, Western,

M   but we're good people.

W   Exactly. We are we are we are good people yes we

are. Good.

310   Are we?

M   You can't think about that stuff.

W   No I know. It's not our responsibility. And any way, so much about it is unknown. And what if this kid, this hypothetical what if she, or he, this imaginary

315 little Edwin or Hannah

M   Edwin?

W   What if she or he was the person to work it all out and save everything, everyone, the world, polar bears, Bangladesh, everything, we don't know so

320 M   no, but

W   or we could plant a forest. We could work out the carbon footprint of the expanding nappies in the landfill and the Baby Gap hoodies flown in from the Congo or wherever and we could plant trees, entire

325 forests, make something pure and and and oxygenating, so

M   how do you factor that in?

W   Exactly.

M   The world is going to need good people in it.

330   With everything that's happening. We can't just leave it to the people who don't think, the people who just have child after child without ever properly examining their their their their capacity for love. I mean, that's what's wrong with everything isn't it?

335 W   Yes. I know. Exactly. Hang on what? Are you saying some people are too stupid to have children?

M   No. No of course not. But yes. Some people, lots of people, aren't thinking it through, not fully, and maybe the smartest, most caring, most informed

340 people aren't having children.

W   Right.

M   So it's their genes that aren't surviving. So things are getting less caring and less informed and more savage.

345 W   So, to save the planet it'll be, what, eugenics or

M   no, no.

W   Sterilise? Exterminate?

M   Not what I'm saying.

W   Camps? Enforced

350 M   no. Of course not I'm not I don't have the answers.

    Yes, some people are saying that maybe that will happen but we'll be long dead by the time that's

    I mean, you know more about this stuff than I

355 do. You're the one doing the PhD.

    But, yes, if we're being honest, really, teen mothers in tracksuits with fags in their mouths, smacking their kids in supermarkets, being a gran by thirty, multiplying like rats,

360 W   rats?

M   Meanwhile the people who read books, the people who think and try to help and I know I'm being a bit fascist here, I'm just playing Devil's advocate here of course I am but there are some thoughtful people who

365 are waiting for the perfect circumstances and it'll never happen there's no such thing as perfect so the

    world is overcrowded and people think well I don't want to bring my child into this world full of crack dealers and pimps and homeless, and I know

370 this sounds reactionary but let's not be politically, you know, correct about this for a second, there are some people who just shouldn't have children. They just shouldn't.

    And would it be such a great loss if those people,

375 you know, couldn't have children? Or I mean,

    isn't this what you were saying? I'm only carrying on from what you were saying.

W   I think I'm going to be sick. No I'm not. I am actually I think yes.

380 M   Do you want me to

W   I know that's what I feel, what I think sometimes, but when you say it out loud it sounds like the worst, cruellest, sickest, most hateful

M   what do you want me to do?

385 W   Just a cuddle and shut up for a bit I think would be good actually.

[…]

M   Good morning.

W   You're cheerful.

M   I think spring's here.

390 W   You made breakfast.

M   We should move. Go to Brighton. Isn't that what people do? Get some outdoor space. Fresh air. Room for goalposts. Trampoline. Paddling pool. Trees. We should plant some trees. Put a bit more oxygen into

395 the world. Like you said. Do our bit.

W   We should get married.

M   Let's think about it.

W   You don't want to?

M   One thing at a time maybe.

400 W   I'll make coffee.

M   You should get a job.

W   Once I've got my PhD my / prospects will be

M   we can't both be

W   I know this isn't very feminist of me but actually

405 sweetheart I think you should, if we're serious about

this, you should get something a bit more full-time and

        I know you get free records and time off to do

gigs but we've both got to make sacrifices and I'm not

going to be able to work once I get bigger and then

410 for a lot of that first year and we're going to need to

M   plenty of musicians have children.

W   Plenty of successful musicians have children.

        Sorry. I didn't mean that. It's just the

        economy is in freefall and nobody's buying vinyl

415 anymore. You really don't want to get married?

    […]

W   What's wrong?

M   Nothing.

        ,

        You should quit smoking.

420   ,

        If you're serious / about

W   yes you're right.

M   You're going to be a home, an ecosystem and

you're / polluting

425 W   I've said yes shut up yes I've said yes alright so /

please just

M   it doesn't make sense to me that you could want

to be a mother and still be smoking.

W   You don't understand because you've never been

430 addicted to anything.

M   Those two impulses seem to me to be completely

W   you're right.

        So shut up.

        ,

435   Good luck.

M   I'm doing it for you.

W   For us.

M   That's what I mean.

    […]

M   How long does it say?

440 W   A minute. Two minutes.

M   Alright.

W   Let's leave it for three just to make sure.

M   Check it each minute but then keep checking.

W   Good good yes good. I'll come and get you.

445 M   Right okay. What?

W   I can't go when you're right there.

M   You've peed in front / of me before, you've

W   I know but I've got performance anxiety

as it is and

450 M   some water I could get you some

W   please yes but then will that count if it's come /

straight through you

M   or will it have to sort of percolate I see what

you're saying.

455 W   It doesn't say in the instructions.

M   Do I really have to leave?

W   This isn't one of the special bits. Pissing on a

plastic stick isn't one of the sacramental

M   yes. I want to, I want to see all of it I think it's all

460 W   fine okay okay okay run the tap or

M   how's that?

W   Ssshhh.

M   Gush or a trickle?

W   Please.

465 M   Sorry.

        ,

        Shouldn't keep it running like this.

W   Can we not think of the planet for one second?

M   Sorry.

470 W   Okay that's

        I think

        yes,

        ,

        right.

475   Now we wait.

        ,

        How long's that been?

M   Thirty seconds.

W   Really? Wow.

480 M   A minute.

W   How about

M   two minutes.

W   Right.

M   Three.

485 W   Okay,

here we go.

,

M   Where's my phone?

W   You hate your parents.

490 M   That's not true.

W   Okay, I hate your parents but
I mean they're not like mine, mine are

M   you could have called them already.

W   I'm going to dial. Do you want to speak to them?

495 M   No.

W   After, I mean, they'll want to speak to you.

M   Why?

W   I don't know, they might, they might want to say,
you know

500 M   I could call mine at the same time.

W   You could of course you could, just let me, I just,
let's just get this first call done and then, you know,
then people know, then it's out and

M   you want them to be the first to know.

505 W   Is that okay?

M   Before mine.

W   I just
yes.

M   Okay.

[…]

510 W   Oh.
Oh no.

M   Blood.

W   Not this. Not to us.

M   Hospital. Now.

515 W   I can't bear this.

M   I'll wait outside.

W   No. I need you.

M   Okay.

,

520 W   At least I can start smoking again.

M   Oh sweetheart. Shit.

W   You were right. We shouldn't have got excited.

M   Don't be silly.

W   We shouldn't have told anyone. We knew this
525 could happen.
Do you have change for the coffee machine?

M   Give me the keys.

W   I'm not an invalid.

M   Talk to me.

530 W   I don't want to.

M   Hold my hand then.

W   It's for the best probably isn't it? Would have
completely taken over our lives. So much time and
money, so much that could go wrong. End up sleepless
535 with worry or with our heads in the sand. The
world. Who'd want to have a child now? We should
be happy. This is a relief it is it is it is we should be
relieved we should take a deep breath and give a huge
sigh of thank fuck for that because we're not going to
540 add to any of it, we're not going to add yet one more
lost person into this crowded little world so good for
us. Let's go on holiday. Let's fly somewhere.
Let's spend our money on us before the global
economy completely implodes. Let's crack open some
545 champagne. When the riots start let's join in. Let's
smash something. Start some fires. If we see an
electric car with a baby on board sticker let's ram it off
the road the fucking hypocrites. The damage they're
doing. It's a relief for you I suppose.

550 M   Why would you say that?

W   Just
you never quite seemed as

M   that's not true.

W   It wasn't as necessary or

555 M   it was my idea.

,

W   Yeah. I'm just trying to
I'm just trying

,

560 M   get some sleep.

,

I'm here.
I heard you get up, can I sit with you?
You fell asleep. I brought you in here.

565 Goodnight.
Good morning.
Goodnight.
I made some tea.
I'll see you after work.

570 Have you been sat there all day?
It's getting dark.
It's getting light.
Come to bed.
You fell asleep.

575   I woke up and you were gone.
      You've not said a word to me for days.

      ,

      Baby.

      ,

580   What's wrong?

W   Please don't. Don't ask me that.

M   I want to know.

[...]

M   I kissed someone else. At work.
      The new girl. The temp. I didn't talk to her about
585 you and I don't know why, didn't say I had a

      ,

      she was nice to me. She was nice to me. We
talked about music.

      And she kissed me and I didn't stop her.

590   However hurt you feel and raw and angry that's
how I'm feeling too and that I love you more than
anything. I'd cut off my arms for you. I'd pull my eyes
out. And I'm sorry. And I know that if I go back in on
Monday and she's there I might do it again.

595   I could see our future together, this picture of
what our lives were going to be like and it feels like
I've been burgled and I have to live in this stupid
angry version of the world where the person I adore,
my best friend in the world can't even look at me and
600 where I can't look at myself.

      I miss you.

      I want to sit opposite you in a restaurant, share
a bottle of wine. I want to go to the cinema and hold
your hand. Run around in the park.

605   We can try again.
      Adopt maybe.

      ,

      Why are you smiling?

W   For the first time in ages I feel a little clarity.

610   I'm sad. I've been really sad and I don't know
if that's ever going to go away completely. I'm sorry
I've not been able to tell you what I've needed. I don't
know what I needed.

      Yes I do.

615   I needed you to be patient with me. To wait as
long as it took. I needed you to be braver than me and
put your own feelings second and to understand. To
try to imagine what it's like to miscarry. To realize that

there are certain feelings I'm trying to cope with and
620 protecting you from and I'm working hard.

      Most of all I needed you to not kiss someone
else.

      So, I'm being sensible for both of us. That's it.
Lucky we don't have kids.

625   ,

      So there you are.

M   You look good.

W   No I don't, shut up. Thank you.

M   No, it's

630 W   thanks for meeting me.

M   Oh, it's no, of course. I was surprised when you
asked

W   right.

M   Starbucks.

635 W   Oh. Yeah. Well. You know.

M   Didn't seem like you.

W   Beard.

M   I know.

W   It's good.

640 M   Oh. Yeah.

W   I didn't know who else to tell.

M   No, I'm glad you did.

W   Mum was very fond of you.

M   I thought she hated me.

645 W   Yeah.

      ,

M   How was the funeral?

W   It's tomorrow.

M   Oh.

650 W   Come with me. Will you come with me? I mean,
if / you want to.

M   Really? Because

W   weird? Too weird, forget it. Sorry.

M   Of course, I'll, yeah if you want me to.

655 W   I do yeah that would be good. You don't need to
check with

M   check with what? What?

W   Nothing.

      ,

660 M   My dad died. Few months back.

W   You never said.

M   No, I know I didn't know if

W   oh, no, that's

665 We're getting to that age now.
Scary. Be just us left soon.

Fuck. Look at you.
M   You too.
670 W   Just want to just
take just a second.
Mental picture.
Click.
M   It's alright.
675 W   No, I know. I know.
M   Oh, please don't
you don't need to oh.
W   I'm sorry, I promised myself I wouldn't
M   it's okay. It's okay.
680 W   Mess. Already. Brilliant. Well done me.
M   You're okay, just
you're okay.

W   How are you anyway? How's life? How's work?
685 Good? Everything good?
M   Yeah / it's
W   how's the temp?
M   Oh. Yeah. No, we're not
W   no?
690 M   No we're, we, / I mean we
W   that's really I'm really I'm sorry about that.
M   No no no, I mean after we, you and I once we I
just wasn't
I didn't have the energy for another
695 not right away, not
W   so you didn't I mean with the
temp
that didn't you didn't
M   oh, well, yeah but I mean, that was just
700 fucking hell.
That was this whole other
W   right.
M   Thing.
W   Right. Yeah.
705 M   How about you?
W   Do we really want to talk about this? I mean, I
don't want to talk about this. I know that we're not that
you and I are no longer but I still don't want to hear

about your your your sex life or
710 M   no okay.
W   So you're not together now?
M   No. Fuck. No. No. No.
No.
W   Right. Okay.
715 M   Now I'm with
W   oh okay.
M   Yeah.
W   You don't have to
M   I don't mind.
720 W   I don't want to hear it.

So okay.
This is horrible.
I don't know what I was expecting.
725 I think I might leave before we start talking about
the weather.
M   It's fucked.
W   It is. It's impossible. Sweat's pouring off me like
M   everything's shut down. City can't cope with it.
730 W   Keep passing out.
M   What?
W   Dehydration or I carry a bottle around with me
but I just go through it like
M   yeah.
735 W   So I take two but then I'm just lugging around all
this water and it's
M   I know I'm the same it's
W   we weren't right together were we?
We were good people, weren't we, but
740 it just wasn't meant to be.
M   You don't believe in any of that predetermination,
destiny stuff.
W   I do now.
M   Oh, sorry. Really?
745 W   Yes. No.
I think what with the world how it is, I think if I
didn't think someone was going to fix it all, that some
superhuman genius was going to work out how to
fix it
750 all then
I think I'd just entirely lose my mind.
I don't know.
I'm different.

We both are.

755 I quit smoking.

M Yeah?

W It's shit. I feel so much better.

M I started.

W You're kidding.

760 M I look cool.

W No.

No.

M How about your course?

W Oh. Yeah. Finished. Done.

765 M You're a doctor.

W Technically.

,

M I've been playing again. Couple of gigs in a
friend's band. Nothing big.

770 W Yeah?

M It's a sort of electronic thing, a new direction.

W Right.

M I think I've got stupider. Since we

,

775 I don't know what books to read, I don't really
read anything.

I have no idea what's happening in the world.

W It's fucked.

M I can't remember how to think.

780 And it feels, you know, really

wonderful.

Not having to worry about stuff I have no
control over. I used to get so angry at people who
didn't read or think or care about anything but I
785 completely get it now.

[…]

W Well well well.

M That was

W it was. It really was.

M I don't feel bad about this.

790 W You, what? You don't

M not at all.

,

W Oh.

M What?

795 W Nothing.

M What?

W No, nothing I'm

I was being

I was thinking something.

800 M What?

W Just

letting myself get carried away for a bit. I forgot
for a second. About her.

M Oh. No, I didn't mean

805 W it's fine.

M I no I'm I wasn't thinking, I was just

W no of course.

M Just talking just

W it's just it felt right. Didn't it? I mean to me anyway.

810 M Yeah, no, of course it was yes.

It did.

,

It did.

But

815 W can we save the buts? I think we both know.

Can we just for a minute just lie here and
pretend that we're years ago and nothing's happened.
That we'll get the papers and maybe go to the pub for
a roast. Play the quiz machine. Have a quarrel about
820 some book I've been reading that I explain badly and
sound like I'm advocating

I don't know, compulsory euthanasia of the old or
you know, I kept a drawer of your socks and
things.

825 It's stuffy in here. Sorry. Can't breathe. I'd open the
window but it's just as bad out there.

I've not slept with anyone else since you.

You don't need to know that. It doesn't matter.
It doesn't matter that you slept with two people.

830 ,

What, more?

M We were apart for

W no I know. I know. It doesn't matter. How many?
It doesn't matter.

835 M You want to know?

W Yes. No. I've not so much as kissed anyone else.
I'm crying again. Shit.

I tried to. I went for a drink with this guy. But
he was

840 horrible.

,

Don't tell me her name. Your girlfriend.

M Fiancée.

845 ,

W Oh.

M Yeah.

,

W Let's never see each other again. Okay?

850 ,

You look startled.

M You said we shouldn't see each other.

W Yet here I am. Why might that be?

M It's raining.

855 W Do I look different?

M You've not got a coat. Different?

W I thought I might, yes look
different.
Glowing maybe.

860 ,

M You mean

W yep.

,

So, okay, that's as far as I planned. I got

865 as far as telling you then I hoped you'd maybe
jump in and save the day, be all manly and know what
happens next because this is
I mean,
come on Superman. Swoop down. Save the day.

870 Anything.

,

Nothing.
I've broken you. You've shut down. It's too
much. Can I come in at least? I'm drenched.

875 ,

It'll be born by the time you've said something.
It'll plop out of me and be slippering, squirming
around in the afterbirth can I at least come in or

M listen,

880 W it speaks.

M Okay, listen, I'm sorry but can I
can we talk later? I'll come round, I'll

W she's here isn't she?
Of course she is. I'm an idiot. This is horrible.

885 I'm going.

M Wait, just

W I can't do this.

M Please.

W Don't.

[…]

890 M And I please, shut up for a second. I'm sorry, just
give me a chance here.

,

Thank you.

,

895 Right.
So okay, let's get married.

W No.

M Why?

W Okay, one, because you're already engaged to

900 someone else. Two, because that's the least romantic
proposal in the entire sad sorry two hundred thousand
year history of the human race and three,
because I don't want to. Fucking hold your horses
I don't even know whether I'm going to keep it yet so

905 let's not get ahead of ourselves.

M You're not / going to

W I've not decided yet and don't tell me your opinion
because it's fucking irrelevant. What's your opinion?

[…]

M I'm going to talk to her. Now. Face to face.

910 Okay? I'm doing it.

,

Can I come to yours once I've seen her?

W Why?

M Because I want to.

915 And I'll have nowhere else to go.

W Okay but
can we just have a second? Without talking. You
and me.
You, me and the little speck The ten thousand

920 tonnes of CO_2 waiting to be unleashed onto the planet.
Just a second.
The three of us.

M Okay.

[…]

W I must be insane. You clearly can't be trusted.

925 M I

W you're clearly unable to overrule your prick.

M I'm not entirely to blame for

W yes actually yes fucking yes you fucking are, yes.

M It was both of us who

930 W I'm not engaged to her.

M Nor am I now.

W Touché.

,

Touché.

935 ,

M So what now? We just what? Go back to normal?

W Normal? What normal? What?

M No, just

W we're not a couple.

940 M Oh.

W We're not we're not going to be like

M no, right.

W Not like before. We need to start fresh. If at all.

M I just sorry, I thought

945 W I don't know you. You're a fucking stranger now. A fucking deceitful, immature evil little stranger.

M I just assumed.

W Well don't. This is all just going at a hundred miles an hour and I need a second to breathe.

950 M No. If we think about it too much we won't do it.

W Do what?

M This. Now. Us.

Yes it's not the perfect circumstances, but let's go into this with open arms. I love you. Okay? I always

955 have. When I'm away from you I forget how to enjoy anything and when I'm with you I feel at home.

We've never worked out how to be together without making each other feel a bit shit and I want to find a way to not do that. You've got to stop being

960 angry with me and I've got to stop giving you reasons to be.

You've needed me to know what to do. To know how I'm feeling and to put it in the right words. You've needed me to grow up. So that's what's happening. I'm

965 putting it in the right words. I'm growing up.

We're not going to overthink this.

We're doing this.

We're going to get the books and go to classes and work out how to be parents. And we're going to

970 grow old together and look back on all this and laugh because it will seem like a different lifetime.

And we'll have a conversation and we'll just try to do the right thing. Because we're good people. Right?

And we'll plant forests. I mean it. We'll cycle

975 everywhere. We'll grow our own food if we have to. We'll never take another plane. We'll just stay right here. And we'll plant forests.

,

W Thank you.

980 I needed to hear that.

,

I'll think about it.

,

M Breathe in.

985 W Okay.

M Breathe.

W They're getting more frequent.

M Every few minutes.

W Get the keys.

990 M We're here.

W Don't leave me.

M I'm right here.

W I'm scared.

M You're so brave.

995 W Hurts.

M I forgot the camera.

W Here it comes.

M He's so beautiful.

W Let me hold him.

1000 M Of course.

W We're a family.

M I'm so tired.

W It's your turn.

M Shall I bring him in with us?

1005 W He's got to wean.

M I know.

W The books all say so.

M Good marks all round.

W I'm so proud of him.

1010 M I forgot my camera.

W There he goes.

M Don't cry.

W He's never slept away from home.

M We're going to be fine.

1015 W You shouldn't let him see that.

M I'll talk to him.

W He needs to hear it from his father.

M Are we going up this weekend?

W I just want to see him before he's off because,

1020 what with the world as it is,

M   I know.

W   Have you got your camera?

M   Let's get married.

W   I do.

1025 M   We need to be prepared.

W   It won't be as bad as they're saying.

M   He hasn't called.

W   They've suspended all flights.

M   It's so hot.

1030 W   The planet's fucked.

M   He looks so different.

W   He wants to help out.

M   We're fine.

W   That's what I told him.

1035 M   It's a standard operation.

W   I know.

M   Just goes with old age.

W   He's going to drive you.

M   I'm going to be okay.

1040 W   I'm scared.

M   You're fine.

W   He's found me a home. They have classes and things there. Art and things. It's nearer to him so a long way from here. He gets cross with

1045 me sometimes. You know how he is. I think a lot of people are angry at me. At us. Those of us still around. I forget more and more. I don't know what they're so upset about.

I miss talking to you. Here I am talking to myself.

1050 Your forests have gone. I don't watch the news any more, it all just gets worse and worse.

Everything's covered in ash. He tells me to stop dusting. Snaps at me.

I'm tired. Fed up. But I'm okay. Listen to me

1055 moaning on. It's a nice cool day today, like we used to have. Fresh air. No sirens. No noise. Nothing. It's good.

,

Anyway, I just thought I'd stop by. Change the flowers.

1060 I don't know if I'll get much of a chance to pop back here so

anyway.

,

I love you.

1065 ,

Lights out.

_____

(6617 words)

Source: Macmillan, Duncan. *Lungs*. Oberon, 2011.

Initial Insight

1. What is the play about? Write down anything that intuitively comes to you.

A couple who break up due to complications and try to work things out.

2. What factual information do you know about the characters?

W is working on her PhD
M has a job
W has a miscarriage
M and W have a break up

3. What is the mood and atmosphere of the play? Write down any adjectives you associate with it.

Quick, sad, nervous, anxious, exciting

Reader's Response

Consider the following questions. Discuss your answers with one or more partners.

1. After reading the play, what do you think its title refers to?

2. Did you find it challenging to keep track of the narrative situation (setting and time) in the play? Why or why not?

3. While reading the play, did you find it easy or difficult to imagine the characters and how they would deliver the text? Explain why.

4. Which character did you find the most likeable? The least likeable? Explain your reasons.

5. What are your thoughts on the representation of gender roles in the play?

6. Do you consider the play to have a "happy ending"? Why or why not?

MyBookshelf > My eLab
> Exercises > Part II: Drama
> Chapter 11: Lungs
> Vocabulary Comprehension

Close Reading

As you read the text again, pay attention to elements that seem significant to understanding and interpreting the story. The following guided reading questions will help you.

1. Where do the characters have an argument at the very beginning of the play? What exactly is it about?

Ikea, having a baby

2. Why does W say she reacts so strongly to M's suggestion to have a baby?

Because her life plan is becoming very real

3. What are W's most important hesitations about parenthood? Circle all the correct answers.

(a) She is worried about the enormous responsibility it implies.

b) She is unsure she loves M sufficiently.

c) She is aware that having a child has a negative impact on the environment.

(d) She is scared that, in the future, her child will not be able to have a good life.

4. According to M, why should they have a child in spite of W's reservations?

Because the most intelligent people don't have kids, even though they're the smartest. They think too far ahead and end up backing out.

5. What are the two main concessions W and M feel the other person should make to prepare for having a child?

Getting married, quit smoking,

6. What happens after W has a positive pregnancy test?

(a) W has a miscarriage.   b) W and M get married.   c) W has an abortion.

7. What is the direct cause of the couple breaking up?

M kisses a temp at work

8. Who or what has changed when W and M meet again? Circle all correct answers.

a) M has started smoking.   c) The climate has deteriorated.

b) W has abandoned her PhD.   d) W and M both have new partners.

9. Why does W go to see M after deciding they should not see each other again?

10. What event does not take place in the last moments of the play (lines 984–1065)?

a) M dies.   c) M and W's son is in a plane crash.

b) W and M marry.   d) W is in a care home.

MyBookshelf > My eLab
> Exercises > Part II: Drama
> Chapter 11: Lungs > Close
Reading: Additional Questions

THE LANGUAGE OF LITERATURE

The effect of any text is to a very large extent determined by the author's diction and use of figures of speech and other literary devices. Use the following questions to focus your attention on how the author uses language in the play.

1. Explain why W's monologue (lines 194–279) can be considered a soliloquy of sorts.

2. What is the following excerpt an example of?

W	A conversation that you're deciding to start now.
M	Yes.
W	In Ikea.
M	I hadn't planned to.
W	No. Okay. Yes. Okay.

a) aside   b) dramatic irony   c) repartee   d) metaphor

3. Explain the meaning of the metaphor "Can we put it back in the box?" (line 66). Why is this metaphor especially effective given the setting of the scene?

Analytical Reading

After making specific observations, you are ready to analyze the subject of your close reading. The following questions will help you look for thematic patterns, establish relationships and identify specific examples of literary devices or principles.

1. What genre and sub-genre of play does *Lungs* belong to (see page 107 for a list)? Explain your answer.

2. Explain how the stage directions make *Lungs* respect the law of three unities, at least in appearance.

3. Closely consider the two examples of ellipses that occur in the play on lines 74 and 285. Underline any textual evidence in the immediate context that allows you to confirm this change of setting (place and/or time).

4. Even though the play is not divided into acts and scenes, it still has a conventional plot structure. Which event can be considered the climax of the play? Explain.

5. Are M and W flat or round, static or dynamic characters? Explain.

6. If W and M are considered dual protagonists, then who or what are the play's antagonist forces?

7. How does M show his support to W throughout their relationship? Why does she feel this is inadequate? Is there a change throughout the play? Closely consider the characters' respective monologues at lines 194 and 952 to inform and support your answer.

8. What is the symbolic meaning of smoking as the characters either take it up or (try to) quit?

9. How does the depiction of the environment evolve throughout the play? Support your answer with precise quotes from the text.

10. The play both stretches out time and condenses it. What can you observe about the speed at which time passes as the play evolves? How does the playwright convey the changes in setting in the absence of dramatic conventions or stage props? How do these changes affect the atmosphere and mood of the play?

Food for Thought

The following questions encourage you to turn a critical eye to your earlier observations and analyses. They introduce elements and considerations that will lead you to formulate new questions and set tentative hypotheses. Discuss these to further your insight into the text.

1. **a.** The play is called *Lungs*. *Breathe* is the third word of the play. What is the significance of the title? Which of the play's themes does it relate to, and how?

   b. The play's French title is *Des arbres* (i.e., *Trees*); does this title support your interpretation of the English title? Explain.

2. The characters are very concerned with whether they are good people, good enough to pass on their DNA and raise a child. What does it mean to these characters to be "good enough"—what do they value?

3. In the secondary text—i.e., the stage directions—the playwright specifies that:

   - The characters don't have names, other than "M" and "W."
   - The play is to be performed on a bare stage.
   - There are no light or sound effects to indicate scene changes.

   What is the impact of these descriptions and stage directions? In what way(s) would the play be different with costume, set and lighting changes to show a change of scene and time?

4. In which way(s) do the characters conform to gender stereotypes, and in which way(s) is their behaviour different?

5. Why do you think the play covers such a long period at the end?

6. How would the storyline be affected if some of the non-gender specific actions and behaviours were inversed—for example, if M had serious doubts about wanting a child, or if W had been the one to cheat? Discuss your hypotheses with a partner.

Presenting an Analysis

Writing | Analyzing Dramatic Treatment of a Theme

Centred around two characters, the plot of *Lungs* is quite straightforward. The dramatic treatment of the central conflict and its related themes is what elevates the play to a thought-provoking theatrical experience. This includes the stage directions and descriptions provided in the secondary text, the treatment of time and setting in the play, the use of dramatic devices and the rendering of natural speech. Select one or more of these contributing dramatic elements. Investigate how they contribute to the development of the central conflict and themes.

Prepare an analytical essay focusing around a thesis statement that investigates the contribution of one or more dramatic devices or elements to the central conflict and themes.

Example:

By eliminating visual references to time and place from the play, Macmillan emphasizes the universality of the situations and questions depicted in *Lungs*, which sees two characters ponder their future and that of their hypothetical child.

In each of the body paragraphs, provide evidence and examples from the text to point out the importance of your chosen elements/devices. Refer to the work you did in the other sections of this chapter. Make sure to provide clear examples from the text to illustrate and support your analysis.

(Refer to Part V, Writing about Literature, on page 271 for more information on essay format and structure.)

MyBookshelf > My eLab
> Exercises > Grammar and
Accuracy

Speaking | Explicating Thematic Duality

Since *Lungs* is structured as an ongoing conversation, language is particularly dense as the two characters exchange their thoughts and opinions. Several thematic concepts are evoked to explain the couple's hesitations and worries: the environment, overpopulation, the uncertainty of the future, being good parents, being responsible citizens, etc. Select one such thematic concept and zoom in on it by explicating salient excerpts that illustrate both characters' points of view on this theme. Then, explain how they each use it to contribute to the ongoing reflection—whether or not to bring a child into the world. Point out any contrasts you observe, either between the characters' opinions, or between the beginning and ending of the play.

Prepare a cohesive presentation in which you demonstrate insight into the play through your selection and discussion of relevant passages. Pay particular attention to the characters' use of language, including the speech features identified in Language Focus, as well as any figures of speech you identify. Make sure to effectively include relevant passages in your presentation.

(Refer to Appendix 2 on page 297 for more information on presentation format and structure.)

PART III
Poetry

ELEMENTS OF ANALYSIS

Poetry distinguishes itself from prose through its form and its dense use of language and literary devices. Poems are not generally involved with developing a plotline, but rather revolve around a theme that appeals to the reader's feelings. They express their meaning in much less space than a novel or even a short story. They are written in **verse**—writing arranged in relatively short lines with a more or less regular rhythm that usually also includes some form of rhyme. These rhythmic elements can often be analyzed into formal patterns. As a result of its relative concision, poetry also makes more concentrated use of figures of speech, sound patterns, symbols and imagery. Obviously, not all poems use all these elements; contemporary poems especially use poetic conventions more freely. Nonetheless, most poetry depends on the aesthetic effects of formalized language use to evoke an emotional response in the reader.

Engaging with Poetry

Because of its formal characteristics, poetry is often more difficult to make sense of than prose—at least, at first glance. It might be helpful to keep in mind that although all poems have a subject—what the poem is about in a literal sense—their ultimate purpose is to develop an underlying theme. The **thematic structure** represents the way in which this theme is taken up throughout a poem, similar to how the plot represents how conflicts unfold in a short story. The poem's **formal structure** concerns its use of rhythmic and rhyme patterns and its division into stanzas. Although these elements do not express any meaning as such, they contribute to the mood and theme of the poem by establishing sound patterns that draw attention to certain words.

Formal literary analysis requires careful study of all the elements and structures that allow you to understand how a poem is crafted. Similar to how you deepen and fine-tune your thinking process as you write and rewrite the different drafts that lead up to a final version of an essay, you continually develop your understanding of a poem as you read and reread it. This will help you bridge the gap between subjective interpretations and objective analyses.

You will approach each poem in this section through three "drafts," each focused on a specific type of reading:

- **Exploratory Reading** allows you to approach a poem without any specific objectives or expectations. Not all poems reveal themselves without some effort, and you may want to read through a poem several times to get a feeling of what it is about. Read through the poem slowly and attentively, but do not break the flow by dwelling on difficult words or looking them up in a dictionary at this stage. Reading the poem out loud or sounding it in your mind will help you appreciate its musicality, which contributes to the overall mood and atmosphere of the text. Finally, take stock of your emotional response to the poem.
- **Close Reading** allows you to gain a more precise understanding of a poem by paying specific attention to its language and how this is organized into a formal structure. This is where you gather elements that you can draw on in your forthcoming analysis. One effective

technique to gain better insight into a poem is to **paraphrase** it line by line. This involves restating the poem's ideas and images in your own words, and stating explicitly what the poem might only suggest. The purpose of this activity is not to trivialize or banalize the meaning of the text but, on the contrary, to make it clearer and more digestible. Looking up challenging words in a reputable dictionary at this point will allow you to write accurate and enlightening paraphrases. Then, **scansion**—the act of scanning a poem to identify rhythm and rhyming structures—will give you valuable insight into the poem's form.

- **Analytical Reading** is informed by the two previous steps. Once you have identified one or more significant elements of focus for your analysis, reread the entire poem or specific passages from this vantage point to critically reconsider your observations, corroborate your inferences, establish new links and deepen your analysis of the poem's thematic and formal structures.

PRACTICE

A. Read the poem "Composed Upon Westminster Bridge, September 3, 1802" (W. Wordsworth) on page 162 and paraphrase it line by line in the right margin or on a separate sheet of paper.

B. Discuss your paraphrase with a partner and try to explain passages that you find challenging.

Poetic Genres

Based on the thematic and formal structures of a poem, different genres can be identified:

Lyric poems are comparatively short, non-narrative poems in which a single speaker presents a state of mind. Originally, these poems were meant to be sung to the music of a lyre, and the genre retains some of this musicality. Lyric poems can further be divided in the following categories:

- **Elegy**, the formal lament for the death of a particular person or a meditation on death in general
- **Ode**, a long lyric poem with a serious subject written in an elevated style
- **Sonnet**, originally a poem musing on love, although later poets also wrote sonnets on other topics. The genre originated in Italy and became popular in Renaissance England. See Structural Conventions (page 163) for a more detailed explanation of the sonnet form.

Narrative poems tell a story in verse, by relating a series of events that may involve different characters. Although they are less commonplace today, narrative poems were very popular in the Middle Ages. One of the oldest surviving texts in the English language, *Beowulf*, is a narrative poem, as are Homer's famous epic poems the *Iliad* and the *Odyssey*. Narrative poems can further be divided into the following categories:

- **Epic**, a large-scope text focusing on a topic of great importance and often involving a heroic quest and/or supernatural elements
- **Ballad**, a narrative folk story, originally transmitted orally in the form of song, and adapted for literary uses from the sixteenth century onwards

Dramatic poems, also called dramatic monologues, are written in the form of a speech delivered by a character. They can be written to be performed as part of a play, for instance in the form of a soliloquy, or to be read as any other form of poetry.

Didactic poems state a lesson or explicitly teach something. This can take the form of very specific instructions, or more abstract moral and theoretical knowledge.

Speaker and Tone

Just as it is often misleading to identify the author of a novel or short story with its narrator, you should never assume that the author of a poem is identical with its speaker, which is referred to as a **persona**. Even lyric poems, written from a first-person point of view, should not automatically be treated as expressions of the poet. While in many cases the poet may indeed be the speaker, this can only be established based on contextual elements that are external to the poem itself.

Much like a speaker's tone of voice, the poem's **tone** conveys the attitude of the speaker (persona) toward its theme. This can be achieved through diction, including figures of speech, as well as through rhythm. Tone can be positive or negative and cover a wide range of feelings. For instance, from its very opening line, Edgar Allan Poe's "The Raven" evokes negative feelings, which might be associated with sadness and resignation: "Once upon a midnight dreary, while I pondered, weak and weary."

PRACTICE

Read through "Composed Upon Westminster Bridge, September 3, 1802" (W. Wordsworth) on page 162.

1. How would you describe its tone? With one or more partners, discuss the elements that motivate your reading.

_____

_____

2. In this poem, what contextual information suggests that the speaker might directly represent the poet?

_____

_____

_____

Prosody, Rhythm and Rhyme

Prosody is the study of speech rhythms. Most poetry makes use of rhythmic elements that are natural to language: alternation of stressed and unstressed syllables (referred to as **poetic foot**), vowel and consonant combinations and pauses (also called **cæsuræ**). These have an impact on the poem's reader—or listener. The purpose of the analysis of formal structure—more specifically meter, rhythm and rhyme—is to determine the function they perform in the poem.

Poetry uses sound patterns that are also present in prose and natural speech:

- **Alliteration** is the repetition of the initial letter or sound of words found close to one another (e.g., *pleasant poem*);
- **Assonance** is the repetition of vowel sounds, which evokes an effect similar to a rhyme (e.g., *monotonous to stop*);
- **Consonance** is the repetition of consonant sounds (e.g., *still the best establishment*);
- **Onomatopoeia** imitates the sound associated with an object, concept or action (e.g., *the buzzing of the bees*).

These sound patterns can create **euphony**, a harmonious arrangement of sounds, or **cacophony**, in which a discordant sound creates an effect that is unpleasant to the ear, usually to draw attention to these particular word(s). Through **repetition**, these effects can be reinforced.

Read the last stanza of Edgar Allen Poe's "Annabel Lee"—if possible, out loud. Pay attention to its sounds.

> For the moon never beams, without bringing me dreams
>   Of the beautiful Annabel Lee;
> And the stars never rise, but I feel the bright eyes
>   Of the beautiful Annabel Lee;
> 5 And so, all the night-tide, I lie down by the side
>   Of my darling—my darling—my life and my bride,
>   In her sepulchre there by the sea—
>   In her tomb by the sounding sea.

1. Which vowel sounds repeat often?

_____

_____

2. Which consonant sounds repeat often?

_____

_____

3. On lines 3 and 5, underline the words that present assonance.

4. On lines 7 and 8, underline the words that present alliteration.

5. With a partner, discuss what image the alliteration on lines 7 and 8 evokes.

Rhyming Patterns

Rhyming is based on the use of (near-)identical vowel sounds, followed by similar consonant sounds (if any), in two or more words:

- In an **exact rhyme**, both the vowel sounds and following consonant sounds are identical: *walk* and *talk*, *trick* and *quick*, *historical* and *categorical*.

- In a **slant rhyme**, the vowel sounds making up the rhyme are similar but not identical: *sun* and *moon*, *pact* and *picked*, *faces* and *houses*. Slant rhyme is typically used to create a specific effect and should not be considered an imperfect form of rhyme.

A rhyme is thus a repetition of similar-sounding words, which usually occur in a poem at the end of lines. This is called **end rhyme**. **Internal rhyme** occurs when words within the same line create a rhyme. In the nursery rhyme "Humpty Dumpty," "Humpty" and "Dumpty" form an internal rhyme on the first two lines, while the last words of each line—"wall" and "fall," "men" and "again"—form two different end rhymes:

> Humpty Dumpty sat on a wall,
> Humpty Dumpty had a great fall.
> All the king's horses and all the king's men
> Couldn't put Humpty together again.

Recurring rhyming patterns in a poem allow the reader to observe a **rhyme scheme**, usually indicated by assigning a capital letter to each different rhyme. In "Humpty Dumpty," the rhyme scheme can be identified as AA-BB.

Establish the rhyme scheme of "Composed Upon Westminster Bridge, September 3, 1802" (page 162):

1. Write the rhyme scheme using capital letters:

_____

2. Which two lines have a slant rhyme rather than an exact rhyme?

_____

Rhythmic Patterns

Meter is the arrangement of syllables and stress patterns in poetry. While these patterns are also present in everyday speech—think of the word *banana*, in which only the middle syllable is stressed and pronounced as an "a" sound—poetry uses them to construct regular patterns:

- **Accentual meter** occurs when each line has the same number of stresses but a variable total number of syllables.
- **Syllabic meter** occurs when each line has the same number of syllables but a variable number of stressed syllables.
- **Accentual-syllabic meter** occurs when each line has the same number of stressed and unstressed syllables in a fixed order. This is the most common type of metrical verse in English.
- **Free verse** occurs when a poem has irregular patterns of stress and syllables. Many contemporary poems employ a form of free verse.

The identification and visual representation of the distribution of stressed and unstressed syllables is called **scansion**. Depending on the notation system, stressed syllables are marked by the symbol ´ or the number 1, while unstressed syllables are indicated with the symbol ˘ or the number 0: bă na̅ nă or ba^0 na^1 na^0. In the examples below, the symbol • indicates where a word has been split into syllables.

English has five main types of **poetic feet**—regular combinations of stressed and unstressed syllables:

Two-syllable combinations

Iambic foot (an iamb)	unstressed-stressed	bĕ•gín, ă start
Trochaic foot (a trochee)	stressed-unstressed	pó•em, líke us
Spondaic foot (a spondee)	stressed-stressed	sún•sét, cóme báck

Three-syllable combinations

| Dactylic foot (a dactyl) | stressed-unstressed-stressed | é•le•phánt, bláck or white |
| Anapestic foot (an anapest) | unstressed-unstressed-stressed | un•der•stánd, in the book |

Observe the distribution of stressed and unstressed syllables in the following excerpts and complete their scansion by placing a ˘ or ´ mark above each syllable. Then, identify the type of poetic foot they use.

Note: The slash mark " / " indicates a line break in the original poem.

1. Bŭt soft, what light through yon•der win•dow breaks? (W. Shakespeare)

a) iambic   b) trochaic   c) spondaic   d) dactylic   e) anapestic

2. And the sheen of their spears were like stars on the sea (L. Byron)

   a) iambic   b) trochaic   c) spondaic   d) dactylic   e) anapestic

3. Dou•ble dou•ble toil and trou•ble, / fi•re burn and caul•dron bub•ble
   (W. Shakespeare)

   a) iambic   b) trochaic   c) spondaic   d) dactylic   e) anapestic

4. Half a league, half a league, / Half a league on•ward (A. Tennyson)

   a) iambic   b) trochaic   c) spondaic   d) dactylic   e) anapestic

5. Slow, slow, fresh fount, keep time with my salt tears (B. Jonson)

   a) iambic   b) trochaic   c) spondaic   d) dactylic   e) anapestic

In accentual-syllabic verse, the number of poetic feet on a line determines its meter, named after the Greek numeral system. The following adaptations of the first line of Edgar Allan Poe's "The Raven"—"Once upon a midnight dreary, while I pondered, weak and weary"—illustrate the different types of meter that can be distinguished. Each foot is delimited by a vertical slash mark: |.

Monometer (1 foot)	mid•night
Dimeter (2 feet)	mid•night | drea•ry
Trimeter (3 feet)	Once u | pon a | mid•night
Tetrameter (4 feet)	Once u | pon a | mid•night | drea•ry
Pentameter (5 feet)	mid•night | while I | pon•dered | weak and | wea•ry
Hexameter (6 feet)	mid•night | drea•ry | while I | pon•dered | weak and | wea•ry
Heptameter (7 feet)	Once u | pon a | mid•night | while I | pon•dered | weak and | wea•ry
Octameter (8 feet)	Once u | pon a | mid•night | drea•ry | while I | pon•dered | weak and | wea•ry

The **rhythmic pattern**, or **meter of a poem**, is usually indicated by combining the name of the stress pattern and the number of repetitions of this pattern (expressed in feet) per line: "The Raven" is written in trochaic octameter, because each line contains eight repetitions of a stressed-unstressed syllable pair (a trochee). Iambic pentameter—a line that contains five repetitions of an unstressed-stressed syllable pair (an iamb)—is often considered the most prevalent rhythmic pattern in English poetry (followed by iambic tetrameter), since the iamb is a base element of natural language use (e.g., a book, to sleep). An iambic hexameter is also called an Alexandrine, a form very popular in French poetry. The meter lengths at both extremes of the table above are less common in English. If a poem has meter but no rhyme pattern, it is called **blank verse**: "I bump'd the ice into three several stars, / Fell in a doze; and half-awake I heard / The parson taking wide and wider sweeps …" (A. Tennyson, "The Epic").

It is not always easy to determine a rhythmic pattern, especially as a series of syllables may allow for more than one stress pattern. Consider the first line of "A Dream Within A Dream" by Edgar Allan Poe: "Take this kiss upon the brow!" Each of the first three words could be stressed. When continuing scansion of the line, it becomes clear that "brow" is stressed, which makes it possible to scan the line as follows: "Take this kiss u •pon the brow!" You may also take into consideration the lines around a challenging or problematic line when deciding on the meter. The basic rule is that unless there are clear arguments against it, that line should be scanned so it fits the pattern of the surrounding lines.

Free verse, often used in contemporary poetry, does not use any particular stress pattern or number of syllables per line. Although it does not contain regular meter, it remains verse, organized around certain rhythmic effects. These may include word or sound repetitions, pauses and line breaks. For instance, the first stanza of "Morning at the Window" by T. S. Eliot does not contain any regular rhythmic pattern, but each line represents a phrase or clause of one sentence. Each line ends on a noun, with "housemaids" and "gates" representing a form of assonance, creating a type of slant rhyme:

> They are rattling breakfast plates in basement kitchens,
> And along the trampled edges of the street
> I am aware of the damp souls of housemaids
> Sprouting despondently at area gates.

PRACTICE

A. Analyze the stress patterns you identified in the exercise on page 160 and place a vertical slash mark "|" between each foot. Then, write each example's rhythmic pattern below. Pay attention to the slash mark indicating a line break in two of the examples.

1. _____   **4.** _____

2. _____   **5.** _____

3. _____

B. Scan "Composed Upon Westminster Bridge, September 3, 1802" by William Wordsworth.

> Earth has not anything to show more fair:
> Dull would he be of soul who could pass by
> A sight so touching in its majesty:
> This City now doth, like a garment, wear
> 5 The beauty of the morning; silent, bare,
> Ships, towers, domes, theatres, and temples lie
> Open unto the fields, and to the sky;
> All bright and glittering in the smokeless air.
> Never did sun more beautifully steep
> 10 In his first splendour, valley, rock, or hill;
> Ne'er saw I, never felt, a calm so deep!
> The river glideth at his own sweet will:
> Dear God! the very houses seem asleep;
> And all that mighty heart is lying still!

1. First, mark the stressed (´) and unstressed (˘) syllables of the last line. What is its rhythmic pattern?

_____

2. Can you readily apply the same rhythmic pattern to the other lines? If not, which problem(s) do you encounter? Provide examples.

_____

_____

_____

Structural Conventions

Through the combination of specific rhythmic and rhyme patterns, poems can conform to **closed-form** structures. Apart from representing an artistic challenge, these structures also allow the poet to craft a particular mood and develop a theme throughout the different parts of a poem. These parts are called **stanzas** and are made up of two or more lines of verse sharing a rhythmic or rhyme pattern.

Rhyming stanzas of two lines are also referred to as **couplets**. Other common patterns are **tercets** (three rhyming lines), **quatrains** (four rhyming lines), **sestets** (six rhyming lines) and **octaves** (eight rhyming lines).

These stanza patterns can be combined into highly formalized patterns that have become poetic categories in their own right. One such category is the **sonnet**. This structural pattern originates from Italy, where it was made famous by Francesco Petrarch in the fourteenth century. **Petrarchan sonnets** consist of an octave and a sestet, each with a different rhyme pattern—usually ABBAABBA CDCDCD, although the pattern of the sestet may differ (e.g., CDECDE). In the sixteenth century, sonnets became popular in England, where poets adapted their rhyme pattern to better fit the English language. **Shakespearean sonnets** (also called Elizabethan sonnets) usually follow the pattern ABAB CDCD EFEF GG, which means they include three quatrains and a couplet. All sonnet types include a **volta**, or thematic turn, which is usually in line 9 for Petrarchan sonnets and in the last quatrain or the rhyming couplet in Shakespearean sonnets.

Free-verse poetry has an **open-form structure** without any apparent rhyme patterns, although all verse has an inherent rhythm based on stress patterns, pauses and line length.

PRACTICE

A. Based on the rhyme pattern of the last stanza of Edgar Allen Poe's "Annabel Lee" (page 159) it is made up of:

a) four couplets   b) a quatrain and two couplets

c) an octave   d) a sestet and a couplet

B. Reconsider your analysis of the rhythmic and rhyme patterns of "Composed Upon Westminster Bridge, September 3, 1802" (page 162). Is it a Petrarchan or a Shakespearean sonnet? Divide it up accordingly into stanzas.

_____

_____

C. Examine "The Heart" by Stephen Crane, a free-verse open-form poem.

In the desert
I saw a creature, naked, bestial,
Who, squatting upon the ground,
Held his heart in his hands,
5 And ate of it.
I said, "Is it good, friend?"
"It is bitter—bitter," he answered;
"But I like it
Because it is bitter,
10 And because it is my heart."

1. What do you notice about the line length? Are there any patterns?

_____

_____

2. What do you observe about the use of punctuation?

_____

_____

3. How do line length and punctuation help establish the rhythm?

_____

_____

_____

_____

Language and Poetic Devices

Language

Although poetry is especially dense in its construction of images, moods and themes, it is made up of words just like prose. No single word is innately prosaic or poetic. Rather, poets combine words to create particular effects based on sounds (as explained above) and meanings. This word choice, which, especially in poetry, should never be considered accidental, is called **diction**.

- Words can be more **concrete** (tree, kiss) or more **abstract** (nature, affection).
- Words not only have **denotation**—their literal meaning easily found in a dictionary—but also **connotation**—the suggested meaning based on associations and the contexts in which the word is or has been used. For instance, while the denotation of the word "desert" is a dry area of land, usually covered by sand, its connotations may include solitude, an inhospitable environment and barrenness.
- Words are typically part of a **register** or level of language, ranging from the formal (or high diction) to the informal (or low diction). These levels can be used to create contrasts.

PRACTICE

Consider the language use in the following excerpt of "London," by William Blake.

> I wander thro' each charter'd street,
> Near where the charter'd Thames does flow.
> And mark in every face I meet
> Marks of weakness, marks of woe.
>
> 5 In every cry of every Man,
> In every Infants cry of fear,
> In every voice: in every ban,
> The mind-forg'd manacles I hear

1. Identify three examples of abstract diction.

_____

2. In a reputable dictionary, look up the following words and write down their denotation. Then, establish what connotation(s) all of these words might share.

a. Chartered (cf. a charter): _____

_____

b. Ban: _____

_____

c. Manacles: _____

_____

d. Connotations: _____

_____

3. How does the connotation of the above words inform the comparison between the city and its inhabitants?

_____

_____

4. What effect does the repetition of the word "every" have?

_____

_____

Poetic Devices

The different types of meanings that can be inferred from language, as described in the previous section, also contribute to the construction of **imagery** and **symbolism**. Images are words or phrases that evoke different sensory experiences (vision, sound, taste or touch), while symbols are images that call up a deeper meaning, either by convention (e.g., a rose referring to love) or in context (e.g., a heart referring to life rather than to love).

Words can also be used as **figures of speech** to create a non-literal meaning that differs from their primary usage:

- A **simile** expresses a comparison between two elements through the use of the words *as*, *like* or equivalent expressions: "My mistress' eyes are nothing like the sun" (W. Shakespeare, "Sonnet 130").
- A **metaphor** evokes a likeness without any explicit comparison: "Hope is the thing with feathers / That perches in the soul" (E. Dickinson).
- A **personification** attributes human qualities to an object or concept: "Earth felt the wound, and Nature from her seat / Sighing through all her works gave signs of woe" (J. Milton, *Paradise Lost*).
- In an **apostrophe**, a poem's speaker addresses a dead or absent person, an inanimate object or concept: "Twinkle, twinkle, little star, / How I wonder what you are!" (J. Taylor)
- An **oxymoron** brings together two ideas that are opposites: "And faith unfaithful kept him falsely true" (A. Tennyson, "Lancelot and Elaine").
- A **hyperbole** exaggerates an image to emphasize a point; "And I will love thee still, my dear, / Till a' the seas gang dry" (R. Burns, "A Red, Red Rose").

MyBookshelf > My eLab
> Exercises > Part III: Poetry
> Elements of Analysis

A. Read "Composed Upon Westminster Bridge, September 3, 1802" again (page 162).

1. What figure of speech does the first line contain?

a) oxymoron   b) apostrophe   c) hyperbole   d) metaphor

2. Identify five examples of personification.

_____

_____

3. Find an example of a simile in the poem.

_____

4. On line 13, what is "Dear God!" an example of?

_____

B. Read "The Heart" again (page 164):

1. Which sense(s) does the poem's imagery appeal to? Explain.

_____

2. With one or more partners, discuss the possible meanings of the following symbols:
- the desert   ■ the naked creature   ■ the heart

_____

_____

_____

_____

Theme and Mood

All of the aforementioned elements play a role in the development of the poem's **theme(s)**, developed in its thematic structure. A poem can have one or more themes, which are comprehensive statements of a deeper meaning that extend beyond the subject matter of the poem and its first-level meaning. They usually require being summarized in more abstract terms. While the subject matter can be observed directly, a theme consists of deeper issues that require analysis to be uncovered.

To determine the theme(s) of a poem, you might therefore ask, "What point does the poet make through the subject matter of the poem?" When answering this question, it may be helpful to distinguish between broad **thematic concepts** that appear in many different poems—for instance, love or death—and narrow **thematic statements**, which concern the particular point the author expresses about such a concept (e.g., true friendship lasts, regardless of distance).

The **mood** refers to the atmosphere that is prevalent in the poem. Elements such as the setting, tone, voice and theme help establish this atmosphere. As a result, the mood evokes certain feelings and emotions in the reader, such as passion, pride or moroseness. A poem generally has one dominant overall mood.

For instance, while both Wordsworth's "Composed Upon Westminster Bridge, September 3, 1802" (page 162) and Blake's "London" (page 164) express the speaker's description of the city of London, the mood of the first poem is positive and contemplative as its theme likens the beauty of the city to the beauty of nature, while the second poem's mood is negative and pessimistic as its theme evokes humanity's lack of strength and freedom.

PRACTICE

A. Re-examine the last stanza of "Annabel Lee" (page 159).

1. Love and death are important thematic concepts in this stanza; combine them in a thematic statement or fully developed theme.

_____

_____

2. Based on the poem's theme and diction, what word best captures its mood?

a) bright   b) scary   c) gloomy   d) upbeat

B. Read "The Heart" again (page 163).

1. Which words (diction) stand out?

_____

2. When interpreted as symbols, how do these keywords translate into a theme? Write down one or more possibilities and discuss them with a partner.

_____

_____

_____

3. How would you describe the mood of the poem in one word? Share your answer with one or more partners.

_____

CHAPTER 12

Poems on Love

This chapter focuses on the following:

- Rhythm, rhyme and meter
- Imagery and diction
- Symbolism
- Language Focus: syllable stress
- The Language of Literature: poetic devices
- Theme

The poems in this chapter, which span exactly four hundred years, take up the concept of love from a variety of angles that reflect the many different ways in which we can love others. The first and last poems are written in sonnet form, illustrating the endurance of structural conventions and poetic devices regardless of how language itself has changed over the centuries.

So you can fully appreciate each poem, the **Exploratory Reading** section first invites you to read it one or more times without interruption, before answering the **Initial Insight** and **Reader's Response** questions below the poem. These intuitive reactions form the foundation for more in-depth analysis. To undertake this analysis, read the poem again, this time more slowly, paying attention to specific elements that seem significant to understanding and interpreting it. **Paraphrase** each line in the margin; look up challenging words as needed. Then, answer the **Close Reading** questions to validate your understanding. The **Analytical Reading** and **Food for Thought** questions will help you look for thematic patterns, identify specific examples of poetic devices or principles and turn a critical eye to your observations. At the end of this chapter, the **Comparative Insight** questions prompt you to compare and contrast thematic and formal patterns across poems, before expressing the fruit of your analyses in speaking and writing.

Connect with the Text

A. Discuss your opinions on the following questions with one or more partners.

    1. How would you describe and define love? Be as precise as possible.

    2. Apart from romantic love, what other types of love exist? Give examples.

    3. Is it possible to truly express love in words? Why or why not?

    4. What metaphors, symbols and clichés do you typically associate with love?

B. Do a web search on the concept of romantic love and how it has manifested itself in Western societies since the seventeenth century. Remember to record your sources. Then, answer and discuss the following questions.

    1. Has the concept of romantic love evolved over the centuries? Explain.

    2. What differences can you observe in the social conventions on courtship, sexuality and marriage between the seventeenth century and today?

    3. What do you think was the role of love poetry in earlier centuries? Can you think of any contemporary genres that have a similar role?

Sonnet 18

Text in Context

While William Shakespeare was a well-respected playwright of his time (see page 119), evidence indicates that he turned to poetry for lasting fame—his plays were not published until after his death. Shakespeare most likely composed his sonnet sequence, comprising 154 poems, in the 1590s, but it remained unpublished until 1609. Each sonnet deals with personal and sentimental themes, and can be analyzed independently or in relation to the sonnets around it. Although it is tempting to consider them autobiographical, not enough is known about Shakespeare's life to affirm this beyond any doubt. It is generally considered that sonnets 1–126 are addressed to a beloved male friend and sonnets 127–152 to a woman the speaker loves in spite of himself.

Exploratory Reading

Sonnet 18   **William Shakespeare**

Shall I compare thee to a summer's day?
Thou art more lovely and more temperate:
Rough winds do shake the darling buds of May,
And summer's lease hath all too short a date:
5 Sometime too hot the eye of heaven shines,
And often is his gold complexion dimm'd,
And every fair from fair sometime declines,
By chance, or nature's changing course untrimm'd:
But thy eternal summer shall not fade,
10 Nor lose possession of that fair thou ow'st,
Nor shall death brag thou wander'st in his shade,
When in eternal lines to time thou grow'st,
So long as men can breathe, or eyes can see,
So long lives this, and this gives life to thee.

Source: Shakespeare, W. "Sonnet XVIII." *Shakespeare's Sonnets*, Thomas Thorpe, 1609, www.gutenberg.org/ebooks/1041.

Initial Insight

1. What is the central image taken up and developed throughout the poem?

_____

_____

2. Who might "thee" refer to?

_____

_____

_____

Reader's Response

Working with one or more partners, discuss your answers to the following questions.

1. Imagine this poem were addressed directly to you. What feelings does it evoke in you?

2. Are all of the images the poem calls up positive? Explain.

3. Do you believe this poem expresses romantic love or platonic love? Explain.

THE LANGUAGE OF LITERATURE

The effect of a poem is to a very large extent determined by the poet's use of poetic devices and structural patterns. Use the following questions to focus your attention on the effect of the poet's diction.

1. Consider the last word of each line to determine the poem's **rhyme scheme**. Use capital letters to represent it.

2. How does the rhyme scheme allow you to break up the poem in **stanzas**?

3. Based on the formal structure identified in questions 1 and 2, what genre does this poem represent (see page 157)?

   a) Petrarchan sonnet   b) Shakespearean sonnet   c) ode   d) elegy

4. Consider the first four lines of the poem. Determine the rhythmic pattern by establishing the type of **foot** and the number of repetitions in each line.

5. In what way are the words "and" and "nor" used at the beginning of certain lines to evoke a contrast between opposing ideas?

   a) They introduce hyperboles.   b) They are part of alliterations.   c) They represent repetitions.

Close Reading

1. How do the ideas in lines 1 and 2 logically connect to each other?

_____

2. What is the denotation of "temperate" in line 2?

_____

3. In lines 3 and 4, what point does the speaker make about summer?

_____

_____

4. In line 5, what figure of speech is "the eye of heaven" an example of? What does it refer to?

_____

5. In line 7, what is the meaning of the word "fair"? Look to the context line 6 provides.

   a) honest and impartial   b) of average quality   c) light and bright

6. After the description of summer, what is the word that signals a shift in the poem? What is this thematic turn also called?

_____

_____

7. Which concept is personified in the poem?

_____

_____

MyBookshelf > My eLab
> Exercises > Part III: Poetry
> Chapter 12: Poems on Love
> Sonnet 18 — Vocabulary
Comprehension

8. In the last line of the poem, the demonstrative pronoun "this" is repeated twice. What does it refer to?

_____

MyBookshelf > My eLab
> Exercises > Part III: Poetry
> Chapter 12: Poems on Love
> Sonnet 18 — Close Reading:
Additional Questions

Analytical Reading

1. How is the idea of the addressee being "temperate" developed throughout the poem? Is it presented as a positive or a negative quality?

2. Analyze the **thematic structure** of the poem. Use the identified divisions as a guide, and refer to your answers to Close Reading questions 1 and 6.

3. What is the theme of Shakespeare's Sonnet 18? Provide textual evidence in your response.

Food for Thought

1. What other extended metaphor(s) could be used, instead of a summer's day, to express the poem's theme?

2. How does the presumed gender of the addressee and their relationship with the speaker affect your analysis of the poem?

3. Is this poem an expression of love to a person, to poetry or to both?

How Do I Love Thee? (Sonnet 43)

Text in Context

As a child, Elizabeth Barrett (1806–1861) was encouraged by her father to read widely and shared her brothers' classical tuition, which was highly unusual in privileged circles at the time. In spite of her ill-health, Browning went on to become a renowned and respected poet, and the first female poet in England to be considered for the prestigious post of poet laureate. Browning's work is critical to understanding the ways in which a woman poet empowers herself to speak. She secretly wrote her sonnet cycle *Sonnets from the Portuguese* to her future husband, Robert Browning, during their courtship, and published it after their marriage.

Exploratory Reading

How Do I Love Thee? (Sonnet 43)　　**Elizabeth Barrett Browning**

How do I love thee? Let me count the ways.
I love thee to the depth and breadth and height
My soul can reach, when feeling out of sight
For the ends of Being and ideal Grace.
5　I love thee to the level of every day's
Most quiet need, by sun and candle-light.
I love thee freely, as men strive for Right.
I love thee purely, as they turn from Praise.
I love thee with the passion put to use
10　In my old griefs, and with my childhood's faith.
I love thee with a love I seemed to lose
With my lost saints. I love thee with the breath,
Smiles, tears, of all my life; and, if God choose,
I shall but love thee better after death.

Source: Barrett Browning, E. "How Do I Love Thee?" (Sonnet 43). *Sonnets from the Portuguese*, Doubleday, 1850, www.poemhunter.com/poem/how-do-i-love-thee/.

Initial Insight

1. What word would you use to describe the love expressed in this poem?

_____

2. Which words and other elements in the text suggest that the speaker is religious?

_____

_____

Reader's Response

Working with one or more partners, discuss your answers to the following questions.

1. Could you imagine yourself expressing your love for someone in a manner similar to the speaker? Why or why not?

2. How old do you imagine the speaker to be? Why?

3. Do you associate the tone of the poem with a new relationship or an established relationship? Explain.

Close Reading

1. How many ways of loving does the speaker list throughout the poem?

_____

_____

2. What type of imagery do "depth," "breadth" and "height" evoke regarding the speaker's soul?

_____

3. Is the speaker in the presence of the person she addresses, or not? Cite the (part of) the line that supports your answer.

_____

4. What does "by sun and candle-light" metaphorically refer to?

_____

5. What figure of speech can be found in line 7? Which other line contains this figure of speech?

_____

_____

6. What can you infer about the speaker's past from lines 9–12?

_____

_____

MyBookshelf > My eLab > Exercises > Part III: Poetry > Chapter 12: Poems on Love > How Do I Love Thee? (Sonnet 43) – Vocabulary Comprehension

7. How is the metaphor "I love thee with the breath, / Smiles, tears" different from the images evoked earlier in the poem?

_____

_____

MyBookshelf > My eLab > Exercises > Part III: Poetry > Chapter 12: Poems on Love > How Do I Love Thee? (Sonnet 43) – Close Reading: Additional Questions

8. How long does the speaker expect her love to last? Cite from the poem to support this answer.

_____

Analytical Reading

1. How does the opening question suggest the speaker's attitude toward verbalizing love?

2. How would you describe the tone of the poem?

3. How does the repetition of "I love thee" contribute to the poem's tone and theme?

4. Examine the words _Being, Grace, Right, Praise_ and _God_ and their context. Why are they capitalized? What does this suggest about the speaker's love?

5. In which way do lines 5 and 6 provide a contrast to lines 2–4? What does the speaker emphasize through this contrast?

6. What is the type and length of poetic foot used in the poem? What type of rhyme scheme do you observe? Use this information to determine the type of sonnet and discuss the thematic structure of the poem.

Food for Thought

1. Consider the sonnet's opening question again. If you imagined another line to precede it, what could it state or ask?

2. Sonnet 43 was published in 1850 and written a few years earlier, which places it in the Victorian era. How do the ideas about love the sonnet conveys correspond with Victorian morals and values on love and the social role of women? Refer to the work you did in Connect with the Text or do a web search.

3. Considering that Elizabeth Barrett Browning was disinherited by her father for choosing to marry Robert Browning, what might be the meaning of the line, "I love thee freely, as men strive for Right"?

To My Mother

Text in Context

While Edgar Allan Poe (1809–1849) is mostly remembered for his short fiction (see Chapter 1), his first love as a writer was poetry. He started to write poems as early as adolescence, inspired by English romantic poets, such as Byron and Keats. Several of his poems are narrated by a young man who deplores the untimely death of his beloved. Like his short stories, his poems often convey a dark mood, expressing emotional torment and despair. Beyond rhyme, Poe's poetry often has a musical quality due to the poet's extensive use of poetic devices such as repetition, alliteration and assonance.

Exploratory Reading

To My Mother   **Edgar Allan Poe**

> Because I feel that, in the Heavens above,
> The angels, whispering to one another,
> Can find, among their burning terms of love,
> None so devotional as that of "Mother,"
> 5 Therefore by that dear name I long have called you—
> You who are more than mother unto me,
> And fill my heart of hearts, where Death installed you
> In setting my Virginia's spirit free.
> My mother—my own mother, who died early,
> 10 Was but the mother of myself; but you
> Are mother to the one I loved so dearly,
> And thus are dearer than the mother I knew
> By that infinity with which my wife
> Was dearer to my soul than its soul-life.

Source: Poe, E. A. "To My Mother." 1849. *Leaflets of Memory, or, Illuminated Annual for MDCCCL*, edited by R. Coates, E. H. Butler.

Initial Insight

1. To whom is the poem "To My Mother" dedicated?

_____

_____

2. On what occasion might the poem have been written? Cite from the poem to support your interpretation.

_____

_____

Reader's Response

Discuss your answers to the following questions with one or more partners.

1. Did you experience positive or negative feelings while reading the poem? Explain.

2. How would you describe the type of love expressed in the poem?

3. Did you find the poem to be more abstract or more concrete? Provide examples.

Close Reading

1. In the opening lines, which image illustrates that the speaker has a Christian conception of life and death?

_____

2. What is the speaker's appreciation of the term "mother"?

_____

3. Why does the speaker value the addressee more than his own mother?

_____

_____

4. What is the meaning of the phrase "my heart of hearts"?

_____

5. What is an example of personification in the poem?

_____

6. What is "setting my Virginia's spirit free" a euphemism for?

_____

MyBookshelf > My eLab
> Exercises > Part III: Poetry
> Chapter 12: Poems on Love
> To My Mother – Vocabulary
Comprehension

7. In lines 9 and 10, what rhythmic feature do the dash, comma and semicolon represent?

   a) internal rhyme   b) cæsura   c) accentual meter

MyBookshelf > My eLab
> Exercises > Part III: Poetry
> Chapter 12: Poems on Love
> To My Mother – Close
Reading: Additional Questions

8. What poetic device are the last two lines of the poem an example of?

   a) register   b) oxymoron   c) hyperbole

Analytical Reading

1. Establish the rhyme scheme of the poem. Does it correspond to a specific closed-form structural pattern? If so, which one?

2. Scan line 3. What is its meter? Is this meter regular throughout the poem?

3. What is the meaning of the last line, "Was dearer to my soul than its soul-life"?

4. What is the theme of the poem?

5. Which adjective and which other words used in the poem can describe the poem's tone?

Food for Thought

1. Research information on Poe's life and marriage. Does this information affect your interpretation of the poem? If yes, how?

2. Explain how, although it is directed at only one particular woman, the poem expresses love and admiration toward three women in Poe's life.

Wild Nights – Wild Nights! (269)

Text in Context

Emily Dickinson (1830–1886) is considered one of the most original American poets of the nineteenth century. Even though she spent her entire life in her birth town, in rural Massachusetts and never married, she did have rich emotional relationships, mostly experienced through correspondence and poetry. She wrote hundreds of poems, only seven of which were published during her lifetime. Rather than traditional rhyme schemes and punctuation, Dickinson used irregular meter, unusual diction, dashes and random use of capitalization to express complex thoughts and emotions. These features contribute to the riddling quality of her poems, often allowing for various interpretations.

Exploratory Reading

Wild Nights – Wild Nights! (269)   **Emily Dickinson**

> Wild Nights – Wild Nights!
> Were I with thee
> Wild Nights should be
> Our luxury!
>
> 5 Futile – the Winds –
> To a Heart in port –
> Done with the Compass –
> Done with the Chart!
>
> Rowing in Eden –
> 10 Ah – the Sea!
> Might I but moor – Tonight –
> In Thee!

Source: Dickinson, E. "Wild Nights – Wild Nights!" *The Complete Poems of Emily Dickinson*, edited by Thomas H. Johnson, Little, Brown, 1960.

Initial Insight

1. What images does the exclamation "Wild Nights!" make you think of? What would you say the poem is about?

_____

_____

2. What is the predominant metaphor that is repeated throughout the poem?

_____

Reader's Response

Discuss your answers to the following questions with one or more partners.

1. What were your initial feelings when you read this poem?

2. What is your experience of the poem's musicality, rhythm and use of space? Did you feel it invited you to read it quickly or slowly?

3. What do you think about the unconventional use of capital letters and punctuation? What impression do they give you about the speaker?

Close Reading

1. What sound device is the opening line "Wild Nights – Wild Nights!" an example of?

    a) alliteration   b) assonance   c) cacophony

2. Which pronouns indicate the speaker directly addresses someone in the poem?

_____

_____

3. In line 2, what verb form indicates the relationship referred to is imaginary or hypothetical rather than real?

_____

4. In the second stanza, the "Heart in port" is

    a) a metaphor   b) a simile   c) an onomatopoeia

5. Identify five words in the poem that constitute nautical images.

_____

6. What is the poem's meter?

    a) monometer   b) dimeter   c) trimeter   d) pentameter

7. What can you observe about the type of poetic foot and rhyme scheme used in the poem?

    a) There is no rhythmic or rhyme pattern.

    b) The rhythmic and rhyme pattern are irregular.

    c) The rhythmic and rhyme pattern correspond to a typical sonnet.

8. In lines 6 and 8, what do the words "port" and "chart" form an example of?

a) exact rhyme   b) blank verse   d) slant rhyme

MyBookshelf > My eLab
> Exercises > Part III: Poetry
> Chapter 12: Poems on Love
> Wild Nights! – Wild Nights!
– Vocabulary Comprehension

MyBookshelf > My eLab
> Exercises > Part III: Poetry >
Chapter 12: Poems on Love
> Wild Nights – Wild Nights!
– Close Reading: Additional
Questions

Analytical Reading

1. What type of foot is the first line an example of? How does it reinforce the emphasis the speaker places on "Wild Nights!" by using an exclamation mark? What other poetic device is used to reinforce the emphasis?

2. In the second stanza, which word symbolizes the "wild" aspect of the nights the speaker alludes to? Does the word mean this symbol is wanted or unwanted?

3. Why might the speaker metaphorically say she is "done" with the Compass and the Chart?

4. What might be the meaning of "Rowing" and "moor / … In thee!" interpreted as a) erotic metaphors, and as b) spiritual metaphors?

5. What may "Eden," "the Sea" and "tonight" be symbols for? Do a web search for common symbols in poetry, if need be. Remember to record your sources.

Food for Thought

1. Look at the following meanings of the word "luxury": 1) a condition of abundance and great comfort; 2) something inessential generating pleasure or satisfaction; and 3) lust (archaic today, but in use in the nineteenth century). How do they inform the overall interpretation of the poem?

2. Consider the recurrence of words rhyming with "thee." Where in the poem do such words occur? In which way does this support the thematic structure of the poem?

3. How does the type of poetic foot and the poem's meter contribute to its nautical imagery? How does this rhythm and imagery reveal the theme?

4. Research biographical information on Emily Dickinson. Based on the information you find, which interpretation of the poem makes the most sense to you? Explain your argument.

5. Consider the last stanza. Do the dashes and other punctuation make it easier to connect the different images and symbols evoked? Explain why or why not.

Blowing the Fluff Away

Text in Context

Born in New York to Canadian parents, Robyn Sarah (1949–) grew up in Montreal, where she still lives. She is known for finding inspiration in everyday experience or, in her words, "making much of something small." As a graduate of the *Conservatoire de musique du Québec*, she considers her ear to be her guide as she composes a poem. Accent, rhythm and rhyme therefore play an important role in her poetry.

Exploratory Reading

Blowing the Fluff Away   **Robyn Sarah**

For E. B.

The sprig of unknown bloom you sent last fall
spent the long winter drying on my wall,
mounted on black. But it had turned to fluff
some months ago. Tonight I took it down
5 because I thought that I had had enough
of staring at it. Brittle, dry and brown,
it seemed to speak too plainly of a waste
of friendship, forced to flower, culled in haste.

So, after months of fearing to walk past
10 in case the stir should scatter it to bits,
I took it out to scatter it at last
with my own breath, and so to call us quits.
—Fooled! for the fluff was nothing but a sheath,
with tiny, perfect flowers underneath.

Source: Sarah, R. "Blowing the Fluff Away." *Poetry*, 2009, www.poetryfoundation.org/poetrymagazine/poems/52677/
blowing-the-fluff-away.

Initial Insight

1. What kind of relationship does the speaker have with the addressee, and what can be
observed about the state of that relationship?

2. What extended metaphor does the speaker use to describe this relationship?

Reader's Response

Discuss your answers to the following questions with one or more partners.

1. What emotions did this poem spark in you?

2. What images came to mind as you read the poem?

3. Did the poem's ending surprise you? Why or why not?

4. Did you find the metaphorical comparison expressed in the poem apropos? Explain.

LANGUAGE FOCUS

The iambic foot is the most prevalent rhythmic pattern in English poetry, since the iamb is a base
element of natural language use (e.g., the sprig, tonight). Scan "Blowing the Fluff Away," and mark
the unstressed syllables as they occur in natural language:

• Identify function words, such as articles, pronouns and prepositions.

MyBookshelf > My eLab
> Exercises > Part III: Poetry
> Chapter 12: Poems on Love
> Blowing the Fluff Away —
Vocabulary Comprehension

Close Reading

1. What does the phrase "mounted on black" indicate about the "sprig of bloom"?

_____

2. What is the denotation of the word "fluff" in this context? How does another meaning of this word contribute to the word's connotation in the poem?

_____

_____

_____

3. Which senses do the images "Brittle, dry and brown" appeal to?

_____

4. In the first stanza, which line contains alliteration, and which words make it up?

_____

5. In line 8, which word starts with a discordant sound that creates an effect of cacophony?

_____

6. What did the speaker intend to mark by "blowing the fluff away"?

_____

7. Who or what is fooled at the end of the poem?

_____

MyBookshelf > My eLab
> Exercises > Part III: Poetry
> Chapter 12: Poems on Love
> Blowing the Fluff Away —
Close Reading: Additional
Questions

8. What poetic device does the exclamation "Fooled!" introduce?

a) a stanza   b) a persona   c) a volta   d) an apostrophe

Analytical Reading

1. The poet identifies "Blowing the Fluff Away" as a sonnet. Does it conform to the close-form structure of a Petrarchan or Shakespearean sonnet? Support your answer by determining the poem's rhyme scheme and division into stanzas.

2. In line 3, explain how the poet uses a sound device to emphasize the word "black" (see page 158). How does the colour black foreshadow the remainder of the stanza?

3. In line 8, does the phrase "forced to flower, culled in haste" describe the "sprig of bloom" or the "friendship"? Explain.

4. What is the theme of this poem?

Food for Thought

1. Do you interpret the poem to have a positive or a negative ending? Explain the metaphor of the hidden flowers to support your answer.

2. Which elements suggest that the speaker may indeed be the poet, addressing an old friend?

Comparative Insight

1. Consider the thematic structure of Shakespeare's Sonnet 18 and Barrett Browning's Sonnet 43. How are they similar? How are they different?

2. Compare the formal structure of Shakespeare's Sonnet 18 and Barrett Browning's Sonnet 43. What impact do their rhythmic and rhyme patterns have on the ways in which the themes are developed?

3. Which elements contribute to the ambiguity in Shakespeare's Sonnet 18 and Dickinson's "Wild Nights – Wild Nights!"?

4. How do the different types of love expressed in Poe's "To My Mother" and Dickinson's "Wild Nights – Wild Nights!" affect the tone of these poems?

5. Dickinson's "Wild Nights – Wild Nights!" and Sarah's "Blowing the Fluff Away" both break with more traditional, closed-form structural patterns. How do these stylistic decisions convey the tone and message they seek to express?

Presenting an Analysis

Writing | Analyzing the Interaction between Formal and Thematic Structure

The poems in this chapter either conform to closed-form structural patterns, such as the sonnet, or knowingly break away from them. Choose one of the poems in this chapter, and prepare an analytical essay focusing around a thesis statement that investigates the link between the poem's formal structure and thematic structure. Explain how they work together in the development of the poem's tone and theme. Pay attention to rhythmic patterns and rhyme scheme, and highlight how they affect the treatment of the subject matter and the poetic devices used. (Refer to Part V, Writing about Literature, on page 271 for more information on essay format and structure.)

Speaking | Comparing Internal and External Context

It is generally assumed that the speakers of the poems in this chapter represent—at least to a certain extent—the poets' voices. Choose one of the poems in this chapter and present an analysis of it. Divide your presentation in two parts:

- First, analyze the theme and explicate any lines you consider important by explaining images, symbols and other poetic devices. Consider only elements contained in the poem itself.
- Then, present salient biographical information on the poet, and point out how this knowledge of external context may alter the interpretation of (parts of) the poem.

Make sure to record the sources you use to research biographical information, and clearly mention them in your presentation. If you use visual support, apply MLA guidelines to present these references on your slides.

(Refer to Appendix 2 on page 297 for more information on presentation format and structure.)

MyBookshelf > My eLab
> Exercises > Grammar and Accuracy

MyBookshelf > My eLab
> Documents > Chapter 22: Writing a Literary Essay
> MLA Referencing Guidelines

CHAPTER 13

Poems on Life

This chapter focuses on the following:

- Rhythm and sound devices
- Diction and figures of speech
- Symbolism
- Language Focus: euphemisms
- The Language of Literature: imagery
- Theme

The poems in this chapter explore the meaning of life in all of its different facets. From small observations on daily life to big questions pondering the elements of a satisfying life, the passing from life to death and cultural and racial cohabitation, they evoke the quintessence of our existence. Mirroring the diversity of the human experience, these poems are written in a variety of genres, which the activities will allow you to explore and analyze.

So you can fully appreciate each poem, the **Exploratory Reading** section first invites you to read it one or more times without interruption, before answering the **Initial Insight** and **Reader's Response** questions below the poem. These intuitive reactions form the foundation for more in-depth analysis. To undertake this analysis, read the poem again, this time more slowly, paying attention to specific elements that seem significant to understanding and interpreting it. **Paraphrase** each line in the margin; look up challenging words as needed. Then, answer the **Close Reading** questions to validate your understanding. The **Analytical Reading** and **Food for Thought** questions will help you look for thematic patterns, identify specific examples of poetic devices or principles and turn a critical eye to your observations. At the end of this chapter, the **Comparative Insight** questions prompt you to compare and contrast thematic and formal patterns across poems, before expressing the fruit of your analyses in speaking and writing.

Connect with the Text

Take stock of your opinions on the following questions. Discuss them with one or more partners.

1. What impulse do you feel most people's lives are driven by? What does it mean to you to live a *good* life? What image or metaphor would you use to describe your life (e.g., a competition, a circus, etc.)?

2. How much does language affect our thinking? Why do you think there is no global language?

3. Despite their differences, are people essentially the same? Why or why not? Would the world be a better or worse place if everyone looked the same? Is criticizing a different culture the same as being racist?

4. When, if ever, is taking a human life justified? Should life be considered sacred? Should people be able to decide over their own life and death? Explain.

If—

Text in Context

Rudyard Kipling (1865–1936) was born in Bombay, India. He became one of the most popular late-Victorian poets and story writers when he moved to London in 1889. He wrote several stories for children, his most famous collection undoubtedly being *The Jungle Books*, inspired by some of the tales he himself read as a child in India. He was awarded the Nobel Prize for literature in 1907, though his unpopular political views, including his support for British imperialism, led to critical neglect following his death. In 1995, however, his poem "If—," written in the form of paternal advice, was voted the United Kingdom's favourite poem in a BBC opinion poll.

Exploratory Reading

If—   **Rudyard Kipling**

    If you can keep your head when all about you
        Are losing theirs and blaming it on you,
    If you can trust yourself when all men doubt you,
        But make allowance for their doubting too;
5 If you can wait and not be tired by waiting,
        Or being lied about, don't deal in lies,
    Or being hated, don't give way to hating,
        And yet don't look too good, nor talk too wise:

    If you can dream—and not make dreams your master;
10   If you can think—and not make thoughts your aim;
    If you can meet with Triumph and Disaster
        And treat those two impostors just the same;
    If you can bear to hear the truth you've spoken
        Twisted by knaves to make a trap for fools,
15 Or watch the things you gave your life to, broken,
        And stoop and build 'em up with worn-out tools:

    If you can make one heap of all your winnings
        And risk it on one turn of pitch-and-toss,
    And lose, and start again at your beginnings
20   And never breathe a word about your loss;
    If you can force your heart and nerve and sinew
        To serve your turn long after they are gone,
    And so hold on when there is nothing in you
        Except the Will which says to them: 'Hold on!'

25 If you can talk with crowds and keep your virtue,
        Or walk with Kings—nor lose the common touch,

If neither foes nor loving friends can hurt you,
　　If all men count with you, but none too much;
If you can fill the unforgiving minute
30　With sixty seconds' worth of distance run,
Yours is the Earth and everything that's in it,
　　And—which is more—you'll be a Man, my son!

Source: Kipling, R. "If—." *Rewards and Fairies*, Doubleday, 1910, www.poetryfoundation.org/poems/46473/if---.

Initial Insight

1. Why do many of the poem's lines start with "if"?

_____

_____

2. Whom does the speaker address the poem to?

_____

Reader's Response

Consider the following questions. Discuss your answers with one or more partners.

1. Did you find the poem inspiring or moralizing? Why?

2. Did you find it easy or difficult to understand the direction in which the poem was going? Explain.

3. Do you consider all of the qualities mentioned in the poem to be virtues? Why or why not?

Close Reading

1. Anaphora is a poetic device that consists of repeating a word or phrase at the beginning of successive lines to create emphasis. What is an example of anaphora in the poem?

_____

_____

2. In line 1, what figure of speech is "if you can keep your head" an example of? What does it mean?

_____

3. In the first stanza, which line represents an example of assonance?

_____

_____

4. What level of language do "talk too wise" and "build 'em up" represent?

　　a) high diction　　　b) low diction

5. Based on the context, what does "pitch-and-toss" refer to?

a) a gambling game   b) a fight or quarrel   c) going bankrupt

6. Identify three examples of personified concepts in each of stanzas 2 and 3.

_____

_____

MyBookshelf > My eLab
> Exercises > Part III: Poetry
> Chapter 13: Poems on
Life > If— – Vocabulary
Comprehension

7. Cite three lines in which the speaker develops a contrasting, paradoxical idea to highlight desirable qualities the addressee should aspire to.

_____

8. Is "If—" a narrative poem or a didactic poem? Explain.

_____

_____

MyBookshelf > My eLab
> Exercises > Part III: Poetry
> Chapter 13: Poems on Life
> If— – Close Reading:
Additional Questions

Analytical Reading

1. What is the poem's rhyme scheme? What is its meter? Explain how these elements, along with the level of diction identified in Close Reading question 4, contribute to the poem's tone.

2. Match each of the values listed with the line from the poem that expresses it.

1. composure	a. "If you can trust yourself when all men doubt you"
2. determination	b. "But make allowance for their doubting too."
3. forgiveness	c. "Or being hated, don't give way to hating"
4. hard-working	d. "If you can make one heap of all your winnings …"
5. humility	e. "And never breathe a word about your loss."
6. righteousness	f. "If you can force your heart and nerve and sinew …"
7. risk-taking	g. "If all men count with you, but none too much"
8. stoicism	h. "If you can fill the unforgiving minute …"

3. What point does the poem make about patience, either explicitly or implicitly?

4. What does the speaker mean when he says one should treat Triumph and Disaster "just the same"? How does this line reveal the poem's theme?

Food for Thought

1. As it reflects the values of the society and era in which it was written, the poem "If—" is considered a fine example of Victorian stoicism. Research this term (remember to record your sources) and discuss both the associated values and how they are taken up in the poem.

2. In which way does "If—" offer a worldview that is at the same time based on disillusion and hope?

3. Feminist readings of the poem point out its inherent sexism. Which aspect(s) of the poem could be considered sexist? How do they reflect Victorian gender roles? Do a web search if need be (remember to record your sources).

Morning at the Window

Text in Context

Thomas Stearns Eliot (1888–1965) grew up in St. Louis, Missouri, but settled in England when, as a Harvard graduate student, he travelled to Europe in 1914. Eliot wrote prose, essays and plays, but it is his poetry that brought him literary fame. His break from the Romantic poets and his modernist experiments with new poetic rhythms and themes resonated with the 1920s intellectuals of the so-called Lost Generation and established him as a pioneering poet. It is remarkable that Eliot, even though he had published twenty-five titles by age forty, could never write for more than three hours a day as he maintained a day job in publishing. In 1948, he received the Nobel Prize in Literature for his poetry.

Exploratory Reading

Morning at the Window   T. S. Eliot

They are rattling breakfast plates in basement kitchens,
And along the trampled edges of the street
I am aware of the damp souls of housemaids
Sprouting despondently at area gates.

5 The brown waves of fog toss up to me
Twisted faces from the bottom of the street,
And tear from a passer-by with muddy skirts
An aimless smile that hovers in the air
And vanishes along the level of the roofs.

Source: Eliot, T. S. "Morning at the Window." 1914. *Prufrock, and Other Observations, The Egoist,* 1917, www.poets.org/poetsorg/poem/morning-window.

Initial Insight

1. What contextual meaning does the title bring to the poem?

_____

_____

2. Does the poem describe a scene, evoke more abstract feelings or both? Explain.

_____

_____

Reader's Response

Consider the following questions. Discuss your answers with one or more partners.

1. Keeping in mind the poem was written in 1914, does it strike you as realistic or imaginary? Explain your point.

2. If you were to associate "Morning at the Window" with a season, which one would it be, and why?

3. If you woke up to the scene described, would it have a positive, negative or neutral impact on your day's mood? Explain your reasons.

THE LANGUAGE OF LITERATURE

The effect of a poem is to a very large extent determined by the poet's use of poetic devices and structural patterns. Use the following questions to focus your attention on the effect of the poet's diction.

The poem "Morning at the Window" is rich in imagery, appealing to the different senses. As a literary device, imagery consists of descriptive language that can function as a way for the reader to better imagine the world of the piece of literature and also add symbolism to the work. Seven major types of imagery can be distinguished, each corresponding to a sense, feeling, action or reaction. For each type of image, identify a word, phrase or line in the poem that evokes it.

1. Auditory (sound): _____

2. Gustatory (taste): _____

3. Kinesthetic (movement): _____

4. Olfactory (smell): _____

5. Organic (feeling inside): _____

6. Tactile (touch): _____

7. Visual (sight): _____

Close Reading

1. From the context, who might "they" refer to?

_____

_____

_____

2. Which word in the first stanza informs the reader on the emotional state of "they," or the people observed? What is that state?

_____

3. Which sound device is **not** used in lines 3 and 4 of the poem? Explain.

   a) assonance   b) consonance   c) internal rhyme   d) alliteration

_____

_____

4. Where is the speaker positioned in relation to the people on the street? Which two words signal this?

_____

5. In the second stanza, which colour is evoked twice, once explicitly and once implicitly? What does it characterize?

_____

_____

6. Which inanimate phenomenon is personified twice in the second stanza? Which verbs help establish this personification?

_____

_____

7. Who or what "tear[s] from a passer-by ... / ... an aimless smile"?

_____

_____

8. True or false? The passer-by's smile is directed at the speaker.

a) True   b) False

MyBookshelf > My eLab > Exercises > Part III: Poetry > Chapter 13: Poems on Life > Morning at the Window — Vocabulary Comprehension

MyBookshelf > My eLab > Exercises > Part III: Poetry > Chapter 13: Poems on Life > Morning at the Window — Close Reading: Additional Questions

Analytical Reading

1. How would you describe the tone of the poem?

2. The denotation of the word "damp" includes "humid, in an unpleasant manner" and "depressed." What connotation do they share? How do these meanings contribute to the metaphor "damp souls"?

3. How can the image of the fog be read as representing the differences between the living conditions of working-class and higher-class citizens?

4. Which poetic devices does the speaker use to depict the working-class people as non-defined, ghost-like beings? How does this affect the mood of the poem?

Food for Thought

1. "Morning at the Window" is an example of imagist poetry, characterized by its attempt to isolate a single image to reveal the essence of its theme. With a partner, distill the imagery in the poem into a single scene by describing or sketching it. How does this scene reveal the poem's theme?

2. The form of "Morning at the Window" is associated with the Spenserian stanza—a fixed-verse form invented by Edmund Spenser for his epic poem "The Faerie Queene." A Spenserian stanza contains nine lines in total: eight lines in iambic pentameter followed by a single Alexandrine—a line written in iambic hexameter. The rhyme scheme of these lines is ABABBCBCC. Does "Morning at the Window" follow each of these formal criteria? Do a web search on the "characteristics of modernist poetry" to explain your observations.

Edge

Text in Context

Sylvia Plath (1932–1963) published her first poem at age eight and grew to become one of the most admired American poets of the twentieth century. During her university studies, Plath began to suffer the symptoms of bipolar disorder and severe depression. In a style called confessional poetry, she explored her own mental anguish, her troubled marriage and her unresolved conflicts with her parents. Her typical imagery uses personal and nature-related symbols; for example, the moon, blood, hospitals and skulls. Plath wrote her last poem, "Edge," six days before she committed suicide.

Exploratory Reading

Edge   Sylvia Plath

The woman is perfected.
Her dead

Body wears the smile of accomplishment,
The illusion of a Greek necessity

5 Flows in the scrolls of her toga,
Her bare

Feet seem to be saying:
We have come so far, it is over.

Each dead child coiled, a white serpent,
10 One at each little

Pitcher of milk, now empty.
She has folded

Them back into her body as petals
Of a rose close when the garden

15 Stiffens and odours bleed
From the sweet, deep throats of the night flower.

The moon has nothing to be sad about,
Staring from her hood of bone.

She is used to this sort of thing.
20 Her blacks crackle and drag.

Source: Plath, S. "Edge." 1965. *Collected Poems*, HarperCollins, 1992, www.poetryfoundation.org/poems/49009/edge-56d22ab50bbc1.

Initial Insight

1. What is the scene described in the poem?

_____

2. What do you observe about the type of diction and level of language used?

_____

Reader's Response

Consider the following questions. Discuss your answers with one or more partners.

1. Did you find the images the poem calls up to be beautiful or morbid? Explain.

2. Do you find the poem transparent or opaque? Give examples to support your point.

3. Do you consider this to be a poem about life or about death? Why?

LANGUAGE FOCUS

Although the poem is clearly concerned with death, the concept is only brought up explicitly twice through the use of its adjective, "dead." Throughout the ages, death has been a concept that is often referred to implicitly, without directly naming it. This can be achieved through the use of symbols and euphemisms—inoffensive substitutions for a more direct or upsetting word. Which euphemisms to refer to death and dying do you know? Use a dictionary or do a web search to complete your answers if necessary.

MyBookshelf > My eLab >
Exercises > Part III: Poetry
> Chapter 13: Poems on
Life > Edge — Vocabulary
Comprehension

Close Reading

1. What poetic genre does "Edge" belong to (see page 157)? Explain your choice.

_____

_____

2. What is the formal structure of the poem? How is it divided into stanzas, and how do stanza divisions relate to the thoughts and sentences that make up the poem?

_____

_____

3. Which two things is the body said to "wear"?

_____

4. What figure of speech is "Pitcher of milk"? What body part does it refer to?

_____

5. In the seventh stanza, what is an example of internal rhyme?

_____

6. What colour contrast does the speaker use as a symbol?

_____

_____

7. In the last stanza, what is the antecedent of "She" and "Her"?

a) the moon   b) the woman   c) the rose

8. Which adjective best represents the tone of the poem?

a) deranged   b) dramatic   c) hysteric   d) sad   e) serene

MyBookshelf > My eLab > Exercises > Part III: Poetry > Chapter 13: Poems on Life > Edge – Close Reading: Additional Questions

Analytical Reading

1. What are the two possible meanings of the past participle "perfected" in the first line? How do these meanings create a sense of ambiguity, further reinforced by a similar duality carried by the word "accomplishment"?

2. How is the poem's title, "Edge," reflected in both the formal and thematic structure of the poem?

3. How is the dead body likened to a statue and a garden? Cite from the poem to highlight the words creating these two comparisons.

4. How is the symbol of the moon used to construct an anticlimax—a poetic device that introduces a transition from an important idea to a trivial one?

Food for Thought

1. Research information on the myth of Artemis (remember to record your sources). How does Artemis connect most of the symbols used in the poem?

2. The symbols of garden and flowers are typically associated with love and desire. Why does the poet associate them with death here?

3. How do you interpret the meaning of "Each dead child coiled, a white serpent, / … back into her body as petals"?

Theme for English B

Text in Context

James Mercer Langston Hughes (1901–1967) was born in Joplin, Missouri, and grew up in different places across the United States and Mexico. While attending Columbia University in New York, he became a part of the Harlem Renaissance, a period during the 1920s and 1930s characterized by the emancipation of African American writers, musicians and other artists. Langston Hughes contributed to this movement by infusing his poems with the rhythms of jazz, the vernacular and social concerns of the African American community. Not only was Hughes a very prolific writer, he also acted as a mentor for many aspiring artists, leading him to become one of the most influential African American literary voices of the twentieth century.

Exploratory Reading

Theme for English B   **Langston Hughes**

The instructor said,

   Go home and write
   a page tonight.
   And let that page come out of you—
5 *Then, it will be true.*

I wonder if it's that simple?
I am twenty-two, coloured, born in Winston-Salem.
I went to school there, then Durham, then here
to this college on the hill above Harlem.
10 I am the only coloured student in my class.
The steps from the hill lead down into Harlem,
through a park, then I cross St. Nicholas,
Eighth Avenue, Seventh, and I come to the Y,
the Harlem Branch Y, where I take the elevator
15 up to my room, sit down, and write this page:

It's not easy to know what is true for you or me
at twenty-two, my age. But I guess I'm what
I feel and see and hear, Harlem, I hear you:
hear you, hear me—we two—you, me, talk on this page.
20 (I hear New York, too.) Me—who?
Well, I like to eat, sleep, drink, and be in love.
I like to work, read, learn, and understand life.
I like a pipe for a Christmas present,
or records—Bessie, bop, or Bach.
25 I guess being coloured doesn't make me *not* like
the same things other folks like who are other races.
So will my page be coloured that I write?

Being me, it will not be white.
But it will be
30 a part of you, instructor.
You are white—
yet a part of me, as I am a part of you.
That's American.
Sometimes perhaps you don't want to be a part of me.
35 Nor do I often want to be a part of you.
But we are, that's true!
As I learn from you,
I guess you learn from me—

although you're older—and white—
40 and somewhat more free.

This is my page for English B.

Source: Hughes, L. "Theme for English B." 1951. *The Collected Poems of Langston Hughes*, Knopf and Vintage, 1994, www.poets.org/poetsorg/poem/theme-english-b.

Initial Insight

1. What is the speaker's reason for crafting his text?

He is a college student who received an assignment

2. Examine the information in Text in Context. Can we conclude that the poem is autobiographical? Explain.

Reader's Response

Consider the following questions. Discuss your answers with one or more partners.

1. Do you associate the poem more with a prepared speech or a stream of thoughts? Why?
2. Do you feel the theme of the poem still resonates strongly today, or did you find it difficult to connect with? Explain.
3. What is your experience of the poem's musicality and use of verse? How does it correspond or differ from what you expect poetry to sound like?

Close Reading

1. Why are lines 2–5 represented in italics?

2. Which word, evoked by the instructor, does the speaker essentially ponder throughout the poem?

3. What are five facts you know about the speaker after reading lines 6–15?

4. Why does the third stanza end (line 15) on a colon?

5. Which two sound devices contribute to the musicality of lines 18–20?

_____

_____

6. What point do the speaker's examples on lines 21–24 illustrate?

_____

_____

7. Which poetic device in lines 27–28 contributes to the pun based on the words "coloured" and "white"?

a) metaphor   b) connotation   c) oxymoron

8. How does the poem's use of rhyme differ in the last stanza?

_____

_____

Analytical Reading

1. How does the narrative position of the speaker in regard to the addressee shift between the beginning and end of the poem? How does this aspect of the poem's formal structure support its thematic structure?

2. The pronoun "you" features repeatedly in lines 16–30. Does it always refer to the same person or entity? Explain.

3. To which effect does the speaker use enjambment—the carrying over of a phrase or sentence to the next line—for instance, in lines 25–26 and 29–33?

4. The assignment instructions start with "Go home." What can you infer from the poem about the speaker's conception of "home," as it relates to physical place but also to society?

5. In which ways does the speaker compare and contrast learning at school and learning in life?

6. How does the speaker use black and white imagery throughout the poem? More specifically, discuss the meaning of the images used in the following lines to highlight difference and identity.

Line	Meaning of Imagery
"I am the only coloured student in my class."	
"I guess being coloured doesn't make me not like / the same things other folks like who are other races."	
"So will my page be coloured that I write? / Being me, it will not be white."	

"You are white— / yet a part of me, as I am a part of you."	
"although you're older—and white— / and somewhat more free."	

Food for Thought

1. Do a web search for the word "coloured," or its American spelling variant "colored." What connotation does the word have today? How was it used at the time the poem was written (1949)? Discuss why the poet might have chosen to use it.

2. Do a web search to find out who or what the records of "Bessie" and "bop" refer to. If you have the opportunity, listen to a few samples. How do they connect with the musicality and themes of the poem?

3. How would you describe the tone of the poem? Pay attention to the level of diction and the use of poetic devices. Cite from the text to support your answer. How does this use of tone contribute to the development of the poem's theme?

4. Do a web search to inform yourself on the Harlem Renaissance. What is the movement's importance, and how is this reflected in the poem's theme?

5. How might this poem be different if it were written today? Explain your argument.

A Different History

Text in Context

Sujata Bhatt (1956–) was born in India, where she spent her childhood until she and her family moved to the United States when she was twelve years old. The multicultural perspectives on language, culture and nature she explores in most of her poetry find origin in her own life experiences. "A Different History," for instance, reflects on Bhatt's relationship with her mother tongue, Gujarati, as an expression of her Indian identity, and English, the language she speaks and writes every day. Bhatt has been recognized as a distinctive voice in contemporary and postcolonial poetry.

Exploratory Reading

A Different History   Sujata Bhatt

Great Pan is not dead;
he simply emigrated
   to India.
Here, the gods roam freely,

5 disguised as snakes or monkeys;
    every tree is sacred

History

    and it is a sin
    to be rude to a book.
    It is a sin to shove a book aside
10   with your foot,
    a sin to slam books down

Culture

            hard on a table,
    a sin to toss one carelessly
            across a room.
15 You must learn how to turn the pages gently
    without disturbing Sarasvati,

Language

    without offending the tree
    from whose wood the paper was made.

    Which language
20   has not been the oppressor's tongue?
    Which language
    truly meant to murder someone?

identity

    And how does it happen
    that after the torture,
25   after the soul has been cropped
    with the long scythe swooping out
        of the conqueror's face—
    the unborn grandchildren
    grow to love that strange language.

Source: Bhatt, S. "A Different History." *Brunizem*, Carcanet, 1988.

Initial Insight

1. How is the poem's title, "A Different History," taken up and reflected in the poem?

_____

_____

_____

2. What is the attitude of the speaker toward the two aspects of Indian culture evoked?

_____

_____

Reader's Response

Consider the following questions. Discuss your answers with one or more partners.

1. Did you feel the two stanzas of the poem are connected or disconnected? Why?

2. What social, cultural or political issues did the poem make you reflect on?

3. Did you find the images and symbols used in the poem easy or difficult to understand and relate to? Why?

Close Reading

1. Who or what is "Great Pan"?

    a) a deity   b) another name for India   c) a person   b) the speaker

2. According to the speaker, why are the gods able to roam freely in India?

_____

3. In lines 8 to 14, how is the word "book" used?

    a) As a form of personification   c) As a hyperbole

    b) As a metaphor   d) As an item, according to its denotation

4. In line 15, who might "you" refer to?

_____

_____

5. How does the speaker link the symbols of the "tree" and the "book"?

_____

6. What are two examples of rhetorical questions in the poem?

_____

7. Which four words carrying negative connotations are associated with "language"?

_____

_____

8. What is unusual about the punctuation mark ending the poem?

_____

MyBookshelf > My eLab
> Exercises > Part III: Poetry
> Chapter 13: Poems on Life
> A Different History
– Vocabulary Comprehension

MyBookshelf > My eLab >
Exercises > Part III: Poetry >
Chapter 13: Poems on Life >
A Different History – Close
Reading: Additional Questions

Analytical Reading

1. What is the poem's predominant theme?

2. How does the repetition of the phrase "a sin to" in lines 7–14 contribute to one and the same metaphor? What might this metaphor be?

3. In the second stanza, which metaphor repeats the idea of "murder"? Why does the speaker use such violent images?

4. Who are the "unborn grandchildren" in line 28? How does this mention represent a shift in the time frame considered by the speaker?

Food for Thought

1. What is the significance of "Great Pan" emigrating to India instead of dying? Do a web search if necessary. Remember to record your sources.

2. Why does the speaker focus on language as a symbol for the oppressor's culture and values?

3. What might be the "soul" that "has been cropped"? How does this metaphor relate to the poem's title and its division in two stanzas?

Comparative Insight

1. Compare the allusions to gods and mythology in "Edge" and "A Different History." What do they refer to? How do the symbols they represent contribute to the construction of theme in these two poems?

2. Compare the imagery in "Morning at the Window" and "Edge." How does it relate to the overall effect of the poems? Pay attention to the level of diction—is it more concrete or abstract?

3. How is the addressee—"you"—used as a rhetorical device in "If—" and "Theme for English B"? What are the similarities and differences in the relationship between the speaker and addressee in these poems?

4. How do "Theme for English B" and "A Different History" develop the thematic concept of racial/cultural identity?

Presenting an Analysis

Writing | Analyzing the Development of Theme and Mood

The poems in this chapter are generally rich in imagery, symbolism and figures of speech. Choose one of them and prepare an analytical essay focusing around a thesis statement that investigates how the diction and poetic devices contribute to the theme and mood of the poem. Refer to the poetic devices identified in Elements of Analysis on pages 165–166 as well as the work you have done in this chapter to identify pertinent elements, and highlight how they help transform the subject matter into a specific theme and mood.

(Refer to Part V, Writing about Literature, on page 271 for more information on essay format and structure.)

Speaking | Examining Sound Devices in Free Verse Poetry

With the exception of "If—," the poems in this chapter are written in free verse, with little or no rhyme. In the absence of rhyme patterns, how does the poet craft verse that supports the development of theme in the poem? Choose one of the four free verse poems in this chapter and present an explication that focuses on the use of sound devices and rhythmic patterns in the poem. Read (parts of) the poem out loud to illustrate your explication, and point out how these sound devices affect the figures of speech they draw attention to.

(Refer to Appendix 2 on page 297 for more information on presentation format and structure.)

MyBookshelf > My eLab > Exercises > Grammar and Accuracy

CHAPTER 14

Poems on Nature

This chapter focuses on the following:

- Rhythm, rhyme and meter
- Imagery and symbolism
- Diction and figures of speech
- Language Focus: cultural references
- The Language of Literature: poetic devices
- Theme, tone and mood

The poems in this chapter meditate on nature and the human experience of it, constructed either in the presence or absence of a speaker. The imagery deployed directly contributes to each poem's tone, leading the reader to experience very different moods, regardless of similar subject matter. This is reinforced by their different formal patterns and sound devices.

So you can fully appreciate each poem, the **Exploratory Reading** section first invites you to read it one or more times without interruption, before answering the **Initial Insight** and **Reader's Response** questions below the poem. These intuitive reactions form the foundation for more in-depth analysis. To undertake this analysis, read the poem again, this time more slowly, paying attention to specific elements that seem significant to understanding and interpreting it. **Paraphrase** each line in the margin; look up challenging words as needed. Then, answer the **Close Reading** questions to validate your understanding. The **Analytical Reading** and **Food for Thought** questions will help you look for thematic patterns, identify specific examples of poetic devices or principles and turn a critical eye to your observations. At the end of this chapter, the **Comparative Insight** questions prompt you to compare and contrast thematic and formal patterns across poems, before expressing the fruit of your analyses in speaking and writing.

Connect with the Text

A. Take stock of your opinions on the following questions. Discuss them with one or more partners.

1. How important is nature to you? Do you try to get close to nature? Where do you go? Share an anecdote (e.g., about encountering an animal in the wild, hiking in a remote area or travelling to an unusual place).
2. What is your favourite season, and why?
3. If you were asked to write a poem about nature, what precisely would you write about?
4. How have nature and the environment changed since you were a child? Give a specific example.
5. How may seeing ourselves as separate from or as a part of nature change our attitudes toward the environment? How are houses and cities similar to or different from animal habitats?

B. Do a web search on the effect nature imagery has on people's mood.

   1. Do you need to physically be in nature to get its benefits?

   2. What are the effects of being exposed to nature imagery?

   3. What type of nature imagery has been shown to have an impact on people's mood?

I Wandered Lonely as a Cloud

Text in Context

William Wordsworth (1770–1850) was born and lived much of his life in the English Lake District, an area which today still is one of rugged beauty. Impressed by the democratic ideals of the French Revolution, he left on a walking tour across France, Switzerland and Italy in 1790. After fathering an illegitimate child in France, he returned to England where he frequented radical political circles sympathetic to the ideas of the Revolution. He identified with what has later been called Romanticism: a conviction that people should follow ideals rather than imposed conventions, stressing the importance of authentic personal feelings.

Such emotions, often associated with natural themes, are predominant in his work. In 1802, "I Wandered Lonely as a Cloud" resulted from a walk in the Lake District. Wordsworth's wife, Mary Hutchinson, contributed lines 21–22. He added the second stanza years later, in 1815. The poem is said to be the most anthologized poem in the world.

Exploratory Reading

I Wandered Lonely as a Cloud   **William Wordsworth**

   I wandered lonely as a cloud
   That floats on high o'er vales and hills,
   When all at once I saw a crowd,
   A host, of golden daffodils;
5 Beside the lake, beneath the trees,
   Fluttering and dancing in the breeze.

   Continuous as the stars that shine
   And twinkle on the milky way,
   They stretched in never-ending line
10 Along the margin of a bay:
   Ten thousand saw I at a glance,
   Tossing their heads in sprightly dance.

   The waves beside them danced; but they
   Out-did the sparkling waves in glee:
15 A poet could not but be gay,
   In such a jocund company:

I gazed—and gazed—but little thought
What wealth the show to me had brought:

For oft, when on my couch I lie
20 In vacant or in pensive mood,
They flash upon that inward eye
Which is the bliss of solitude;
And then my heart with pleasure fills,
And dances with the daffodils.

Source: Wordsworth, W. "I Wandered Lonely as a Cloud." 1807. *Poems, in Two Volumes*, Longman, Hurst, Rees, and Orme.

Initial Insight

1. What element of the landscape is central to the scene the speaker describes?

_____

2. What event does the last stanza describe?

_____

Reader's Response

Working with one or more partners, discuss your answers to the following questions.

1. What colour(s) does the poem make you think of? Why?
2. Which one of your senses does the poem appeal to the most? Explain which part(s) of the poem contribute to this.
3. Do you feel that observing a field of daffodils merits such a strong emotional reaction?

THE LANGUAGE OF LITERATURE

The effect of a poem is to a very large extent determined by the poet's use of poetic devices and structural patterns. Use the following questions to focus your attention on the effect of the poet's diction.

In his "Preface to *Lyrical Ballads*" (1800), Wordsworth wrote that poetic devices "cannot be necessary here, either for elevation of style, or any of its supposed ornaments: for, if the Poet's subject be judiciously chosen, it will naturally, and upon fit occasion, lead him to passions the language of which, if selected truly and judiciously, must necessarily be dignified and variegated, and alive with metaphors and figures."[1] In the poem, find two examples of each of the following figures of speech. Include the line number.

1. Hyperbole: _____

_____

2. Metaphor: _____

_____

_____

1. Wordsworth, W. "Preface to Lyrical Ballads." 1802. University of Pennsylvania, Penn Arts & Sciences, www.english.upenn.edu/~mgamer/Etexts/lbprose.html.

3. Personification: _____

_____

4. Simile: _____

_____

Discuss which feelings you believe the poet conveys by using these figures of speech.

Close Reading

1. What is the poem's rhyme scheme? Is it regular?

_____

2. What is the predominant meter of the poem?

a) iambic pentameter   c) trochaic pentameter

b) iambic tetrameter   d) trochaic tetrameter

3. What genre does the poem best fit into?

a) lyric poems   c) dramatic poems

b) narrative poems   d) didactic poems

4. What part of the meaning of "wandering" does the qualifier "as a cloud" reinforce?

a) The speaker has no particular aim or destination.

b) The speaker has a very light step, as if he floats.

c) The speaker feels very isolated and alone.

5. In the second stanza, what does the speaker describe?

_____

_____

_____

6. In line 13, what do the "waves" refer to?

a) the movement of the daffodils in the wind

b) the movement of stars sparkling in the sky

c) the movement of the water in the lake

7. In the third stanza, what does the reader learn about the speaker?

_____

8. In the last stanza, which word best describes what feeling the memory of daffodils brings to the speaker?

_____

_____

MyBookshelf > My eLab
> Exercises > Part III: Poetry
> Chapter 14: Poems on
Nature > I Wandered Lonely
as a Cloud — Vocabulary
Comprehension

MyBookshelf > My eLab
> Exercises > Part III: Poetry
> Chapter 14: Poems on
Nature > I Wandered Lonely
as a Cloud — Close Reading:
Additional Questions

Analytical Reading

1. How does the speaker's state of mind change as the poem unfolds?

2. How does the wind enhance almost every visual aspect of the images brought up in the first three stanzas? Cite from the poem to support your answer.

3. What do daffodils mean to the speaker? Cite from the text to support your analysis.

4. How does the poet use alliteration, assonance and consonance to create an effect of euphony? Provide at least one example for each sound device. How does this sound effect contribute to the construction of the poem's mood? How does it fit in with the poem's imagery?

Food for Thought

1. In classical thought, the four elements are earth, water, air and fire. Aristotle added a fifth element, ether, which describes what is beyond the material world. How is each of these elements represented in the poem's imagery?

2. As pointed out in The Language of Literature, Wordsworth strongly believed poetic devices have to naturally fit into a poem's theme rather than function as mere style or ornament. If he had used the word "walked" instead of "wandered" in the first line, how would this have affected the poem's theme? Explain your answer.

3. How does the poet evoke a sense of communion between human and nature? Be specific on the images and other poetic devices that contribute to this construction.

Indian Summer

Text in Context

Archibald Lampman (1861–1899) was born in Kent County, Ontario. His family, who had French, Dutch, German, Swiss, Scottish and English roots, mostly lived in small, rural communities. Lampman dedicated his childhood to study and enjoying the outside. Influenced by his father's fondness for what was called *belles lettres,* he took a particular interest in the work of Keats and Wordsworth, which was to influence his own poetry, associated with Romanticism. After graduating from college, Lampman entered the civil service. Although he was unsatisfied with his career, he did little to change it. His poetry, which was heavily focused on nature and idealized communities and relationships, was his escape from his daily routine.

Exploratory Reading

Indian Summer   Archibald Lampman

> The old grey year is near his term in sooth,
> And now with backward eye and soft-laid palm
> Awakens to a golden dream of youth,
> A second childhood lovely and most calm,

5 And the smooth hour about his misty head
　An awning of enchanted splendour weaves,
　Of maples, amber, purple and rose-red,
　And droop-limbed elms down-drooping golden leaves.
　With still half-fallen lids he sits and dreams
10 Far in a hollow of the sunlit wood,
　Lulled by the murmur of thin-threading streams,
　Nor sees the polar armies overflood
　The darkening barriers of the hills, nor hears
　The north-wind ringing with a thousand spears.

Source: Lampman, A. "Indian Summer." 1899. *Canadian Poetry*, Canadian Poetry Press, www.canadianpoetry.ca/
confederation/Archibald Lampman/alcyone/indian_summer.htm.

Initial Insight

1. Which two seasons are evoked and contrasted in the poem?

_____

_____

2. Who or what is the poem's central persona?

_____

Reader's Response

Working with one or more partners, discuss your answers to the following questions.

1. Which of your senses did the poem appeal to the most?
2. How do you think the speaker feels about fall, winter and the Indian summer? Explain.
3. Which of the poem's images do you associate the most with the Indian summer? Why?

Close Reading

1. How does the poet use verbs and pronouns to personify the concept of the year? Cite two examples for each grammatical category.

_____

_____

_____

2. Which two noun phrases does the poet use as metaphors to refer to the Indian summer?

_____

3. What colour-palette is the poem built around? Cite from the poem to support your answer.

_____

_____

4. Scan the poem. What is its meter?

_____

5. What is the rhyme scheme of the poem? What type of closed form does this represent (see page 163 for a list)?

_____

MyBookshelf > My eLab
> Exercises > Part III: Poetry
> Chapter 14: Poems on Nature
> Indian Summer – Vocabulary
Comprehension

6. Which poetic device is not found in the poem? Provide an example for each other option.

a) alliteration   b) assonance   c) metaphor   d) repetition   e) simile

Examples: _____

MyBookshelf > My eLab
> Exercises > Part III: Poetry
> Chapter 14: Poems on Nature
> Indian Summer – Close
Reading: Additional Questions

Analytical Reading

1. Which poetic devices does the poet use to express the inevitability of winter?

2. What is the predominant theme of the poem?

3. Which structural elements make "Indian Summer" a sonnet?

Food for Thought

1. Which images reflect the poet's Canadian roots and his association with the "Confederation Poets" movement?

2. Critics observe that, as a Romantic poet, Lampman "speaks about the difficulty of coming to terms with nature, of taming the unpredictable, cruel and often meaningless landscape."[2] How is this theme revealed in "Indian Summer"?

Fall, Leaves, Fall

Text in Context

Emily Brontë (1818–1848) was born in rural Yorkshire, England. Her father was an Anglican reverend who had a keen interest in literature and writing. It should then come as no surprise that she and two of her sisters, Charlotte and Anne, also wrote prose and poetry. From an early age, she made drawings of natural subjects such as birds, plants and landscapes, which would later also become a significant part of her poetry. Emily Brontë's innovative writing style uses natural and mystical elements to convey intense energy and emotion. Her writing, including her novel _Wuthering Heights_, which is now considered a classic of English literature, was not well-received during her lifetime. The only poems by Emily Brontë published in her lifetime were included in a slim volume by her and her sisters, which sold a mere two copies.

---

2. M. Domines Veliki, "Archibald Lampman's 'Nature' Poetry as Reflecting the (Im)possibility of Construing Canadian Identity," _The Central European Journal of Canadian Studies_, 2008, vol. 6, no. 1, pp. 143–153.

Exploratory Reading

Fall, Leaves, Fall   **Emily Brontë**

Fall, leaves, fall; die, flowers, away;
Lengthen night and shorten day;
Every leaf speaks bliss to me
Fluttering from the autumn tree.
5 I shall smile when wreaths of snow
Blossom where the rose should grow;
I shall sing when night's decay
Ushers in a drearier day.

Source: Brontë, E. "Fall, Leaves, Fall." 1923. *The Complete Poems of Emily Jane Brontë*, Hodder and Stoughton, www.poetryfoundation.org/poems/52330/fall-leaves-fall.

Initial Insight

1. What is the speaker's main wish regarding the fall?

_____

2. Whom or what does the speaker address?

_____

Reader's Response

Discuss your answers to the following questions with one or more partners.

1. What were your initial feelings when you read this poem?
2. Do you think the speaker truly yearns for winter to come? Explain.
3. How would you describe the speaker's state of mind? Explain.

Close Reading

1. What poetic device is used twice in the opening line?

  a) an allusion   b) an apostrophe   c) a metaphor

2. What play on words can you perceive in the first line?

_____

_____

3. What verb form is used repeatedly in the first and second lines? _____

4. Which two grammatical elements does the speaker use to include herself in the poem? Do they include her explicitly or implicitly?

_____

_____

5. Do the following words have a positive or negative connotation? Write *P* or *N* next to each word.

bliss _____   decay _____   dreary _____   sing _____

blossom _____   die _____   fall _____   smile _____

6. Which two sound devices do lines 5 and 7 employ to underscore their message?

_____

_____

_____

MyBookshelf > My eLab
> Exercises > Part III: Poetry
> Chapter 14: Poems on Nature
> Fall, Leaves, Fall -- Vocabulary
Comprehension

7. Who or what is the subject of "ushers in"?

_____

8. What is the rhyme scheme of the poem?

_____

MyBookshelf > My eLab
> Exercises > Part III: Poetry
> Chapter 14: Poems on Nature
> Fall, Leaves, Fall — Close
Reading: Additional Questions

Analytical Reading

1. How does the poet use verbs and imagery to confer a more active role to winter and a more passive role to fall?

2. How does the rhyme scheme support the poem's thematic structure?

3. What is the poem's tone? What is the poem's mood?

4. What is the theme of the poem?

5. How does the poet use light as visual imagery to support the poem's theme?

Food for Thought

1. This poem allows for two levels of interpretation: one that easily reveals itself as being related to the thematic concept of nature, and a second one that is more abstract. What other thematic concept may be inferred from the poem? Cite from the poem to support this analysis.

2. In Close Reading question 2, you identified a play on words. Research the etymology of the word "fall" and explain whether or not you believe this to be intentional on the poet's part.

Spirit Bear

Text in Context

Dan MacIsaac (1959–) grew up on Vancouver Island and now lives in Victoria, British Columbia. He is a lawyer and also served for ten years on the board of the Environmental Law Centre at the University of Victoria. His poetry, translations and fiction have appeared in a variety of literary journals and magazines, and he has received praise for his use of vivid metaphors. *Cries from the Ark*, the volume that contains "Spirit Bear" and "Garbage Bear," is his first poetry collection.

Exploratory Reading

Spirit Bear   Dan MacIsaac

Ursus americanus kermodei

At the river's black mouth, the white bear waits
for the swimmer.
He crashes into shallows, seizing the quick fish,
5 glisten of silver
along cinder lips.
A cedar twig
cracks.
He lunges
10 for the far shore
murky with hemlock.
He vanishes–
froth spattered
on dark rock.

Source: MacIsaac, D. "Spirit Bear." *Cries from the Ark*, Brick, 2017.

Initial Insight

1. What is the setting of the poem?

_____

2. How is the bear portrayed in the poem?

_____

_____

Reader's Response

Discuss your answers to the following questions with one or more partners.

1. How did reading this poem make you feel? Be precise.
2. If this poem were a visual, would it be a photo or video? Explain.
3. Is this a scene you would like to witness? Why or why not?

Close Reading

1. Which three names are used in the poem to refer to the bear?

_____

2. How does the poet create a contrast in the first line?

_____

3. How is the reference to "the swimmer" used as a metaphor?

_____

_____

MyBookshelf > My eLab
> Exercises > Part III: Poetry
> Chapter 14: Poems on Nature
> Spirit Bear – Vocabulary
Comprehension

4. In line 8, what poetic device is the word "cracks" an example of?

a) a metaphor   b) an onomatopoeia   c) an oxymoron

5. What does the image "froth spattered / on dark rock" represent?

_____

MyBookshelf > My eLab
> Exercises > Part III: Poetry
> Chapter 14: Poems on Nature
> Spirit Bear – Close Reading:
Additional Questions

Analytical Reading

1. In which way does the poet use sound to point out the normality and harmony of the bear hunting and eating a fish?

2. How is the word "cracks" (line 8) used to reinforce the thematic structure of the poem? What is the function of the period that follows it?

3. What is the theme of the poem?

4. What is the tone of the poem? Which sound devices are used to emphasize this tone? Give examples.

Food for Thought

1. Which pronoun is used to refer to the bear? What impact does this have on the reader's perception of the animal?

2. Read the Text in Context section again (page 207). Do a web search for "spirit bear." Beyond the interest of the poem as a description of nature, what other message(s) might it convey?

Garbage Bear

Exploratory Reading

Garbage Bear   **Dan MacIsaac**

Quarter-ton vermin
toppling steel bins,
brash and ruinously loud
as a steel band,
5 bursting into a bruin buffet
of stale-dated Spam,
spattered antifreeze,
and gouts of chain oil.

Putrid smorgasbord,
10 spoils not fit for a goat,
bolted down.
It knows
want, close cousin
to the foul horn of plenty.

Source: MacIsaac, D. "Garbage Bear." *Cries from the Ark*, Brick, 2017.

Initial Insight

1. What is the setting of the poem?

_____

2. How is the bear portrayed in the poem?

_____

_____

Reader's Response

Discuss your answers to the following questions with one or more partners.

1. How did reading this poem make you feel? Be precise.

2. Without the title, what else could this poem be about?

3. Is this a scene you would like to witness? Why or why not?

LANGUAGE FOCUS

Cultural references are words and ideas that point to a specific culture, associated with a time period, a place or both. Unless the reader is informed about these cultures, the reference remains opaque. Consider the following words that act as cultural references in the poem. What is their denotation? What is their connotation? How does your understanding of them affect your interpretation of the poem?

1. Buffet: _____

_____

2. Spam: _____

_____

3. Antifreeze: _____

_____

4. Smorgasbord: _____

_____

MyBookshelf > My eLab
> Exercises > Part III: Poetry
> Chapter 14: Poems on Nature
> Garbage Bear – Vocabulary
Comprehension

Close Reading

1. What type of verse is the poem written in?

    a) blank verse   b) free verse   c) metered verse

2. In the poem, which two words are used to refer to the bear?

_____

3. What is an example of a simile in the poem?

_____

4. Which line contains a clear example of alliteration?

_____

_____

5. In line 13, is the word "want" used as a noun or a verb?

_____

6. What is the meaning of the expression "close cousin / to"?

_____

MyBookshelf > My eLab > Exercises > Part III: Poetry > Chapter 14: Poems on Nature > Garbage Bear — Close Reading: Additional Questions

Analytical Reading

1. In which manner is the bear portrayed in the first lines of the poem? Explain the diction and imagery used to achieve this.

2. In the first stanza, what are two examples of sound devices (assonance and alliteration) to reinforce the poem's diction?

3. What is the meaning of the metaphor "want, close cousin / to the foul horn of plenty"?

Food for Thought

1. Which pronoun is used to refer to the bear? What impact does this have on the reader's perception of the animal?

2. Read the Text in Context section again (page 207). Do an online image search for "garbage bear." Beyond the interest of the poem as a description, what other message(s) might it convey?

Comparative Insight

1. Consider the presence of the speaker in "I Wandered Lonely as a Cloud" and "Fall, Leaves, Fall." How are they similar? How are they different? What is their rapport with the nature scenes they describe?

2. "Fall, Leaves, Fall" and "Indian Summer" both explore the transition of fall into winter. Does this lead to thematic statements that are similar or different? How do each poem's tone and mood contribute to these themes?

3. "I Wandered Lonely as a Cloud" and "Fall, Leaves, Fall" may have deeper themes underlying the ones involving nature. What are those themes, and how are they revealed in the poem through the use of poetic devices? Are there implicit and/or explicit references to these themes?

4. Both "Indian Summer" and "Spirit Bear" contemplate nature in the absence of a speaker. What are the similarities and differences in the development of thematic structure? Which poetic devices are used to craft tone and mood?

5. "Spirit Bear" and "Garbage Bear" focus on the same subject matter—the bear—but place it in different contexts to construct different thematic statements. How do these contexts and the images used to evoke them lead to the development of thematic statements? What do they have in common?

Presenting an Analysis

Writing | Analyzing the Contribution of Imagery to Tone and Mood

The poems in this chapter are rich in natural imagery, but each poem uses it to construct a very different tone and mood. Choose one of the poems in this chapter, and prepare an analytical essay focusing around a thesis statement that investigates the link between the poem's use of imagery and how it contributes to the construction of a particular tone and mood. Also pay attention to the use of sound devices to support the use of this imagery throughout the poem.

ByBookshelf > My eLab
> Exercises > Grammar and
Accuracy

(Refer to Part V, Writing about Literature, on page 271 for more information on essay format and structure.)

Speaking | Revealing Themes Underlying Natural Description

The poems in this chapter, whether they explicitly feature a speaker or not, reveal themes that underpin the more directly observable natural descriptions and themes. Choose one of the poems in this chapter and present a reader's response analysis of it. Divide your presentation in two parts:

- First, analyze the first-level natural theme. Explicate the poem, drawing attention to the images, symbols and other poetic devices used.
- Then, proceed with a second-level analysis, explaining how these same elements may act as symbols to reveal a deeper, underlying theme. Use a reader's response approach to point out how these images inform your analysis of their interpretation as symbols.

(Refer to Appendix 2 on page 297 for more information on presentation format and structure.)

PART IV
Other
Genres

ELEMENTS OF ANALYSIS

While written in verse or prose like the other literary genres presented in this book, the texts in the following chapters blend genres and/or formats. Songs are constructed around a melody to provide an aural experience that brings together the sounds of music and language. Spoken word also makes musicality central through a performance element, which enhances the effect of poetic devices through the artist's use of voice and even body language. Graphic novels develop a plot line not only through the use of narration and dialogue, but also through visual information in the form of illustrations, colours and layout. Finally, speeches deploy rhetorical devices and rely on narrative techniques to convey a nonfiction message.

Engaging with Other Genres

Analyzing multimodal texts—which blend genres and/or formats—requires insight into the different elements that compose them in order to better grasp and appreciate how those aspects piece together cohesively into a multimodal experience requiring the reader to also be a listener or viewer. In all of these texts the author or speaker uses subject matter—what the text is about on a first level—to develop a more abstract underlying theme. This is achieved through literary devices and thematic or narrative structures, but also through formal structures that extend beyond the use of language to include musical and visual arrangements.

Formal literary analysis requires careful study of all the elements and structures that allow you to understand how a blended text is crafted. Similar to how you combine distinct ideas into one cohesive essay as you write and rewrite different drafts, you continually develop your understanding of a blended text as a holistic experience when you engage with it repeatedly. Applying such a parts-to-a-whole approach will help you bridge the gap between subjective interpretations and objective analyses.

You will approach each text in this section through three "drafts," each focused on a specific type of reading and/or listening:

- **Exploratory Reading/Listening** allows you to approach a text as a cohesive entity, without any specific objectives or expectations. Read or listen to the text without interruption; try to let the work guide your attention rather than making a conscious effort to focus on particular features. Afterwards, take stock of your initial reaction to the text, which may be a combination of rational and emotional considerations. Appreciate how the verbal and non-verbal elements of the text have contributed to its effect on you.
- **Close Reading/Listening** allows you to gain a more precise understanding of the different aspects of a multimodal text by paying specific attention to each element as it contributes to the overall form and development of the text's subject matter and theme. This is where you gather elements that you can draw on in your forthcoming analysis. Close reading can help you distinguish between verbal and non-verbal features and pinpoint their function in the text. This section introduces the concepts and terminology needed to do so.

- **Analytical Reading/Listening** is informed by the two previous steps. Once you have identified one or more significant elements of focus for your analysis, reconsider the entire text or specific passages from this vantage point to critically reconsider your observations, corroborate your inferences, establish new links and deepen your analysis. This will allow you to avoid merely summarizing what is in the text or making assumptions.

Shared Elements across Different Genres

Narrative Voice and Tone

Literary analysis recognizes that there is no direct and transparent connection between the author's intended meanings and the reader's or listener's experience. The narrator or speaker is always a **discursive construct**, observable through traces in the text, but is distinct from the author. For instance, it is unlikely that all of a prolific pop artist's lyrics are based on autobiographical experiences; in many cases, the songs performed by a singer have been written by others. Even in a nonfiction text such as a speech, the **narrative voice** represents only the part of the author revealed to the reader or listener through the text.

This can be determined by the narrator's or speaker's use of pronouns used to tell the story. For instance, a song, spoken word poem or speech can directly involve the artist or speaker, making them a **first-person narrator**, or it can relate the story of other characters, from a **third-person point of view**. In graphic novels, the visuals support the construction of point of view, as explained on page 225.

The text's **tone** conveys the attitude of the speaker or narrator toward its theme, be it directly through tone of voice, through diction (including figures of speech) or through rhythmic or graphic elements. Tone can be positive or negative and cover a wide range of feelings. For instance, a speech on climate change may have a serious and ominous tone, while a children's song on the environment may be constructed as bright and cheerful.

PRACTICE

Consider the following excerpts, and answer the questions that follow.

"Till We Meet Again," a song by R. Whiting and R. B. Egan, originally released in 1918

There's a song in the land of the lily
Each sweetheart has heard with a sigh
Over high garden walls this sweet echo falls
As a soldier boy whispers goodbye

5 Smile the while you kiss me sad adieu
When the clouds roll by I'll come to you
Then the skies will seem more blue
Down in Lover's Lane, my dearie

Queen Elizabeth II, Christmas Speech 1952

Each Christmas, at this time, my beloved father broadcast a message to his people in all parts of the world. Today I am doing this to you, who are now my people. My father, and my grandfather before him, worked all their lives to unite our peoples ever more closely, and to maintain its ideals which were so near to their hearts. I shall strive to carry on their work. […] Already you have given me strength to do so. For, since my accession ten months ago, your loyalty and affection have been an immense support and encouragement. I want to take this Christmas Day, my first opportunity, to thank you with all my heart.

1. For each, identify the narrative voice: is the narrative told from a first-person or third-person point of view?

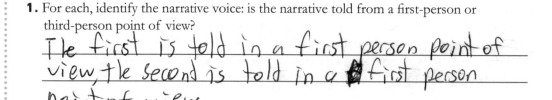

The first is told in a first person point of view, the second is told in a first person point of view

2. Both excerpts also contain the second-person pronoun "you." Whom does it refer to?

-In the song it is to whoever the writer is talking about
-In the speech it is to the father

3. How would you describe the tone of each excerpt? With one or more partners, discuss the elements that motivate your reading.

Prosody, Rhythm and Rhyme

Prosody is the study of speech patterns, present in prose, poetry and natural speech. Through **repetition**, these effects can be reinforced.

- **Alliteration** is the repetition of the initial letter or sound of words found close to one another (e.g., pleasant poem).
- **Assonance** is the repetition of vowel sounds, which evokes an effect similar to a rhyme (e.g., monotonous to stop).
- **Consonance** is the repetition of consonant sounds (e.g., still the best establishment).

Rhyme is a repetition of similar-sounding words, which usually occur in a song or spoken word poem at the end of lines. **Internal rhyme** occurs when words within the same line create a rhyme. Recurring rhyming patterns in a poem allow the reader to observe a **rhyme scheme**, usually indicated by assigning a capital letter to each different rhyme.

- When both the vowel sounds and following consonant sounds are identical, there is **exact rhyme**: *walk* and *talk*, *historical* and *categorical*.
- If the vowel sounds are (slightly) different while the consonants are identical, or vice versa, there is **slant rhyme** (also referred to as half rhyme or imperfect rhyme): *sun* and *moon*, *sun* and *thumb*.

The arrangement of syllables and stress patterns in verse is referred to as meter. While these patterns are also present in everyday speech—think of the phrase *a literary analysis*, in which only the syllables "li-" and "-na-" are fully stressed and pronounced with more emphasis than the other syllables that make up the phrase—they can be used more consciously to construct regular patterns—for instance, in speeches, songs and spoken word.

Most contemporary spoken word poems and songs are written using a form of free verse, which has irregular patterns of stress and syllables and may or may not include a rhyme scheme. Although it does not contain regular meter, it remains verse, organized around certain rhythmic effects. These may include word or sound repetitions, pauses and line breaks.

PRACTICE

A. Read the lyrics to the song "Goin' Home" (W. Fisher, 1922), and answer the questions below.

> Goin' home, goin' home, I'm a goin' home;
> Quiet-like, some still day, I'm jes' goin' home.

It's not far, jes' close by,
Through an open door;
5 Work all done, care laid by,
Goin' to fear no more.
Mother's there 'spectin' me,
Father's waitin' too;
Lots o' folk gather'd there,
10 All the friends I knew,
All the friends I knew.

Home, I'm goin' home!

Nothin' lost, all's gain,
No more fret nor pain,
15 No more stumblin' on the way,
No more longin' for the day,
Goin' to roam no more!
Mornin' star lights the way,
Res'less dream all done;
20 Shadows gone, break o' day,
Real life jes' begun.
There's no break, there's no end,
Jes' a livin' on;
Wide awake, with a smile
25 Goin' on and on.

Goin' home, goin' home, I'm jes' goin' home,
goin' home, goin' home, goin' home!

1. Consider the following line of the song: "Wide awake, with a smile." Which sound
patterns can you identify? Explain.

  a) assonance   b) consonance   c) alliteration

~~assonance:~~
alliteration: Wide, With

2. Discuss the use of repetition in lines 10–11 and 14, 15 and 16. How is it different?

It is used to emphasize a point in the
14, 15, 16. In 10-11, it is to do the same

3. What can you observe about the repetition of "goin' home"? What is its function?

It's function is to emphasize a point
he is trying to make

4. Write the rhyme scheme using capital letters:

AABCBC

5. Which lines can be said to have a slant rhyme rather than an exact rhyme?

10,11,12,21,22

6. Which two consecutive lines form an example of a slant internal rhyme?

11,12

Diction

No single word is innately prosaic or poetic. Rather, authors combine words to create particular effects based on sounds (as explained above) and meanings. This word choice, which, when conducting literary analysis should never be considered accidental, is called diction.

- Words can be more **concrete** ("flower," "kiss") or more **abstract** ("nature," "love").
- Words not only have **denotation**—their literal meaning easily found in a dictionary—but also **connotation**—the suggested meaning based on associations and the contexts in which the word is or has been used. For instance, while the denotation of the word "whisper" is to speak very softly, its connotations may include to share a secret, or to express words of love or comfort.
- Words are typically part of a **register** or level of language, ranging from the formal to the informal. Informal language use also includes contracted verb forms (*ain't, gonna*) or word clippings (*'cause* or *'cos* for *because*). These levels can be used to create contrasts.

PRACTICE

A. Identify examples of concrete and abstract diction in the following excerpt of the Speech in Favour of Confederation, delivered in 1865 by Hon. George Brown (a Canadian politician and one of the Fathers of Confederation). This speech represented the culmination of his fifteen-year campaign for constitutional reform leading to the 1867 Confederation of Canada. Brown described Confederation as a great reform designed to clear away the constitutional problems that had plagued Canada and lead to national unity and greatness.

> Have we not then, Mr. speaker, great cause of thankfulness that we have found a better way for the solution of our troubles than that which has entailed on other countries such deplorable results? And should not every one of us endeavour to rise to the magnitude of the occasion, and earnestly seek to deal with this question to the end in the same candid and conciliatory spirit in which, so far, it has been discussed? [...]

> I perfectly agree with you, but it could not be done. Whether we ask for parliamentary reform for Canada alone or in union with the Maritime Provinces, the French Canadians must have their views consulted as well as us. This scheme can be carried, and no scheme can be that has not the support of both sections of the province.

Examples of abstract diction: _____

_____

Examples of concrete diction: _____

_____

B. In a reputable dictionary, look up the following words from the song "Till We Meet Again" (page 215) and write down their denotation. Then, establish their connotation(s) in light of the song's context.

1. Wall: Denotation: _____

     Connotation: _____

2. Adieu: Denotation: _____

     Connotation: _____

3. Clouds: Denotation: _____

     Connotation: _____

C. With what register of language do you associate the song "Goin' Home" (pages 216–217)? Give examples to support your answer.

_____

_____

_____

Literary Devices

The different types of meanings that can be inferred from language, as described in the previous section, also contribute to the construction of **imagery** and **symbolism**. Images are words or phrases that evoke different sensory experiences (vision, sound, smell, taste or touch), while symbols are images that call up a deeper meaning, either by convention or in context.

Words can also be used as **figures of speech** to create a non-literal meaning that differs from their primary usage:

- A **simile** expresses a comparison between two elements through the use of the words *as*, *like* or equivalent expressions: "You lived your life / Like a candle in the wind" (E. John, "Candle in the Wind").
- A **metaphor** evokes a likeness without any explicit comparison: "Baby, you're a firework" (K. Perry, "Firework").
- A **personification** attributes human qualities to an object or concept: "You start to freeze as horror looks you right between the eyes" (M. Jackson, "Thriller").
- In an **apostrophe**, a poem's speaker addresses a dead or absent person, an inanimate object or concept: "But you don't really care for music, do you?" addressed to God (L. Cohen, "Hallelujah").
- An **oxymoron** brings together two ideas that are opposites: "The sound of silence" (Simon & Garfunkel, "The Sound of Silence").
- A **hyperbole** exaggerates an image to emphasize a point: "Cry me a river" (J. Timberlake, "Cry Me a River").

For contextualized practice on literary devices, see question C on page 224 and question B on page 231.

MyBookshelf > My eLab > Exercises > Part IV: Other Genres > Elements of Analysis

Theme and Mood

The text's **mood** refers to the atmosphere that is prevalent. While the author creates tone using particular diction and other elements, the mood is the feeling that the text evokes in the reader. Elements such as the setting, imagery, tone, voice and theme help establish this atmosphere.

As a result, the mood evokes certain feelings and emotions in the reader, such as passion, pride or sadness. A text may have one dominant mood, or evoke contrasting moods as it unfolds.

All of the aforementioned elements play a role in the development of the text's **theme(s)**, developed in its thematic structure. A text can have one or more themes, which are comprehensive statements of a deeper meaning that extend beyond the subject matter and its first-level meaning. They usually require being summarized in more abstract terms. While the subject matter can be observed directly, a theme consists of deeper issues that require analysis to be uncovered.

To determine the theme(s) of a text, you might therefore ask, "What point does the author or speaker make through the subject matter?" When answering this question, it may be helpful to distinguish between broad **thematic concepts**—for instance, *freedom*—and narrow **thematic statements**, which concern the particular point the author expresses about such a concept (e.g., In order to gain civil freedom, women require voting rights).

PRACTICE

Re-examine the following three texts: 1) "Till We Meet Again" (page 215), 2) Christmas Speech 1952 (page 215) and 3) "Goin' Home" (page 216–217). *Sad*

1. How would you describe the mood of the poem in one word? Share your answer with one or more partners.

2. What are the thematic concept(s) evoked in these texts?

Goodbye's

3. For each text, write one thematic statement.

1) *Goodbye to a loved one*

2) *Goodbye to a father*

3) *Goodbye to his current life*

Song Elements

Musical rhythm is the repeated movement of sounds through time. In songs, the words usually match the musical rhythm, made up of the beat, accent and tempo of the song.

- **Beat** is the regular pulse (comparable to the ticking of a clock, or the measure of a metronome).
- **Accent** is where the strongest emphasis is placed as in *one*, two, three, *one*, two, three.
- **Tempo** is the speed of the music—how fast or slow it is.

Melody is the tune. The tune is made up of musical notes or pitches that make up a pattern. When you add words to a melody, it becomes a song. Notes are situated on a spectrum between high and low. Their height is called the **pitch**. This pitch determines the height of a note in relation to the others around it. When two or more notes are produced at the same time—for instance, by combining two voices, or voice and music—a harmony is created. This also contributes to the song's **texture**—the layering of instruments and/or voices to create a light or fuller sound.

The use of typical instruments, sound combinations, melody and rhythm determines the **genre**, or style of music. This allows the listener to distinguish, for instance, between jazz, rock, hip hop or pop music.

Pop songs usually consist of the following formal elements:

The **introduction** is a unique section at the beginning of the song, which usually only contains music and no words. It creates the atmosphere of the song.

A **verse** can be compared to a poem's stanza and consists of lyrics that convey the narrative of the song—its story. It often rhymes, following an AABB or ABAB rhyme scheme. Pop songs usually have two or more verses that have almost identical music but different lyrics.

An optional section that may occur after the verse is the **pre-chorus**, which connects each verse to the repeated chorus, both musically and lyrically.

The **chorus** or refrain is the element of the song that repeats at least once in (near-)identical form. It is almost always of greater musical and emotional intensity than the verses. It expresses the main message or theme of the song and is the most memorable element of the song for listeners.

The **bridge** is a section that appears toward the end of the song and creates a contrast by breaking up the repetitive musical and lyrical pattern of the song.

The **conclusion** of a song serves a purpose similar to the introduction; it signals the end of the song and usually contains only music or lyrics that slowly fade out. It brings a sense of harmonious closure.

PRACTICE

A. Consider the lyrics to the well-known song "Happy Birthday." First, read them as you would a prose text or a poem. Then, sound the melody of the song in your head.

Happy Birthday to You
Happy Birthday to You
Happy Birthday Dear (name)
Happy Birthday to You

1. How does the addition of melody enhance the meaning of the lyrics?

It enhances the word birthday and You, which makes it more specific

2. If you were to clap along, how would the words fit the song's rhythm? Mark the words or syllables that carry accent. Is the tempo slow or fast?

Hap —> birth —> day —> to —> you
clap —> clap —> clap —> clap —> clap

3. Which notes have higher pitch? Write down the corresponding words. What do you notice about the placement of these higher-pitched notes?

Birth, To, Dear

They are in the middle of the line

B. In the pop song lyrics below, identify these formal elements: bridge, chorus, pre-chorus and verse. Some elements appear more than once. Then, answer the questions underneath.

Beggar
(Concept: Andy Van Drom; lyrics: Laura Roklicer)

Running down your lane   *verse*
I don't feel too sane
You're holding back on me

Burning memories
5 I'm passing like the wind
A movie badly trimmed
You're stepping out of us
Say you don't like the fuss

I paint us back in time   _chorus_
10 Like silhouettes that rhyme
You sometimes dream of me
Falling on my knees

I'm just a beggar in your eyes   _verse_
A lousy gambler in disguise
15 I stand defeated in your eyes
You used to wait to be my prize
I'm just a beggar in your eyes
You used to say you choose them wise

I'm hoping for the rain   _verse_
20 To walk away unstained
I'll be a different man
I'll find another plan
And when I hitch a ride
You'll let me have my pride
25 'Cause baby I can't grow
When you hold me down so low

I paint us back in time   _chorus_
Like silhouettes that rhyme
You sometimes dream of me
30 Falling on my knees

I'm just a beggar in your eyes   _verse_
A lousy gambler in disguise
I stand defeated in your eyes
You used to wait to be my prize
35 I'm just a beggar in your eyes
You used to say you choose them wise

We've gone too deep, deep   _bridge_
Into this mess
We're falling asleep
40 Becoming too tense
We're selling cheap, cheap
For a regress
Falling too deep, deep
Into this mess

45 I'm just a beggar in your eyes   _conclusion_
A lousy gambler in disguise
I stand defeated in your eyes
You used to wait to be my prize
I'm just a beggar in your eyes …

1. What do you think this song would sound like in terms of rhythm and melody? Which words should receive emphasis through higher or lower pitch? Discuss your thoughts with one or more partners.

2. How would you express the thematic statement of the song? Which poetic devices are used to develop this theme? Discuss your answers with one or more partners.

Spoken Word Features

Spoken word (also referred to as performance poetry) emphasizes sound and performance aspects and may exist in writing only after transcription—for instance, at a poetry slam, a competitive event where poets perform within certain restrictions, such as theme. Slam poetry is a term used to refer to poems performed at slams but is not a genre in its own right. Most slam poetry is spoken word, but not all spoken word poems are written to be performed at slams.

Under the influence of musical genres such as rap and hip hop, spoken word tends to demonstrate a heavy use of rhythm, rhyme, repetition, word play and literary devices (see pages 215–220 under "Shared Elements across Different Genres" and Elements of Analysis on pages 158–165), but also performance-related aspects such as voice projection, enunciation and body language.

PRACTICE

A. Read the spoken word poem in silence. Answer the questions on page 224.

Horizon Line
(Concept: Andy Van Drom; words and performance: Matthew Madonia)

I've run with tornados for tour mates
My health record been taking L's
Like panther skates
I dance on breaks with every chance I take
5 When you don't have a leg to stand on
Tell me what stance you take

When the nerves shake your bones beyond bass tones
You might as well let out an Earthquake
Break down the mountains that taunted you into rubble
10 I fell onto the right path every time that I stumbled
I was built from cookie crumble
I was constructed from stardust just like you
Tell the shadow of death to stay humble

Cause I've been staring at the event horizon
15 Where suns set for the final time
Wondering if death is simply a portal
Through time
To a past life
Future life
20 This life

Made me fearful of those lights
Most nights
I watch Netflix 'cause it's safer than the theatre
Safer than the corner store

25 Safer than walking home
Safer than filling my car
Standing at the metre
How am I supposed to be a leader
When I'm afraid to be a speaker in public?
30 Is it my fault or the republic's?
The food that they feed us
Is that the reason my immune system has been eating my stomach?

Let's discuss it

My entire generation is on antidepressants
35 Are we just supposed to wait for everyone to die
Before we are given a chance?

So it's fight or flight
Most nights those are the same thing
Spread my wings and I could be anything

40 So it's fight or flight
Or medicate until everything's alright
If I could jump through this horizon line
I would go back in time
And make all of this right

1. What emotions do you expect the speaker's tone of voice to convey? What words suggest these emotions?

2. Which words, phrases or lines especially stood out for you?

3. How do you expect the speaker to deliver the text? Do you imagine them to speak fast or slowly? Do you think they respect the line breaks or not?

B. Listen to the complete spoken word performance in My eLab. How does the recording correspond to or differ from your expectations? How does it enhance the meaning of the words? Discuss your answers.

MyBookshelf > My eLab > Documents > Part IV: Other Genres > Elements of Analysis

C. Referring to the explanations under "Literary Devices" on page 219, identify an example of each of the following figures of speech. Validate and discuss your answers with one or more partners.

1. Hyperbole: _____

_____

2. Metaphor: _____

_____

3. Personification: _____

_____

4. Simile: _____

_____

Graphic Novel Elements

The basic building blocks of comics and graphic novels alike are **panels**—single visual frames organized into a sequence. These panels usually have rectangular **borders** (or frames). Although they can have any shape, or remain implicit, there is always some sign of where one panel ends and another begins. The area between borders (usually blank or a uniform colour) is called the **gutter**. Panels are generally read in the same sequence as text (i.e., in Western countries from left to right, and top to bottom).

Canadian Identity (Roddy Thorleifson)

Not all graphic novels include text, but most do. This includes narration, dialogue and sound effects, expressed in three distinct manners:

Text boxes (or captions) contain narrative elements that provide context to the scene that is depicted. The language and shape of the text boxes indicate their distance from the principal narration, but the parallel text provides an ironic commentary on the main scene.

Text balloons contain utterances associated directly with the characters. Dialogue is indicated in **speech balloons**, which are connected to a character with a tail, while **thought balloons** are indicated with a series of bubbles between the character and the text balloon. Different fonts or font sizes can be used to indicate emphasis or volume.

Sign text is part of the imagery used to construct a panel. It may identify a visual—for instance, by labelling a container as "honey" or marking a building as a hospital. It may also draw attention to sounds that occur in the scene—for instance, by adding onomatopoeia like *bang*.

In graphic novels, *how* narrative information is presented is often as important as *what* that information is. When approaching a page, first consider the organization, shape and size of the panels.

Analyzing **artistic style** is probably the most difficult aspect of analyzing graphic novels, since there are few guidelines for talking about different types of drawings and how they create meaning. Remain attentive to the artist's use of colour, the level of realism of the drawing style, the level of detail of backgrounds and the type of images. Image types are usually described in terms of distance, angle and movement, using the film studies terminology:

- A **long shot** shows the entire subject or character depicted, as well as some surroundings.
- A **medium shot** shows the character from head to waist.
- A **close-up shot** shows only (part of) the character's face, usually to express emotion.

In each panel, objects and characters can be depicted in the **foreground, midground** or **background**. They can be at **eye level** (horizontal), or the scene can be rendered from a **high angle** (from above) or from a **low angle** (from below).

PRACTICE

Consider the graphic novel page below, which is adapted from the short story "The Magic Shop" (see Chapter 3). Then, answer the questions that follow the excerpt.
(Concept: Andy Van Drom; illustrations: Svetlana Kiseleva)

1. How many panels does the excerpt have? What is the colour of the borders and the gutter?

_____

_____

2. Which part of the page was your attention drawn to first?

_____

_____

_____

3. What is the function of the text boxes in the first and last panels?

_____

_____

4. In which four different ways are the characters' words included in the panels?

_____

_____

_____

_____

5. What are two examples of sign text?

_____

_____

_____

6. How do body language and facial expressions support the boy's mental state?

_____

_____

_____

7. What is the colour palette of the page? Do you observe a difference between the scenes inside the magic shop and the other panels?

_____

_____

_____

8. How would you describe the artistic style? Is it cartoonish, abstract, realistic, …?

_____

_____

_____

9. What types of shots are used in each of the panels? Describe the distance and the angle of the shots. What purpose do they serve?

_____

_____

_____

_____

_____

_____

10. In the last panel, what inference do your observations about the use of colour allow you to make? How do they reinforce the contrast between what is depicted in the foreground and background?

_____

_____

Speech Elements

A speech is a formal address delivered to an audience. While speeches can be written for many purposes and delivered in many different ways, they generally share the same basic format:

- **The introduction** grabs the audience's attention and previews the topic of the speech.
- **The body** includes the speaker's main points supported by facts, details, examples and counter-arguments.
- **The conclusion** reminds the audience of the key points made and ends with a final, powerful thought or a specific call to action.

Analysis of a speech is based on the principle of the text as a rhetorical transaction. It is necessary to consider the relationship between speaker, audience, message, purpose, theme, tone and mood:

- What is said (**logos**/message): These are the ideas the speaker constructs and argues through the careful selection and exposition of evidence.
- Who is saying it (**ethos**/speaker): What does the speaker reveal about themselves, why is it important and how does it shape their point of view? Information external to the text may be needed to fully answer these questions.
- Who is listening (**pathos**/audience): When delivering a speech, the speaker establishes an emotional connection with the audience. Understanding this relationship is essential to the analysis of the speech.
- Where/when it is being said (**kairos**/context): Speeches do not occur in a vacuum. Writers are influenced by the **larger occasion**: an environment of ideas, attitudes and emotions on a broad issue. Speeches often concern an **immediate occasion**: an event that triggers a response. For example, a speech concerning civil rights violations is a larger occasion; someone being killed unjustly by a police officer would be an immediate occasion.
- Why it is being said (purpose/theme): A speaker engages their audience with a central idea to attain one or more of three objectives: to **inform**, to **persuade** the audience of a specific interpretation of this information and to **motivate**—for instance, by a call for action.
- How it is being said (tone, mood): The speaker uses tone and rhetorical devices to express the shared values and interests that determine the speech's mood.

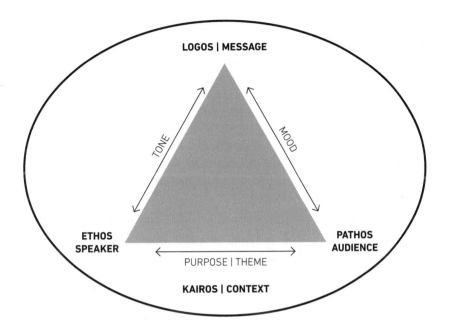

PRACTICE

A. Read the Freedom or Death Speech delivered by Emmeline Pankhurst, a leader of the British women's suffrage movement. She delivered the speech in front of the Connecticut Women's Suffrage Association on November 13, 1913, in Hartford (USA). Then, answer the questions that follow the text.

I am here as a soldier who has temporarily left the field of battle in order to explain—it seems strange it should have to be explained—what civil war is like when civil war is waged by women. I am not only here as a soldier temporarily absent from the field at battle; I am here—and that, I think, is the strangest part of my coming—I am here as a person who, according to the law courts of my country, it has been decided, is of no value to the community at all: and I am adjudged because of my life to be a dangerous person, under sentence of penal servitude in a convict prison. So you see there is some special interest in hearing so unusual a person address you. I dare say, in the minds of many of you—you will perhaps forgive me this personal touch—that I do not look either very like a soldier or very like a convict, and yet I am both. […]

A great many of you have been led to believe, from the somewhat meagre accounts you get in the newspapers, that in England there is a strange manifestation taking place, a new form of hysteria being swept across part of the feminist population of those Isles, and this manifestation takes the shape of irresponsible breaking of windows, burning of letters, general inconvenience to respectable, honest business people who want to attend to their business. It is very irrational you say: even if these women had sufficient intelligence to understand what they were doing, and really did want the vote, they have adopted very irrational means for getting the vote. "How are they going to persuade people that they ought to have the vote by breaking their windows?" you say. Now, if you say that, it shows you do not understand the meaning of our revolution at all, and I want to show you that when damage is done to property it is not done in order to convert people to woman suffrage at all. It is a practical political means, the only means we consider open to voteless persons to bring about a political situation, which can only be solved by giving women the vote. […]

Well, then the shopkeepers who could not understand why we should break the shopkeepers' windows. Why should we alienate the sympathy of the shopkeepers?

Well, there is the other side of the question, gentlemen—why should the shopkeepers alienate the sympathy of their customers by refusing to help them to get political power, some power to make the condition of the woman who helps to earn the shopkeeper's money by serving in his shop, easier than it is at the present time? Those women broke shopkeepers' windows, and what was the situation? Just at the beginning of the winter season when all the new winter hats and coats were being shown, the shopkeepers had to barricade all their windows with wood and nobody could see the new winter fashions. Well, there again is an impossible situation. The shopkeeper cannot afford to quarrel with his customers, and we have today far more practical sympathy amongst the shopkeepers of London than we ever had when we were quiet, gentle, ladylike suffragists asking nicely for a vote. […]

So here am I. I come in the intervals of prison appearance: I come after having been four times imprisoned under the "Cat and Mouse Act," probably going back to be re-arrested as soon as I set my foot on British soil. I come to ask you to help to win this fight. If we win it, this hardest of all fights, then, to be sure, in the future it is going to be made easier for women all over the world to win their fight when their time comes.

1. Identify the Introduction, body and conclusion of the speech.

_____

_____

_____

_____

2. Which two forms of address does the speaker use to refer to her audience? How might this be surprising?

_____

_____

_____

3. Which strategy does the speaker use to rebut any possible objections her audience may have?

_____

_____

_____

4. Analyze the speech as a rhetorical transaction based on the following questions.

a. Logos: What is the central message the speaker wishes to convey?

_____

_____

b. Ethos: What does the speaker reveal about herself, and how does it shape her point of view?

_____

_____

_____

_____

_____

c. Pathos and Kairos: Since the speech mentions little information about the context of the speech and the audience present, do a web search to inform yourself on the larger and immediate occasion of this speech and on the audience to which it was delivered. Discuss your answers with one or more partners.

5. Summarize each of the speech's three objectives in one sentence each.

a. Inform: _____

_____

b. Persuade: _____

_____

c. Motivate: _____

_____

B. Referring to the explanations under "Literary Devices" on page 219, find three metaphors related to the concept of warfare. How does the speaker use them to describe her quest for women's rights?

_____

_____

_____

CHAPTER 15

Songs

This chapter focuses on the following:

- Formal structure
- Rhythm and rhyme
- Figures of speech
- Language Focus: non-standard language use
- The Language of Literature: sound patterns
- Theme, tone and mood

Connect with the Text

Take stock of your opinions on the following questions. Discuss them with one or more partners.

1. When listening to a song, do you find it more important to appreciate the music or the lyrics? Why?
2. Does it matter to you if an artist writes his or her own songs? For what reasons?
3. Do you like pop music? How does it differ from other music genres? What features or stereotypes do you associate with pop music?
4. The term "pop music" is usually traced back to the 1950s. How are pop songs now similar or different from the ones in previous decades? Research and listen to some examples.
5. Have you ever taken a road trip, travelled alone or simply contemplated a landscape? What thoughts and feelings did it inspire in you? Share your experience.

Text in Context

Matt Holubowski grew up in a bilingual home in Hudson, Quebec. He learned the guitar by himself at age seventeen, and discovered his singing and song-writing talents in the process. While studying political science at Concordia University, Holubowski played his music in bars across Montreal. He also travelled extensively through Africa and Southeast Asia, which would serve as inspiration for his music. In 2014, Holubowski put his ambition to become a teacher on hold to work on his first album *Ogen, Old Man*. He wrote not only the lyrics and music to all songs, but also played all the instruments, including guitar, ukulele, mandolin and harmonica, and created a handmade art pouch. In 2015, he went on to be a finalist on *La Voix*, Quebec's version of the singing contest, *The Voice*. His unexpected success led him to personally package and send over thirteen thousand copies of the album. His second album, *Solitudes*, has attained gold status in Canada and brought the artist international acclaim.

Exploratory Reading

First, listen to the song as you would for enjoyment. Keep an open mind and take a mental note of your emotional reactions. Listen a second time while following along with the lyrics below. Soak up the atmosphere of the music and language without looking for any specific elements. When you are finished, answer the questions below the text.

MyBookshelf > My eLab > Documents > Part IV: Other Genres > Chapter 15: Songs

On Trains   **Matt Holubowski**

Nimbus clouds surround the mountains now.   _____
Can't tell who resides this wooden town.
There's a makeshift mystery
that's going down.

5 The plains below me here now live in peace,
where farmer grows his rice and Chinese tea.
Never has a man seemed so damn free to me.
So damn free to me.   _____
So damn free to me.
10 Darkness comes now as it please,   _____
then light comes back to me so suddenly,
as we tunnel through to further majesty.

The sight of smoke, and sound
of ringing bells,
15 the ones we've come to love, and know so well
calms our qualms, and
make us feel so swell.
Make us feel so swell.   _____
Make us feel so swell.

20 Well honey, maybe you don't know this,   _____
but life's a train ride and we are all on it.
Well honey, maybe you don't know this,
but life's a train ride and we are all on it.
Well honey, maybe you don't know this,
25 but life's a train ride and we are all on it.

Pretty homes all made of marble stone   _____
line up one by one to say hello, hello.
They are beautiful, and
they don't even know.

30 They don't even know,   _____
they are beautiful.

Well honey, maybe you don't know this,
but life's a train ride and we are all on it.
Well honey, maybe you don't know this,
35 but life's a train ride and we are all on it.
Well honey, maybe you don't know this,
but life's a train ride and we are all on it.

    When I am on trains,
    I feel safe.

40 The city lights are now coming in sight.
They shine on me with
all their pretty might,
but I can't tell, because I'm sleeping
oh so tight.

45 Conductor calls us all to come on out,
we've reached the platform,
now it's time for solid ground,
and remember where it is that we are bound.

    Where it is we're bound.
50 Where it is we're bound.

    Well honey, maybe you don't know this,
but life's a train ride and we are all on it.

Source: Holubowski, M. "On Trains." *Ogen, Old Man*, Audiogram, 2014.

Initial Insight

1. What is the song about? Write down anything that intuitively comes to you.

_____

2. What is the mood and atmosphere of the song as a whole?

_____

_____

Reader's Response

Consider the following questions. Discuss your answers with one or more partners.

1. Which aspects of the song did you like and/or dislike? Be precise in your description.

2. What visual images came to mind as you were listening to the song?

3. How did the song make you feel? Pinpoint a precise emotion and explain.

LANGUAGE FOCUS

To better fit the rhythm, melody or tone of a song, artists sometimes use language in a non-standard manner, for instance by bending grammar rules or changing the pronunciation of a word.

A. For each of the following lines from the song, pinpoint the non-standard language use. With one or more partners, discuss why you think it has been phrased this way. Consider what changes are needed to make it conform to standard grammar patterns.

1. Can't tell who resides this wooden town.

_____

_____

_____

2. where farmer grows his rice and Chinese tea.

_____

3. Darkness comes now as it please,

_____

4. calms our qualms, and / make us feel so swell.

_____

_____

B. In which way(s) is the pronunciation of certain words or syllables altered (in comparison with spoken language use) for the purpose of the song's musicality? Give examples.

_____

_____

_____

Look up any words you are unsure of.

MyBookshelf > My eLab
> Exercises > Part IV: Other
Genres > Chapter 15: Songs
> Vocabulary Comprehension

Close Reading

As you read the lyrics again, pay attention to specific elements that seem significant to understanding and interpreting the song. The following guided reading questions will help you.

1. What is the formal structure of the song? Identify the verses, pre-chorus, chorus and bridge in the spaces provided next to the song (page 233).

2. What is the "makeshift mystery" the singer alludes to?

_____

3. Where is the singer travelling? Cite from the lyrics to support your answer.

_____

4. Why do light and darkness alternate?

_____

5. Does the singer address someone in particular? If yes, who?

_____

6. In which way does the singer personify the houses he observes?

_____

_____

_____

7. Why is the singer unaware of the city lights?

_____

8. What happens to the passengers at the end of the song?

_____

MyBookshelf > My eLab
> Exercises > Part IV: Other
Genres > Chapter 15: Songs
> Close Reading: Additional
Questions

THE LANGUAGE OF LITERATURE

The effect of a song's words is to a very large extent determined by the singer's use of sound devices and rhyme to make the words fit with the song's melody and rhythm. Use the following questions to focus your attention on the effect of these devices.

1. What do you observe about the use of rhyme in the song? Is there a formal rhyme scheme?

_____

_____

2. In the following excerpt of the song, identify at least one example each of assonance, consonance and alliteration.

> Nimbus clouds surround the mountains now.
> Can't tell who resides this wooden town.
> There's a makeshift mystery
> that's going down.
>
> The plains below me here now live in peace,
> where farmer grows his rice and Chinese tea.
> Never has a man seemed so damn free to me.

Assonance: _____

Alliteration: _____

Consonance: _____

3. How does the singer use repetition throughout the song?

_____

_____

Analytical Reading

After making specific observations, you are ready to analyze the subject of your close reading. The following questions will help you look for thematic patterns, establish relationships and identify specific examples of literary devices or principles.

1. What is the song's subject matter? What is its theme? How do the two relate?

2. How does the singer use the chorus to reveal and support the song's theme?

3. How do the song's melody, rhythm and structure highlight the train ride imagery evoked through the lyrics?

4. In which manner does the singer turn the people mentioned in the song—the farmer and the conductor—into characters, suggesting they might act as symbols rather than representing one specific individual?

5. Almost every verse contains a form of personification. Identify seven different examples of personification, and explain how they personify an inanimate object or concept.

6. In which manner does the bridge reinforce the mood of the song?

Food for Thought

The following questions encourage you to turn a critical eye to your earlier observations and analyses. They introduce elements and considerations that will lead you to formulate new questions and set tentative hypotheses. Discuss these to further your insight into the text.

1. How does the singer use metaphor and personification to suggest there is more to life than we might suspect at first glance?

2. Considering that the song links the observation of an actual train ride to a more abstract theme of life being like a train ride, discuss the deeper metaphorical meanings that each verse may represent.

3. In Analytical Reading question 3, you investigated how the song's melody and rhythm contribute to its imagery and theme. Discuss the impact any changes to these musical elements would have on the song's mood and theme; for instance, if the song were faster-paced or in a different musical genre (dance, hard rock, hip hop ...). Can all music styles be used to express any mood and theme? Why or why not?

4. Why do you think the song is called "On Trains" even though the singer-songwriter only mentions one particular train ride?

5. All of the songs on the *Ogen, Old Man* album are thematically connected. In the words of Holubowski, the album is "a story of the transition of youth into old age. It's a journey that we all have to go through, and this album is a reflection about how best to do it in your own way." Compare "On Trains" with one or more other songs on the album. What similarities and differences in their subject matter, themes and mood do you observe?

Presenting an Analysis

Writing | Analyzing the Development of Mood and Theme through the Combination of Words and Music

The lyrics of "On Trains" are rich in imagery, sound devices and figures of speech. The song's melody and rhythm complement these lyrics—and vice versa—to lead to a cohesive listening experience. Prepare an analytical essay focusing around a thesis statement that investigates how the musical and verbal elements contribute to the theme and/or mood of the song. Refer to the work you have done in this chapter to guide you while identifying pertinent elements, and highlight how they help transform the subject matter into a specific theme and mood.

(Refer to Part V, Writing about Literature, on page 271 for more information on essay format and structure.)

Speaking | Comparing a Listener's Responses to Different Songs

Humans have been making music for thousands of years, and the combination of voice and instruments to form one cohesive rhythm and melody has the capacity to deeply affect the listener. Depending on their theme, melody and rhythm, songs can instantly put people in a good mood, or move them to tears.

First, present a response to the "On Trains." What impact did it make on you? What was your reaction to the music and the lyrics? Which images speak to you, and which ones do not?

Then, present another song that either deals with the subject matter of trains or with the theme of life. Explain why you have chosen this particular song and discuss the impact it has on you. Compare these observations to the ones pertaining to "On Trains." How are they similar; how are they different? Explain what you consider these similarities and differences to be based on. Do they relate to the music, the lyrics or both? Give precise examples, quoting or playing passages of the songs.

(Refer to Appendix 2 on pages 297 for more information on presentation format and structure.)

MyBookshelf > My eLab > Exercises > Grammar and Accuracy

CHAPTER 16

Spoken Word

This chapter focuses on the following:

- Performance
- Rhythm and rhyme
- Figures of speech
- Language Focus: vernacular and pronunciation
- The Language of Literature: sound patterns
- Theme, tone and mood

Connect with the Text

A. Before you listen to and read "To Blossom in the Shadow" by Kate Tempest, do a web search to find the answers to the questions below. This will help you understand the roots of the spoken word genre and how it distinguishes itself from other forms of poetry and song. Remember to record your sources so you can use them as references, should you decide to include this information in an essay or presentation.

  1. Why can spoken poetry be considered the original form of poetic creation?

  2. What is the distinction between page poetry and performance poetry?

  3. Are performance poetry and spoken word the same genre? Explain.

  4. What is the link between the ancient Greek rhapsodes and the Olympic Games on the one hand, and modern-day poetry slams on the other?

  5. How did the Harlem Renaissance contribute to the interaction between literary and musical artists? How did the civil rights movement, to which it laid the foundation, further the recognition of spoken word as a rhetorical genre?

B. Take stock of your opinions on the following questions. Discuss them with one or more partners.

  1. What activities allow you to express your emotions and state of mind, whether positive or negative?

  2. How important is it for you to belong to a group or community? Explain.

  3. Do you think people can achieve more through competition or collaboration? Why?

  4. What do you consider more important: getting along with others or respecting your own feelings and opinions? Explain.

Text in Context

Kate Tempest (1985–) was born Kate Calvert in London, UK. At the age of sixteen, the poet, novelist and spoken word artist began performing at open mic nights on the London rap and hip hop scene. While completing a degree in English Literature at Goldsmiths, University of London, she went on to win prestigious

poetry slams in London and New York and opened shows for renowned British spoken word artists John Cooper Clarke and Scroobius Pip. Her first collection of poems and songs, *Everything Speaks in Its Own Way*, which features "To Blossom in the Shadow," came out in 2012. She has since been recognized as one of her generation's most acclaimed performance artists, drawing large crowds and receiving prestigious literary awards. Tempest's work explores issues such as inequality, the failure of modern politics and the quest for identity. She cites influences ranging from the Romantic poet William Blake to the hip hop formation Wu-Tang Clan. In 2018, Tempest received an honorary doctorate in letters from the London Metropolitan University.

Exploratory Reading

First, listen to the performance for enjoyment. Keep an open mind and take a mental note of your emotional reactions. Listen a second time while following along with the text below. Soak up the rhythm and atmosphere of the piece without looking for any specific elements. When you are finished, answer the questions on page 241.

MyBookshelf > My eLab > Documents > Part IV: Other Genres > Chapter 16: Spoken Word

To Blossom in the Shadow   Kate Tempest

Old friends with new faces—time don't heal, time softens;
Time just blocks out the problems
So why bother waiting when the drink does the same much quicker?
In the absence of a mic, I'll clutch liquor;
5   And raise a salute to the three that gave me the strength to be Katie.
Things change, people make gravely damaging decisions that lead to mistakes,
So now I'm sitting here thinking it all must have been a piss take
A big old hoax, the elements cracking jokes watching us tie ourselves into knots
    like our ropes were enchanted. Last night I awoke in the darkness of predawn,
    and I watched as the sky gave way to the day:

The moon sat peaceful in the West (right). And the sun sent emissaries to herald
    his approach,
10 And gradually he rose, to beam across the sky at his sister. He sent his colours out
    to whisper that he'd missed her.
And for a short while the two shared the same sky—both of them glorious, both of
    them perfect.
And I couldn't help but think of us lot in the days gone by—
We didn't want to fit the Earth, and so we made the Earth fit us.
We were big souls in a small dimension. Our wits told us to walk, direction unimportant,
    we thought we'd be safe, we performed with an awkward grace, we were sure there
    was more to this place.

15 If only we'd have known (ah but the journey is paramount), that behind our backs,
    the snake hands had their daggers out.

Days passed, we blazed, laughed, drank dragon stout,

Every time we had our doubts—we made sure we had 'em out

And yeah, we played a few shows, it were nothing much to brag about,

But in within that grouping there was some kind of solution that made us all sure we
    were moving through confusion to lucidity—made bigger by each other's abilities.

20 Those days are the blood in my lyrical capillaries.

I, too, is the blood in my lyrical capillaries.

You see—'what happens in love occurs beyond good and evil'.

We did what we did, we was people, truly.

And as I keep progressing on my path I often think of them friends that gave my own
    style to me.

25 So I move through life, every tiny little moment, building on the others, contributing
    to the now,

And I get it: if we'd have all stayed allies, never shifted to opponents, we wouldn't be
    the people that we are, anyhow, what I'm saying is—watching the sky this morning,
    I saw perfect harmony, and it was so beautiful,

And I thought about us lot, and the nature of companions, and that day when we all piled
    into the mic booth for that chorus on that old track in that studio—

No egos, just childish enjoyment imagining itself as maturity.

This morning it dawned on me I still feel the foundations that we built then supporting me,

30 And I still hear the words of our young raps calling me,

As I struggle on to be what I was born to be—better.

So when you rise, I'll smile. I'll greet you warmly, and for a short while, I will shine out,

But shortly I'll start to sink slowly and happily away—

Coz every good Moon moves to make room for the Day

35 Every good Moon makes room for the Day

So you lot, you do your thing, and I'll do mine.

It's important we give each other space to shine,

Coz when the morning arrives, there'll be a space in time,

When we can shine out together, and glory in each other's glow.

Source: Tempest, K. "To Blossom in the Shadow." *Everything Speaks in Its Own Way*, Zingaro, 2012.

Initial Insight

1. What is the spoken word piece about? Write down anything that intuitively comes to you.

_____

2. What is the mood and atmosphere of the piece as a whole?

_____

_____

_____

_____

Reader's Response

Consider the following questions. Discuss your answers with one or more partners.

1. How did listening to the performance make you feel? Pinpoint a precise emotion and explain.

2. Did you prefer listening to the piece, reading it or doing both at the same time? Explain.

3. Which aspects of the performance did you like and/or dislike? Be precise in your description.

4. Did you connect with the speaker? Do you feel you were able to fully grasp the piece's story and message? Explain.

LANGUAGE FOCUS

While page poetry creates rhythm and sound patterns in writing, the spoken word artist's speech particularities are an integral part of a performance. Kate Tempest's origins lie in East London, associated with the cockney vernacular. Thus, the use of cockney pronunciation contributes to the speaker's authenticity and often serves a strategic purpose in the piece's use of rhyme and sound devices.

A. Listen to the poet's pronunciation of the sounds indicated in bold. How are they different from your own pronunciation? How does this pronunciation serve the rhyme or sound devices?

1. **T**ime / m**y** / r**i**se / sm**i**le / wh**i**le

2. Bo**th**er / **th**ree / streng**th** / Ear**th**

3. Ka**t**ie / lucidi**t**y / abili**t**ies / li**tt**le

4. Thinki**ng** /sitti**ng** / watchi**ng** / groupi**ng**

5. En**ch**anted/ la**s**t / predaw**n** / pa**ss**ed / laugh**ed**

B. What do you notice about the pronunciation of words ending on –*r*?

Look up any words you are unsure of.

MyBookshelf > My eLab > Exercises > Part IV: Other Genres > Chapter 16: Spoken Word > Vocabulary Comprehension

Close Reading

As you read the text again, pay attention to specific elements that seem significant to understanding and interpreting the spoken word piece. The following guided reading questions will help you.

1. Who or what are the "Old friends with new faces" referred to in line 1?

_____

2. In which line does the speaker express how important performing is to her?

_____

_____

3. Which two elements in the first verse allow the listener/reader to establish a clear link between the speaker and the poet?

_____

_____

_____

4. How are the sun and moon personified?

_____

_____

5. Which metaphor does the speaker use to refer to the inspiration for her writing?

_____

6. Who do the expressions "us lot" and "you lot" refer to?

_____

_____

7. What does the speaker say about her friendships? Check all that apply.

a) Some of her friends have become rivals.

b) She feels let down and disappointed by some of her old friends.

c) Even though they are no longer friends, some people still inspire her.

d) She feels better than her old friends.

MyBookshelf > My eLab > Exercises > Part IV: Other Genres > Chapter 16: Spoken Word > Close Reading: Additional Questions

8. Which word or phrase best summarizes the idea expressed in the last verse?

a) collaboration   b) competition   c) individual success   d) mutual respect

THE LANGUAGE OF LITERATURE

The effect of a spoken word piece is to a very large extent determined by the speaker's use of sound devices, rhythm and rhyme to make the words resonate with the audience. Use the following questions to focus your attention on the effect of these devices.

1. In the first verse, identify two examples each of end rhyme and internal rhyme. For each example, determine if it is a form of exact rhyme or slant rhyme.

End rhyme: _____

_____

Internal rhyme: _____

_____

2. In the third verse, identify at least one example each of assonance, consonance and alliteration. First, work from the text. Then, listen to the recording to change or add to your answers if need be. Precise answers may vary.

Assonance: _____

_____

_____

Consonance: _____

_____

Alliteration: _____

_____

3. In the second verse, how does the speaker use volume and rhythm to draw attention to certain words and phrases?

_____

_____

_____

_____

_____

Analytical Reading

After making specific observations, you are ready to analyze the subject of your close reading. The following questions will help you look for thematic patterns, establish relationships and identify specific examples of literary devices or principles.

1. How does the speaker alternate between concrete and abstract diction?

2. How would you summarize the meaning of the extended metaphor constructed around the personification of the sun and the moon, and the relationship they have?

3. What is the piece's subject matter? What is its theme? How do the two relate?

4. How does the piece's title reflect its theme?

5. In the following lines, how does the speaker use rhythm to reinforce the rhymes and sound devices and support the meaning of the words? "But in within that grouping there was some kind of solution that made us all sure we were moving / through confusion to lucidity— made bigger by each other's abilities."

Food for Thought

The following questions encourage you to turn a critical eye to your earlier observations and analyses. They introduce elements and considerations that will lead you to formulate new questions and set tentative hypotheses. Discuss these to further your insight into the text.

1. One of the most abstract and opaque passages of the piece comes near the end of the performance: "Coz every good Moon moves to make room for the Day / Every good Moon makes room for the Day." What do you think the artist means by this? Discuss your interpretation with one or more partners.

2. Consider the artist's comment that follows the spoken word performance. Read the Text in Context section again. How do these elements inform your interpretation of the piece's theme and meaning and, more specifically, the meaning of the sun and moon metaphor?

3. Consider how the diction and delivery of the spoken word piece complement each other.

a. What words or phrases are powerful on their own? Why do you think those words are powerful?

b. What words or phrases are powerful because of how the artist says them? What did the artist do to give those words power? How did that make you feel?

4. Watch a video recording of a Kate Tempest performance. Some of these include only spoken word, while others are set to music. How does the artist's body language add to the performance? How does music add to the performance? Discuss your observations and opinions.

Presenting an Analysis

Writing | Analyzing the Contribution of Performance to the Development of Mood and Theme

While the verse that makes up "To Blossom in the Shadow" is rich in imagery, poetic devices and sound patterns, the performance of the piece actively contributes to the impact of these elements. The speaker's pronunciation and enunciation complement the words to elevate the piece to an effective aural experience. Prepare an analytical essay focusing around a thesis statement that investigates how the performance elements contribute to the tone, theme and mood of the spoken word piece. Refer to the work you have done in this chapter to guide you while identifying pertinent elements, and highlight how they help transform the subject matter into a specific theme and mood.

(Refer to Part V, Writing about Literature, on page 271 for more information on essay format and structure.)

Speaking | Comparing Spoken Word Performances

While page poetry is based on literary devices that call up images—including sounds—for the reader, allowing for different experiences, spoken word pieces are performed in a specific manner by the poet to resonate as much as possible with the audience. Such performance elements include pronunciation, enunciation (projection and tone of voice), rhythm and, in certain contexts, body language and the use of percussion or music.

Choose a spoken word performance and analyze it in a manner similar to the analysis of "To Blossom in the Shadow" you have undertaken in this chapter. Focus on the use of figures of speech, sound devices and performance elements and analyze how they contribute to the development of the piece's subject matter, theme, tone and mood.

Present your analysis of this performance by comparing and contrasting it with your analysis of "To Blossom in the Shadow." For instance, if you watched a video recording or a performance set to music, you can discuss how the addition of this element enhances the performance aspect. If you listen to the performance of a poet with a different accent, tone of voice or speech rhythm, you may investigate how these differences do or do not affect the performance and impact of the spoken word piece. Give precise examples, playing passages of the performances to highlight similarities and differences.

MyBookshelf > My eLab
> Exercises > Grammar and
Accuracy

(Refer to Appendix 2 on page 297 for more information on presentation format and structure.)

CHAPTER 17

Graphic Novels

This chapter focuses on the following:

- Imagery and symbolism
- Plot and narrative
- Language Focus: onomatopoeia
- The Language of Literature: visual elements
- Theme, tone and mood

Connect with the Text

A. Take stock of your opinions on the following questions. Discuss them with one or more partners.

1. Intuitively, how would you define comic books and graphic novels? How are they similar? How are they different? Explain.

2. Do you associate graphic novels more with young readers or adults? Why?

3. Do you consider graphic novels to be forms of literature? Explain.

4. Like prose, graphic novels are not limited to fiction. Do you think they are effective tools to teach or inform readers on nonfiction issues? Why or why not?

5. Do you prefer to read text-only or graphic novels? Why?

6. In which way(s) do you think the presence of visual elements affects one's experience of a story's characters, plot and atmosphere?

B. Before you read the two graphic novel excerpts in this chapter, do a web search to find the answers to the questions below. This will help you contextualize the story and its themes. Remember to record your sources so you can use them as references, should you decide to include this information in an essay or presentation.

1. Who was Louis Riel? What are his origins and upbringing? What is his connection with the Métis and with French Canadians? What was his role in the Red River Rebellion? How did he contribute to the foundation of Manitoba? Why was Riel hanged?

2. Who was Chanie Wenjack? What are his origins and cultural heritage? What happened to him? What are Indian residential schools and why are they condemned today?

Louis Riel

Text in Context

Chester Brown (1960–) grew up in the Montreal area but moved to Toronto at age nineteen, where he started self-publishing photocopied comics. A few years later, Brown started working full time as a cartoonist. His cult black comedy *Ed the Happy Clown* was first published as a serial, before being turned into a graphic novel in 1989. In the 1990s and 2000s, Brown wrote several autobiographical graphic novels, including the controversial *Paying for It*. His best-known work is also biographical in nature, focusing on the life of Métis leader Louis Riel. The 2003 publication of *Louis Riel: A Comic-Strip Biography* led Brown to receive the 2004 Harvey Award for best writing and best graphic novel. It is often considered to be the first Canadian best-seller in the graphic novel genre. Instead of drawing complete pages, Brown usually draws individual panels and then assembles them into pages. He uses a sparse drawing style and tends to provide detailed annotations and end notes documenting his research and artistic choices.

Exploratory Reading

First, explore the graphic novel excerpt as you would for enjoyment. Allow your eyes to be drawn across the pages to soak up the visual style and atmosphere of the excerpt without looking for any specific elements. Take a mental note of your emotional reactions. When you are finished, answer the Initial Insight questions below.

Louis Riel   Chester Brown

(See pages 248–249.)

Source: Brown, C. *Louis Riel: A Comic-Strip Biography*. Drawn and Quarterly, 2003.

Initial Insight

1. In which two places is the excerpt set?

_____

_____

_____

2. What is the link between the events taking place in these two locations?

_____

_____

_____

Reader's Response

Consider the following questions. Discuss your answers with one or more partners.

1. How is the excerpt similar to or different from what you know or expect from a graphic novel?

2. Which aspects stood out to you, either positively or negatively? Explain.

3. Do you feel a graphic novel like this one could be used to teach history? Why?

THE LANGUAGE OF LITERATURE

The effect of a graphic novel is to a very large extent determined by the author's use of visual elements as part of a cohesive style. Use the following questions to focus your attention on the effect of the author's visual choices.

1. How many panels does each page have? How are they separated from each other?

_____

2. Which two types of precision are provided in text boxes?

_____

_____

3. What type of shot is not used in the excerpt?

a) long shot   b) medium shot   c) close-up shot

4. From which angle(s) are the scenes in the excerpt rendered? Check all that apply.

a) eye level   b) high angle   c) low angle

5. How do the colour schemes of the first and second pages contrast?

_____

_____

Close Reading

As you read the text again, pay attention to specific elements that seem significant to understanding and interpreting the graphic novel excerpt. The following guided reading questions will help you.

1. What is the defining feature used to depict John A. Macdonald?

_____

2. Which two conditions do the Hudson's Bay Company representatives set for selling their land?

_____

3. How is the representatives' agreement visually represented in the fourth panel?

_____

4. How does the last panel on the first page identify the setting for the scene on the second page?

_____

5. Which punctuation mark is used when Louis Riel and his fellow settlers speak with each other?

_____

6. How is movement of the human and animal characters on the second page visually indicated?

_____

_____

MyBookshelf > My eLab > Exercises > Part IV: Other Genres > Chapter 17: Graphic Novels > Louis Riel – Close Reading: Additional Questions

7. In the last panel, what is particular about the spelling of the [th] sound?

_____

Analytical Reading

After making specific observations, you are ready to analyze the subject of your close reading. The following questions will help you look for thematic patterns, establish relationships and identify specific examples of literary devices or principles.

1. How do the panels on the first and second page visually contrast with one another? Focus on the use of colour and the depiction of the characters. What implicit comment do these elements make about the events that unfold?

2. On the second page, how does the author indicate the passing of time and distance? Which visual strategy is used twice to signal the start of a scene?

3. How are types of shots and angles used to focus the attention of the reader on the characters' actions and words and to support the plot line?

4. Which typographical effect does the author use to signal the language barrier between the settlers and the surveyors?

5. Which of Riel's actions and reactions depict him as a leader? How is this similar to or different from the depiction of John A. Macdonald on the first page?

Food for Thought

The following questions encourage you to turn a critical eye to your earlier observations and analyses. They introduce elements and considerations that will lead you to formulate new questions and set tentative hypotheses. Discuss these to further your insight into the text.

1. Chester Brown took certain liberties with some of the story's details. These discrepancies are pointed out in endnotes. For example, although the first page portrays John A. Macdonald in England negotiating in person with the Hudson's Bay Company representatives, he never went to London. Moreover, the acreage was not mentioned in the original agreement. Why exactly do you think Brown changed these details? Does this change your appreciation of the graphic novel? Explain.

2. Scholars argue that the historical image of Louis Riel has been constructed as a symbol of cultural conflict and as representative of a clash of regions.[1] How are both of these perceptions illustrated in the graphic novel?

---

1 Douglas Owram, "The Myth of Louis Riel," _The Canadian Historical Review_, vol. 63, no. 3, 1982, pp. 315–336, _Project MUSE_, muse.jhu.edu/article/571310.

3. Although the sequential nature of graphic novels may encourage readers to interpret events in a strict chronological manner, Brown's portrayal of Riel can be read as a more symbolic representation of key moments in Riel's rebellions. Discuss the organization and narrative structure of the excerpt to express your agreement or disagreement with this statement.

Secret Path

Text in Context

Gordon "Gord" Downie

Jeff Lemire

Gordon "Gord" Downie (1964–2017) was a musician, singer-songwriter, writer and activist from Ontario, best known as the lead singer for the band The Tragically Hip. Downie is considered one of the most influential artists in the Canadian music scene. Jeff Lemire (1976–) was born in Essex County, Ontario—a region he wrote several award-winning graphic novels about. He is also a prolific cartoonist for Marvel and DC comics, and has co-authored several superhero comics, most notably in the *Batman* and *X-Men* series. In 2016, Downie collaborated with Lemire on *Secret Path*, a cross-media project that includes text, music and illustrations. It was later also turned into an animated film. *Secret Path* tells the story of Chanie Wenjack, a twelve-year-old Indigenous boy who died in 1966 while running away from an Indian residential school in the hope of finding his family, which he had been taken away from, over 600 km away.

Exploratory Reading

First, explore the excerpt as you would for enjoyment. Allow your eyes to be drawn across the pages to soak up the visual style and atmosphere of the graphic novel excerpt without looking for any specific elements. Take a mental note of your emotional reactions. When you are finished, answer the Initial Insight questions below.

Secret Path   **Gord Downie and Jeff Lemire**

(See page 253.)

Source: Downie, G. and J. Lemire. *Secret Path*. Simon & Schuster, 2016.

Initial Insight

1. In one sentence, how would you summarize this passage of the graphic novel?

_____

_____

2. Who or what receives the focus in the excerpt? Is this the same or different between the text and the illustration?

_____

_____

SEVEN MATCHES

She gave me matches
Seven wooden matches
She put them into a small slim glass jar
With a screwtop lid

I fingered that jar
I put it in my pocket
She said, "Can't go into the woods without them."
I smiled at her and left

And I kept them dry
And as long as there were six
I'd be fine
As long as there were five

Matches in that jar
Mile after mile
On the chick-chick chick-chick sound of the matches
On the memory of her smile

I kept them dry
And as long as there were five
I'd be fine
As long as there were four

Matches in a jar
With a screwtop lid
I know she did not mean to hurt my feelings
But that's what she did

And I kept them dry
And as long as there were three
I'd be fine
As long as there were two

Matches in that jar.

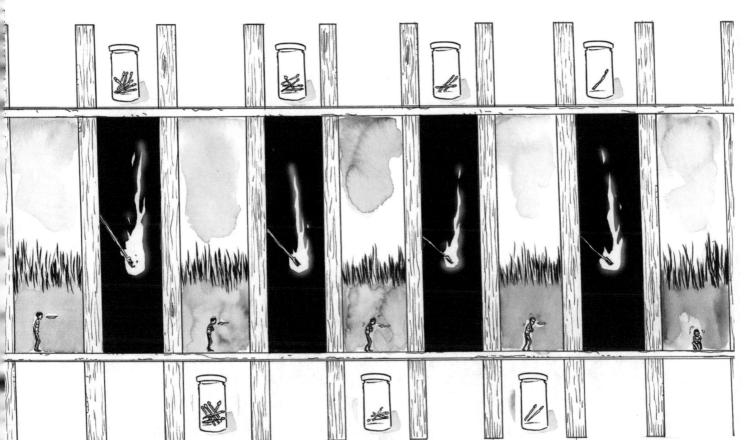

Reader's Response

Consider the following questions. Discuss your answers with one or more partners.

1. How did the excerpt make you feel? Use precise adjectives and explain your choices.

2. Which aspect of the graphic novel made the biggest emotional impact on you; the text or the illustration? Why?

3. What did you like/dislike about the text and the artwork? Be precise.

Close Reading

As you read the text again, pay attention to specific elements that seem significant to understanding and interpreting the graphic novel excerpt. The following guided reading questions will help you.

1. Who do the pronouns *I* and *she* refer to in the text?

_____

_____

2. How many matches are there, and how are they kept together?

_____

3. Which two sound devices does the phrase "small slim glass jar" contain?

_____

4. Which repetition, in the form of anaphora, indicates the passing of time?

_____

_____

5. How is this repetition visualized in the illustration?

_____

_____

6. Which objects act as the gutters that separate the different panels in the illustration?

_____

7. Which two types of shots are used in the illustration? See page 225 for a list.

_____

MyBookshelf > My eLab
> Exercises > Part IV:
Other Genres > Chapter 17:
Graphic Novels > Secret Path
— Close Reading: Additional
Questions

LANGUAGE FOCUS

Onomatopoeia imitates the natural sounds of things or actions. This sound effect can make a description more expressive or evocative, and even appeal to imagery that transcends sounds. For instance, writing that a drink *fizzes* not only describes the sound produced by a carbonated beverage but also evokes the sensation this creates on the tongue when drinking it.

1. Which onomatopoeia is used in the excerpt? Apart from sound, which other image(s) does the onomatopoeia call up?

_____

_____

_____

2. Think of examples of four other onomatopoeia, each appealing to another sense beside sound
—i.e., sight, taste, smell and touch.

Look up any words you are unsure of.

MyBookshelf > My eLab
> Exercises > Part IV: Other
Genres > Chapter 17:
Graphic Novels > Vocabulary
Comprehension

Analytical Reading

After making specific observations, you are ready to analyze the subject of your close reading. The following questions will help you look for thematic patterns, establish relationships and identify specific examples of literary devices or principles.

1. How is the repetition of words and visual images used to indicate the passing of time?

2. What do you observe about the figure of the boy in the illustration? For each of the seven matches, pinpoint an emotion that might be associated with it. For instance, the first match may symbolize hope.

3. What is the colour scheme of the illustration? What does the white line in front of the boy's face represent? What do you observe about the boy's body language? How do all of these elements inform the reader about the weather and the temperature?

4. How does the visual representation of the matches highlight their importance for the boy's survival? Apart from their physical capacity, how do they help him?

Food for Thought

The following questions encourage you to turn a critical eye to your earlier observations and analyses. They introduce elements and considerations that will lead you to formulate new questions and set tentative hypotheses. Discuss these to further your insight into the text.

1. The number 7 has a strong symbolic value in Ojibwe (Anishinaabe) culture, which Chanie Wenjack was a part of. Do a web search for the Teaching of the Seven Grandfathers. What are they? How can they be related to the matches in the story?

2. The graphic novel is based on historical events. How does knowing this affect your interpretation and emotional response to it? What message do you think anyone can infer from the "Seven Matches" excerpt, regardless of their origin and situation?

3. The words and illustrations are entirely separate in this graphic novel. How do you think their integration would impact the reader's experience of the story?

4. The text also exists in the form of song, and the illustrations exist in the form of an animated cartoon. Consult one or both of these versions. How do they alter your experience of engaging with the story, either in a positive or negative manner? Give specific examples.

Presenting an Analysis

Writing | Analyzing the Development of Plot in Graphic Novels

In graphic novels, textual and visual elements are combined to construct one cohesive narrative experience. Prepare an analytical essay focusing around a thesis statement that investigates how the author strategically uses different elements to construct the plot and move it forward. You can focus on one of the graphic novel excerpts or compare and contrast them both. Refer to the work you have done in this chapter to guide you while identifying pertinent elements, including the use of panels, types of shots and angles, the integration of text and illustration, the depiction of characters and the expression of time and action. Highlight how they help transform the individual panels into a cohesive story.

(Refer to Part V, Writing about Literature, on page 271 for more information on essay format and structure.)

Speaking | Examining the Visual Construction of Tone, Mood and Atmosphere

The graphic novel excerpts in this chapter represent different visual styles and approaches to the construction of tone, mood and atmosphere. This is achieved through the use or absence of colour, the drawing style, the level of detail, the depiction of characters, the combination of words and illustrations and the strategies used to render the action, either implicitly or explicitly.

Focus on one of the graphic novels in this chapter or compare both. Present a reader's response analysis of it by explaining how their visual style contributed to your experience and interpretation of the tone, mood and atmosphere of the story and its characters. Focus on one aspect at a time; describe it and then point out the impact it had on you as a reader.

MyBookshelf > My eLab
> Exercises > Grammar
and Accuracy

(Refer to Appendix 2 on page 297 for more information on presentation format and structure.)

CHAPTER 18

Speeches

This chapter focuses on the following:

- Rhetorical devices
- Figures of speech
- Language Focus: Canadianisms
- The Language of Literature: the rhetorical transaction
- Theme and purpose

Connect with the Text

A. Take stock of your opinions on the following questions. Discuss them with one or more partners.

  1. What does it mean to be educated?

  2. Why is education important? Is it a right or a privilege? Support your point of view.

  3. What defines Canadians? Which values do you associate with Canada?

  4. Would you move to another country all by yourself? For which reason(s)?

  5. How can learning about other cultures teach us more about ourselves? Give an example.

B. Before you read the speeches, do a web search to find the answers to the questions below. This will help you contextualize the speakers and their stories. Remember to record your sources so you can use them as references, should you decide to include this information in an essay or presentation.

  1. Who is Malala Yousafzai? What are her origins and upbringing? Why is she well known?

  2. Why is access to education in Pakistan problematic, especially for girls? What role does the country's social and political situation play in this issue? Do such problems exist elsewhere?

  3. Malala spoke at the United Nations headquarters and was awarded the Nobel Peace Prize. What are the UN and the Norwegian Nobel Committee, and why are they significant?

  4. What are the historical reasons for Chinese immigration to Canada in the nineteenth century? What was the Chinese head tax? Why could the Chinese not immigrate to Canada between 1923 and 1947?

  5. What do you know about Chinatowns? How many of them exist in Canada, and how did they come about?

  6. How can someone become a Canadian citizen if they were born a different nationality? What does the application procedure consist of today?

Speech at the Youth Takeover of the United Nations

Text in Context

Malala Yousafzai (1997–) was born in Pakistan, and was attending the school founded by her father, when the area began to change as the Taliban tried to take control. In 2008, she gave a first talk, entitled "How dare the Taliban take away my basic right to education?" She also started blogging for the BBC and became an advocate for women's right to education. In response, the Taliban issued a death threat against her, and on October 9, 2012, a gunman boarded the school bus she was on and shot her in the head. Nine months after being shot, on her sixteenth birthday, Malala gave a speech at the United Nations where she repeated her commitment to education and women's rights, urging world leaders to change their policies. This day—July 12—was named "Malala Day" by UN secretary Ban Ki-moon. In 2014, Yousafzai received the Nobel Peace Prize, and in 2017 she was given honorary Canadian citizenship. She currently studies at Oxford University.

Exploratory Reading

Read the speech a first time without interruption. Keep an open mind and take a mental note of your reactions and observations. Take in the information given by the speaker and the way she presents it, without looking for any specific elements. When you are finished, answer the questions below the text.

Speech at the Youth Takeover of the United Nations
Malala Yousafzai

1 In the name of God, The Most Beneficent, The Most Merciful.
Honourable UN Secretary-General Mr. Ban Ki-moon,
Respected President General Assembly Vuk Jeremic
Honourable UN envoy for Global education Mr. Gordon Brown,
Respected elders and my dear brothers and sisters;

2 Today, it is an honour for me to be speaking again after a long time. Being here with such honourable people is a great moment in my life.

3 I don't know where to begin my speech. I don't know what people would be expecting me to say. But first of all, thank you to God for whom we all are equal and thank you to every person who has prayed for my fast recovery and a new life. I cannot believe how much love people have shown me. I have received thousands of good wish cards and gifts from all over the world. Thank you to all of them. Thank you to the children whose innocent words encouraged me. Thank you to my elders whose prayers strengthened me.

4 I would like to thank my nurses, doctors and all of the staff of the hospitals in Pakistan and the UK and the UAE government who have helped me get better and recover my strength. I fully support Mr. Ban Ki-moon the Secretary-General in his Global Education First Initiative and the work of the UN Special Envoy Mr. Gordon Brown. And I thank them both for the leadership they continue to give. They continue to inspire all of us to action.

5 Dear brothers and sisters, do remember one thing. Malala day is not my day. Today is the day of every woman, every boy and every girl who have raised their voice for their rights. There are hundreds of Human rights activists and social workers who are not only speaking for human rights, but who are struggling to achieve their goals of education, peace and equality.

Thousands of people have been killed by the terrorists and millions have been injured. I am just one of them.

6 So here I stand ... one girl among many.

7 I speak—not for myself, but for all girls and boys.

8 I raise up my voice—not so that I can shout, but so that those without a voice can be heard.

9 Those who have fought for their rights:
- Their right to live in peace.
- Their right to be treated with dignity.
- Their right to equality of opportunity.
- Their right to be educated.

10 Dear Friends, on the 9th of October 2012, the Taliban shot me on the left side of my forehead. They shot my friends too. They thought that the bullets would silence us. But they failed. And then, out of that silence came, thousands of voices. The terrorists thought that they would change our aims and stop our ambitions but nothing changed in my life except this: Weakness, fear and hopelessness died. Strength, power and courage was born. I am the same Malala. My ambitions are the same. My hopes are the same. My dreams are the same.

11 Dear sisters and brothers, I am not against anyone. Neither am I here to speak in terms of personal revenge against the Taliban or any other terrorist […] group. I am here to speak up for the right of education of every child. I want education for the sons and the daughters of all the extremists especially the Taliban.

12 I do not even hate the Talib who shot me. Even if there is a gun in my hand and he stands in front of me[,] I would not shoot him. This is the compassion that I have learnt from Muhammad […] the prophet of mercy, Jesus [C]hrist and Lord Buddha. This is the legacy of change that I have inherited from Martin Luther King, Nelson Mandela and Muhammad Ali Jinnah. This is the philosophy of non-violence that I have learnt from [Mahatma] Gandhi […], Bacha Khan and Mother Teresa. And this is the forgiveness that I have learnt from my mother and father. This is what my soul is telling me, be peaceful and love everyone.

13 Dear sisters and brothers, we realize the importance of light when we see darkness. We realize the importance of our voice when we are silenced. In the same way, when we were in Swat, the north of Pakistan, we realized the importance of pens and books when we saw the guns.

14 The wise saying […] "The pen is mightier than the sword" was true. The extremists are afraid of books and pens. The power of education frightens them. They are afraid of women. The power of the voice of women frightens them. And that is why they killed 14 innocent medical students in the recent attack in Quetta. And that is why they killed many female teachers and polio workers in Khyber [Pakhtunk]hwa and FATA. That is why they are blasting schools every day. Because they were and they are afraid of change, afraid of the equality that we will bring into our society.

15 I remember that there was a boy in our school who was asked by a journalist, "Why are the Taliban against education?" He answered very simply. By pointing to his book[,] he said, "A Talib doesn't know what is written inside this book." They think that God is a tiny, little conservative being who would send girls to the hell just because of going to school. The terrorists are misusing the name of Islam and Pashtun society for their own personal benefits. Pakistan is [a] peace-loving democratic country. Pashtuns want education for their daughters and sons. And Islam is a religion of peace, humanity and brotherhood. Islam says that it is not only each child's right to get education, rather it is their duty and responsibility.

16 Honourable Secretary General, peace is necessary for education. In many parts of the world[,] especially Pakistan and Afghanistan[,] terrorism, wars and conflicts stop children to go to their schools. We are really tired of these wars. Women and children are suffering

in many parts of the world in many ways. In India, innocent and poor children are victims of child labour. Many schools have been destroyed in Nigeria. People in Afghanistan have been affected by the hurdles of extremism for decades. Young girls have to do domestic child labour and are forced to get married at early age. Poverty, ignorance, injustice, racism and the deprivation of basic rights are the main problems faced by both men and women.

17 Dear fellows, today I am focusing on women's rights and girls' education because they are suffering the most. There was a time when women social activists asked men to stand up for their rights. But, this time, we will do it by ourselves. I am not telling men to step away from speaking for women's rights[,] rather I am focusing on women to be independent to fight for themselves.

18 Dear sisters and brothers, now it's time to speak up.

19 So today, we call upon the world leaders to change their strategic policies in favour of peace and prosperity.
- We call upon the world leaders that all the peace deals must protect women and children's rights. A deal that goes against the dignity of women and their rights is unacceptable.
- We call upon all governments to ensure free compulsory education for every child all over the world.
- We call upon all governments to fight against terrorism and violence, to protect children from brutality and harm.
- We call upon the developed nations to support the expansion of educational opportunities for girls in the developing world.
- We call upon all communities to be tolerant—to reject prejudice based on cast, creed, sect, religion or gender. To ensure freedom and equality for women so that they can flourish. We cannot all succeed when half of us are held back.
- We call upon our sisters around the world to be brave—to embrace the strength within themselves and realize their full potential.

20 Dear brothers and sisters, we want schools and education for every child's bright future. We will continue our journey to our destination of peace and education for everyone. No one can stop us. We will speak for our rights and we will bring change through our voice. We must believe in the power and the strength of our words. Our words can change the world.

21 Because we are all together, united for the cause of education. And if we want to achieve our goal, then let us empower ourselves with the weapon of knowledge and let us shield ourselves with unity and togetherness.

22 Dear brothers and sisters, we must not forget that millions of people are suffering from poverty, injustice and ignorance. We must not forget that millions of children are out of schools. We must not forget that our sisters and brothers are waiting for a bright peaceful future.

23 So let us wage a global struggle against illiteracy, poverty and terrorism and let us pick up our books and pens. They are our most powerful weapons.

24 **One child, one teacher, one pen and one book can change the world.**

25 **Education is the only solution. Education First.**

(1487 words)

Source: Yousafzai, M. "Speech at the Youth Takeover of the United Nations." *United Nations*, 2013, www.un.org/News/dh/infocus/malala_speech.pdf.

Initial Insight

1. In one or two sentences, what is the central message of the speech?

_____

_____

_____

2. To whom is the speech mostly addressed?

_____

_____

Reader's Response

Consider the following questions. Discuss your answers with one or more partners.

1. After reading or watching the speech, what impression do you have of Malala? Be precise.

2. Which part(s) of the speech resonated the most with you? Why?

3. Do you think Malala's hopes are realistic? Explain.

THE LANGUAGE OF LITERATURE

The effect of a speech is based on the principle of rhetorical appeals—devices used to establish the rhetorical transaction between a speaker and their audience. Malala's speech contains explicit references to a) ethos, b) pathos, c) logos and d) kairos (see page 228). For each of the excerpts below, establish the corresponding rhetorical appeal by writing the matching letter.

_____ "it is an honour for me to be speaking again after a long time"

_____ "Respected elders and my dear brothers and sisters"

_____ "I am focusing on women's rights and girls' education because they are suffering the most"

_____ "So here I stand ... one girl among many. I speak—not for myself, but for all girls and boys."

For each rhetorical appeal, find at least one more example in the speech. Discuss your answers with one or more partners.

Close Reading

As you read the text again, pay attention to specific elements that seem significant to understanding and interpreting the speech. The following guided reading questions will help you.

1. Whom does the speaker thank first?

_____

2. What are the four rights Malala considers herself to speak up for?

_____

_____

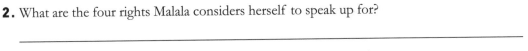

3. What is the only thing the speaker says changed in her life after she was attacked?

_____

_____

4. What figure of speech is "The pen is mightier than the sword"? What does it mean?

_____

5. According to the speaker, what feeling is the reason why extremists commit attacks?

_____

6. Why does Malala focus on women's rights and girls' education, and why does she think it is important she does so?

_____

_____

7. In her call for world leaders to change their policies, which concepts does Malala associate with education? Check all that apply.

a) equality   b) freedom   c) peace   d) prejudice   e) privilege

8. If knowledge is a means of empowerment, then what allows those standing up for their rights to shield and protect themselves?

_____

MyBookshelf > My eLab > Exercises > Part IV: Other Genres > Chapter 18: Speeches > Speech at the Youth Takeover of the United Nations — Close Reading: Additional Questions

Analytical Reading

After making specific observations, you are ready to analyze the subject of your close reading. The following questions will help you look for thematic patterns, establish relationships and identify specific examples of rhetorical devices or principles.

1. What is the speech's immediate occasion? What is the larger occasion? How are the two connected? Refer to the Connect with the Text and Text in Context sections to help you.

2. What events does Malala allude to in the opening lines when she says, "Today, it is an honour for me to be speaking again after a long time"? What does this statement suggest about her activism?

3. In which way does Malala warrant her being the one delivering a speech? How does she represent herself as being different from yet similar to the audience?

4. How does the speaker link the concepts of education, equal rights and peace?

5. Find two examples of the speaker's use of repetition. What particular effect does each example have?

6. In which two ways does the speaker use the metaphor "the pen is mightier than the sword"? What does using this metaphor allow her to achieve?

7. What is the purpose of Malala sharing her own story with the audience at the beginning of the speech?

8. How does the speech fulfill each of the following three objectives: persuade, inform and motivate? Cite specific passages.

Food for Thought

The following questions encourage you to turn a critical eye to your earlier observations and analyses. They introduce elements and considerations that will lead you to formulate new questions and set tentative hypotheses. Discuss these to further your insight into the text.

1. Considering she is speaking up against the Taliban regime, what is the importance of Malala speaking "In the name of God, The Most Beneficent, The Most Merciful"? Which other passage in the speech reinforces this point of view? Do you consider this an effective or ineffective persuasive strategy? Explain your answer.

2. How does Malala's condemnation of violence contrast with the metaphors she uses toward the end of the speech? Do they go against the values she advocates?

3. On December 10, 2014, Malala delivered her Nobel Peace Prize acceptance speech in Oslo, Norway. Watch or read this speech and compare it with the one you have just analyzed. Which rhetorical devices and appeals are shared by both speeches? Pinpoint and explain at least five of them.

Being Canadian

Text in Context

Denise Chong (1953–) is a third-generation Canadian of Chinese descent; she grew up in Prince George, British Columbia. She studied in economics at the University of British Columbia, where she also started her writing career as a journalist on the university's student newspaper. After graduating, she moved to Ottawa where she worked at the Department of Finance before becoming an advisor to Prime Minister Pierre Trudeau. As a young Asian woman, Chong set an example in the white male-dominated world of public administration. At the end of the Trudeau era, Chong became a professional writer and spent several years in China. This inspired her 1994 book *The Concubine's Children*, which tells the story of her grandparents, who moved to Canada in the hope of giving their children a better life. It is a story of courage and survival, celebrating the contributions immigrants have made to a country that initially did not welcome them with open arms. In her speech "Being Canadian," delivered during the 1995 Citizenship Week, Chong draws on her grandparents' example to explain why today she is a proud Canadian citizen. She also wrote books relating to the Vietnam war and the 1989 protests in Tiananmen Square. In 2013, she was named an Officer of the Order of Canada for "writing books that raise our social consciousness."[1]

Exploratory Reading

Read the speech a first time without interruption. Keep an open mind and take a mental note of your reactions and observations. Take in the information given by the speaker and the way she presents it, without looking for any specific elements. When you are finished, answer the questions below the text.

---

1 "Ms. Denise Chong, O.C., M.A., LL.D.," *The Governor General of Canada*, www.gg.ca/en/honours/recipients/146-11554.

Being Canadian   Denise Chong

1 I ask myself what it means to be a Canadian. I was lucky enough to be born in Canada. So I look back at the price paid by those who made the choice that brought me such luck.

2 South China at the turn of the century became the spout of the tea pot that was China. It poured out middle-class peasants like my grandfather, who couldn't earn a living at home. He left behind a wife and child. My grandfather was 36 when exclusion came. Lonely and living a penurious existence, he worked at a saw mill on the mud flats of the Fraser River, where the Chinese were third on the pay scale behind Whites and Hindus. With the door to Chinese immigration slammed shut, men like him didn't dare even go home for a visit, for fear Canada might bar their re-entry. With neither savings enough to go home for good, nor the means once in China to put rice in the mouths of his wife and child there, my grandfather wondered when, if ever, be could return to the bosom of a family. He decided to purchase a concubine, a second wife, to join him in Canada.

3 The concubine, at age 17, got into Canada on a lie. She got around the exclusion law in the only way possible: she presented the authorities with a Canadian birth certificate. It had belonged to a woman born in Ladner, British Columbia, and a middleman sold it to my grandfather at many times the price of the old head tax. Some years later, the concubine and my grandfather went back to China with their two Vancouver-born daughters. They lived for a time under the same roof as my grandfather's first wife. The concubine became pregnant. Eight months into her pregnancy, she decided to brave the long sea voyage back so that her third child could be born in Canada. Her false Canadian birth certificate would get her in. Accompanied by only my grandfather, she left China. Three days after the boat docked, on the second-floor of a tenement on a back alley in Vancouver's Chinatown, she gave birth to my mother.

4 Canada remained inhospitable. Yet my grandparents chose to keep Canada in their future. Both gambled a heritage and family ties to take what they thought were better odds in the lottery of life. The gratitude owed them can perhaps best be expressed by my mother's brother in China—the son of my grandfather and his first wife. In the late 1980s, my mother and I found the family left behind. My uncle pressed a letter into my mother's hand on the last night of our visit. It read, in part, ["]As parents, who would not be concerned about the future of his or her children?['] I hope to get my children out of China to take root in Canada. Then, the roots of the tree will grow downwards and the leaves will be luxuriant. We will be fortunate, the children will be fortunate and our children's children will be fortunate. The family will be glorious and future generations will have a good foundation.

5 My own sense, four generations on, of being Canadian is one of belonging. I belong to a family. I belong to a community of values. I didn't get to choose my ancestors, but I can try to leave the world a better place for the generations that follow. The life I lead begins before and lingers after my time.

6 The past holds some moral authority over us. Rather than forget it, we must acknowledge that we have one, and learn the lessons of it. We have to be vigilant about looking past the stereotypes and seeing the contrasting truths. It means understanding that someone's grandfather didn't change the family name from French to English to forsake his heritage, but to make it easier to find a job. It means lifting the charge against the early Chinese of having no family values by seeing how the laws and history cleaved their families in two. It means going to the Legion and looking at a Sikh and seeing the veteran as well as the turban.

7 If we don't, we won't see that the layers of injustice cut deep. It happened in my own family. My grandfather couldn't afford a concubine. To repay the cost of my grandmother's false papers and passage to Canada, he indentured her as a tea house waitress. In the bachelor societies of the Chinatowns of their day, a *kay toi nen* was seen as one and the same as a

prostitute—both were there to woo men to spend money. My grandmother would spend the rest of her lifetime trying to climb up from that bottom rung of society. I, too, condemned my Popo, until I learned what she had been fighting against all her life.

8   Despite the luck of my mother's birth, discrimination continued to cast a long shadow over her growing-up years. Her parents separated. In neither of their lifetimes would either find work outside Chinatown. My mother knew too well the path to the pawn shop where she accompanied her mother to translate as she bargained her jewellery to pay her gambling debts. The wall on my mother's side of the bed at the rooming house was wallpapered with academic certificates. My mother wanted to become a doctor. She didn't know that it would be years after her time before the faculty of medicine at the University of British Columbia would admit its first Chinese student. Despite the narrow confines of her life, the opportunity of education gave my mother a chance to dream.

9   Eventually exclusion against Chinese immigration was lifted and other barriers of discrimination began to fall. My mother's generation was the last to grow up in Chinatown. Gradually, the Chinese became part of the larger society. In 1947, my mother no longer had to call herself Chinese. With exclusion lifted, and the new citizenship act that Canada brought in that same year, for the first time in her life my mother could call herself Canadian.

10   My parents walked out from the shadow of the past. They were determined to raise their five children as Canadians. In our own growing-up years in Prince George, my mother wanted us to be as robust as our playmates; she enriched the milk in our glasses with extra cream. My parents wanted us to take to heart the Canadian pastimes. They bought us skis to share among us. Every winter they bought us new used skates. There was a piano upstairs on which we learned to play "O Canada" for school assemblies. There was a hockey net in the basement, so my brothers could practise for the pond.

11   My parents wanted us to understand that we were part of Canada's future. They instilled the importance of an education. They encouraged us to believe that individuals could make a difference. I remember when Mr. and Mrs. Diefenbaker came to Prince George. I remember when a dashing Pierre Trudeau made his first visit. My parents made sure we were turned out to greet every visiting dignitary. My grandparents, in their time, were barred from government jobs. I, their granddaughter, would come to work as senior economic advisor to Prime Minister Pierre Trudeau.

12   I am now the mother of two young children. I want to pass on a sense of what it means to be a Canadian. But what worries me as a parent, and as a Canadian, is whether we can fashion an enduring concept of citizenship that will be the glue that holds us together as a society.

13   Curiously, Canadian citizenship elicits the most heartfelt response outside Canada. Any Canadian who has lived or travelled abroad quickly discovers that Canadian citizenship is a coveted possession. In the eyes of the rest of the world, it stands for an enlightened and gentle society.

14   Can we find a strong concept of citizenship that could be shared by all Canadians when we stand on our own soil? Some would say it is unrealistic to expect a symbol to rise out of a rather pragmatic past. We spilled no revolutionary blood, as did France—where the word *citoyen* was brought into popular usage—or America. Some lament the absence of a founding myth; we don't have the equivalent of a Boston Tea Party. Others long for Canadian versions of heroes to compete with the likes of American images that occupy our living rooms and our playgrounds.

15   The one Canadian symbol with universal recognition is the flag. But where does the maple leaf strike a chord? Outside Canada. On the back packs of Canadian travellers. Of late, in Great Britain and Ireland, flying from the masts of boats and local fishermen as a show of support for Canada in its turbot dispute with Spain.

16 Some say Canadian citizenship is devalued because it is too easy to come here. But what sets Canadian society apart from others is that ours is an inclusive society. Canada's citizenship act remains more progressive than many countries. Canadians by immigration have equal status with Canadians by birth. In contrast, in Western Europe, guest workers, even if they descended from those who originally came, can be sent home any time. In Japan, Koreans and Filipinos have no claim to the citizenship of their birth. The plight of the Palestinians in Kuwait after the Gulf War gave the lie to a free Kuwait.

17 Canadian citizenship recognizes differences. It praises diversity. It is what we as Canadians *choose* to have in common with each other. It is a bridge between those who left something to make a new home here and those born here. What keeps the bridge strong is tolerance, fairness, understanding and compassion. Citizenship has rights and responsibilities. I believe one responsibility of citizenship is to use that tolerance, fairness, understanding and compassion to leaf through the Canadian family album together.

18 My family story is about one family living on two sides of the globe, in a village in China and in the Chinatowns of the west coast of Canada. I knew I had to understand my grandparents' difficult and tangled decision to leave China for an unknown land. I had to understand the cultural baggage they brought, in order to see what they shed along the way and what they preserved. I had to see what they created anew as they acquired western sensibilities.

19 I also had to open the windows on the old Chinatowns in Canada. I had first to chip away at the layers of paint that stuck them shut, so intent had the former inhabitants been on shutting out inquiry. Some wondered why I'd want to write the story of my grandfather, who came a peasant and lived out his days alone in a rooming house. And why I'd want to write the story of my grandmother, who lived by the wages and wits that came with being a *kay toi neu*? I see no honour lost in laying down the truth of their lives. It re-visits the once harsh verdict I myself had.

20 The same holds true for other leaves of the Canadian album. Often, the only ones whose memory is preserved are those who either prayed or worked hard, or both. But others are just as real, if not more so, with their strengths and weaknesses, triumphs and foibles. My story happens to take place in dingy rooming houses, alleyways and mah-jong parlours in decaying Chinatowns. The backdrop of others may be the church basement, the union hall, school or hockey rink, or even the front porch. These stories, like mine, serve to illuminate Canada's social history.

21 How we tell our stories is the work of citizenship. The motive of the storyteller should be to put the story first. To speak with authenticity and veracity is to choose narrative over commentary. It is not to glorify or sentimentalize the past. It is not to sanitize our differences. Nor to rail against or to seek compensation today for injustices of bygone times. In my opinion, to try to rewrite history leads to a sense of victimization. It marginalizes Canadians. It backs away from equality in our society, for which we have worked hard to find expression.

22 I believe our stories ultimately tell the story of Canada itself. In all our pasts are an immigrant beginning, a settler's accomplishments and setbacks, and the confidence of a common future. We all know the struggle for victory, the dreams and the lost hopes, the pride and the shame. When we tell our stories, we look in the mirror. I believe what we will see is that Canada is not lacking in heroes. Rather, the heroes are to be found within.

23 The work of citizenship is not something just for the week that we celebrate citizenship every year. It is part of every breath we take. It is the work of our lifetimes.

24 The world is changing, and changing fast. People's lives are on the move. We travel more. We move to take new jobs, to find a bigger house, to live next to the schools we want our children to go to, to find a smaller house when they've grown up and left home. Families are far-flung, even to different continents. Children may have more than one home, a parent in each. Few of us

as adults live in or can even re-visit our childhood home. Some of us cannot even return to the neighbourhoods of our childhood and find the landscape familiar.

25 There are political pressures that could redefine Canada as we know it. Canadians continue to debate the future of the federation and question whether the country is governable. A growing regionalism could fracture the national interest. On a global scale, the trend is integration, economically and culturally. The availability and dominance of American culture crowds our ability as Canadians to find the time and space to preserve our own culture and to share it with each other. Clicking the remote control and finding the television show of our choice is a display of our consumerism, not our Canadianism. Somehow, in this rapidly changing, busy world, we have to satisfy the emotional longing for roots, for understanding who we are, and what we are.

26 If we do some of this work of citizenship, we will stand on firmer ground. Sharing experience will help build strength of character. It will explain our differences, yet make them less divisive. We will yell at each other less, and understand each other more. We will find a sense of identity and a common purpose. We will have something to hand down to the next generation.

27 My grandfather's act of immigration to the new world and the determination of my grandmother, the girl who first came here as a *kay toi neu*, to chance the journey from China back to Canada so that my mother could be born here, will stand as a gift to all future generations of my family. Knowing they came hoping for a better life makes it easy to love both them and this country.

28 In the late 1980s, I would find myself in China, on a two-year stint living in Peking and working as a writer. In a letter to my mother in Prince George, I confessed that, despite the predictions of friends back in Canada, I was finding it difficult to feel any Chineseness. My mother wrote back: "You're Canadian, not Chinese. Stop trying to feel anything." She was right. I stopped such contrivances. I was Canadian; it was that which embodied the values of my life.

(2605 words)
Source: Chong, D. "Being Canadian." *Canadian Speeches: Issues of the Day*, vol. 9, no. 2, May 1995, 17–22.

Initial Insight

1. What are the two principal narrative components that make up the speech?

_____

_____

2. Whom do you consider to be the target audience of this speech?

_____

_____

_____

_____

Reader's Response

Consider the following questions. Discuss your answers with one or more partners.

1. Which part(s) of the speech resonated the most with you? Explain what the part(s) made you reflect on.

2. Did the speech change your opinion on (Canadian) citizenship? Why or why not?

3. Given that it was delivered over twenty years ago, do you find the speaker's family story still relevant today? For what reasons?

Close Reading

As you read the text again, pay attention to specific elements that seem significant to understanding and interpreting the speech. The following guided reading questions will help you.

1. Where was Denise Chong born? And her mother?

_____

2. Why did Chong's grandfather emigrate to Canada? Why did he initially stay?

_____

_____

3. What is a concubine? Whom does Chong refer to when she uses the word?

_____

_____

_____

4. What metaphor does Chong's uncle use to express his belief that his own family would thrive in Canada?

_____

_____

5. Which two hardships did Chong's grandmother suffer to keep her family in Canada?

_____

_____

6. Which pastimes did Chong's parents offer their children to instill in them Canadian culture?

_____

_____

7. What contrast does Chong point out between her parents' status and her own job?

_____

_____

8. According to Chong, where is the symbolic value of Canadian citizenship the strongest?

_____

9. What does Chong say is the one thing all Canadians choose to have in common with each other?

_____

10. Why does Chong consider it important to share her family story?

_____

_____

_____

MyBookshelf > My eLab
> Exercises > Part IV: Other
Genres > Chapter 18: Speeches
> Being Canadian — Close
Reading: Additional Questions

LANGUAGE FOCUS

The speaker uses several terms, such as *kay toi neu*, to refer to concepts that relate to Chinese culture. In a similar fashion, Canadianisms are words that are specific to Canadian English (although they may be used elsewhere) and often refer to cultural realities associated with identifying as Canadian, a feeling Chong so well describes.

A. Research the meaning and origin of the following Canadianisms.

   1. tuque/toque: _____

   _____

   2. lacrosse: _____

   _____

   3. parkade: _____

   _____

   4. serviette: _____

   _____

   5. anorak: _____

   _____

B. Think of or research five more examples of Canadianisms and discuss their meaning and origin with one or more speaking partners.

Look up any words you are unsure of.

MyBookshelf > My eLab
> Exercises > Part IV: Other
Genres > Chapter 18: Speeches
> Vocabulary Comprehension

Analytical Reading

After making specific observations, you are ready to analyze the subject of your close reading. The following questions will help you look for thematic patterns, establish relationships and identify specific examples of rhetorical devices or principles.

1. What is the meaning of the metaphor of "South China at the turn of the century" being "the spout of the tea pot that was China"?

2. In her story, which character trait(s) does Chong associate with her grandparents? Which value does the Canadian experience represent in spite some of its adversity?

3. What is the underlying theme Chong develops through her family's story and the observations she makes about Canadian citizenship?

4. How does Chong link the history of her grandparents to the need to be proud of Canadian citizenship today?

5. In spite of the family story she shares with the audience, Chong concludes her speech on the fact that she finds it difficult "to feel any Chineseness." What is the importance of this observation at the end of the speech?

Food for Thought

The following questions encourage you to turn a critical eye to your earlier observations and analyses. They introduce elements and considerations that will lead you to formulate new questions and set tentative hypotheses. Discuss these to further your insight into the text.

1. What are the observations Chong makes about Canadian society and the values that she associates it with? How do these elements resemble or differ from your own?

2. As Chong points out, the Canadian experience is one of diversity. Reflecting on your own family history and background, what stories and examples inspire your own identity? How is this similar to or different from Chong's experience?

3. The story Chong shares with her audience is not a recent one. How do you believe it is still relevant today, in light of contemporary immigration movements and policies? Compare and contrast examples from Chong's grandparents' story with specific contemporary examples.

Presenting an Analysis

Writing | Analyzing a Rhetorical Transaction

Although they can often be consulted by others at a later moment, speeches bring together a speaker and an audience in a particular context. This leads to the construction of a rhetorical transaction, where the speaker seeks to inform, persuade and/or motivate the audience on an issue that usually transcends the immediate context. In other words, the underlying theme usually concerns a larger occasion.

Prepare an analytical essay focusing around a thesis statement that investigates the development of one of the speeches presented in this chapter as a rhetorical transaction. Refer to the diagram and explanations on page 229 to inform your analysis, using the appropriate terminology. Also refer to the work you have done in this chapter to guide you while identifying pertinent elements. Focus on explaining how these elements come together and are used by the speaker in the development of an underlying theme.

MyBookshelf > My eLab > Exercises > Grammar and Accuracy

(Refer to Part V, Writing about Literature, on page 271 for more information on essay format and structure.)

Speaking | Examining Personal Stories Underpinning Societal Issues

In both speeches, the speaker presents a personal story to develop a broader underlying theme. Focus on one of the speeches in this chapter or compare both. Present salient passages from the speaker's personal story and explain how they are used to explain or illustrate a broader issue or thematic concept. Focus on one element at a time and describe how it is used to make a point. You may also wish to point out the impact it had on you as a reader. Conclude your presentation by highlighting how these different examples connect to develop the speech's underlying theme.

(Refer to Appendix 2 on page 297 for more information on presentation format and structure.)

PART V

Writing about Literature

The other sections in this book give you the opportunity to explore different literary genres and show you how to connect with them using a multi-draft reading approach (exploratory reading, close reading and analytical reading). Actively engaging with a text in this manner leads you to question the text and make observations about plot, themes and characters that can inform various literary essay formats. The chapters in this section will help you turn these observations and ideas into a cohesive literary essay. They will guide you through the different stages of the writing process and elaborate on several text types and the paragraphs that constitute them. Note that although this section focuses on writing, the presented strategies and formats also apply to the preparation of oral presentations. (See Appendix 2 on page 297 for oral presentation guidelines.)

CHAPTER 19

The Writing Process

Everyone has experienced writer's block. You may have been sitting in class, given a writing assignment and thought, "I have no idea what to write about." All writers have experienced this moment of panic. Envisioning writing as a process rather than a product will help you focus, plan and write an essay you are proud of.

Although everyone follows his or her own writing process in a way that feels most natural, breaking up the act of essay writing in a step-by-step approach will make you more aware of your own needs and the aspects of writing that require more attention. This is especially helpful when you struggle with a challenging assignment.

Although the process, when broken down, may seem linear, it is important to consider it as being recursive. This means that as your essay starts taking shape, you may wish to revisit previous steps—for instance, to brainstorm more ideas or fine-tune your thesis statement. It requires you to continually self-reflect and critically assess your work. Finding and expressing ideas cannot be rushed; make sure to plan ahead, so you have enough time to write a satisfying essay within the time constraints you are given.

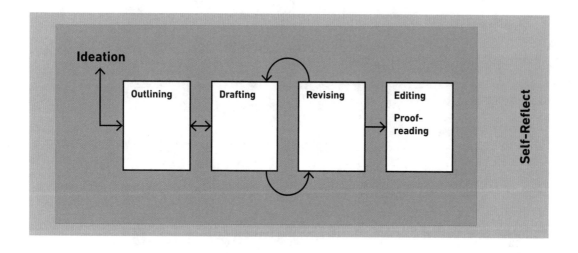

1. Ideation

This step begins with the assignment itself. If you have been given a question or a writing cue, it is important to first understand what is expected of you. If you have been given an open-ended assignment, you may wish to start by asking yourself general questions such as, "After reading the text, what do I want to write about?" or, "What do I want my audience to learn about the text?"

Ideation, or finding ideas, includes taking and referring to your notes, thinking, talking to others and gathering information. In some cases, writing a literary analysis means presenting your own original analysis; other assignments may require you to research credible sources to support your ideas.

The immediate objective of this step is to develop a working thesis, but you will continue generating ideas throughout the writing process. Only at the very end of the writing process should you consider your working thesis to be final—an affirmative sentence that expresses the main argument or point of view put forward in the essay.

→ See page 280 for ideation strategies and practice.

2. Outlining

Once you have brainstormed ideas and distilled them into a working thesis, the next crucial step is to produce a plan. These come in different types, including informal mind maps and formal outlines, which use letters, numbers and indentation to reflect the structure and organization of the essay being planned. The most appropriate format depends on the length and complexity of the assignment as well as the amount of time available.

FORMAL OUTLINE

Thesis statement

I. Topic sentence 1
   A. Supporting detail 1
   B. Supporting detail 2
      1. Quotation X
      2. Quotation Y

II. Topic sentence 2
   A. Observation 1
   B. Observation 2
      1. Supporting detail 3
      2. Quotation Z

MIND MAP

Thesis

Main Idea 1 —logical consequence→ Main Idea 2

• Support A
• Support B

• Counter-argument
• Refutation + support

Quotation par. X
Quotation par. Y

refer back to

At this point, your ideas are probably still in the order in which they occurred to you. The visual aspect of an outline makes it easier to rearrange the raw material of your essay—the ideas, notes and quotations you have gathered—into an order that best supports your planned analysis or argument.

A complete outline should contain your thesis statement, a topic sentence summarizing each body paragraph's main idea as well as the information you intend to use to support this idea.

Finally, considering your complete outline allows you to validate that your essay structure will be focused, balanced and logically connected. Making adjustments at this point will save you time, as reorganizing the points of an outline is easier than rewriting entire sections of an essay draft.

→ See page 281 for outlining techniques and practice.

3. Drafting

Drafting involves expressing your ideas in full sentences and paragraphs. It allows you to concentrate on explaining, supporting and connecting your ideas. Regardless of the amount of thinking and planning you have done, the mere process of putting your ideas into words is bound to change them, so either make sure you respect your outline or take time to revise it.

The goal of the first draft is to focus on the content and make sure that your ideas are clear and well developed. A draft does not have to be perfect; you should not yet worry about essay mechanics such as diction, grammar or spelling. As you write, continue asking yourself critical questions to further develop and support your thesis.

→ See page 284 for essay drafting guidelines and practice.

4. Revising

Thorough revision is what turns a collection of good ideas into a successful essay. As you revise your first draft, closely consider not only your writing focus and purpose, but also your intended audience's needs and expectations. Peer reviewing may provide you with useful insight from an outside perspective.

While revising, ask yourself questions, such as: Are my thesis statement and topic sentences precise and transparent? How much support is required to convince my readers? Which terms should I explain, and what background information should I provide? Is my organization easy to follow?

Revision may imply adding, omitting and reordering ideas and information as well as reconsidering word choice and sentence structure. At the end of the revision process, your ideas should be fully developed and clearly organized.

→ See page 293 for revision strategies and practice.

5. Editing and Proofreading

Once you are entirely satisfied with the contents of your essay, you are ready to start the final step of the process, which involves polishing your text. First, edit your text for grammar and syntax. Then, proofread for mechanics such as formatting, capitalization, punctuation and spelling. Depending on the context, it may be helpful to spend a few minutes, hours or even days away from your revised draft before editing it.

Editing and proofreading require time and effort. They are most effective if you focus on one category or element at a time, keeping in mind those issues you tend to struggle with the most. For instance, if you know you tend to forget the third-person-singular or if you use commas too sparingly, you may want to read your text focusing on this error only. Glancing over your essay as a whole will inevitably lead you to overlook errors, which are distracting to your audience and negatively impact the reader's impression.

→ See page 294 for editing and proofreading practice.

MyBookshelf > My eLab > Exercises > Grammar and Accuracy

CHAPTER 20

Writing with Purpose

Your immediate reason to write a literary essay is most likely because your teacher assigned it to you. That said, to produce a successful essay, it is crucial to understand the reason behind this assignment and to keep in mind the intended audience (other than your teacher).

Writing about literature allows you to showcase your critical thinking skills to reflect on the plot, themes, characters and setting of a text. Your knowledge of literary and poetic devices and your capacity to identify and explain them will help you achieve this. How you go about this and what you focus on depends on the purpose of the essay. Therefore, before you undertake the writing process, it is important to fully understand the writing cue assigned by your teacher, or if you have been tasked with a free response, to set a clear purpose for yourself.

The nature of the writing assignment will determine not only the ideas and information you include, but also how you structure and present these elements. Below is an overview of the most common writing formats you may be asked to produce. All of these essay types have in common the fact that they are articulated around a thesis statement.

→ See page 284 for more information and practice on thesis statements.

It is important to differentiate these essay types from formats you may be familiar with from high school:

- A literary essay is not a book report, which mostly summarizes the storyline and provides information about the author. It should go beyond the surface and discuss your understanding of the text.
- A literary essay is not a review, which expresses a subjective, personal opinion on your appreciation of a text and its merit. Your observations should be supported and not merely focus on what you consider positive or negative aspects of the text.

1. Reader Response

The reader response essay is often considered the most accessible form of writing about literature because it does not require in-depth study of literary features or external research. Its main objective is to convey your thoughts and feelings about one or more aspects of a text through close reading and critical thinking.

A response essay, as a form of academic writing, should still respect the appropriate formatting conventions and follow good practices for essay and paragraph structure (see page 284).

Because of their personal nature, reader response essays are often written in the first person, as in the example below. To maintain a more impersonal academic tone, your teachers may prefer you to avoid the use of first-person pronouns, so make sure to inform yourself about their expectations.

Sample Paragraph

Although the absurdity of the situation depicted in "The Gift of the Magi" is reminiscent of a melodramatic silent movie, its premise makes me profoundly question the value of our gift-giving customs, especially in Occidental culture influenced by consumerism. The main characters, Della and Jim, sacrifice what is most precious to them in order to have money to buy a gift that will make the other happy. It makes me realize that the gifts we offer one another are often expensive and practical rather than meaningful and that we have thus lost the quality that drives the protagonists as well as the Magi, which they are compared to. If they had been as sensible as we are today, maybe the Three Wise Men would have offered the baby Jesus clothing or a blanket rather than gold and incense. O. Henry shows that rather than dwell on the apparent value of such a gift, we should consider that the true expression of love lies in the thought behind it.

Note: In accordance with MLA guidelines, a complete essay should have a Works Cited list including the short story's reference.

MyBookshelf > My eLab
> Documents > Chapter 22:
Writing a Literary Essay
> MLA Referencing
Guidelines

PRACTICE

Practise the reader response by writing one short paragraph (approx. 250 words) in reaction to one of these writing cues:

- Choose a character from a short story or play that you feel strongly about. Discuss your particular like or dislike of this character based on the words and actions that illustrate his or her personality traits.
- Choose a poem you find particularly challenging and discuss how you connected with it.

2. Explication

Explication is a technique that involves a close analysis of a text. Because of its high level of detail, explication is most pertinent and appropriate when applied to a poem or a relatively short excerpt of prose or drama.

When writing an explication, you usually proceed word by word or line by line to reveal the meanings of the text through the commentary you provide. It is important to distinguish it from mere paraphrasing; the objective is to explain how diction, tone, theme, setting and other relevant elements contribute to the meaning of a text.

An explication is not necessarily a running commentary; for instance, you may wish to discuss elements out of order to uncover contrasts or similarities, or focus on non-contiguous passages.

Sample Paragraph

Hamlet's diction throughout the "To be or not to be" soliloquy from Shakespeare's play *The Tragedy of Hamlet* (act 3, scene 1) gives the reader insight into his conflicting feelings toward life and death. Overall, Hamlet's word choice conveys a negative view on life. The line "Whether 'tis nobler in the mind to suffer / The slings and arrows of outrageous fortune, / Or to take arms against a sea of troubles" (65–67) suggests that Hamlet's doubts make him unable to appreciate the positive aspects of life. In his eyes, life provides nothing but unhappiness and misfortune. Phrases like "suffer," "slings and arrows" and "take arms" all have dark and violent connotations attached to them. The only point in which Hamlet conveys a positive feeling throughout the soliloquy is when he describes death. In the line, "To die, to sleep— / To sleep: perchance to dream: ay, there's the rub! / For in that sleep of death what dreams may come / When we have shuffled off this mortal coil," the reader interprets Hamlet as having a much more positive outlook on death. The word "sleep" evokes a calm and happy feeling. When one is asleep, they are able to escape the struggles of daily life. Lastly, Hamlet goes on to talk about the unknown of the afterlife: "But that the dread of something after death, / The undiscover'd country, from whose bourn / No traveller returns, puzzles the will / And makes us rather bear those ills we have / Than fly to others that we know not of ? / Thus conscience does make cowards of us all" (86–91). It is at this point that the reader is able to see Hamlet's vulnerability. Phrases such as "dread," "undiscover'd country," "no return," "puzzles" and "know not of" display the ambiguity of afterlife in the eyes of Hamlet. He is fearful of not knowing what to expect when he dies, and these words represent his trepidations. Shakespeare's word choice is an effective way to give the reader insight into Hamlet's feelings about what the future will bring for him and whether he will decide to kill himself and deal with the bewilderment of the afterlife or continue to bear the hardships of daily life.

Note: In accordance with MLA guidelines, the parenthetical references to the play indicate line numbers. Forward slashes (/) indicate line breaks in the original text. A complete essay should have a Works Cited list including the play's reference.

MyBookshelf > My eLab > Documents > Chapter 22: Writing a Literary Essay > MLA Referencing Guidelines

PRACTICE

Practise explication by writing one short paragraph (approx. 250 words) in reaction to one of these writing cues:

- Choose a short poem and explicate how its figures of speech contribute to the mood it conveys.
- Choose a key monologue or dialogue from a play and explicate how the character's or characters' words and actions impact the storyline.

3. Comparison/Contrast

Rather than focusing on one single text, a comparison-and-contrast essay looks at a collection of two or more texts through the lens of an element that is significant in each of them; for instance, a theme, literary device or rhyming pattern. The aim is to uncover and discuss similarities or differences in the treatment of this common element to gain more insight into each of the texts.

You can organize this type of essay in two ways. In point-by-point, each paragraph zooms in on one specific topic analyzed within each of the selected texts (A and B). In text-by-text, an initial paragraph deals exclusively with the first text (A) to discuss different topics, and is then followed up by a subsequent paragraph that discusses the second text (B) in order to compare it to the first one. When using the text-by-text method, it is important to explicitly show comparison and contrast—by emphasizing the connections between the texts—to avoid writing an essay consisting of two (or more) completely isolated analyses.

Sample Paragraph

"Desirée's Baby" by Kate Chopin and "Theme for English B" by Langston Hughes illustrate how the construction of race has changed and evolved over time, yet still conveys a root of perceived inferiority. In the short story by Kate Chopin, race is looked at as despicable when mixed in marriage. To find out that his wife was not white was enough for Armand to "avoid her presence and that of her child, without excuse" (par. 18). The reason behind this hatred is due to the late-nineteenth-century cultural beliefs and pride that placed everyone in Louisiana above this "race that is cursed with the brand of slavery" (par. 48). While the slavery label no longer has as strong an impact on freedom or choices for people of colour, in the work by Langston Hughes, colour remains an obstacle separating people from mutual agreement and harmony. The speaker in the Hughes poem points out in a more forceful way the problem in the Chopin story: white and black people can have the same likes or dislikes, the same desires. "I like to eat, sleep, drink, and be in love," are just a few of the statements that depict the idea of goals and values everyone has, regardless of race (21). A pivotal moment occurs after it is mentioned that "being coloured doesn't make me not like / the same things …" (25–26). When the speaker says, "As I learn from you, / I guess you learn from me" (37–38), he suggests that allowing races to influence each other positively creates a new ground for understanding and knowledge, which is still very much needed in today's society. Both Chopin's short story and Hughes' poem are thus indicative of the racial tension and lack of equal treatment observed by the author in the time period they were written.

Note: In accordance with MLA guidelines, the parenthetical references to "Desirée's Baby" indicate paragraph numbers, while "Theme for English B" is referenced using line numbers. Forward slashes (/) indicate line breaks in the poem. A complete essay should have a Works Cited list including these two sources.

MyBookshelf > My eLab > Documents > Chapter 22: Writing a Literary Essay > MLA Referencing Guidelines

PRACTICE

Practise comparison/contrast by writing one short paragraph (approx. 250 words) in reaction to one of these writing cues:

- Choose two short stories that share a similar setting. Compare and contrast how the descriptions of this setting lead to similarities or differences in the mood and portrayal of this place.
- Choose a short story, play or film in which two characters react very differently to a situation or event. Compare and contrast these reactions to provide insight into the characters' personality traits.

4. Argumentation

Literature can also be analyzed within a broader sociocultural context. In such an argumentative essay, the thesis statement does not directly concern the literary work, but quotations and insight from the text are used to support observations or claims that concern the real world.

This type of essay allows you to demonstrate a deep understanding of a text's theme or characters, especially if they have a historical, social or political significance. Further research is usually needed to support the central argument.

Sample Paragraph

In recent Women's Marches throughout America after president Donald Trump's inauguration, women have protested dressed as handmaids from the novel *The Handmaid's Tale* (Nussbaum), leading people to compare gender inequality in America under the Trump presidency to its dystopian society of Gilead. In Margaret Atwood's novel, women are assigned jobs purely based on their sexuality and struggle to survive in their male-dominated world. In Gilead, the public sphere is limited only to the men, who are able to be employed and work. All women are part of the private sphere, where they are hidden from society, only allowed into the public sphere for domestic reasons. The Women's Marches make Atwood's novel relevant today, and they act as a reminder for us to not take for granted the respect and freedom women have fought so hard to attain.

Works Cited

Atwood, Margaret. *The Handmaid's Tale*. Anchor Books, 1998.

Nussbaum, Emily. "A Cunning Adaptation of *The Handmaid's Tale*." *The New Yorker*, 22 May 2017, https://www.newyorker.com/magazine/2017/05/22/a-cunning-adaptation-of-the-handmaids-tale.

Note: In accordance with MLA guidelines, the Works Cited list includes all sources referred to in the essay. It should be placed after the conclusion.

MyBookshelf > My eLab > Documents > Chapter 22: Writing a Literary Essay > MLA Referencing Guidelines

PRACTICE

Practise explication by writing one short paragraph (approx. 250 words) in reaction to one of these writing cues:

- Choose a short story from another time period and analyze its theme to make observations on the sociocultural context in which it was written.
- Choose a dystopian short story or novel and discuss its significance in contemporary society.

5. Literary Analysis

The purpose of a literary analysis essay is to carefully examine one or more aspects of a work of literature, including characterization, theme, symbolism or tone. This requires you to first do a close reading of the text in order to pinpoint its different meaningful components. This is not an end in itself but rather a process to help you better understand the entire text. In other words, a successful analysis relates the aspect it focuses on to the meaning of the whole.

For instance, a short story analysis might focus on the protagonist's character traits and their impact on the central theme. Analyzing a poem might deal with its imagery or with the relationship between the form and content. When analyzing a play, you might look at how a character's verbal and non-verbal behaviour complement or contradict each other. The chapters in this book guide you toward meaningful analysis of the story, poem or play they present.

The importance of the element under analysis and its relationship with the other components that make up the literary work are expressed through the thesis statement. For instance, the sample analysis paragraph below could be part of an essay with the following thesis statement, in which "doubling" and "irony" are the analyzed elements and the underlined sentence parts express their meaning in regard to the story as a whole:

> "The instances of doubling in 'The Black Cat' provide situational irony to <u>act as projections of the narrator's guilt</u> and <u>create symmetry in the story</u> to <u>suggest a sense of justice based on the law of talion, or an eye for an eye</u>."

→ See page 284 for more information and practice on writing thesis statements.

Sample paragraph

One of the main functions of doubling in "The Black Cat," a short story by Edgar Allan Poe, is to provide situational irony, which acts as justice to the narrator. In the beginning, the narrator hangs his cat Pluto. He later finds and adopts another black cat and starts making delusional parallels. He doubles the two cats based on their physical appearance; the more time he spends with the new cat, the more he fears it. He explains: "I avoided the creature; a certain sense of shame, and the remembrance of my former deed of cruelty, preventing me from physically abusing it" (par. 17). The occurrence of a second cat is thus significant because it brings out his feelings of guilt about killing Pluto. Near the end of the story, the narrator is apparently sentenced to death by hanging because he is found guilty of murdering his wife. This doubling of hanging and then being hanged provides a sense of karma, in the form of situational irony, in the story. It underlines justice and shows that the narrator suffers the consequences of his own actions.

Note: In accordance with MLA guidelines, the parenthetical references to "The Black Cat" indicate paragraph numbers. A complete essay should have a Works Cited list including the short story's reference.

MyBookshelf > My eLab > Documents > Chapter 22: Writing a Literary Essay > MLA Referencing Guidelines

PRACTICE

Practise analysis by writing one short paragraph (approx. 250 words) in reaction to one of these writing cues:

- Choose a short story with a clear central theme. Analyze how one particular aspect of the text (e.g., symbolism, irony, etc.) contributes to the construction of this theme.
- Choose a poem written from a first-person point of view and addressed to one persona. Analyze the elements that reveal insight into the speaker or addressee of the poem.

CHAPTER 21

Generating and Developing Ideas

Ideation Strategies

"Brainstorming" is rarely an act of sitting idle, waiting for an idea to come to you. It requires actively engaging and thinking about the text you are planning to write about, questioning yourself and questioning the text. The following methods and strategies may help you in the process of coming up with ideas:

- **Taking notes** or maintaining a **reading log** is essential to keeping track of any observations or questions that come to you while you read. In order to turn these annotations into coherent ideas and topics for writing, it is necessary to reconsider and restructure them.

- **Freewriting** involves giving yourself a predetermined amount of time and then writing down or typing up anything that comes to you in regard to your topic during that time. It is important not to interrupt the process or stop writing, even if your mind goes blank momentarily. Once the time is up, read over your notes and highlight what seems useful or meaningful. If needed, you can then use the highlighted topics as a starting point for another freewriting session. This is often referred to as **looping**, which is a good strategy for quickly narrowing down your topic.

    Example:

    I can't think of anything to say about the novel *1984*, so I am just going to keep on putting these words on the paper until I can start working on this analysis, which I clearly do not feel inspired about. My teacher is walking around and looking at what everyone writes, which unsettles me a bit. Actually, the novel picks up on that because people, including the protagonist Winston, are constantly under surveillance by Big Brother. I suppose this also happens in real life, because through our use of the Internet and our cellphones, it is easy for governments to know what everyone is doing at any given point. Is that ethical? Maybe that is something George Orwell was trying to criticize …

- **Clustering** is a more visual form of ideation. It allows you to structure ideas as they come to you. Start a cluster by writing in the middle of a sheet of paper the title of the work, an idea you have or a broad topic. Then, add ideas that come to you, trying to connect them in a meaningful way with what is already on the page. Use different shapes, arrows and colours to organize your ideas or bring out patterns and links.

    Example:

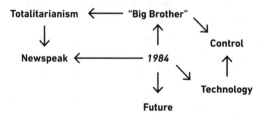

- Listing is most effective when using single words or short phrases. Make a first list by writing down ideas and topics that have come from your notes or that have occurred to you after close reading the text. Then, start regrouping these items in new lists that convey logical relationships. Add new items to these lists to reflect more deeply on your topic.

Example:

1984	Rewriting History	Surveillance
Dystopia	Controlling the past = controlling the future	...
Totalitarianism		
Big Brother/surveillance	Propaganda	
Impossible love	Media control	
Rewriting history	Importance of language	

PRACTICE

A. On a separate sheet of paper, choose one of the following broad topics and brainstorm using at least two different methods from the ones presented above. Take note of the method that seemed to work best for you.

- Fairy tales teaching a valuable moral lesson
- The role of rhythm and rhyme in lyrical poems
- Characters with a message

B. Work in a small group. Choose one of the writing cues from Chapter 20, and give yourself a set amount of time. Working individually, each member of the group should use a different method to brainstorm ideas for a possible essay. When time is up, present the results of your ideation strategy and explain your thinking process. Discuss with your partners any similarities and differences between the ideas you have brainstormed.

Outlining Techniques

An outline is a way of formally arranging and developing ideas. It helps organize your essay by visualizing if and how ideas connect to each other, or whether certain points need more support. To make this possible, an outline needs to follow a consistent set of formatting rules. The standard structure of an outline is:

I. Large Roman numerals (I, II, III, etc.)
    A. Capital letters (A, B, C, etc.)
        1. Arabic numerals (1, 2, 3, etc.)
            a. Small letters (a, b, c, etc.)
                i. Small Roman numerals (i, ii, iii, etc.)

A decimal outline follows the same structure but uses added decimals to indicate different levels (1, 1.1, 1.1.1, etc.).

Steps Toward an Outline

- Write your working thesis statement at the top of the outline.
- Group related points you have noted (ideas, quotations) under headings that summarize their underlying connection. These are the topic sentences that introduce the paragraphs of your essay-to-be.
- Using large Roman numerals, create enough headings to match the number of idea groups.

- Make sure all topic sentences are of equal importance and that they clearly relate to the thesis statement and connect with one another. At this point, rearrange or omit idea groups if needed, keeping in mind the projected length and focus of your planned essay.
- Identify the subpoints in each idea group. Place them in the order in which you wish to address them. Create deeper sublevels if there are at least two details you wish to add for a more general point.
- Evaluate and compare the number of levels and sublevels in different paragraphs to ensure your essay will be balanced.

Although the introduction (including a hook, context and a thesis statement) and conclusion (including a recap of main ideas and a concluding statement) are usually not part of a formal outline, you can jot down ideas you wish to take up in these sections at the top and bottom of the outline once it is complete. If you are handwriting the document, leave sufficient space for this.

Outline Template

Note: The labels used in this template are usually not mentioned in the outline. Replace them with your actual text. It is preferable to use only phrases or short sentences in your outline, although you may wish to copy quotations in full. The number of levels and sublevels will depend on the complexity and structure of your analysis or argument.

Hook

Context

Thesis Statement

I. Topic Sentence 1

    A. Supporting Idea 1

        1. Evidence (relevant detail and/or quotation)

        2. Explanation of the evidence

    B. Supporting Idea 2

        1. Evidence (relevant detail and/or quotation)

        2. Explanation of the evidence

II. Topic Sentence 2

    A. Evidence (relevant detail and/or quotation)

    B. Evidence (relevant detail and/or quotation)

    C. Explanation of the evidence

Recap

Concluding Statement

PRACTICE

Refer to the literary analysis sample essay on page 291 to produce a reverse outline based on the ideas put forward in this text. First, on a separate sheet of paper, draw an informal mind map (see page 273) visualizing the main ideas and how they relate to one another. Then, complete the formal outline template underneath with the necessary information.

"The Gift of the Magi" – Outline

Hook: _____

Context: _____

Thesis statement: _____

I. (topic sentence) _____

   A. (supporting idea 1) _____

      1. (quotation) _____

      2. (explanation) _____

      3. (quotation) _____

      4. (explanation) _____

   B. (supporting idea 2) _____

      1. (evidence) _____

      2. (explanation) _____

II. (topic sentence) _____

   A. (supporting idea 1) _____

   B. (supporting idea 2) _____

      1. (quotation) _____

      2. (explanation) _____

Recap: _____

Concluding Statement: _____

CHAPTER 22
Writing a Literary Essay

Drafting Guidelines

All of the literary essay types presented in Chapter 20 share a set of common structural characteristics:

- They are focused around a precise thesis statement.
- The central thesis is broken down into topic sentences, each of which is developed into one body paragraph.
- The body paragraphs are preceded by an introduction and followed by a conclusion.
- They have an engaging and meaningful title.

Thesis Statement

A thesis statement expresses the main argument or point of view put forward in an essay. Typically, the thesis statement is one affirmative sentence located at the very end of the introductory paragraph.

A thesis statement can be broken down into a topic (the narrow subject the essay deals with) and one or more controlling ideas (what the essay will set out to prove or discuss in regard to the topic). The structure of the thesis statement gives a preview of your rationale and the organization of your essay.

Example 1:

In "The Gift of the Magi," O. Henry uses irony to contrast the rationality and foolishness involved in giving generously and loving unconditionally.

In this thesis statement, the topic or narrow subject is the use of irony in the short story "The Gift of the Magi." The controlling idea is that this irony impacts on the theme of the story—the relationship between giving generously and loving unconditionally. The preview of the rationale is expressed through the verb "contrast" and the four concepts the writer will investigate, presumably in the order they appear in the thesis statement.

Example 2:

While Hamlet's obsessive thoughts in his "To be or not to be" speech are specific to his own situation, they preview what happens to other characters in the play, giving the audience insight into Hamlet's influence.

In this thesis statement, the topic or narrow subject is Hamlet's speech in the Shakespeare play of the same name. The controlling idea concerns Hamlet's thoughts and their effect. The rationale and structure are indicated in the words "preview" and "giving … insight," which suggest that the writer will first establish links between the speech and subsequent events in the play, before pointing out how this allows the audience to better understand Hamlet.

A successful thesis statement therefore helps the writer to narrow down the essay's topic and think about the essay's structure, while allowing the reader to get a clear understanding of the essay's topic and purpose from its first few lines.

A thesis statement is **not successful** if:

- It is not precise enough in light of the type, length and purpose of your essay. An insufficiently focused thesis statement will lead to an essay that is not cohesive and a rationale that is difficult for your reader to follow.

  Example: In "Désirée's Baby," Kate Chopin draws attention to racism.

- It does not present an idea that is debatable. If you state a fact or something that is obvious, it will be impossible to develop an essay around it.

  Example: In "The Gift of the Magi," O. Henry writes about the misadventures of a young couple trying to find the perfect Christmas gift for each other.

- It expresses a personal opinion. The point of a literary essay is to use objective information and examples to convince your reader of the point you wish to make. Focus should be on the topic rather than on you as a writer.

  Example: I strongly believe that the main character in Edgar Allan Poe's "The Black Cat" suffers from mental illness.

- It merely announces the topic you will write about. As a result, your controlling idea and rationale will not be clear to the reader.

  Example: The topic of this paper is the importance of Hamlet's "To be or not to be" speech in regard to what happens to the characters in the play.

- It is formulated as a question. This will not allow your reader to understand the purpose of your essay.

  Example: Why does Edgar Allan Poe use irony in the short story "The Black Cat"?

These sentences announce or evoke the thesis but are not suitable substitutes for it.

PRACTICE

A. Consider the following sentences used as thesis statements, and determine whether they are successful (S) or unsuccessful (U).

For an unsuccessful thesis statement, pinpoint the problem it presents, referring to the list above. With a partner, brainstorm ways to improve it.

For a successful thesis statement, double underline the topic and underline the controlling idea(s). With a partner, discuss the rationale—or the logical steps of your argument—and essay structure you expect based on the thesis statement.

1. _____ "The Gift of the Magi" is the most touching Christmas story I have ever read.

2. _____ "To be or not to be?" that is the question this essay will investigate.

3. _____ Kate Chopin uses irony to emphasize the unfounded nature of the injustice that is racism in "Désirée's Baby."

4. _____ Both "The Black Cat" and "A Dog's Tale" use an animal as a form of symbolism.

5. _____ What do we know about the speaker in Shakespeare's Sonnet 18?

6. _____ Sonnets can have different rhyming schemes.

7. _____ Through her use of metaphor and simile, Maya Angelou has written the empowering poem "Still I Rise."

8. _____ In the short story "The Lottery," Shirley Jackson uses stones as symbols to assert that social values are heavily dependent on individuals' desires and expectations.

B. Think of a literary work you have read and write three different thesis statements about it. Exchange your work with a partner; double underline the topic and underline the controlling idea(s) in each other's statements. Using the criteria listed above, determine if the thesis statements are successful or not, and make suggestions on how to improve them if necessary. Then, discuss your observations with each other. Finally, based on this feedback, revise your own thesis statements to improve them.

MyBookshelf > My eLab > Exercises > Part V: Writing about Literature > Chapter 22: Writing a Literary Essay > Thesis Statements

Introduction and Conclusion

The beginning of your essay determines the first impression you make on your reader. Therefore, it should start with an engaging **hook**—one or a few sentences that capture your readers' interest and make them want to read the remainder of the essay. The hook may take the shape of a worthwhile or surprising fact about the work, a key quotation, a definition or an anecdote.

This is followed by background information allowing readers to understand the context of your essay and its purpose. This **context** should also allow for a smooth transition into your thesis statement.

Because of its intimate link with the topics developed in the body of the essay, it may be a good strategy to write the introduction after developing the body paragraphs. At the very least, you should revisit the introduction and the thesis statement at the end of the writing process to validate their cohesion with the paragraphs that follow them.

Similar to the introduction, your conclusion provides a last opportunity to capture your readers' attention and to convince them of the worth of your analysis or argument.

The conclusion recaps the main ideas and reminds the reader of strong points you have put forward in your essay, yet it should avoid merely repeating or restating them. A good conclusion ends on a **closing statement** that leaves readers with something to think about.

Visualize your introduction and conclusion as mirrored triangles allowing your reader to smoothly transition into and out of the heart of your essay. After providing context, the introduction becomes narrower, until you get to your thesis. The conclusion does the opposite; it reminds the reader of your central points, then ends on a more general thought.

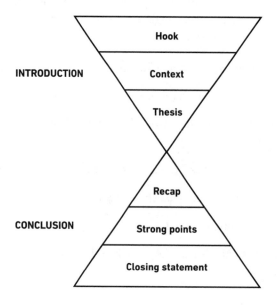

PRACTICE

A. Consider the following hooks, and determine which means they use to introduce the topic: a worthwhile fact (F), an anecdote (A), a key quotation (Q) or a definition (D).

1. _____ While even Bart Simpson has recited Hamlet's famous "To be or not to be" soliloquy in an episode on *The Simpsons*, the importance of the speech as a plot device in the Shakespeare play is far greater than what pop culture references may suggest.

2. _____ "Still I Rise." This mantra from the eponymous Maya Angelou poem will resonate with anyone who has ever overcome difficulty or adversity in life.

3. _____ While today, reading J. D. Salinger's *The Catcher in the Rye* can almost be considered a rite of passage for high school students, it was actually banned by many schools and libraries for its use of swear words when it was published in 1951, even though these are essential to the depiction of the main character.

4. _____ Modernism is the period spanning the first half of the twentieth century and marked a break with traditions such as Christianity and cultural uniformity. Virginia Woolf's classic novel *Mrs. Dalloway* is an exemplary modernist novel characterized by elements such as caustic pessimism, resignation and an overbearing melancholy.

B. Consider the introduction to the literary analysis sample essay on page 291. Rewrite the hook and context of the introduction using the four strategies listed above. You needn't change the thesis statement. Work in a small group or with a partner to discuss which types of hooks you find most engaging, and why.

C. Work individually to propose three alternative closing statements to the literary analysis sample essay on page 291. Then, work with a partner to put your ideas together and devise what you consider the absolute best closing statement to this essay.

Body Paragraphs

A paragraph is your fundamental unit of composition. It cohesively groups together different sentences on one single topic and allows you to clearly structure your text. All body paragraph types share the same structure to bring focus and unity to your ideas. This structure mirrors that of the essay: introduction, development and conclusion.

The **topic sentence** presents the central point of your paragraph. It is made up of the topic and a controlling idea (what you point out about the topic). It is usually the first sentence of the paragraph.

The body of the paragraph develops your central point with **supporting ideas**. These vary depending on the type and purpose of your paragraph. For instance, you can use direct quotations from the text to illustrate a point, use logical reasoning to connect different aspects of a text or refer to external sources to appeal to authority. If the development feels incomplete or unconvincing, elaborate further or narrow your topic sentence.

The **concluding sentence** summarizes the central point and may include a reflection or observation on that point to help you transition to the next paragraph. Although the topic sentence and concluding sentence share a common purpose—to focus the paragraph—they should not be identical. Think of them as the front and back cover of a book; although they both serve the same purpose—to hold together and protect the book's pages—they do not have the exact same format or shape.

A. Read this analytical paragraph on "A Tell-Tale Heart" by Edgar Allan Poe. Then, determine which of the options listed represents the best topic sentence and concluding sentence for the paragraph. Compare your answers with a partner and explain your choices.

Throughout the passage, the author repeats words—usually reinforced by "very" or "so"—to indicate that the narrator is conscious of his surroundings, and he responds with a heightened sense of alertness: "I moved it slowly—very, very slowly." Poe reveals that the cautious, alert nature of the narrator ultimately caused him to murder the old man. He is aware of trivial things, such as the old man's eye. Rather than being able to ignore the eye, he cannot help but notice and feel threatened by it. Not only does Poe repeat words, but he also includes parallel structure in many of the passage's sentences. The usage of parallel structure is a technique Poe uses to explore the narrator's sanity, more particularly to show when the narrator defends his sanity: "The disease had sharpened my senses—not destroyed—not dulled them." Ultimately, the narrator is saying the same thing, but by repeating it and adding emphasis with dashes, Poe exemplifies that the narrator is trying to rationalize his behaviour to convince himself of his saneness.

1. The most suitable topic sentence is:

a) The narrator repeats many words and sentences, which illustrates his unstable mental state.

b) Poe highlights the narrator's unstable mental state through the use of repetition of words and parallel sentence structures.

c) Why does Poe use the literary devices of repetition and parallel structure?

d) This paragraph discusses the use of literary devices linked with the narrator's mental state.

e) The narrator's language use is an indicator of his unstable mental state.

2. The most suitable concluding sentence is:

a) Repetition and parallel structure are used to signal the author's poor mental state.

b) Poe's language use generates a realistic depiction of someone with mental health issues.

c) There are also other indicators of this insanity, which are analyzed in the next paragraph.

d) The narrator clearly struggles with his mental state, and these two forms of repetition in his recounting of the events are used as literary devices to externalize this struggle and his instability.

e) Maybe this also suggests that the narrator talks to himself, which may be a symptom of delusional behaviour.

B. Complete the following paragraph with a topic sentence and a concluding sentence. Refer to the words in bold and ask yourself the following questions to inspire you:

- What type of literary device is the lottery?
- What does the lottery represent? What point does Jackson make in regard to this?
- What can you conclude about the concept represented by the lottery?

Shirley Jackson's "The Lottery" _____

_____.

It is a grim tale of villagers annually sacrificing one of their own by random selection in the name of **tradition**. The tradition entails a communal killing justified by archaic superstitions: "Used to be a saying about 'Lottery in June, corn be heavy soon.' First thing you know, we'd all be eating stewed chickweed and acorns. There's *always* been a lottery" (Jackson 4). By the overruling authority and historical significance of it, the ritual of the lottery is **never questioned**. When Tessie Hutchinson expresses her **resistance** toward her ill fate, she is not given a voice but brutally murdered by her compatriots. Even small children partake in Tessie's death, as children are encouraged to participate in the event. In this way, Jackson illustrates _____

_____ .

Work with a speaking partner or in a small group to discuss your sentences. Which ideas in the paragraph did you refer to when developing them? Explain to each other how exactly you crafted your topic sentence and concluding sentence.

MyBookshelf > My eLab > Exercises > Part V: Writing about Literature > Chapter 22: Writing a Literary Essay > Topic Sentences

Title

Once your essay stands complete, you are ready to craft a suitable title. It is used primarily to catch the interest of potential readers and should differ from your thesis statement. It should be concise and original.

Example of a title lacking originality: Analysis of the Use of Irony in "The Gift of the Magi"

Example of a title that is too complex and wordy: In "The Gift of the Magi," O. Henry contrasts the rationality and foolishness involved in giving generously and loving unconditionally through the use of irony.

Example of a suitable title: O. Henry's "The Gift of the Magi," an Ironic Ode to the Perfect Foolishness of Love

This title is clear on the text being analyzed as well as the essay's focus on the use of irony to construct the theme of love. The topic is expressed in a creative manner.

PRACTICE

Think of an engaging title to accompany the paragraphs on "A Tell-Tale Heart" and "The Lottery" in the previous activity. Work with a speaking partner or in a small group to present and explain your titles.

Referencing and Plagiarism

Whether referring to the text you are discussing or to external research, it is imperative to signal the words and ideas in your essay that are not your own. Failing to do so will be considered a form of **plagiarism**. There are three ways to reference: through direct quotations, paraphrases or summaries.

Direct quotations are words, phrases or sentences taken directly from another source, using the identical language found in the original. Sometimes you might need to add or change words to make a quotation grammatical or suitable for your essay. Use square brackets to indicate this. Make sure the change does not alter the meaning of the quotation.

Use direct quotations to illustrate a point you are making with examples from the literary work, or to draw attention to figures of speech or other language items from the text. Direct quotations must be indicated within quotation marks and followed by a parenthetical reference mentioning the author and page, paragraph number or line number where the particular utterance can be found.

Original passage: "Maybe the hairs of my head were numbered," she went on with sudden serious sweetness, "but nobody could ever count my love for you." ("The Gift of the Magi," par. 33)

Quotation: Della draws attention to the theme that the value of true love cannot be measured in money when she says, "Maybe the hairs of my head were numbered […] but nobody could ever count my love for you" (par. 33).

Paraphrases take a passage from the original text and express it in your own words. Paraphrases are usually shorter or of similar length than the original. Use paraphrases when the idea you wish to convey is more important than the words used to do so in the original. Paraphrasing allows you to avoid breaking the flow of your own writing. Paraphrases must be followed by a parenthetical reference mentioning the author and page(s), paragraph or line number(s) where the particular idea or information you are paraphrasing can be found.

Original passage: One dollar and eighty-seven cents. That was all. And sixty cents of it was in pennies. Pennies saved one and two at a time by bulldozing the grocer and the vegetable man and the butcher until one's cheeks burned with the silent imputation of parsimony that such close dealing implied. Three times Della counted it. One dollar and eighty-seven cents. And the next day would be Christmas. ("The Gift of the Magi," par. 1)

Paraphrase: At the outset of the story, the narrator points out that the day before Christmas, Della only has a dollar and eighty-seven cents to her name (par. 1).

Summaries express a text's main idea(s) or story line in your own words, in a condensed format. Although a literary essay is based on the idea that the reader is familiar with or has access to the literary work, and therefore should never summarize the text as a whole, it may be useful to summarize certain plot elements to provide your reader with the necessary context to understand your ideas. Although summaries also need to be attributed to the author, this may be done implicitly if it is clear you are referring to the literary work being written about.

Summary: "The Gift of the Magi" takes place at Christmas and tells the story of Jim and Della, a young married couple who don't have enough money to buy each other Christmas gifts. They each sell their most prized possession to pay for a gift for the other, effectively rendering each other's gifts useless.

→ See the MLA referencing guidelines in My eLab Documents.

MyBookshelf > My eLab > Documents > Part V: Writing about Literature > Chapter 22: Writing a Literary Essay

PRACTICE

Consider the following original passage as well as the direct quotations and paraphrases referring to it. Each item contains an error. Find and correct it.

Original passage:

To be or not to be, that is the question:

Whether 'tis nobler in the mind to suffer

The slings and arrows of outrageous fortune,

Or to take arms against a sea of troubles

And by opposing end them.

(Shakespeare, *The Tragedy of Hamlet*, 3.1.64–68)

1. In act 3, scene 1, Hamlet delivers the infamous words, to be or not to be (64).

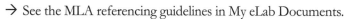

Error: _____

2. Hamlet likens life to "a sea of troubles" in his soliloquy.

Error: _____

3. Hamlet wonders if it would be better for him to continue suffering or commit suicide.

Error: _____

4. Hamlet asks if one should "suffer [...] a sea of troubles" (3.1.65–67).

Error: _____

5. "To be or not to be, that is the question."

Error: _____

MyBookshelf > My eLab > Exercises > Part V: Writing about Literature > Chapter 22: Writing a Literary Essay > Quotations, Paraphrases and Plagiarism

MyBookshelf > My eLab > Documents > Part V: Writing about Literature > Chapter 22: Writing a Literary Essay > MLA Referencing Guidelines

Sample Literary Analysis Essay

O. Henry's "The Gift of the Magi," an Ironic Ode to the Perfect Foolishness of Love

According to Pew Research, over 2 billion people in more than 160 countries consider Christmas to be the most important holiday of the year. While it is a time of celebrating and embracing loved ones, individuals paradoxically also spend a great deal of time and money shopping for the "perfect" Christmas present. In "The Gift of the Magi," O. Henry highlights this apparent paradox by contrasting the rationality and foolishness involved in giving generously and loving unconditionally.

Della and Jim Dillingham Young's characters are used to demonstrate the true meaning of love through "sacrifice" (par. 45). In the beginning of the story, they worry over the small amount of money they have to spend on Christmas Eve. Then, the protagonists have a selfless idea. To understand the importance of their actions, the reader must understand that "there were two possessions of the James Dillingham Youngs in which they both took a mighty pride. One was Jim's gold watch that had been his father's and his grandfather's. The other was Della's hair" (par. 9). Della sells her hair to be able to buy Jim a heartfelt gift, a watch chain. This is not just any chain, though. O. Henry writes, "It surely had been made for Jim and no one else" (par. 19). When he walks into the house, Jim glares at Della with an unreadable expression and this scares her. Eventually, Della learns that Jim is acting this way because the gift he has for her is a set of hair combs. When Della, in response, offers Jim her gift, he confesses to his wife that he sold his prized belongings in order to have enough money to purchase her gift (par. 38). The whole situation is ironic, considering both Della and Jim sold their own valued possessions in order to buy each other a deserving Christmas present.

"The Gift of the Magi" is thus a classic example of irony in literature. The irony here works both on a practical and on a deeper, more sentimental level. Both Della and Jim buy each other a gift that ultimately seems financially foolish. However, what they get is something they don't expect: a more intangible gift that reminds them how much they love each other and are willing to sacrifice to make each other happy. In the resolution, O. Henry underlines this paradox by comparing Della and Jim to the Magi, or Three Wise Men, in the Bible's nativity story:

The Magi, as you know, were wise men—wonderfully wise men—who brought gifts to the newborn babe in the manger. Being wise, their gifts were no doubt wise ones, possibly bearing the privilege of exchange in case of duplication. And here I have lamely related to you the

MyBookshelf > My eLab > Documents > Part V: Writing about Literature > Chapter 22: Writing a Literary Essay > The Gift of the Magi (complete version)

uneventful chronicle of two foolish children in a flat … who most unwisely sacrificed for each other the greatest treasures of their house. But in a last word to the wise of these days, let it be said that of all who give gifts, these two were the wisest.

O. Henry uses irony to emphasize the thematic difference between wisdom and foolishness in relation to the value of self-giving love. The Magi were wise in a practical sense. The comical reference to their gifts being exchangeable relates to the pragmatic side of thoughtfulness in gift-giving. Jim and Della, on the other hand, despite their apparent foolishness, are wise in another sense—that is, in their ability to appreciate the sentimental meaning behind gift-giving that goes deeper than a gift's material worth.

Essentially, "The Gift of the Magi" represents something much more than just a young couple giving up something of their own to buy a gift for the other. This story portrays the themes of unconditional love and, through the use of irony, highlights that, while from a rational point of view, money cannot buy love, love has the power to make someone go to any extent to make their loved one happy. This apparent foolishness, rather than the worth of a gift, is where the true value of love lies. This is an especially sentimental message during the Christmas season when the rush to buy presents and get all of the shopping done sometimes makes people forget this simple truth.

Works Cited

Henry. O. [William Sydney Porter]. "The Gift of the Magi." *Project Gutenberg*, 5 April 2015, www.gutenberg.org/cache/epub/7256/pg7256.txt. Accessed 16 July 2018.

Lipka, Michael and David Masci. "5 Facts about Christmas in America." *Pew Research Center*, 18 December 2017, www.pewresearch.org/fact-tank/2017/12/18/5-facts-about-christmas-in-america. Accessed 16 July 2018.

CHAPTER 23

Revising and Editing an Essay

Revision Strategies

Once your ideas have taken the shape of words in the first draft of your essay, evaluate the development, structure and clarity of your writing, and rewrite passages as necessary.

Development

☐ Check that your thesis statement is appropriately focused for the length of your essay and that it is correctly formatted.

☐ Check that each body paragraph presents sufficient evidence to support its topic sentence, and that it does so using logical arguments.

☐ Check that you have a convincing introduction and conclusion.

PRACTICE

Work with a partner or in a small group. In the following paragraph, evaluate the topic sentence, the type and amount of evidence given and the quality of the arguments. Discuss the problems this paragraph presents and discuss how it can be improved. Focus on strategies to apply rather than concrete information to change or add.

> The theme of the short story is presented through the lives of Mr. and Mrs. Dillingham Young. Their lives are what makes the story and the theme come about. The theme of the short story is love conquers all. The story shows that in a relationship, there are many sacrifices that each party involved must understand. This couple sacrificed their favourite things for each other, showing their true love for each other.

Structure

☐ Check that each paragraph focuses on only one specific idea.

☐ Check that the topic sentence of each paragraph clearly and directly contributes to the thesis statement.

☐ Check that you have used transitional words and expressions to signal logical relationships between your ideas.

PRACTICE

Work with a partner or in a small group. In the following paragraph, evaluate the cohesion of the ideas presented, their link with the topic sentence and the clarity of transitional words, which have been underlined. Discuss the problems this paragraph presents and discuss how it can be improved. Focus on strategies to apply rather than concrete information to change or add.

The Magi are three wise men in the Bible who have gone on a long journey to bring sacrificial gifts to the son of God. When making a comparison between the couple and the Magi, O. Henry points out the reason for that. Both of them buy each other a gift that is ultimately useless. <u>Obviously</u>, they waste money on things that cannot be used while every penny saved is extremely valuable to them. <u>Consequently</u>, from an entirely practical perspective, their gifts do not make any sense. <u>Actually</u>, calling the couple "foolish children," O. Henry brings humour to his story to ease the seriousness of the characters' situation. <u>Hence</u>, the writer indicates his sympathy for the impoverished couple.

Clarity of Writing

☐ Check that you have expressed your ideas using precise language.
☐ Check that you have expressed your ideas in varied sentence structures.
☐ Check that you have included parenthetical references where needed.

PRACTICE

Work with a partner or in a small group. In the following paragraph, evaluate the precision of the words and phrases used, their level of language and the clarity of the sentences. Discuss the problems this paragraph presents and discuss how it can be improved. Propose specific suggestions of words and sentences when possible.

> In the short story "The Gift of the Magi" by O. Henry, they both personify the theme that love is stronger than anything. In the story, the author uses imagery to make the story more interesting and to highlight the story's main points. "So now Della's beautiful hair fell about her rippling and shining like a cascade of brown waters." He is using imagery for emphasis. In the last part of the story, the author goes on to say "They are the magi," which is a metaphor meaning that they resemble the wise and compassionate gift-giving creatures since they have such a strong passion toward one another, so in the end nothing matters except the fact that they love each other.

Editing and Proofreading

Once you have expressed all of your ideas precisely and cohesively, the last step of the revision process involves improving grammar, spelling and punctuation to make for an enjoyable, convincing read.

☐ Check that each idea is expressed concisely. Omit any words that seem redundant.
☐ Check that none of your word choices express bias or prejudice against a certain group.
☐ Check that you have used pronouns gender-neutrally. Avoid using only male or female pronouns when referring to individuals that might be of either gender.
☐ Check grammar and syntax. If you know that you tend to make certain types of errors, check separately for each kind of error. For instance, read your essay once to check for sentence fragments; read it again to be sure subjects and verbs agree, and a last time to trace pronouns to antecedents.
☐ Check spelling and punctuation. Making your text less recognizable, for instance, by reading it backwards, skipping alternating sentences, or covering up the lines you are not proofreading, may help you identify mistakes you have previously glanced over. Pay specific attention to homonyms (e.g., "they're," "their" and "there") and certain typos (like "he" for "the"), which even electronic spelling checkers tend to miss.

PRACTICE

Edit the following body paragraphs of an explication essay for grammar and syntax, then proofread it for spelling and punctuation. Each paragraph contains four errors. Underline them and correct them.

In the first stanza of her poem the fight, Sara Teasdale compares two lovers lives to that of two eagles flying together. This metaphor provides the reader with a vision of these powerful birds flying gracefully through the air. In lines 3 and 4, they are described as flying "under the heavens" and over the mountains." Which gives the reader a vision of blue skies and a sense of childhood playfulness.

In lines 5 through 9, Teasdale introduces four different parts of nature, each element she discusses seem to affect the two eagles in a physical sense. However, these descriptions also describe differents emotions that one experiences throughout life. For example, in line 5, "Stretched on the wind" initially made the reader think of an eagle's wings outstretched as it glides through the wind. Upon further investigation, it also describes the strains being put on their relationship, trying to blow them away from other. Teasdale's careful selection of words evokes a physical meaning and a deeper metaphorical meaning.

In the second stanza, Teasdale is using the eagles as a simile rather then a metaphor. Instead of saying that they are two eagles, she describes them as being like eagles. The the whole tone of the poem changes following this distinction. It is as though she has realized that they are mortal and this life of living in the clouds cant last forever.

The last four lines of the poem begin with the same word "let." The reader can envision the speaker on her knees, praying that He allow her to reunite with her lover again. While asking for this fate, she uses three metaphors to describe live. First, she asks for the flight to be ended Once again, she refers to the life of these two eagles flying together. Next, in line 16, she asks, "Let the fire blacken." Not only is the colour black associated with death, but also in the case of fire, dark smoke typically means the fire is going out. In the final line of the poem, she asks, "Let the book close." She obviously feels as tough she is on her last chapter and is ready to be done with the story of life.

[…]

MyBookshelf > My eLab
> Exercises > Part V: Writing
about Literature > Chapter 23:
Revising and Editing an Essay

APPENDIX 1:
ESSAY CHECKLIST

☐ The essay has an introduction that generates interest, provides context and transitions to the thesis statement.

☐ The thesis statement at the end of the introduction is clear, precise, debatable and supportable. It is expressed as an affirmative sentence that includes a topic and one or more controlling ideas.

☐ Each body paragraph begins with a topic sentence that focuses on only one major point that helps support the thesis.

☐ Each body paragraph includes evidence in the form of quotations, paraphrases, facts or logical reasoning to provide specific support for the point being made in the paragraph.

☐ Quotations and paraphrases are integrated correctly following MLA guidelines, and are preceded and/or followed by an explanation of their meaning, relevance and importance.

MyBookshelf > My eLab
> Documents > Chapter 22:
Writing a Literary Essay
> MLA Referencing Guidelines

☐ The conclusion restates the essay's main points and expands on their strength, and ends on a concluding statement that leaves the reader with food for thought.

☐ The text being analyzed or discussed is included in a Works Cited section. If any other external sources have been used, they are listed as well, in alphabetical order and following MLA guidelines.

☐ There are no traces of plagiarism in the essay (credit is clearly provided for any words or ideas that come from someone else).

☐ The essay has been thoroughly edited and proofread.

APPENDIX 2: PRESENTATION CHECKLIST

PREPARE

☐ After brainstorming ideas and analyzing the text(s), I have sufficient material and it is precise enough for the length of the presentation.

☐ I have taken note of all the references I plan to use, including the precise lines, paragraphs or page numbers of the source text I will cite.

☐ I have imagined myself as part of the audience to understand what elements they might find challenging and/or interesting.

☐ I have developed a through line, which is similar to the thesis statement in an essay. I use it to ensure my presentation is focused on a specific topic.

☐ I have structured my presentation carefully:

- I start with a strong hook to capture the audience's interest.

- I provide context and introduce the topic, avoiding a "Today, I will" announcement.

- I have divided the topic into a sequence of precise points that are clearly connected and provide in-depth analysis or insight.

- I end with a short summary of the most important points and a thought-provoking concluding statement.

☐ I have prepared an outline following this structure, containing only keywords and direct quotations as memory aids.

☐ If required, I have designed a visual aid to illustrate and strengthen my information. It is effective and not heavy on text, colour or animations. I have carefully proofread it and included a Works Cited list on the last slide.

☐ I have looked up the pronunciation of challenging words and paid particular attention to the delivery of passages from the literary text.

☐ I have practised extensively (using my visual support, if applicable) and made sure my presentation respects the time restrictions I have been given.

PRESENT

☐ I am well prepared; I can deliver my entire presentation with a natural flow.

☐ I have tested my visual or aural support beforehand to avoid last-minute stress because of technical reasons.

☐ I speak naturally and do not read from prepared notes or a script. I pronounce clearly and accurately and avoid the use of slang or informal speech.

☐ I mention my references, as I would in writing.

☐ I speak loudly enough and vary the tone of my voice to keep listeners interested.

☐ I make eye contact with my audience to engage with them.

A sample MLA-style slideshow presentation and a modifiable presentation outline template are available in My eLab Documents.

MyBookshelf > My eLab > Documents > Appendix 2: Presentation Checklist

GLOSSARY

A

Abstract diction
Words describing qualities that cannot be perceived with the five senses

Act
A group of scenes that form an important and cohesive part of a play's plot

Addressee
The person explicitly addressed by the persona of a first-person poem

Allegory
Work that conveys a hidden meaning—usually moral, spiritual or political—through the use of symbolic characters and events

Alliteration
Repetition of the initial letter or sound of words found close to one another

Allusion
Implicit reference to someone or something outside of the text, such as other literary works, historical figures or events, etc.

Anapestic foot
Metrical pattern in poetry in which two unstressed syllables are followed by a stressed syllable

Anaphora
Repetition of words at the beginning of successive clauses, phrases or sentences

Antagonist
Person, collective or abstract force opposing the main character (protagonist) of a story

Anthropomorphism
Presenting animals or other non-human things as having human characteristics, emotions and behaviours

Antihero
Protagonist with common or negative character traits

Antithesis
Juxtaposition of two contrasting ideas

Apostrophe
Address to someone or something that cannot respond, usually because the entity is dead, imaginary or absent from the narrative

Aside
Direct address to the audience, unheard by the other characters in a play

Assonance
Repetition of the same vowel sound within a group of words

Atmosphere
Emotional mood a text evokes

B–C

Balloon
Graphic bubble presenting the words or thoughts of a character in a graphic novel or comic

Blank verse
Poetry that has meter (usually iambic pentameter) but does not rhyme

Bridge
Section of a song that breaks up the song's repetitive musical and lyrical pattern

Cacophony
Combination of words sounding unpleasant or harsh together

Cæsura
Pause that occurs within a line of poetry, usually marked by punctuation

Characterization
Representation of the traits, motives and psychology of a character in a narrative

Chorus
In classic drama, a group of unnamed individuals standing to the side of the stage, commenting on the action

In contemporary music, the refrain of a song that is repeated several times

Cliché
Phrase that, due to overuse, is considered to lack in substance or originality

Climax
Moment of peak tension or conflict in a plot, representing the story's turning point

Close-up
In a graphic novel or film, a perspective that shows only (part of) the character's face to emphasize emotions

Comedy
Dramatic genre implicitly reassuring the audience that the play's outcome will be positive

Concrete diction
Words referring to tangible things that appeal to one of the five senses

Conflict
The opposition of different characters or forces in a story, and which can take the shape of character vs. human, character vs. self, character vs. nature and character vs. society

Connotation
Emotions and ideas suggested by a word in addition to its dictionary definition

Consonance
Repetition of the same consonant sound within a group of words

Couplet
Two lines of poetry that rhyme or are visually separated from other lines

D–E

Dactylic foot
Metrical pattern in poetry in which a stressed syllable is followed by two unstressed syllables

Denotation
Literal meaning or dictionary definition of a word

Dénouement
Final section of a story's plot, which brings a sense of resolution

Dialogue
Exchange of spoken words between two or more characters

Diction
The writer's choice and arrangement of words

Didactic poem
Poem that states a lesson or explicitly teaches something

Drama
Theatrical production written to be performed by actors through dialogue and action

Dramatic irony
Plot device that highlights the difference between a character's understanding of a situation and that of the audience

Dramatis personae
List of characters appearing in a play, usually accompanied by essential traits or relationships that link the characters

Dynamic character
Character that undergoes substantial internal changes throughout a story

Elegy
Poem of serious reflection, especially one in which a speaker mourns the loss of someone who died

Ellipsis
Omission of a part of a story

End rhyme
Rhyme that occurs in the final words or lines of poetry

Enjambment
Continuation of a sentence or clause across a line break

Ethos
Rhetorical appeal emphasizing the speaker's credibility and authority

Euphony
Combination of words that sound pleasant together

Exact rhyme
Rhyme in which both the vowel sounds and following consonant sounds of the words involved are identical

Exposition
Description or explanation of background information at the beginning of a story

Extended metaphor
Metaphor that unfolds across multiple lines or passages of a text by developing a central implicit comparison between two elements

F–I

Falling action
Section of the plot following the climax, where tension gradually decreases toward the conclusion

Fiction
A literary work that only describes imaginary events

Figure of speech
Literary device in which language is used in an unusual way to produce a stylistic effect

Flat character
Character that is one-dimensional or lacks in complexity

Foreshadowing
Literary device that (often implicitly) provides a clue on later plot developments

Formal structure
A poem's use of rhythmic and rhyme patterns and its division into stanzas

Free verse
Poetry without strict meter or rhyme scheme

Graphic novel
Literary genre combining words and images to develop a story; usually considered a longer and more complex form of comic strip

Gutter
Space, which is usually white or a solid colour, between the borders that delineate the panels of a comic or graphic novel

High angle
Scene illustrated or filmed from above, looking down at the subject

Hyperbole
Exaggeration for the sake of emphasis

Iambic foot
Metrical pattern in poetry in which one unstressed syllable is followed by a stressed syllable—the closest pattern to natural speech

Imagery
Descriptive language that engages the senses (sight, sound, smell, taste and touch)

Inciting incident
Event that signals the beginning of a story's main conflict

Internal rhyme
Rhyme that occurs within lines of poetry rather than at the end

Irony
Literary device in which what things appear or are expected to be is very different or opposite from how they actually are. *See also* dramatic, situational, verbal irony

K–N

Kairos
Context of a rhetorical transaction, such as a speech, made up of an immediate occasion (trigger event) and a larger occasion (broad issue)

Law of the three unities
In drama, a convention stating that a play should only have one single plot line, taking place in a single place over the span of one day

Limited narrator
Narrator who can only relay what happens in one given place at one given time

Logos
Rhetorical appeal that concerns the strength and logic underpinning the message and arguments of the speaker

Long shot
In a graphic novel or film, a perspective that shows the entire subject or character depicted, as well as some surroundings

Low angle
Scene illustrated or filmed from below, looking up at the subject

Lyric poem
Comparatively short, non-narrative poem in which a single speaker presents a state of mind

Lyrics
The words that accompany the music of contemporary songs

Medium shot
In a graphic novel or film, perspective that shows the character from head to waist

Melody
Pattern of musical notes and pitches

Metaphor
Figure of speech that implicitly compares two different things by saying that one thing is the other

Meter
Regular pattern of stressed and unstressed syllables used to describe the rhythm of poetry, usually expressed in poetic feet

Mood
General atmosphere or emotional complexion of a text as experienced by the reader

Musical rhythm
The repeated movement of sounds through time, made up of the beat, accent and tempo of the music

Narrative
Structured account of connected events

Narrative poem
Poem using verse to relate a series of events that may involve different characters

Narrative voice
Discursive construct representing the perspective from which a story is told. *See also* narrator *and* persona

Narrator
The character from whose perspective a literary text is told

O–Q

Octave
Eight-line stanza

Omniscient narrator
Narrator knowledgeable about the actions and thoughts of all the characters

Onomatopoeia
Device in which words are used to evoke the sound of the thing they refer to or describe

Oxymoron
Figure of speech in which two contradictory terms or ideas are paired to make a point

Page poetry
Poetry written to be published in text form

Panel
Single visual frame of a comic or graphic novel, usually delimited by a border

Paradox
Figure of speech that seems to contradict itself but contains a core of truth

Parallelism
Repetition of the same grammatical structure across sentences

Paraphrase
Restating a text's ideas and images in your own words

Pathos
Rhetorical appeal to the audience's emotions

Pause
Interruption of a narrative to make room for narratorial observations

Performance poetry
Genre of poetry written to be performed out loud rather than read on a page

Persona
Character assumed by a poet in a first-person poem

Personification
Attribution of human qualities to an object or concept

Plot
Sequence of interconnected events within a narrative, organized for effect

Poetic foot
Measure to indicate a poem's rhythmic structure in meter

Poetry slam
Competitive event where poets perform their work to an audience

Point of view
Perspective that the narrator holds in relation to the events of the story

Primary text
The lines of a play delivered by the actors

Prose
Language use that follows the natural flow of speech and grammatical structure

Prosody
Study of rhythmic and metrical patterns in prose and verse

Protagonist
Main character, often considered the hero or heroine, who propels the central action in a literary work and who is often in conflict with an antagonist

Pun
Play on words that sound similar but mean different things

Quatrain
Four-line stanza of poetry

R–S

Register
Level of language, ranging from the formal to the informal

Repartee
A brief, usually witty, response between two characters in a literary work

Repetition
Word, phrase, sentence or image that comes back several times throughout a text

Rhetorical question
Question asked for a reason other than to get an answer—usually to persuade

Rhyme
Repetition of similar sounds at the end of two or more words

Rhyme scheme
Pattern according to which end rhymes are repeated in a poem

Rising action
Section of the plot leading up to the climax

Round character
Lifelike or complex character

Satire
Use of humour, irony or sarcasm to criticize something or someone

Scansion
Act of scanning a poem to identify its rhythm and rhyming structures

Scene
Part of a play or narrative during which the action occurs in a single place without a break in time

Secondary text
Texts allowing the playwright to communicate ideas to future performers of the play, including scene descriptions and stage directions

Sestet
Six-line stanza of poetry, usually the last six lines of a sonnet

Setting
Where and when a story or scene takes place

Sign text
Textual information integrated into the illustrations of a graphic novel or comic to identify sounds or objects

Simile
Figure of speech that explicitly compares two things using a connecting word

Situational irony
Type of irony based on a discrepancy between what is expected to happen and what actually happens

Slant rhyme
Type of rhyme in which two words end in similar but not identical syllables containing slightly different consonant or vowel sounds

Soliloquy
Dramatic device in which a character speaks alone, relating his/her innermost thoughts and feelings as if thinking out loud

Sonnet
Type of fourteen-line poem written in iambic pentameter. Petrarchan and Shakespearean sonnets differ in rhyme scheme

Spoken word
A form of performance poetry, influenced by hip hop and rap music, that makes heavy use of rhythm, rhyme, repetition and word play

Spondaic foot
Metrical pattern in poetry in which both syllables are stressed

Stage business
Non-verbal action that draws the attention of the audience to a character through gestures and/or to an element of the setting through a character's interactions with a stage prop

Stanza
Group of lines that form a smaller unit within a poem because of their rhyme pattern or visual separation through line breaks

Static character
Character that does not undergo any substantial internal changes throughout a story

Stream-of-consciousness
Writing technique that captures the natural flow of a character's extended thought process

Style
Sum of a text's linguistic characteristics, including the use of syntax and diction

Subject matter
What the story is about on a primary, concrete level

Symbol
Literary device that uses a physical object or phenomenon to represent something more abstract

T–V

Tercet
Three rhyming lines of verse

Text box
Textual information that provides background to a panel in a graphic novel or comic without being a part of the scene it depicts

Thematic concept
Universal idea that can be taken up in many different literary works. E.g, Love

Thematic statement
The particular point an author expresses about a more universal thematic concept. E.g., Love is worth travelling around the world for.

Thematic structure
The way in which a theme is taken up throughout a literary work

Theme
Underlying idea or message explored throughout a literary work. *See also* thematic statement

Tone
General character or attitude the author takes toward the subject matter

Tragedy
Play that typically involves intense action and conflicts, arouses emotions such as pity and fear and ends in a catastrophe

Tragicomedy
Play that draws on the conventions of tragedy and comedy

Trochee
Two-syllable metrical pattern in poetry in which a stressed syllable is followed by an unstressed syllable

Understatement
Ironic type of speech in which something is deliberately expressed less strongly than would be expected

Verbal irony
Literary device making a character say the opposite of what they actually mean

Verse
In one sense, writing arranged in relatively short lines with a more or less regular rhythm that may include some form of rhyme; in another sense, any form of poetic composition, including poetry without strict meter or rhyme scheme. *See also* free verse

INDEX

The majority of the terms listed below are either explained or mentioned in the Elements of Analysis sections. Page numbers that are in italics indicate the most pertinent references within the chapters, including the exercises.

A

abstract diction 164, 218, *244*
act 110, *132*
active character *23*
addressee *171*, *194*, *198*
allegory 57
alliteration 12, 116, 158, 216, *236*, *243*
anapestic foot 160
anaphora 184, *254*
antagonist 10, 112
anthropomorphism 57
antihero 10
apostrophe 165, 219
aside 108, 117
assonance 12, 77, 116, 158, 216, *236*, *243*
atmosphere 11, *48*, 115, 166, 219

B–C

balloon 225
blank verse 161
bridge 221
cacophony 158
caesura 158
characterization 10, *25*, *58*, *68*, *70*, *77*, 113
chorus 117, 221
climax 9, *101*, 110
close-up 225
colloquialism *99*
comedy 107
concrete diction 164, 218, *244*
conflict 8, *22*, *77*, 110, *132*
connotation 12, *78*, 116, 164, *188*, 218
consonance 12, *77*, 116, 158, 216, *236*, *243*
couplet 163

D–E

dactylic foot 160
denotation 12, 116, 164, *188*, 218
dénouement 9, 110
dialogue 8, *75*, 116, 225
diction 12, *84*, 116, 164, 218, *244*
didactic poem 157

drama 106
dramatic irony 32, 117
dramatis personae 106, 111
dynamic character 10, 113
dystopia 80, *86*
elegy 157
ellipsis 8, 108
end rhyme 159, *243*
enjambment *194*
ethos 228, 229
euphemism 101, *190*
euphony 158, *203*
exact rhyme 159, 216
exposition 8, 9, 110
extended metaphor *69*, *244*

F–I

falling action 9, *33*, 110
fiction 4, 106
figure of speech 12, 116, 165, *201*, 219
flat character 10, 113
foreshadowing 8, 21, *78*
formal structure 156, *181*, *190*, 214, *235*
free verse 160, 162, 163, *198*, *203*, 216
graphic novel 225
gutter 225
high angle 225
hyperbole *132*, 165, *201*, 219
iambic foot 160, 161, *179*
imagery 11, *45*, *76*, 115, 165, *187*, *194*, 219
inciting incident 8, 9
internal rhyme 159, 216, *243*
irony 12, 32, *58*, 117

K–N

kairos 228, 229
law of the three unities 111, *152*
limited narrator 6
logos 228, 229
long shot 225
low angle 225
lyric poem 157
lyrics 215, 221

medium shot 225

melody 220

metaphor 12, *67*, 116, *131*, 165, *178*, 219

meter 160, 161, 162, *176*, 216

mood 11, *47*, *48*, 115, 166, 167, *198*, *212,* 219, 220, 228, *238*, *244*

musical rhythm 220

narrative 5, 8, *68*, 108, 110, 215

narrative poem 157

narrative voice 5, 215

narrator 5, 6, 8, *85*, *92*, 108, 158, 215

O–Q

octave 163

omniscient narrator 5, 108

onomatopoeia 158, 225, *254*

oxymoron 165, 219

page poetry 239, 242

panel 225, *250*, *251*

paraphrase 157

passive character *23*

pathos 228, 229

pause 8, 108, 163, 216

performance poetry 223

persona 158

personification 57, 165, 219

plot 8, 9, *33*, *46*, *85*, *101*, 108, 110, 111, *132*, *256*

poetic foot 158, 160, 161, *178*

poetry slam 223

point of view 5, 6, 7, 108, 158, 215, 228

primary text 106

prose 4, 115, 156, 216

prosody *91*, 158, 216

protagonist 5, 10, 107, 112, *152*

pun 117

quatrain 163

R–S

register 12, 116, 164, 218

repartee 116

repetition 12, *67*, 116, 158, 161, 216, *236*

rhyme 158, 159, 163, 216, 221, *236*

rhyme scheme 159, *170*, *175*, 216, 221, *236*, *243*

rising action 9, *33*

round character 10, 113

scansion 157, 160

scene 8, *91*, 108, 110, 225

secondary text 106

sestet 163

setting 10, 11, *22*, *34*, *48*, *102*, 114, 115

sign text 225

simile 12, *67*, 116, 165, 219

situational irony 32, *58*

slant rhyme 159, 162, 216

soliloquy 108, 113, 116, *132*

sonnet 157, 163, *180*

spoken word 216, 223, *243*, *245*

spondaic foot 160

stage business 115

stanza 156, 163, *170*, *188*, 221

static character 10, 113

stream-of-consciousness 60, 65

style 12, 21, 115, 220, 225

subject matter 13, 117, 166, *212*, 214, 220, *236*

symbol 11, *34*, *45*, *67*, *91*, *103*, 115, 165, 219

T–V

tercet 163

text box 225, *250*

thematic concept 13, *59*, *79*, *104*, 117, 166, *198*, 220

thematic statement 13, 117, 166, 220

thematic structure 156, 166, *181*, 220

theme 9, 12, 13, *25*, *35*, *59*, *70*, *79*, 115, 117, *135*, *153*, 166, *198*, *207*, *212*, 219, 220, 228, 229, *238*, *244*

tone 12, 32, *36*, 115, 158, 166, *212*, 215, 219, 228, 229

tragedy 107

tragicomedy 107

trochee 160

unreliable narrator *24*, *91*, *93*

verbal irony 32

verse 115, 156, 160, 161, 162, 163, 216, 221

volta 163

CREDITS

PHOTO CREDITS

Adams, S. p. 87: © Anneliese Mackintosh.

Alamy pp. 26, 189: © The History Collection; p. 37: © Historic Images; p. 48 top, left: © Classic Stock; bottom: © Chronicle; p. 49: © AF Archive; pp. 60, 191, 205: © IanDagnall Computing; p. 80: © Baqsso Cannarsa/Opale; p. 171: © Hilary Morgan; pp. 176, 186: © Lebrecht Music & Arts; p. 183: © Archive Pics; p. 195: © M-dash News Archive; p. 240: © Gary Doak.

Bannerji, H. p. 71.

Brick Books p. 207.

Chong, Denise p. 263: © Danielle Schaub.

Drawn & Quarterly p. 247: © Catherine Liu.

Flickr.com pp. 136 right, 154: © Flickr.com/Shehal Joseph.

Library and Archives Canada p. 203: © Topley Studio Fonds / Library and Archives Canada / PA-025726.

Macmillan, D. p. 136 left: © Effie Woods.

Naponse, D. p. 94.

Pexels p. 48 middle, right.

Pixabay p. 48 top, right.

Sarah, R. p. 178.

Shutterstock p. 14: © The Arts; p. 48 middle, left: © Oleg Golovnev; right: © dboystudio; pp. 119, 200: © Georgios Kollidas; p. 252 left: © Paul McKinnon; p. 258: © JStone.

Simon & Schuster p. 252 right: © Jamie Hogge.

Teman, Esther p. 232.

TEXT CREDITS

p. 7: "The Appointment in Samarra" from the play *Sheppey* (1933) reprinted by permission. p. 61: "The New Dress" from *Mrs. Dalloway's Party* by Virginia Woolf. Copyright © 1973, renewed 2001 by Quentin Bell and Angelica Garnett, copyright 1944 and renewed 1973 by Houghton Mifflin Harcourt Publishing Company. Reprinted by permission of Houghton Mifflin Harcourt Publishing Company. All rights reserved. p. 72: "The Other Family" by Himani Bannerji reprinted by permission. p. 81: "We Ate the Children Last" by Yann Martel (*Grain*, Volume 31, Number 4, 2004). Copyright © 2004 Yann Martel; reprinted by permission. p. 88: "Wide and Deep" by Socrates Adams reprinted with permission. p. 95: "She Is Water" by Darlene Naponse reprinted with permission. p. 137: *Lungs* © Duncan Macmillan, 2011, reprinted by kind permission of Oberon Books Ltd. p. 179: "Blowing the Fluff Away" from *Pause for Breath* (2009) by Robyn Sarah, reprinted with permission of the poet and Biblioasis Press. p. 189: "Edge" by Sylvia Plath reprinted with permission.
p. 192: "Theme for English B" from *The Collected Poems of Langston Hughes*, published by Knopf and Vintage Books; copyright © 1994; reprinted by permission of Harold Ober Associates Incorporated; copyright 1994 by the Langston Hughes Estate. p. 195: "A Different History" by Sujita Bhatt reprinted with permission.
pp. 208, 209: "Spirit Bear" and "Garbage Bear" by Dan MacIsaac reprinted with permission. p. 221: "Beggar," lyrics by Laura Roklicer used with permission. p. 223: "Horizon Line," words and performance by Matthew Madonia used with permission. p. 226: Graphic novel page adapted from "The Magic Shop" by Svetlana Kiseleva; used with permission. "On Trains" by Matt Holubowski used with permission. p. 240: "To Blossom in the Shadow" by Kate Tempest used with permission. p. 247: "Louis Riel" by Chester Brown used with permission by Drawn & Quarterly; copyright Chester Brown. p. 252: "Secret Path" by Gord Downie and Jeff Lemire used with permission. p. 258: "Speech at the Youth Takeover of the United Nations" by Malala Yousafzai used with permission. p. 264: "Being Canadian" by Denise Chong used with permission.